DISCARDED

CHILDREN'S SEARCHING:

The Development of Search Skill and Spatial Representation

CHILDREN'S SEARCHING:
The Development of Search Skill and Spatial Representation

Edited by

HENRY M. WELLMAN
The University of Michigan

 LAWRENCE ERLBAUM ASSOCIATES, PUBLISHERS
1985   Hillsdale, New Jersey   London

Copyright © 1985 by Lawrence Erlbaum Associates, Inc.
All rights reserved. No part of this book may be reproduced in
any form, by photostat, microform, retrieval system, or any other
means, without the prior written permission of the publisher.

Lawrence Erlbaum Associates, Inc., Publishers
365 Broadway
Hillsdale, New Jersey 07642

Library of Congress Cataloging in Publication Data
Main entry under title:

Children's searching.

Bibliography: p.
Includes index.
1. Searching behavior in children. 2. Space
perception in children. I. Wellman, Henry M.
BF723.S2C48 1985   155.4′13   84-25914
ISBN 0-89859-567-3

Printed in the United States of America
10 9 8 7 6 5 4 3 2 1

Contents

Contributors　vii

Preface　ix

Introduction　xi

1. Beyond Egocentrism: A New Look at
the Beginnings of Spatial Representation
   —*Clark C. Presson and Susan C. Somerville*　1

2. Spatial Knowledge and Its Manifestations
   —*Barbara Landau and Elizabeth Spelke*　27

3. Active Movement and Development of
Spatial Abilities in Infancy
   —*J. Gavin Bremner and Peter E. Bryant*　53

4. The Logical Search Skills of Infants
and Young Children
   —*Susan C. Somerville and Robert J. Haake*　73

5. The Origins of Search and Number Skills
   —*Paul L. Harris*　105

CONTENTS

6. The Early Development of Planning
   —*Henry M. Wellman, William V. Fabricius, and Catherine Sophian* 123

7. Memory-Based Searching by Very Young Children
   —*Judy S. DeLoache* 151

8. A Developmental Model of Search: Stochastic Estimation of Children's Rule Use
   —*Catherine Sophian, Jill H. Larkin, and Joseph B. Kadane* 185

9. A Comparative Description of Representation and Processing During Search
   —*C. Donald Heth and Edward H. Cornell* 215

10. Mathematical Models of Search
    —*David R. Cross and Henry M. Wellman* 251

11. Controlling Sources of Variation in Search Tasks: A Skill Theory Approach
    —*Roberta Corrigan and Kurt Fischer* 287

Author Index   319

Subject Index   325

Contributors

J. Gavin Bremner
Department of Psychology
University of Lancaster
Bailrigg, Lancaster, England

Peter E. Bryant
Department of Experimental
 Psychology
University of Oxford
Oxford, England

Edward H. Cornell
Department of Psychology
University of Alberta
Edmonton, Alberta, Canada

Roberta Corrigan
Department of Educational
 Psychology
University of Wisconsin—Milwaukee
Milwaukee, Wisconsin

David R. Cross
Department of Psychology
The University of Michigan
Ann Arbor, Michigan

Judy S. DeLoache
Department of Human Development
 and Family Ecology
University of Illinois
Champaign, Illinois

William V. Fabricius
Department of Psychology
The University of Georgia
Athens, Georgia

Kurt Fischer
Department of Psychology
University of Denver
Denver, Colorado

Robert J. Haake
Institute of Child
 Development
University of Minnesota
Minneapolis, Minnesota

Paul L. Harris
Department of Experimental
 Psychology
University of Oxford
Oxford, England

C. Donald Heth
Department of Psychology
University of Alberta
Edmonton, Alberta, Canada

Joseph B. Kadane
Department of Psychology
Carnegie-Mellon University
Pittsburgh, Pennsylvania

Barbara Landau
Department of Psychology
Columbia University
New York, New York

Jill H. Larkin
Department of Psychology
Carnegie-Mellon University
Pittsburgh, Pennsylvania

Clark C. Presson
Department of Psychology
Arizona State University
Tempe, Arizona

Susan C. Somerville
Department of Psychology
Arizona State University
Tempe, Arizona

Catherine Sophian
Department of Psychology
Carnegie-Mellon University
Pittsburgh, Pennsylvania

Elizabeth Spelke
Department of Psychology
University of Pennsylvania
Philadelphia, Pennsylvania

Henry M. Wellman
Center for Human Growth
  and Development
The University of Michigan
Ann Arbor, Michigan

Preface

The chapters collected here represent contemporary research and thinking on children's searching—their developing skills at finding missing or unavailable items and locations. This is a topic of classic as well as current interest in developmental psychology. Several of the chapters were presented in preliminary form at a symposium held at the meetings of the Society for Research in Child Development in Detroit in 1983. Considerable excitement and insight were generated at that symposium. At the same time, it became apparent that research on this topic was both varied and extensive. This led to the conception of a volume on children's searching, the solicitation of additional chapters, and, eventually, the publication of this book. The present chapters exemplify just why children's searching is an exciting and informative new, as well as classic, area of investigation, and they are authored by many of the persons who have been responsible for the renewed interest in this topic.

Publication of this volume would have been impossible save for the efforts of a great many persons. Special thanks are due to the chapter authors, who were especially efficient and effective; to the staff of the Center for Human Growth and Development at the University of Michigan—especially Kim Marentay and Laura Skidmore; and to the publication staff at Lawrence Erlbaum Associates, Inc. Acknowledgement is also due to NICHHD, who provided me with a research career development award at the time I was editing this work.

H.M.W.
Ann Arbor, Michigan

Introduction: The Importance of Studying Children's Searching

Henry M. Wellman
The University of Michigan

Children's searches for missing and unavailable things—objects, people, spatial locations—have long been studied (e.g., Hunter, 1917; Piaget, 1954). However, interest in this topic has also recently been rekindled (e.g., Harris, 1983; Wellman & Somerville, 1982). Why has search reemerged as a vital area of developmental investigation? Why study children's searching? There are four excellent reasons for doing so.

First, search activities confront all of us, and often. Even infants and toddlers misplace their toys, clothes, and implements, lose sight of mother, wander from their familiar home bases, and must find these things again. Older children and adults are notorious for lost keys, books, money, contact lenses, pets, etc. Searching for things is a frequent, important, and universal human behavior. Investigating the development of important, universal acquisitions is an essential part of developmental psychology, at least for many of us.

Second, specific search activities—retrieving a hidden toy, finding a lost pet—face the person with specific search problems. That is, they require problem solving, where the problem to solve is recovering or acquiring a missing or currently unavailable item. In fact, not only are various search activities instances of problem solving, but in contemporary cognitive psychology searching forms the basic metaphor for all problem solving. As argued by Newell and Simon (1972), solving *any* problem requires searching—searching for the problem solution in a theoretical problem space. For studying the development of problem solving (a further important, universal development), children's searching seems a particularly direct and informative domain of investigation.

Third, search tasks are understood, enjoyed, and readily undertaken by young children, and indeed by children of almost all ages. Infants, toddlers, and preschoolers, like adults, easily comprehend what is required of them if presented with tasks requiring them to find hidden or missing objects and locations. This turns out to be extremely useful methodologically; it provides the investigator with a means of studying the often difficult-to-research very young child. Better yet, search tasks at times allow the researcher to investigate infants, toddlers, and older children all in one programmatic effort. All too often our research methods are discontinuous. Contiguous but distinctly different ages—the infant and toddler, the toddler and preschooler, etc.—are not studied together on the same tasks. Search tasks afford an opportunity to overcome this methodological and theoretical shortcoming.

Fourth and finally, researching search can provide an index to other important underlying developments. This is the classic place of research on search in developmental psychology. Indeed, until recently search tasks were employed solely as a method for investigating some other topic. For example, children's retrieval of immediately hidden objects was investigated in order to infer their conceptions of space and objects, as for example in Piagetian object permanence studies. Part of the new interest in search is an expanded vision as to what search tasks may be able to tell us in this regard. That is, if appropriately controlled, research into children's searching can inform us not just about object concepts but also about the child's developing memory, logical-inferential abilities, planning, etc. At the same time investigators have become increasingly aware that the link between the child's search behavior and his or her knowledge of objects and space is an indirect one (Harris, 1983). If we wish to use children's performances in search tasks to infer their spatial (or other) knowledge, then we must carefully distinguish the effects on performance of spatial knowledge from spatial strategies and problem solving. To do so requires knowledge of the child's search processes themselves, as well as theoretical care and empirical precision.

These several advantages are not mutually exclusive. Research on children's searching, at its best, is ecologically important, methodologically advantageous, and theoretically informative.

The chapters in this volume all invoke and trade upon these rationales, typically in combination. To preview, the chapters by Presson and Somerville, by Landau and Spelke, and by Bremner and Bryant consider the nature of young children's spatial knowledge, as revealed in search tasks. Presson and Somerville and Landau and Spelke, specifically, carefully distinguish spatial knowledge from the uses to which that knowledge is put—e.g., in finding hidden objects. In doing so, they independently offer new but converging accounts as to the nature of young children's understanding of space. The chapters by Somerville and Haake, by Harris, by Wellman, Fabricius and Sophian, by DeLoache, and by Sophian, Larkin and Kadane all address, in part, a serious lacuna in our current theories and descriptions of development—the toddler. Moreover, they do so by invoking similar tasks and procedures in order to study infants and toddlers together (Somerville and Haake; Harris; Sophian et al.) or toddlers and preschoolers together (DeLoache; Wellman et al.).

Many of the chapters consider children's search activities and skills themselves and thus offer insight into the development of this ubiquitous and important activity. In addition, almost all the chapters use children's early search competencies to reveal and discuss other topics of fundamental concern for a comprehensive theory of cognitive development. These include, at a general level, knowledge and representation (Presson and Somerville; Landau and Spelke; Bremner and Bryant; Somerville and Haake), problem solving (Wellman et al.; DeLoache; Heth and Cornell; Cross and Wellman), and general cognitive skills (Corrigan and Fischer; Sophian et al.). At a more specific level, the topics covered include logical inferences (Somerville and Haake), number concepts (Harris), planning (Wellman et al.), and memory (DeLoache). The content of these chapters fully attest to the value of studying children's searching.

REFERENCES

Harris, P. L. (1983). Infant cognition. In M. M. Haith & J. J. Campos (Eds.), *Handbook of child psychology: Vol. 2. Infancy and developmental psychobiology*. New York: Wiley.

Hunter, W. S. (1917). The delayed reaction in a child. *Psychological Review, 24,* 74–87.

Newell, A., & Simon, H. (1972). *Human problem solving*. Englewood Cliffs, NJ: Prentice-Hall.

Piaget, J. (1954). *The construction of reality in the child*. New York: Ballatine Books.

Wellman, H. M., & Somerville, S. C. (1982). The development of human search ability. In M. E. Lamb & A. L. Brown (Eds.), *Advances in developmental psychology* (Vol. 2). Hillsdale, NJ: Lawrence Erlbaum Associates, pp. 41–84.

CHILDREN'S SEARCHING:

The Development of Search Skill and Spatial Representation

1 Beyond Egocentrism: A New Look at the Beginnings of Spatial Representation

Clark C. Presson
Susan C. Somerville
Arizona State University

This chapter examines evidence concerning the development of spatial representation in and beyond infancy. The early development of spatial representation is connected with search in two ways. First, the notion of search itself seems naturally to entail a search space (cf. Wellman & Somerville, 1982), for which the searcher may or may not use some form of internal or external representation. Second, historically search tasks have provided the typical means of investigating spatial representation in infants.

Our main purpose is to review the notion of *egocentric* spatial representation in infancy. The prevalent cognitive-developmental view of early spatial representation argues that the infant begins with a representational system which locates objects and events in relation to the body, with no objective awareness of body position (or changes in body position) in a surrounding space. This egocentric coding system is supplanted, toward the end of infancy, by an objective (or allocentric, or geocentric) representational system, which is based on the relations of objects, people, and events to other objects occupying relatively stable positions in space. We examine a growing body of empirical evidence relevant to this view, together with conceptual issues surrounding the meaning of the terms *representation* and *egocentric*. Our conclusion is that the current evidence supports an alternative view, which is also consistent with spatial developments beyond infancy. This alternative view emphasizes changes in the nature of children's developing *uses* of spatial information, rather than changes in the form of stored representations. The solution of search problems is a major source of information about these developments, especially in infancy.

The term *spatial representation* has several meanings in the psychological literature (e.g., Deregowski, 1977; Liben, 1981; Mandler, 1983). If we consider only internal representations, there are two senses of spatial representation that may be distinguished.[1] First, there is spatial information that is stored and available to the person (infant or adult). This sense of spatial representation (or knowledge) is the one on which our discussion of infant spatial development focuses. Second, there is Piaget's (Piaget, 1954; Piaget & Inhelder, 1967) use of the term *representational space* to refer to a form of thought that is attained only when the child acts conceptually in space (e.g., infers a view not perceptually given; reads a map). Clearly, these two senses of the term representation do not have equal developmental status: spatial storage is developmentally prior to spatial thought. While preverbal, presymbolic infants do not engage in conceptual thinking about space or create symbolic artifacts based on their spatial knowledge, there is evidence that they do represent spatial information (Mandler, 1983; Yonas & Pick, 1975).

Spatial storage is the most basic form of representational behavior, since spatial thought presumes and requires stored spatial information. That is, spatial thought is one way in which spatial information may be used (see Mandler, 1983). In discussions of spatial representation as storage, it is critical to maintain a distinction between the information that is stored and how that information may be used. The importance of this distinction stems from the fact that one cannot directly examine the stored spatial representation. Empirical evidence always concerns representations as used to perform a particular function. There is no way to examine directly just the representation itself (Newcombe, 1981; Palmer, 1978). This does not mean that inferences can never be drawn about the stored representation, but that to do so it is necessary also to consider the rules or operations that govern its use. Thus, Palmer (1978) has emphasized the need to focus less on the representation per se and to "consider its functional information content as defined by the processes that use it" (p. 300).

To clarify this distinction between the stored representation of information and its uses, and to introduce the principal ways in which represented spatial information might be used, let us consider a mobile animal traversing some terrain (of a relatively large or small scale). As the animal moves, its relation to objects in the environment changes. To be well adapted, mobile organisms must keep track of where they are (e.g., Krebs, 1978; Menzel, 1973). Doing so, while efficiently maintaining position constancy, requires the representation of information about space since objects go in and out of view. Later, when the animal returns to that space, it will show a benefit from prior encounters. In this case, the gain constitutes evidence of some representation of the spatial information.

---

[1]Our concern with representation as internal knowledge contrasts with a classical use of the term representation to refer to what Deregowski (1977) called spatial artifacts. Although these artifacts (such as drawings, maps, and diagrams) are often used as important evidence about spatial knowledge, they do not directly concern us here. Such external symbols have been referred to variously as "spatial products" (Liben, 1981) or "re-representations" (Kosslyn, Heldmeyer, & Locklear, 1977).

The nature of this representation may be inferred from the nature of the practical gain in the later encounter.[2] There are two things to note. First, the inference about the representation does not reflect only the representation, per se. Rather, it reflects the represented information as utilized by the organism. Second, in most animals and human infants the utilization of spatial information is limited to practical orientation and action.

If the animal crossing the terrain is an adult human, there is a second sense in which we might say he or she uses represented spatial information. The adult may, for example, draw a map that represents the space externally. The creation of such an external representation provides much stronger evidence that some form of stored spatial information exists. At the same time, it requires the capacity to use graphic, verbal, or other symbols, (cf. Piaget & Inhelder, 1967; Siegel & White, 1975; Werner & Kaplan, 1963/1984). The manipulation of such symbols constitutes spatial thought, which under this definition infants do not display. However, although representation in this latter sense of spatial thought develops after infancy, we argue that it draws on the same basic stored spatial representation. Thus to account for developmental changes in infancy and beyond, it is not necessary to postulate changes in the basic form of stored information available to the child. Development may consist primarily of changes in the ways in which stored spatial information can be used.

For the preverbal infant, the evidence of (stored) representation comes from direct action and orientation in space. One important category of actions is the retrieval of hidden or displaced objects, which is required in simple search tasks. There are certain risks involved in making inferences about spatial representation from indirect behavioral evidence (see also Liben, 1982; Yonas & Pick, 1975). Nevertheless, cognitive developmental researchers have considered it likely that the infant does code spatial information in some form (Mandler, 1983). The coding of spatial information is assumed to consist of relations, and the major issue is whether the relations that the system can store are relative to the infant's own body exclusively (i.e., *egocentric*) or relative to other objects or landmarks (i.e., *objective*). In the current literature it is suggested that early development can be accounted for in terms of a major change, toward the end of infancy, in the type of relation that is coded. This change is from an "egocentric" code (body-centered relations) to an "objective" code (relations to other objects) as the basis for spatial representation.

It is this question of the infant's early egocentric coding of spatial information that we consider in greater depth. Although we recognize that the infant's behavior shows dramatic changes, we argue that these observed changes may occur primarily in the way that the same form of stored information is used. Our discussion consists of three major sections. The first deals with the conceptual history of the term *egocentric* as applied to spatial representation. In this section

---

[2]We are indebted to Ed Sadalla for suggesting this example.

we draw attention to some inconsistencies between various uses of the terms egocentric and representation in developmental contexts. In the second major section we review empirical studies of infant spatial development that are relevant to the notion of egocentric representation. As we shall see, in these studies the inferences drawn about spatial representation are based on the infant's ability to search for hidden objects. When we refer to spatial representation we mean the stored spatial information that is available to the infant. Finally, we propose a modified account of infant spatial development that does not require a notion of early egocentric coding.

INFANT EGOCENTRISM: THE CONCEPTUAL PROBLEMS

The terms *egocentrism* and *egocentric* are difficult to define precisely and differ in meaning across research areas (Ford, 1979; Glucksberg, Krauss, & Higgins, 1975; Howard & Templeton, 1966; Piaget, 1954, 1959; Piaget & Inhelder, 1967; Presson, 1980). Piaget (1954, 1959) was the first to give the terms real currency in the developmental literature. He used them initially to describe aspects of the 4- to 7-year-old child's behavior, and subsequently, almost by analogy, to describe the infant's interactions with objects in space (Piaget, 1968, pp. 78–79).

In the 4- to 7-year-old, it is clear that Piaget's term egocentric was intended to describe characteristics of spatial thought rather than of stored spatial information. As applied to infants, the term referred to the logic inherent in the coordination of overt actions. Thus the infant achieved only an understanding of how to act in a "practical space," whereas the older child was capable of performing mental operations in a "conceptual space" as well (Piaget & Inhelder, 1967). Within conceptual space, Piaget described both an early "egocentric" stage and a later stage in which egocentrism was overcome by the coordination of viewpoints and frameworks. Within practical space, no such change from an egocentric to a non-egocentric stage was postulated. In fact, the sensorimotor practical space of the infant was seen by Piaget as "inherently egocentric" (but not in the same sense as the egocentrism of later spatial thought).

There is a sense in which, to act appropriately in space, even an adult must adopt an "egocentric" viewpoint (cf. Howard & Templeton, 1966; Pick, Yonas, & Rieser, 1979). That is, in order to move, reach, or even look in the direction of some object a person requires knowledge of its position in relation to him or herself. Similarly, in using "egocentrism" to discuss infant spatial development, Piaget (1954) referred principally to his claim that, for the young infant, objects were "located" at the disposal of actions rather than being located in space, in their own right. Thus the very young infant "learns how to grasp, hence to localize, objects in relation to himself" (Piaget, 1954, p. 165). Piaget described the early coordinations of actions with respect to objects as "subjective groups," meaning that the localization of an object depended solely on the memory of particular movements made to reach it. Gradually, the infant was said to progress toward the use of more specifically spatial notions in guiding his actions, e.g., "moving away from" or "moving near to" (Piaget, 1954, p. 197), but Piaget stressed that such notions rely on "the relations of objects with the behavior of the subject and still do not apply to the interrelations of objects independently of the action" (Piaget, 1954, p. 198). Thus, according to Piaget, throughout the first year of life the infant lacks any means of coding the relative positions of objects in space, including relations involving the position of his or her own body.[3]

Next, as a result of the mobility attained by infants early in the second year, Piaget considered that the infant succeeded in achieving an objective coordination of the perceived movements of other objects and of his or her own body parts. However, he still maintained that such "objective groups" did not entail the representation of spatial relations by the infant, since "the child does not yet know either how to take account of displacements produced outside the perceptual field (although he does perceive their result) or to locate himself in relation to objects (this operation presupposes that one pictures oneself as a moving object and is not merely aware of one's own movements)" (Piaget, 1954, p. 224).

Thus even the attainment of "objective" groups with respect to immediate, overt actions in space did not signal the end of "egocentrism" in Piaget's account of infant spatial development. Practical space remained "egocentric," in Piaget's sense, throughout. In Piaget's (1954) view it was the attainment of symbolic representational skills, at the end of infancy, which brought about a significant change; "through spatial representation and the capacity to elaborate representative groups, space is constituted for the first time as a motionless environment in which the subject himself is located" (Piaget, 1954, p. 235); "spatial egocentrism . . . tends to disappear from the moment (the infant) locates himself in space as such, instead of perceiving space as a function of himself" (Piaget, 1954, p. 230). For Piaget, then, the "practical space" of the infant was an attempt to characterize the progressive adaptation of the infant's actions to a spatial world. The term egocentrism was not intended to refer to a stored representation or encoding of space in infancy, but rather to a lack of symbolic skill. In Piaget's view it was the attainment of symbolic skills, toward the end of infancy, which enabled the representation of objects (including the self) in space and which freed the infant from his or her sensorimotor egocentrism (see also Butterworth, 1978; Laurendeau & Pinard, 1970).

In recent studies of infants (e.g., Acredolo, 1978; Butterworth, 1977; Rieser, 1979), the term *egocentric* has been used in a variety of senses, ranging from the more descriptive to the more explanatory. On the simplest level, "egocentric"

---

[3]As will be clear from the studies reviewed below, this view no longer seems tenable.

has been used to describe a response that maintains a fixed relation to the infant's body, such as reaching to the right of the body (e.g., Bremner & Bryant, 1977; Cornell & Heth, 1979). Whereas there can be no question about this descriptive use of the term, questions do arise as soon as there is a shift from describing a single response, or a pattern of responses, to describing a general quality of the infant's knowledge. This shift has occurred quite frequently in the literature and has created the impression that the concept of *egocentricity* has considerable explanatory power for infant spatial development (see e.g., Harris, 1975; Pick & Lockman, 1981).

In infant spatial development, in particular, it has proved difficult to avoid explanations in terms of "egocentric coding" or "egocentric representation," meaning that the locations of objects are coded in some system that has the infant's body at its center (Acredolo, 1978, 1979; Bremner, 1978a, 1978b; Butterworth, 1977; Rieser, 1979). Butterworth (1975, 1977) was one of the first to introduce spatial notions into the interpretation of performance on object permanence tasks. He suggested that the 9- to 11-month-old infant "locates the object in a duality of relations between a self-referent body-centered space (i.e., an egocentric spatial code) and the visual field (i.e., an allocentric spatial code . . .)" (p. 399). For Butterworth, the infant's problem was essentially one of making the two codes congruent. Other investigators have viewed the infant as "choosing" between the two codes, with various situational and developmental factors determining whether the chosen code is "egocentric" or "allocentric" (Acredolo, 1978; Bremner, 1978a). Even in the most recent studies, where the evidence for "egocentrism" has become less firm, the notion of two opposing codes has been retained (Acredolo, 1979; Bremner, 1978b; Rieser, 1979). Rieser (1979), for example, examined the visual search behavior of 6-month-old infants. In his discussion the terms *egocentric* and *geocentric* were used in two different senses, the first of which was simply to label two of the infant's response possibilities. However, the results were also interpreted in terms of the relative influence of three factors on visual search, two of the three being "the learned egocentric code and the learned geocentric code" (p. 1088). Rieser's conclusion was that "the egocentric code exerts a stronger influence over the 6-month-olds' visual search than either of the two other factors" (1979, p. 1088).

Harris (1977) proposed that spatial development could be viewed as "a gradual coordination of . . . two types of position specification—the self-related specification on the one hand, the landmark specification on the other" (p. 84). He reviewed evidence indicating that human infants can locate objects in relation to their bodies at an early age. He envisaged a gradual increase in the infant's use of landmarks (the infant's body not included) to specify the positions of objects. Harris thus explained certain search behaviors (the classic Stage IV AB̄ error, described in more detail later) by suggesting that the infant (a) has a tendency to "neglect the more accurate but less stable self-related position code," and also

(b) "treats the landmark code as an overly stable system, and fails to update it even when the object has moved to a new position" (p. 86).

A more continuous view of the development of spatial representation was proposed by Pick and Lockman (1981). They outlined a developmental progression in spatial knowledge from matters concerned with body-body relations (e.g., thumbsucking) through body-object relations (e.g., reaching), to object-object relations; at the same time pointing out that developments in all three continue into adulthood. However, in common with other accounts, their discussion of infant spatial development (and also developments in the preschool years) retained the notion of one (egocentric) reference system, concerned with body-object relations, being used instead of and (gradually) in conjunction with an allocentric or geocentric system, concerned with object-object relations.

In summary, there are interpretive problems associated with current uses of the term egocentric. It is used to describe a response, to refer to a limitation of thought (by Piaget), as well as to refer to a body-centered system of spatial coding. In its most general sense, infant spatial egocentrism is said to entail the use of a separate reference system that is overthrown by an objective (or "allocentric" or "geocentric") one at a later point in development. These interpretive problems led us to examine the empirical evidence pertaining to infant egocentrism more closely and, in particular, to reconsider the question of whether the notion of an egocentric coding or reference system was required by the data. The next section contains a review of the relevant studies.

INFANT EGOCENTRISM: THE EMPIRICAL PROBLEMS

The cognitive developmental tasks that tap spatial knowledge in infancy typically are search tasks and typically are also related to the development of the object concept (Frye, 1980; Lucas & Uzgiris, 1977; Piaget, 1954). Recent paradigms (particularly those pertaining to the Stage IV or AB error) have included some in which an infant remained stationary and the position of a (hidden) object was changed (e.g., Butterworth, 1977); and others in which the infant, as well as or instead of the object, was moved at a particular point in a series of hiding and finding trials (e.g., Bremner & Bryant, 1977). There are many variations on these two basic types of paradigm, each pertaining to a different aspect of the Stage IV error, or to object permanence more broadly defined. A comprehensive review of this literature is beyond the scope of the present discussion. In our review we have selected the studies that are most directly linked to the issue of egocentric spatial representation and coding.

In the traditional Stage IV object permanence task (Gratch, 1975; Piaget, 1954), the infant remains stationary. An object is repeatedly hidden and retrieved at location A and then, in full view of the infant, is hidden at a new location, B.

On B hiding trials, infants aged 9 to 11 months tend to search at location A, making the AB̄ error. There are some interpretations of this error that do not involve spatial coding (at least not directly); for example, the suggestion that the infant has learned a fixed response (Bremner & Bryant, 1977), or that the infant cannot achieve a new coordination of schemes (Frye, 1980). However, the AB̄ error has also been interpreted as providing direct evidence of the infant's processing of spatial information. The error has been attributed, on the one hand, to infants' searching in a fixed place (Gratch, 1975) and, on the other hand, to infants' "egocentric" coding of the event's location (Butterworth, 1975, 1977). The "egocentric coding" hypothesis asserts that the infant locates the object or event in space in relation to his or her body (e.g., the object is "to my right"). The last two interpretations, which postulate spatial coding, are impossible to separate as long as the infant has a constant spatial relation to the array of hiding locations. Can they be separated by procedures in which the infant (or the array) is moved?

Bremner and Bryant (1977) moved the infant 180° around the display (or rotated the array 180°) before hiding the object on the B hiding trials. Bremner and Bryant's 9-month-old infants tended to make the same response (i.e., to search by reaching in the same direction relative to their bodies) which was successful during the A hiding trials. Bremner (1978a) pointed out the two possible interpretations of these results and those of other, similar studies: "It remains to be seen to what extent the infant's perseverative errors in the Stage IV task are simply due to a response habit, or, at a higher level, to an egocentric understanding of space" (p. 83). These interpretations differ in that the latter, but not the former, necessarily implies encoding of the spatial position of the hidden object. Of course, as Bremner and Bryant (1977) indicated, the two alternatives are difficult to distinguish experimentally (see also Acredolo, 1978; Acredolo & Evans, 1980; Rieser, 1979).

Acredolo (1978) investigated the development of infants' spatial orientation abilities, using a longitudinal design. The response required from the infants was a head-turn to the left or right. Anticipatory turns were obtained using a procedure in which a centrally located buzzer signaled the appearance of an experimenter with toys in one of two windows of a small room. After training to criterion, the infant was moved 180° and his or her anticipatory head-turns observed over the course of five extinction trials. The findings indicated that 9-month-old infants turned their heads primarily in the same direction, relative to their bodies, as before. At 16 months, by contrast, the infants oriented to the same window in the room, thus making a different head-turn. As in the Bremner and Bryant (1977) hiding and finding procedure, the only movement that infants underwent was to the opposite side of the room (through 180°).

A recent study by Rieser (1979) extended Acredolo's (1978) methodology in an attempt to establish how very young infants interact with recurring events at a location. He devised an experimental situation such that infants lay beneath a white dome, in which there were four doors. Six-month-old infants viewed an interesting event after looking at the door to the right or up. The infants were then rotated 90° and Rieser observed the direction in which they looked. If the infants turned to the original door that had the interesting event, the response was termed geocentric—preserving the information concerning the externally defined spatial location of the events. This response was made frequently only under two conditions—when gravitational cues were available and when landmarks were placed on the correct ("geocentric") door and the door opposite it.

If the infants, after rotation, made the same eye and/or head movement as previously to view the event, the response was described as egocentric—preserving the initial information in relation to the infant's own body. This response was predominant in the other four conditions, all of which had no gravitational cues, two having no landmarks and two having landmarks placed on the crucial incorrect (egocentric) door and other(s). It is true that this behavior can be described as maintaining the relation of the response to the infant's body. However, Rieser's (1979) use of the term egocentric was not confined to this descriptive sense, but as we have already seen, was extended to imply a form of spatial coding.

There is a presumption in these studies that the experiment is solely concerned with what the infant learns about the location of the event (rather than information about response contingencies). Once this basic presumption is accepted, it is difficult not to treat each possible response as necessarily indicative of a unique spatial coding system. For example, in Acredolo's (1978) two-choice experiment, the infant's response was judged to be evidence of either objective coding or egocentric coding. Let us consider the interpretation of each response. Given that the infant has successfully located the target after being moved (i.e., has searched the same location, making a different motor response) it is presumably impossible to argue that the location was coded egocentrically. In fact most researchers would argue that this response provides evidence of objective spatial coding.[4] By contrast, given that the infant has made the other, so-called egocentric response there is no necessary implication that the event was spatially coded relative to the infant's body.

The making of an "egocentric" response does not provide clear evidence that any coding of location information was involved. Such a response could equally well be based on either of two types of information, only one of which entails coding of the location of an event. The first type of information is spatial coding relative to the infant's body; by which the event in space might be coded as "located to my right." This is the so-called egocentric coding. The second,

---

[4]It is possible that objective responding is not evidence of coding per se. For example, following Gibson (1966), one might argue that objective information about spatial positions would be afforded directly by the optical flow of information from the spatial array, even when the viewer and/or the array is moved. Lasky, Romano and Wenters (1980) have attempted recently to obtain experimental evidence for this position.

alternative information which could underlie the egocentric response is a learned tendency to respond that implies nothing about the event's location. In this case the information might be described as "When I turn my head this way (or to the right) an interesting event occurs." In the second interpretation, the infant has basically mastered a response-event contingency, akin to those described by Bower (1979), Papousek (1969), and Watson (1966).

The main difference between these two possible interpretations of the "egocentric" response is the extent to which one must postulate the infant's knowledge of external events. For the purposes of this discussion let us crudely suppose that there is a pliable envelope adhering to and enclosing the infant. In the case of an egocentric spatial coding, the infant would "know" something about an event external to this envelope. If the situation is described as response learning, then there is no supposition of particular knowledge about a location external to the envelope. The infant might know only that a response would lead to some stimulation. An interpretation in terms of response learning (rather than place learning) is more conservative and also links the procedure and interpretations conceptually to their predecessors in the animal literature (e.g., Montgomery, 1952; Tolman, Ritchie, & Kalish, 1946). In fact Cornell and Heth (1979) have used procedures very similar to those of Acredolo (1978) to argue that between 4 and 15 months there is little change in the ability of infants to use reliable "response cues," but a marked increase in their ability to use reliable "place cues." Such an interpretation denies that "response cue" knowledge involves any spatial information and contrasts with interpretations in terms of a change from one kind of spatial coding (egocentric) to another (objective).

The studies discussed to this point typically have employed procedures that repeatedly required infants to locate an object or event (Acredolo, 1978; Bremner & Bryant, 1977; Cornell & Heth, 1979; Rieser, 1979). We have argued above that such procedures do not provide sufficient evidence to separate a "learned response" interpretation from one of "egocentric spatial coding." Several recent studies of infants, employing somewhat different hiding procedures, have addressed this problem of "egocentric coding" versus response learning more directly (Acredolo, 1979; Bremner, 1978b). In these procedures, an object has been typically hidden in one of two (left versus right) locations, the infant has been moved 180° around a table before being allowed to search, and the question has been whether he or she would respond incorrectly (egocentrically) or correctly (objectively). Since no prior training (or "A" hiding) trials have occurred, the infant could not have explicitly practiced a particular response prior to the test (analogous to "B" hiding) trials.

Bremner (1978b) compared this no-training procedure to the typical procedure with 9-month-olds in their own homes. He reported a large effect of having prior reinforced trials at the original position. Given no A (training) trials, on the first B trial only 6 (of 16) 9-month-olds made the response described as egocentric after they were moved; compared with 14 (of 16) who had experienced five prior A hiding trials. Bremner concluded that: "Although this experiment has shown that the nine-month-old's organization of space need not be egocentric, we are left with the fact that in many cases it is" (1978b, p. 93). Bremner's findings for the procedure with no training trials were replicated by Acredolo (1979) in the "in home" condition. The data from both studies thus demonstrated that 9-month-old infants are capable of coding spatial information using an objective system, at least in their homes. The strong effect of prior training on strategies is consistent with the view that the earlier data on "egocentric" coding might be better explained as response learning.

Acredolo (1979) interpreted Bremner's (1978b) data as evidence against the infant's "dependence on a spatial reference system centered on the body" (p. 666) and proposed that the findings were a result of testing the infants in their homes, where the surroundings provided familiar "landmarks." She suggested that "reliance on an egocentric system would be found if the procedures were carried out in less familiar surroundings" (Acredolo, 1979, p. 666). She therefore repeated the hiding and moving procedure with no training trials, varying the environment in which testing took place. In their homes, the responses of 11 (of 15) 9-month-olds were classified as objective, whereas in both the office (unfamiliar landmarks) and laboratory (no landmarks) the responses of a clear majority were classified as egocentric. The number of "objective" responders in the office and laboratory was 4 (of 20) in each case. Acredolo argued that familiarity was important in determining whether the infants could use landmarks to enable an objective response. Otherwise, Acredolo's (1979) interpretation retained the notion of a basic egocentricity for young infants, "with egocentricity predominating in the laboratory but not in the home" (p. 667).

The procedure used in the home and laboratory by Acredolo (1979) greatly reduced, and perhaps eliminated, the confound of the learned response possibility with egocentric spatial coding, since this procedure had no training trials. However, one aspect of the experimental situation suggests that there may be an alternative interpretation of the results. During the hiding phase, the experimenter sat directly across the table from the infant and the mother was at the infant's position. After the target was hidden, the mother moved with the infant to the opposite side of the table and the experimenter moved to the infant's original position. Then the infant searched. Note that the mother and experimenter both provided landmark information that supported the "egocentric response." This movement of experimenter and mother along with the child occurred in both the home and laboratory testing situations. Yet in the home the 9-month-old infants made the "objective" response, i.e., located the object correctly.

It is reasonable to suppose that the familiarity of landmarks is an important determinant of their use. But given Acredolo's data it would be equally reasonable to claim that in an unfamiliar setting the infants, rather than using no landmarks, used the most salient landmarks of experimenter and mother to locate the target. These landmarks turned out not to be reliable, of course, since they too moved. However, they constituted quite plausible cues to the target's location; and cues that could not be construed as egocentric.

The results of a recent study support the interpretation of Acredolo's (1979) data given above. Presson and Ihrig (1982) taught 9-month-olds to turn in order to view a slide presented to their left or right. Then the infant was rotated 180° for a test trial, remaining in the same position in the room. The key variable manipulated was whether the mother stayed in place (initially in front and to the right of the infant) or moved through 180° with the infant. For the group in which the mothers remained stationary while the infants moved there were fewer egocentric responses than for the group in which the mothers moved with the infants. Thus these infants were sensitive to their mothers' location as a basis for locating the target. It can therefore be suggested that even in Acredolo's (1979) study (where there was apparently strong evidence of egocentricity) the information that infants used was not necessarily body-centered.

Presson and Ihrig (1982) suggested that the effect of environment observed by Acredolo (1979) reflects the use of different landmarks when in a strange, new environment. In a new environment the infants may narrow their attention to only the most salient aspects of the surrounds; and the location of the mother (and perhaps the experimenter) would be a very important feature for 9-month-olds. As the infants became more familiar and comfortable in an environment, their sense of near space would be likely to increase and they would attend to a wider range of features. Such an interpretation is consistent with Acredolo's (1981a) finding that in a laboratory setting infants do not tend to make egocentric responses if given a 15-minute warm-up period of play in the experimental room.

Using a different methodology, McKenzie, Day, and Ihsen (1984) have added still more evidence that task variables are important determinants of egocentric responses. They trained infants as young as 6 months to anticipate an event occurring in a fixed position. The infants were trained from two different starting positions so that infants turned sometimes to the right and sometimes to the left to a fixed target location (through 30° or 60°). After training, and without further reinforcement, the infants were able to locate the target position when rotated to a new starting position. They did not tend to repeat egocentric responses. McKenzie et al. argued that even quite young infants are able to register the place of a target and monitor the direction and extent of their movements so that the target can be located from a different position. In a manner consistent with the current argument, McKenzie et al. attribute arguments that young infants can only use egocentric spatial reference more to experimental limitations than to the children's knowledge.

In summary, we have reviewed studies demonstrating that in a variety of search and orientation tasks infants often do not seem to use all the information that is available to specify the spatial locations of objects. In some situations, infants make errors that have been described as egocentric. However, we have argued that these errors do not require an assumption that infants have a system of spatial representation based on the body as its center. Further, recent studies have made clear that infants in familiar environments do search or orient to objects in an adequate, objective fashion. The presence of egocentric responding is very often a function of specific task elements (Acredolo, 1981a; Bremner, 1978b; McKenzie et al., 1984; Presson & Ihrig, 1982). It therefore seems unnecessary to invoke two separate representational systems, one of which (objective) must overthrow the other (egocentric). Rather it seems reasonable to propose that the representation of spatial information, even in infancy, is uniformly objective. This proposal has the following implications for spatial coding in relation to the infant's body. To the extent that the infant's body might be used, early in infancy, it would be used as one "object" (like others) to locate another object (Bremner, 1982). In fact, for the young infant, in many situations the body may be a better cue than others since it is relatively immobile. This view of the infant's body as an object and a potential landmark would remove the distinctions made by earlier investigators between the "self-related specification" and the "landmark specification" (Harris, 1977), or between "body-object" (i.e., egocentric) and "object-object" (i.e., allocentric) relations (Pick & Lockman, 1981). The progressions described by Pick and Lockman (at least from body-object to object-object relations) would be considered as the gradual broadening of a single form of spatial representation. Developmental changes would occur as this single form of representation was used in different ways. In our discussion we therefore argue that both structure and process components must be considered for an adequate account of spatial development. In fact an emphasis on process, rather than the traditional emphasis on structure, seems necessary for an integrated and parsimonious account of current empirical evidence.

DISCUSSION

The studies of infant spatial development that we have reviewed do not provide compelling evidence for an "egocentric" form of spatial representation. Even infants as young as 6 months are responsive to objective information in certain task situations (Acredolo & Evans, 1980; McKenzie et al., 1984; Rieser, 1979), which conflicts with the notion that infants are necessarily limited to a body-centered coding of spatial information. In some situations the "egocentric" responses of the infant may be based on response habit rather than spatial coding (Bremner, 1978a; Cornell & Heth, 1979). In other tasks, where the case for egocentric coding seemed stronger (Acredolo, 1979) the infants may well have been using nonegocentric landmarks such as mother (Presson & Ihrig, 1982).

We argue that there is little utility in the notion of an "egocentric" coding of spatial information. As we have seen, the specific response that the infant makes could be based on several sorts of underlying information. Researchers have assumed a rather straightforward link between the infant's response and the infant's understanding or knowledge of space. However, the task situation typically affords many interpretations and it is important to recognize that the "meaning" of a response depends in part on the meaning of the task to the infant.

A striking example of how task variables may bias general conclusions about spatial knowledge is the effect of the amount of change in the infant's position. Most studies move the infant (or the display) through 180°, which interchanges responses to the left and right. Studies providing the strongest evidence of egocentric errors have used 180° trials (e.g., Acredolo, 1979; Bremner & Bryant, 1977). By contrast, when smaller rotations have been used there has been less tendency to make egocentric errors and even young infants have shown some objective understanding (McKenzie et al., 1984; Rieser, 1979). It is unsatisfactory to use data obtained only from 180° trials to advance an argument about general spatial knowledge or skills, since 180° changes represent a special case. The 180° rotations lead to changes in left-right relations that may be especially difficult as a result of symmetries in the nervous system (Corballis & Beale, 1976) rather than as a result of limitations in spatial knowledge. Even with older children and adults, right-left reversals and 180° rotations present particularly challenging demands in many spatial tasks (Howard & Templeton, 1966). A familiar example is letter reversals by young school children. The difficulty of 180° changes can be seen even when an underlying task competence may be clearly shown for other transformations (Presson, 1980, 1982a; Pufall, 1975). Thus, infant tasks that use only 180° rotations may serve to mask further the general spatial competence of young infants.

A similar situation regarding the subject's definition of the task would exist if an adult were exposed to a "simple search paradigm," analogous to the Stage IV task, or to one of its variants involving movements in space. There are several meanings that an adult might ascribe to the particular task. If the adult sees the object hidden he is likely to view the game as one involving a hidden object located in one place. However, if the hider were thought to be a magician, or the hiding not witnessed directly, then the adult also might have other hypotheses about what the correct response would be, even though an object initially always appeared at the same "place." The sort of behavioral rule used by the subject would depend largely on the particular aspects of the task on which the subject was focused.

The studies reviewed above indicate that infants are also capable of using a variety of behavioral rules to solve simple search and orientation tasks. Infants may use response rules or even idiosyncratic rules not based on the task contingencies (although infants who used noncontingent rules often would be excluded for failure to meet some training or pre-test criterion). Infants may use position rules based either on relations to specific cues or landmarks (such as the spatial features of the cover or mother's location), or on more complex spatial frameworks, to define position. The typical regularities in infant behavior have been considered to constitute an "egocentric rule," which can be considered as a special case of position rules. Although there may exist important developmental shifts in the type of "rule" primarily used by children, these rule changes do not unequivocally imply changes in the nature of spatial representation. In fact some rules (e.g., response rules or noncontingent rules) would not imply any spatial coding at all. In summary, the rules that infants use do not have clear implications for the nature of spatial representation, but they do indicate how infants use various aspects of information available in tasks presented to them. Interpretive problems have arisen from the use of specific response patterns as direct indicators of representational systems. What is needed is a more explicit focus on the ways in which infants use information in specific task contexts, as illustrated by some of the emerging research on search strategies reported in other chapters of this volume (e.g., Somerville & Haake; Sophian, Larkin & Kadane).

It is also clear that there are important changes in spatial abilities that occur toward the end of infancy. What do these changes entail? Although much of the literature we have discussed speaks of a shift in representation, we feel that the changes are best described in terms of the *uses* of spatial information rather than the nature of represented spatial information itself. Specifically, they can be explained by distinguishing primary versus secondary uses of spatial information.

PRIMARY AND SECONDARY USES OF SPATIAL INFORMATION

As discussed in the introduction, there are two major ways in which humans use spatial information, which we will term *primary uses* and *secondary uses*. Primary uses of spatial information include practical orientation and action in direct relation to aspects of space. Infants are limited to using spatial information in these primary ways, one of the principal ones of developmental interest being searches for hidden objects. Secondary uses of spatial information include symbolic representation and allow older children and adults to think about spatial information to which they are not directly oriented. Secondary uses include aspects of spatial thought (e.g., drawing or reading maps, mental rotation).

This distinction between primary and secondary uses of spatial information is the one Piaget made in distinguishing practical, or sensorimotor, space from conceptual, or representational, space. Piaget used the term representation to refer to aspects of spatial thought, which is a secondary use of information. As we have indicated, this usage sometimes has been confused with the use of representation to refer to coding or storage. That is, Piaget's claim that conceptual space is attained after infancy has been interpreted to mean that the younger infant does not have spatial representation (as storage). More recently people have recognized that using representation to refer to storage is distinct from

Piaget's usage (Mandler, 1983; Mounoud & Vinter, 1981; Nelson, 1981; Newcombe, 1981).

It is important to recognize that Piaget did allow for representation (as storage) in the young infant: "Therein is manifest undeniable memory of position . . . .[but] that which the child *rediscovers* is still only his initial position related to the object" (Piaget 1954, p. 135, italics added). This statement typifies the complexity of Piaget's writing. Although the second part might be used to support a view of egocentric coding, the statement as a whole conveys that when the infant *uses* the information, the result is non-objective. Thus, infant egocentrism is a lack of ability to think or reflect about space, or to use spatial information in a flexible manner, not necessarily a body-centered coding of spatial information.

Piaget and Inhelder's (1967) distinction between practical and conceptual space is important for considering developing uses of spatial information. However, their terminology has not been adopted systematically, in part due to confusion between different meanings of the term representation, and the interpretation has sometimes been made that conceptual space *replaces* practical space, as representation replaces egocentrism. However, the primary uses of spatial information (orientation and action) are not replaced. They are as much a part of the spatial behavior of adults as of young infants. For adults to orient and act in space requires the primary use of their spatial information. The sense of "here" which locates body position relative to some place remains critical as a basis for action. It is also conceptually important for adults (as well as children) to define the "deictic" frame of reference that allows for the communication of ideas like "here" and "there," "this" and "that" and, in some circumstances, "in front of" and "behind" (Miller & Johnson-Laird, 1976).

The primary spatial activities (basic action and orientation) can provide objective information to add to an existing representation of spatial information and, conversely, information in memory can aid action and orientation. Action and orientation, for example when exploring a new place, provide several types of information suitable for constructing a stable knowledge of space: (1) relations as perceived (X was next to Y) and (2) relations as encountered (after reaching X, I also encountered Y). The information from orientation and action are not independent, of course. Certainly the visual-perceptual system is well integrated with movements to guide orientation by the time the infant is mobile (e.g., Bower, 1974). At the same time, when a mature organism is in a familiar area perhaps searching for an object known to move about in certain ways, the primary abilities to orient and to act are aided by drawing on well-known relations from the spatial representation. This information serves to update near space as movement occurs or to extend it beyond the immediate perceptual field.

However, primary spatial activity does not indicate directly the nature of spatial representation. There are other types of short-term information whose spatial content may not be objective in character: (3) memories of state information from orientation (at that time, X was to my right) and (4) action memories (I looked or reached to X on my right). Although specific action memories would play a relatively minor role in long-term spatial representation, they might well interfere with the use of objective information in specific task situations.

When the infant makes a response, for example reaching in a certain direction to search for an object, the response could be based on any of these four types of information at various times. Furthermore, the use of non-objective information does not necessarily mean that more stable, objective information was not available. Any particular response, or set of responses, provides only an indirect index of spatial representation. Even if one considers more complex behavior such as following a route, the behavior might be based on several different types of represented information. Route behavior consists of a series of actions in space organized to achieve a goal. It could be as simple as reaching for an object. Route information contains both temporal and spatial information. Route behavior could thus imply only a series of cues to turn in particular directions, or it might be based on a rather complex map-like representation. The difference is usually thought of in terms of the amount of information about the subparts of the route that is available simultaneously to the individual. However, if an infant follows a route, there is no unambiguous way of knowing the basis for that behavior. This illustrates the general problem of trying to use any single behavioral index to specify the form of an infant's spatial representation. Although performance on a given task may lead to a conclusion that infants do not use objective spatial information in the task, it does not necessarily imply that such information is unavailable.

For infancy we have argued that it is important to examine the task context and the range of spatial (and other) meanings that a given response such as reaching or turning the head may have. This is especially important with infants since their use of spatial information is limited to direct action and orientation. Thus, there is no unique way to identify the nature of the underlying representation. Empirical attempts to specify distinct spatial coding systems have not been successful. The effects of variations in task conditions obtained in recent studies (e.g., Acredolo, 1981a; Bremner, 1978b; Presson & Ihrig, 1982) suggest that developmental changes reflect changes in the way spatial information is used by infants. In short, there are logical and empirical grounds for an interpretation of infant spatial behavior within a framework that emphasizes a developmentally consistent form of representation. In this view only primary uses of that information are available in infancy, and additional, secondary uses develop later.

A further way to assess the usefulness of an interpretive approach emphasizing different uses of information based on a common representation is to examine whether it can also contribute to work on subsequent spatial development. After infancy the child develops new, more abstract ways of using spatial information, which we have termed secondary spatial activities. The secondary spatial activities consist of the functional abilities to gather and manipulate spatial information symbolically. These secondary spatial activities, and the self-awareness that accompanies them, are a powerful complement to the primary uses of spatial information. In addition to acting directly in space, children begin to use information when not oriented directly to it. The attainment of secondary spatial abilities does not entail a new system of representation. Rather, it enables a new, powerful means of using spatial information. These symbolic abilities are not necessary for the attainment of an organized, objective representation of space. O'Keefe and Nadel (1978) referred, in passing, to these human abilities as "optional."

The issues involved in spatial development in older children are at times quite different from those raised in the infant studies we have discussed. Yet, the distinction between primary and secondary uses of spatial information remains of interest, especially when children's failures on tasks are interpreted to indicate a lack of represented knowledge. However, children may have the knowledge and even be able to use it in direct, primary ways. They may fail when it is necessary to use that information in secondary, symbolic ways or to translate information to and from symbolic form. Maintaining the distinction between primary, direct uses of spatial information and secondary, indirect ones, within a more process-oriented task analysis, is important to avoid the static view that the spatial tasks used with older children directly reflect stored spatial knowledge. To examine the implications of recognizing the ways spatial information is used we first review in some detail the classic "perspective-taking task" first presented by Piaget and Inhelder (1967) and often used as evidence for "egocentrism" in children aged 8 or 9 years or even older. A functional analysis of how information is used symbolically in that task can help explicate performance on old and new versions of that task. Finally, we examine how the coordination of primary and secondary uses of spatial information relates directly to search tasks using maps.

The classic perspective-taking task has a subject at one vantage point predict how an array of objects would appear to a viewer in some other position. Piaget and Inhelder (1967) were the first to demonstrate that children tend to act as if the viewer would see the array just as the child currently does. That is, they pick the same photograph to represent what they themselves and the viewer would see. This error Piaget and Inhelder called egocentric, and they stated that the child does not understand that left/right and before/behind are relative to viewing position. This classic view that the egocentric error means that the child's understanding about spatial relations is limited to egocentric, or body-centered, knowledge has guided most interpretations of spatial development in childhood (see e.g., Salatas & Flavell, 1976). Many studies have replicated the basic finding that for the perspective-taking task, errors tend to be of the egocentric type (e.g., Flavell, Botkin, Fry, Wright, & Jarvis, 1968; Laurendeau & Pinard, 1970; Fishbein, Lewis, & Keiffer, 1972). These studies have also demonstrated that the overall task difficulty depends on the nature of the materials used. The more abstract the materials, the more difficult the task. Perspective-taking tasks have been adapted for 3-year-olds (Masangkay et al., 1974) and for 16-year olds (Flavell et al., 1968).

We would argue that performance on the standard perspective-taking task is not a direct index of the child's primary knowledge about space or of his or her practical understanding of the spatial relations. To respond, children must (typically) pick a picture (or model) of how the entire array might look to the viewer. This ability requires a large measure of symbolic understanding about what a photograph or model can convey about the array. Young children have difficulty demonstrating their knowledge because they do not have mastery of secondary spatial skills. They do not separate the "photograph as symbol" from the "photograph as object." Although they do realize that the photograph can stand for the array, they treat it as having only a direct correspondence to how the array would "be" in space. According to this interpretation children who choose the egocentric response may *know* the relation of the array to the viewer implicitly, but they are unable to represent that information symbolically.

Recently, empirical support has been obtained for this distinction between *knowing* the information and being able to choose a symbolic representation to show the information in conventional symbolic form. Huttenlocher and Presson (1979) found that the type of errors made in the perspective-taking task depended on the type of question asked. When models of the whole array were used, children were overwhelmingly "egocentric," as expected. However, if very modest symbolic demands were made on the children (the questions were about individual array elements), the task was much easier and there was no egocentricity overall. Thus, children showed that they knew the information, yet they failed to use it appropriately to pick the correct symbol. Presson (1980) provided further support for this view that the difficulty stems from using spatial symbols rather than lack of knowledge. He showed that the systematic egocentric errors with symbolic pictures were due to the influence of the immediate surrounding spatial field, rather than the picture's relation to the subject (see also, Acredolo, 1981b; Kielgast, 1971; Smothergill, Hughes, Timmons, & Hutko, 1975). Thus, though the children had begun to understand that a picture can stand for the array, they interpreted the symbolic representation as giving information only by its direct orientation as an object.

We would argue, in line with this recent evidence (Huttenlocher & Presson, 1979; Presson, 1980) that these perspective-taking tasks do not demonstrate a new form of internal representation or knowledge about space. Rather they tap the developing symbolic skills of the child, as applied to the abstraction involved in "reading" a picture or model.[5] This interpretation is also consistent with the results of many investigations that have simplified the perspective-taking procedures to show developmental precursors in younger children. The key factor in

---

[5]This argument that children's difficulty in perspective tasks results from more complex symbolic demands, rather than from a lack of knowledge or representation, is further supported by the finding that adults show similar patterns of relative difficulty (Presson, 1982b).

those studies appears to be the decreasing symbolic demands as the task becomes more immediate and closer to a primary spatial task. With fewer symbolic demands, younger children can show their "knowledge" (see e.g., Masangkay et al., 1974).

Finally, the distinction between primary and secondary uses of spatial information can be applied directly to search behavior in the case of map reading. In general, search involves the use of information available about a target's position to guide behavior whose purpose is to locate that target.[6] The relevant question for our discussion of spatial representation concerns the source of that information.

In the hiding studies with infants that we have reviewed, as well as in many of the search tasks presented to older children that are the focus of other chapters, the information to guide search is obtained directly from what the child experiences in the immediate surrounds. Even though the solution of some tasks may depend on the making of inferences (e.g., Somerville & Haake, this volume), these inferences are drawn from information that is directly available. The information so obtained is then also used in a direct way to guide a physical search of the same surrounds. In the case of these tasks, there is no need to consider the distinction between primary and secondary uses of spatial information, because only primary uses seem entailed. However, if the information used to guide the search is obtained from a symbol (such as a map), the translation of the information into direct action is more complex. In using the map to guide a search, the information about the target's location (in the map) cannot always be applied directly to the immediate surrounds. Rather, the coordination of both primary and secondary uses of the information is necessary in order to make adequate use of the map information.

Several studies of map reading have investigated the ability of children and adults to coordinate these primary and secondary uses. Even preschoolers understand that a map has some relation to the critical space, and they typically establish a direct, primary relation in attempting to discover the correspondence between the map symbol and the space. If the map is aligned with the immediate surrounds, this simple correspondence is correct, and young children find it easy to use a marked map to locate a hidden target (Bluestein & Acredolo, 1979; Presson, 1982a). However, just as in the use of spatial symbols to portray "appearance" in perspective tasks, if the map is *not* aligned with the surrounding space, it is much more difficult for young children to use the symbol to locate the target (Bluestein & Acredolo, 1979; Presson, 1982a); with 180° misalignments more difficult than 90° ones (Presson, 1982a). Children appear to use the map marker as a direct index of the target location, and relate the elements in the map to the surrounds in the simplest, one-to-one direct correspondence.

---

[6]If the target's location is known completely, then the search is perhaps more properly called retrieval. More typically, however, only partial information is available, and it specifies a set of possibilities that are used to guide search.

These realistic errors (Presson, 1982a) are very much like the errors in the perspective task with appearance questions, discussed earlier. This difficulty in coordinating the symbolic meaning of the map with the primary, direct relation of the map to the surrounds does not disappear with development. Adults show the same difficulty as do children in using rotated maps, albeit to a lesser degree. If a map is aligned so that there is a direct correspondence between the map and the space, adults can use it effectively to locate a target. However, if the map is misaligned with the space, then adults often treat the map realistically, very much as do children, and make quite large errors (Levine, 1982).

The secondary spatial system does not operate totally independently of the primary spatial system, as is clear from the above discussion of both perspective-taking and map-reading tasks. Studies that deal with spatial symbols (such as maps) must also deal with the fact that the materials used in such tasks have a dual "meaning." First, they are oriented to and perceived directly as objects in primary space. Second, they are treated as symbols of spatial information to represent a hypothetical state of affairs. The use of any information in this way requires different cognitive skills, those we have termed secondary. The beginnings of symbolic understanding are likely to be found in the child's establishment of correspondences between equivalent things. The establishment of spatial correspondence is not difficult if the two aspects are physically aligned; however, it is far more challenging when the two aspects are not in direct alignment (Presson, 1982a; Pufall & Shaw, 1973). It is in the second case that the primary and secondary spatial systems initially conflict and are only coordinated at a later point in development, enabling the child to use symbolic representation maturely.

The coordination between these systems has not been fully explored in any context. However, Minsky (1975) recently dealt in part with the continuing link between the primary and secondary spatial systems, in an artificial intelligence context. He proposed that knowledge be thought of as a set of frames. People have an abstract Global Spatial Frame (GSF), a set of typical locations in an abstract space, of which they are usually in the center. The global frame could contain a set of "view frames" of basic spatial information about the visual appearance and relations of objects. The GSF would be used most often as the basis for what we have termed the primary spatial system, to organize the information about near space. Minsky proposed that it is also used (as part of the secondary system) to imagine oneself oriented in some other place, or to imagine information in some new orientation.

CONCLUSION

When the infant studies reviewed earlier are considered in this broader context, a number of conclusions about spatial development can be drawn. First, there are no compelling theoretical or empirical grounds for retaining the notion of an egocentric system of spatial coding in infancy. Infants' stored representations of spatial knowledge can be regarded as objective throughout, since there are at least some task conditions in which their responses reflect objective knowledge. Second, the fact that regularities in responding are only indirect reflections of stored representations means that our conceptualization of spatial development must be based on spatial knowledge as it is used. For infants in particular, the indices of spatial knowledge are limited to direct action and orientation. Even for older children and adults, there is no way to examine a representational system directly. We have therefore argued that a reorientation toward the uses rather than the structure of spatial representation is necessary for a coherent account of spatial development in and beyond infancy. In particular, this account views the change to a system of symbolic spatial activities, toward the end of infancy, as a change involving the introduction of new uses of the same underlying representation. The earlier primary uses, which guide action and orientation, are not supplanted at this point, but continue to develop in interaction with secondary uses. Finally, an analysis of the performance of older children and adults on more complex spatial tasks also supports an interpretation in terms of the interplay of primary and secondary uses of spatial information. Thus the conceptual framework that has been proposed integrates infant spatial abilities with later developments in a direct and parsimonious way.

Finally, let us consider the points that have emerged from our discussion about the relation between studies of search and studies of spatial representation. Several other chapters in the present volume have emphasized the need to analyze and understand search processes in order to understand the behavior of infants in object permanence tasks. Similarly there is a need to understand what the infant knows about searching when designing search tasks to investigate the development of spatial representation. For infants in particular, we have emphasized the need to investigate the variety of rules that might be applied to the solution of any particular task. Some of these rules, we have argued, will reveal infants' developing uses of spatial information, whereas others will not. Similar arguments apply to the use of symbolic tasks such as map reading or mental rotation to address issues about the development of spatial representation. Thus to study spatial representation requires careful consideration of the knowledge about search that an infant brings to bear on the task. But of course the converse is also true. To study search, one must address issues of object conception and spatial representation at some point. In order to understand search one must understand spatial representations *because* search typically is search for *objects* in a *space* (Wellman & Somerville, 1982). Thus the present analysis can be seen as providing further support to the study of young children's search as an integral part of spatial competence. Given that it is meaningful to talk of infants and young children as in some sense representing item and self in an objective space, then it becomes proper (and necessary) to investigate the search processes they use.

ACKNOWLEDGMENT

Preparation of this chapter was supported in part by NIH Grant HD-13317.

REFERENCES

Acredolo, L. P. (1978). Development of spatial orientation in infancy. *Developmental Psychology, 14*, 224–234.
Acredolo, L. P. (1979). Laboratory versus home: The effect of environment on the 9-month-old infant's choice of spatial reference system. *Developmental Psychology, 15*, 666–667.
Acredolo, L. P. (1981a, April). *The familiarity factor in spatial research: What does it breed besides contempt?* Paper presented at the biennial meeting of the Society for Research in Child Development, Boston.
Acredolo, L. P. (1981b). Small- and large-scale spatial concepts in infancy and childhood. In L. S. Liben, A. H. Patterson, & N. Newcombe (Eds.), *Spatial representation and behavior across the life span* (pp. 63–81). New York: Academic Press.
Acredolo, L. P., & Evans, D. (1980). Developmental changes in the effects of landmarks on infant spatial behavior. *Developmental Psychology, 16*, 312–318.
Bluestein, N., & Acredolo, L. P. (1979). Developmental changes in map-reading skills. *Child Development, 50*, 691–697.
Bower, T. G. R. (1974). *Development in infancy.* San Francisco: Freeman.
Bower, T. G. R. (1979). *Human development.* San Francisco: Freeman.
Bremner, J. G. (1978a). Spatial errors made by infants: Inadequate spatial cues or evidence of egocentrism? *British Journal of Psychology, 69*, 77–84.
Bremner, J. G. (1978b). Egocentric versus allocentric spatial coding in nine-month-old infants: Factors influencing the choice of code. *Developmental Psychology, 14*, 346–355.
Bremner, J. G. (1982). Object localization in infancy. In M. Potegal (Ed.), *Spatial abilities: Developmental and physiological foundations* (pp. 79–106). New York: Academic Press.
Bremner, J. G., & Bryant, P. E. (1977). Place versus response as the basis of spatial errors made by young infants. *Journal of Experimental Child Psychology, 23*, 162–177.
Butterworth, G. (1975). Object identity in infancy: The interaction of spatial location codes in determining search errors. *Child Development, 46*, 866–870.
Butterworth, G. (1977). Object disappearance and error in Piaget's stage IV task. *Journal of Experimental Child Psychology, 23*, 391–401.
Butterworth, G. (1978). Thoughts and things: Piaget's theory. In A. Burton & J. Redford (Eds.), *Thinking in perspective* (pp. 65–89). London: Methuen.
Corballis, M. C., & Beale, I. L. (1976). *The psychology of left and right.* Hillsdale, NJ: Lawrence Erlbaum Associates.
Cornell, E. H., & Heth, C. D. (1979). Response versus place learning by human infants. *Journal of Experimental Psychology: Human Learning and Memory, 5*, 188–196.
Deregowski, J. B. (1977). Pictures symbols and frames of reference. In G. Butterworth (Ed.), *The child's representation of the world.* (pp. 219–236). New York: Plenum.
Fishbein, H. D., Lewis, S., & Keiffer, K. (1972). Children's understanding of spatial relations: Coordination of perspectives. *Developmental Psychology, 7*, 21–33.
Flavell, J. H., Botkin, P. T., Fry, C. L., Wright, J. W., & Jarvis, P. E. (1968). *The development of role-taking and communication skills in children.* New York: Wiley.
Ford, M. E. (1979). The construct validity of egocentrism. *Psychological Bulletin, 86*, 1169–1188.
Frye, D. (1980). Stages of development: The stage IV error. *Infant Behavior and Development, 3*, 115–126.

Gibson, J. J. (1966). *The senses considered as perceptual systems.* Boston: Houghton Mifflin.
Glucksberg, S., Krauss, R., & Higgins, E. T. (1975). The development of referential communication skills. In F. D. Horowitz (Ed.), *Review of child development research* (Vol. 4, pp. 305–345). Chicago: University of Chicago Press.
Gratch, G. (1975). Recent studies based on Piaget's view of object concept development. In L. Cohen & P. Salapatek (Eds.), *Infant perception: From sensation to cognition* (Vol. 2, pp. 51–99). New York: Academic Press.
Harris, P. L. (1975). Development of search and object permanence during infancy. *Psychological Bulletin, 82,* 332–344.
Harris, P. L. (1977). The child's representation of space. In G. Butterworth (Ed.), *The child's representation of the world* (pp. 83–93). New York: Plenum.
Howard, I. P., & Templeton, W. B. (1966). *Human spatial orientation.* London: Wiley.
Huttenlocher, J., & Presson, C. C. (1979). The coding and transformation of spatial information. *Cognitive Psychology, 11,* 375–394.
Kielgast, K. (1971). Piaget's concept of spatial egocentrism: A reevaluation. *Scandinavian Journal of Psychology, 12,* 179–191.
Kosslyn, S. M., Heldmeyer, K. H., & Locklear, E. P. (1977). Children's drawings as data about internal representations. *Journal of Experimental Child Psychology, 23,* 191–211.
Krebs, J. R. (1978). Optimal foraging: Decision rules for predators. In J. R. Krebs & N. B. Davies (Eds.), *Behavioral ecology: An evolutionary approach* (pp. 23–63). London: Blackwell Scientific Publications.
Lasky, R., Romano, N., & Wenters, J. (1980). Spatial localization in children after changes in position. *Journal of Experimental Child Psychology, 29,* 225–248.
Laurendeau, M., & Pinard, A. (1970). *The development of the concept of space in the child.* New York: International Universities Press.
Levine, M. (1982). YOU-ARE-HERE Maps: Psychological considerations. *Environment and Behavior, 14,* 221–237.
Liben, L. S. (1981). Spatial representation and behavior: Multiple perspectives. In L. S. Liben, A. H. Patterson, & N. Newcombe (Eds.), *Spatial representation and behavior across the life-span* (pp. 3–36). New York: Academic Press.
Liben, L. S. (1982). Children's large-scale spatial cognition: Is the measure the message? In R. Cohen (Ed.), *New directions in child development: Spatial cognition* (pp. 51–64). San Francisco: Jossey-Bass.
Lucas, T. C., & Uzgiris, I. C. (1977). Spatial factors in the development of the object concept. *Developmental Psychology, 13,* 492–500.
Mandler, J. (1983). Representation. In J. H. Flavell & E. M. Markman (Eds.), *Handbook of child psychology: Vol. 3. Cognitive development* (pp. 420–494). New York: Wiley.
Masangkay, Z. S., McCluskey, K. A., McIntyre, C. W., Sims-Knight, J., Vaughn, B. E., & Flavell, J. H. (1974). The early development of inferences about the visual percepts of others. *Child Development, 45,* 357–366.
McKenzie, B. E., Day, R. H., & Ihsen, E. (1984). Localization of events in space: Young infants are not always egocentric. *British Journal of Developmental Psychology, 2,* 1–9.
Menzel, E. W. (1973). Chimpanzee spatial memory organization. *Science, 192,* 943–945.
Miller, G. A., & Johnson-Laird, P. N. (1976). *Language and perception.* Cambridge, MA: Belknap Press/Harvard University Press.
Minsky, M. (1975). A framework for representing knowledge. In P. Winston (Ed.), *The psychology of computer vision* (pp. 211–277). New York: McGraw-Hill.
Montgomery, K. C. (1952). A test of two explanations of spontaneous alternation. *Journal of Comparative and Physiological Psychology, 45,* 287–293.
Mounoud, P., & Vinter, A. (1981). Representation and sensorimotor development. In G. Butter-

worth (Ed.), *Infancy and epistemology: An evaluation of Piaget's theory* (pp. 200–235). Brighton, Sussex: The Harvester Press.
Nelson, K. (1981). Social cognition in a script framework. In J. H. Flavell & L. Ross (Eds.), *Social cognitive development* (pp. 97–118). New York: Cambridge University Press.
Newcombe, N. (1981). Spatial representation and behavior: Retrospect and prospect. In L. S. Liben, A. H. Patterson, & N. Newcombe (Eds.), *Spatial representation and behavior across the life-span* (pp. 373–388). New York: Academic Press.
O'Keefe, J., & Nadel, L. (1978). *The hippocampus as cognitive map.* Oxford: Clarendon Press.
Palmer, S. E. (1978). Fundamental aspects of cognitive representation. In E. Rosch & B. B. Lloyd (Eds.), *Cognition and categorization* (pp. 259–303). Hillsdale, NJ: Lawrence Erlbaum Associates.
Papousek, H. (1969). Individual variability in learned responses in human infants. In R. J. Robinson (Ed.), *Brain and early behavior* (pp. 251–266). New York: Academic Press.
Piaget, J. (1954). *The construction of reality in the child.* New York: Basic Books.
Piaget, J. (1959). *The language and thought of the child.* London: Routledge & Kegan Paul.
Piaget, J. (1968). *Six psychological studies.* New York: Vintage Books.
Piaget, J., & Inhelder, B. (1967). *The child's conception of space.* New York: Norton.
Pick, H. L., & Lockman, J. J. (1981). From frames of reference to spatial representation. In L. S. Liben, A. H. Patterson, & N. Newcombe (Eds.), *Spatial representation and behavior throughout the life-span* (pp. 39–61). New York: Academic Press.
Pick, H. L., Yonas, A., & Rieser, J. J. (1979). Spatial reference systems in perceptual development. In M. Bornstein & W. Kessen (Eds.), *Psychological development from infancy: Image to intention* (pp. 115–145). Hillsdale, NJ: Lawrence Erlbaum Associates.
Presson, C. C. (1980). Spatial egocentrism and the effect of an alternate frame of reference. *Journal of Experimental Child Psychology, 29,* 391–402.
Presson, C. C. (1982a). The development of map-reading skills. *Child Development, 53,* 196–199.
Presson, C. C. (1982b). Strategies in spatial reasoning. *Journal of Experimental Psychology: Learning, Memory and Cognition, 8,* 243–251.
Presson, C. C., & Ihrig, L. H. (1982). Using mother as a spatial landmark: Evidence against egocentric coding in infancy. *Developmental Psychology, 18,* 699–703.
Pufall, P. (1975). Egocentrism in spatial thinking: It depends on your point of view. *Developmental Psychology, 11,* 297–303.
Pufall, P., & Shaw, R. (1973). Analysis of the development of children's spatial reference systems. *Cognitive Psychology, 5,* 151–175.
Rieser, J. J. (1979). Spatial orientation of six-month-old infants. *Child Development, 50,* 1078–1087.
Salatas, H., & Flavell, J. H. (1976). Perspective taking: The development of two components of knowledge. *Child Development, 47,* 103–109.
Siegel, A. W., & White, S. H. (1975). The development of spatial representation of large-scale environments. In H. W. Reese (Ed.), *Advances in child development and behavior* (Vol 10, pp. 9–55). New York: Academic Press.
Smothergill, D. W., Hughes, F. P., Timmons, S. A., & Hutko, P. (1975). Spatial visualizing in children. *Developmental Psychology, 11,* 4–13.
Tolman, E. C., Ritchie, B. F., & Kalish, D. (1946). Studies in spatial learning IV: Place learning versus response learning. *Journal of Experimental Psychology, 36,* 221–229.
Watson, J. S. (1966). The development and generalization of "contingency awareness" in early infancy: Some hypotheses. *Merrill-Palmer Quarterly of Behavior and Development, 12,* 123–135.
Wellman, H. M., & Somerville, S. C. (1982). The development of human search ability. In M. E. Lamb & A. L. Brown (Eds.), *Advances in developmental psychology* (Vol. 2, pp. 41–84). Hillsdale, NJ: Lawrence Erlbaum Associates.

Werner, H., & Kaplan, B. (1984). *Symbol formation*. Hillsdale, NJ: Lawrence Erlbaum Associates. (Original work published 1963.)

Yonas, A., & Pick, H. L. (1975). An approach to the study of infant space perception. In L. Cohen & P. Salapatek (Eds.), *Infant perception: From sensation to cognition* (Vol. 2, pp. 3–31). New York: Academic Press.

2 Spatial Knowledge and Its Manifestations

Barbara Landau
Columbia University

Elizabeth Spelke
University of Pennsylvania

Knowledge of space and of the objects that occupy and move through space constitutes a fundamental domain of human cognition. Adults perceive and move smoothly through space, search for and locate objects in spatial layouts, construct and use maps, and even reflect on the nature of their spatial knowledge. As psychologists, however, our understanding of this spatial knowledge is far from complete. What is the nature of this knowledge, and how does it arise?

To begin, we should specify what we mean by spatial knowledge. In our use, spatial knowledge is a system of representations and rules that supports the recording of spatial relationships among objects, and the deduction of new spatial relationships among the same objects. Note that many spatial performances can be explained adequately without reference to such a system. For example, navigation toward a visible or audible object can be explained by appeal to perceptual-motor mechanisms that enable directed locomotion (see, e.g., Hein & Jeannerod, 1983, for examples of such mechanisms). Or, navigation along a previously learned route can be explained by reference to motor memories that specify the muscle movements needed to reach some goal from some starting point. In contrast, some abilities can be captured best by appeal to a system of spatial knowledge. A straightforward example of such an ability is the creation of new routes or detours through a layout. In order to make a detour effectively through a region, one must know the position of the goal and its spatial relationship to the starting point, and one must be able to infer what path or paths will lead efficiently from the starting point to the goal. Construction of such paths requires spatial knowledge—knowledge of the distances and directions among the places in the layout. Adult humans clearly have such knowledge, and other species may have similar systems (Cheng & Gallistel, 1984; Maier, 1929;

Menzel, 1973; Tolman, 1948). Yet, there is surprisingly little evidence that human infants or young children have such knowledge. Why is this so?

First, many demonstrations of young children's spatial *abilities* can be explained adequately without referring to spatial knowledge. For example, infants and children are known to be able to locate objects in space, if sufficient information is provided to aid their search. For infants, this may be a colored cover coincident with the target (Bremner, 1978); for young children, it may be an obvious landmark near the target (Acredolo, 1979). There are interesting developmental changes in children's ability to use such information (DeLoache, 1984; Huttenlocher & Newcombe, 1984). However, efficient location of objects using such information can be explained adequately by one or a set of simple motor-behavioral rules: for example, "go to the red cloth" or "move to the couch, then go forward three steps." Since the performance *can* be explained in this way, there is no need to posit a spatial knowledge system, as described above. Second, existing studies of children's spatial knowledge may underestimate that knowledge by employing tasks that may systematically bias infants and children to fail for reasons other than a lack of spatial knowledge. For example, many experimental tasks require that infants or children find an object after a 180° rotation around an array. Such a task may be hard, however, *not* because there is no spatial knowledge system that could support a 180° transformation; but rather, because an immature motor system may be incapable of producing right-left reversals. In short, an independent constraint on the motor system might interfere with the expression of spatial knowledge.

In this chapter, we argue that a spatial knowledge system may be intact quite early in life, but that children may not always be able to demonstrate that knowledge. We support this argument in two parts, with evidence on the spatial abilities of a young congenitally blind child and normal sighted controls of the same ages. In the first part, we briefly review our previously published evidence for a spatial knowledge system in both the blind child and sighted children. The demonstrations are based on a set of navigation tasks requiring the construction of new routes through a room in the absence of immediate information about the positions of the target locations. The children's successes enable us to expand our description of the nature of the spatial knowledge system. In the second part, we present some new evidence for early spatial knowledge, focusing on one task that has heretofore been used to argue for deficits in the spatial abilities of infants and young children. This is a 180° rotation task, requiring reaching to the left or right before and after rotation. The blind child failed this task systematically through age 5, whereas most of the sighted children succeeded at the youngest ages tested. To explain these differences, we then consider task-specific variables that might lead to success in the navigation task but failure in the rotation task. We propose that one factor, in particular, underlies the dramatic performance differences. Most importantly, we propose that the blind child's difficulty in the rotation task does not in any way stem from deficiencies in her spatial knowledge.

In conclusion, we discuss the possibility that there is very little development in the nature of the spatial knowledge system itself. Instead, developmental changes in spatial navigation seem to reflect an increasing coordination of the knowledge system with action, and with spatial markers in the world. That is, we suggest that development does not change the basic units of the spatial knowledge system; rather, children learn how actions and information in the world can reliably be used to locate particular objects in space.

I. SPATIAL KNOWLEDGE AND THE NAVIGATION TASK

With this general description in mind, we have focused on a young blind child's ability to navigate the environment without benefit of current perceptual information about the locations of objects. The primary motivation for studying a blind child was the logic of forcing reliance on a mental representational system that might be concealed under the more advantageous conditions of looking and searching. Much of children's spatial behavior (as well as that of adults) may be perceptually guided—when we visually search for an object, when we navigate to seen landmarks, there may not be any need to rely on a mental representation of space. For the blind, the situation is different, for they are often without current perceptual information about landmarks and places. Methodologically, the blind child is an especially relevant case, since limitations imposed by blindness can quickly rule out certain hypotheses about the nature of early spatial abilities. Since the blind child's only distance sense is audition, she may be pressed into recruiting spatial representational capacities to locate objects beyond her immediate reach. Two candidates suggest themselves: memorized motor routines, which are burdensome and confined to specific prior experiences; and "cognitive maps" whose formation and use reflect a rule-governed knowledge system that allows endless computation of new spatial relations from the few that are stored in memory. The blind child may thus be especially well suited to revealing the nature of early spatial knowledge.

A second motivation was to discover whether the development of spatial knowledge necessarily involves visual experience. Blindness has often been negatively implicated in the development and use of spatial concepts (see Fraiberg, 1977; Millar, 1975; Potegal, 1982; Warren, 1977). For example, it has been proposed that blindness severely restricts accessibility to spatial information, leading to representational deficits (Fraiberg, 1977); that it biases against the construction of unified spatial representations, leading to difficulties in mental manipulations (Millar, 1975, 1976); and that it denies the perceiver access to a firmly imposed reference system, leading again to difficulties in constructing and manipulating spatial representations (Warren, Anooshian, & Bollinger, 1973). Cited in favor of these views are findings of delays in object location in blind infants and sighted infants who must rely on sound for localization (Bigelow, 1983; Fraiberg, 1977; Freedman, Fox-Kolenda, Margileth, & Miller, 1969); relative difficulties in reversing haptically traced routes in both blind and sighted subjects (Millar, 1975), and the relative superiority on a variety of tasks by late-blinded relative to early-blinded individuals (see Warren, 1977, for review).

Yet conflicting observations come from other sources, suggesting that perhaps blind infants and children have spatial capacities that have not been revealed by the preceding methods. Anecdotal reports suggest that blind infants and toddlers can often find their way about familiar environments (Norris, Spaulding, & Brodie, 1957), and experimental reports have shown that many spatial tasks are solved with close comparability by blind and sighted subjects (Jones, 1975), including apparently difficult tasks such as mental rotation (Carpenter & Eisenberg, 1978; Marmor & Zaback, 1976) and use of maps (Berla, 1982; James, 1982). Convincingly, it has been shown that blind adolescents can use properly constructed tactile maps to guide route and detour formation in unfamiliar geographic regions (Leonard & Newman, 1967). These more positive reports seemed to us consistent with our own naturalistic observations: The blind child we studied appeared to be quite capable of navigating around familiar environments, locating objects in familiar places, taking paths between objects, and predicting the direction of travel to known places from novel locations. Moreover, in related investigations of language learning, we have observed three blind children, none of whom appeared to be lost in space. Rather, they were all quite able to navigate their environments, to locate their favorite toys on command, and later, to verbally direct others in space (see Landau & L. R. Gleitman, in press). These informal observations prompted our experimental work.

In a series of experiments, we investigated the ability of a young blind child to learn paths between objects in a large space, and to use those experiences to generate further, novel paths among the objects.[1] The child, Kelli, was blind due to Retrolental Fibroplasia occurring shortly after birth. Kelli is totally blind, and has been so since approximately 4 weeks of age. We studied her spatial navigation abilities during the age range of 34–60 months.

Initial Experiment

In the first study, Kelli was 34 months old. She was brought into a novel 8' × 10' room, which contained four objects at the positions labeled A–D (see Fig. 2.1). She was seated at A, where she was told she would be shown where some toys were in the room. The ensuing procedures included a training and a testing phase, as follows.

---

[1]The navigation experiments are reported fully in Landau, Gleitman, & Spelke (1981), and Landau, Spelke, & Gleitman (1984). Experiments on Kelli's ability to spontaneously interpret and use simple 3-dimensional tactile maps to guide locomotion are detailed in Landau (forthcoming).

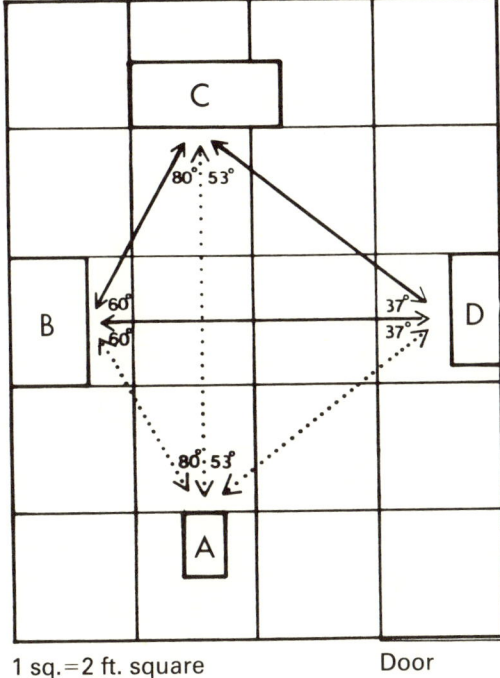

FIG. 2.1. Room layout for navigation task. (Adapted from Landau, Spelke, & Gleitman [1984] by permission of the publisher.)

◄――――► Test Routes
◄········► Trained Routes
A = Mother
B = Pillows
C = Table
D = Basket

During training, she was walked from A to B and back again, twice; then from A to C and back again, twice; finally, from A to D and back again, twice. Each time, Kelli was told where she was at the beginning and end of the route; when she reached the end of the route, she was shown the landmark object from a canonical viewing position, aligned in front and facing the object (see center arrowheads at each landmark in Fig. 2.1). She was allowed to explore the landmarks, and was then turned and guided back to A.

When these routes were completed, Kelli was walked to C, and she was then tested on her ability to find new routes among the three landmarks, B, C, and D. Specifically, she was asked to move from C to B and back again, twice; from C to D and back again, twice, and from B to D and back again, twice; for a total of

12 test trials. Kelli's position at the beginning of each test trial varied unsystematically, in a relationship determined by the route she had just taken. For instance, on the first test trial, she began facing landmark C, and moved to B. Her position on reaching B served as the starting position for the next test trial, moving from B back to C. Sometimes her position at B was identical to her position at B during training, i.e., front and facing B. Other times, however, she reached B at a corner, or a side of the landmark. These times, she was not oriented to front and facing, but rather, was given the next test command from whatever position she occupied at the moment.

For each test trial, Kelli was instructed using simple commands, e.g., "Can you find the pillow?" or "Can you please put this on the table?" When Kelli began moving after each command, the experimenter remained behind her, encouraging her (e.g., "That's good, find the table"), but did not interfere in any way. A trial was terminated when Kelli fell within a 1-foot radius of the block encompassing the target object. Trials were also terminated if Kelli began moving along an inference path that had not yet been tested (e.g., Trials 4, 6, 8), or if she indicated confusion, either by moving in circles, or by explicitly asking for help.In these cases, the trials were always counted as failures (see scoring procedures below). All sessions were videotaped, and Kelli's paths of independent movement were transcribed and used as raw data.

The results were analyzed by a number of methods we devised to determine (a) whether or not Kelli's movements were random with respect to the goal; and (b) whether or not Kelli's movements were directed more toward the goal than toward the other landmarks.

Kelli's paths of locomotion in this experiment are shown in Fig. 2.2. Simple observation of the paths suggests that Kelli did know where she was going and that she moved immediately and directly toward the goal. Her performance was not perfect, however; several trials were terminated upon apparent loss of bearings (Trials 4, 6, 8); and in others, her paths were not completely straight-line, but were somewhat curvilinear. Nevertheless, these simple observations of success in most trials are supported by several statistical analyses of her movement paths, as follows.

First, we analyzed Kelli's initial turns from the source, asking whether these turns were better adjusted to the goal than to the other landmarks. Second, we analyzed Kelli's final positions prior to termination of each trial, asking whether these positions were better adjusted to the goal than to the other landmarks. Finally, we performed a correlational analysis of the relationship between the initial turns and final positions, asking whether accuracy of the initial turn would predict the final position. We assumed that if Kelli knew where she was going, she would make an initial turn that was quite well directed toward the goal, and would then proceed in straight-line fashion to the goal. If this were true, then trials on which her initial turns were accurate would also be those trials for which final position was accurate. Under all of these analyses, Kelli's movement paths were shown to be significantly better than chance: on 11 of 12 trials, Kelli turned

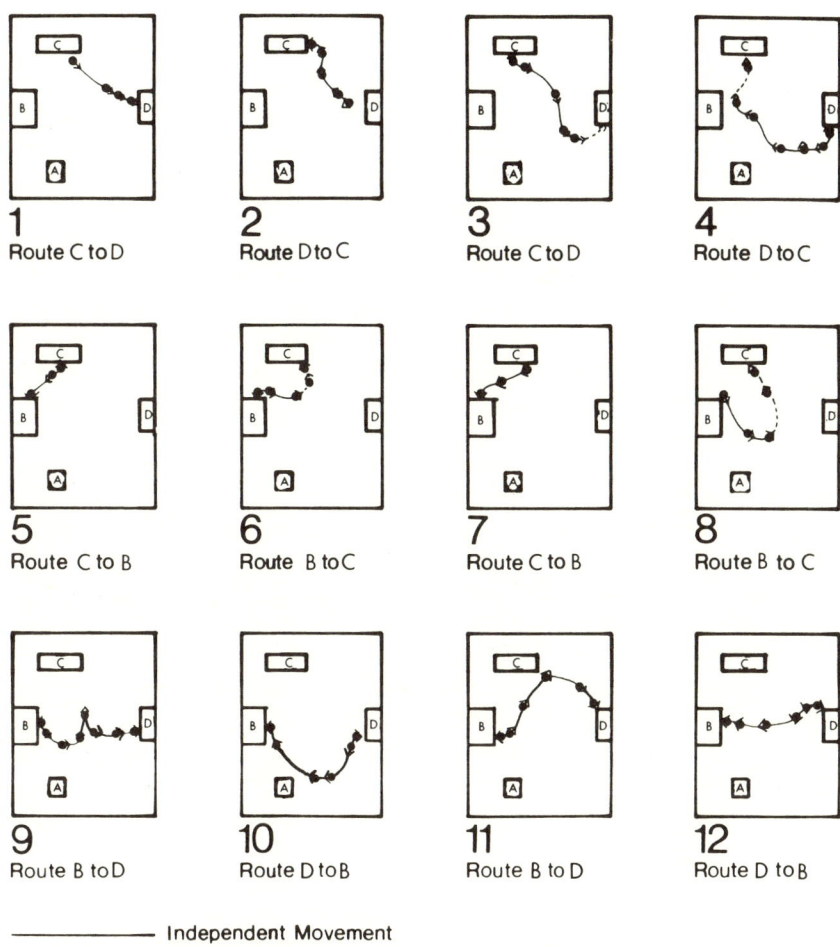

FIG. 2.2. Kelli's paths of movement on navigation test trials. Arrowheads indicate Kelli's frontal directions, and solid circles indicate her positions as she moves. (Adapted from Landau, Spelke, & Gleitman [1984] by permission of the publisher.)

toward the goal (instead of away from it; $p = .0029$, Binomial test); her final position fell within a 40° range subtending the goal on 8 of 12 trials ($p = .0001$, Binomial test). Finally, there was a significant relationship between success or failure on the initial turn, and success or failure on final position, suggesting that the initial turns could predict Kelli's ultimate performance (9 of 12 measures agreed in sign, $p = .05$, Binomial test).

These results suggested that Kelli could indeed use the experience of walking along a set of object-joined paths, to generate new paths among those same objects.

Follow-up Experiments

In later experiments, we sought to contrast Kelli's behavior in this first experiment with her performance under various other conditions. The methods all followed the paradigm of Experiment 1, but the configurations changed slightly and the landmarks changed entirely. In a second experiment (at 43 months), we studied her behavior when the paths were not always object-linked. Here, we removed two of the landmarks (C and D; see footnote 2)[2], and repeated the experiment, training Kelli to move to two places that contained object landmarks (A,B), and to two places containing no landmarks at all (C,D) defined as "your place" and "my place." When she was tested as in the first experiment, her performance showed that she could make inferences relating places in space that were not occupied by landmarks. Her performance was comparable to that in Experiment 1.

We also studied her performance under conditions where we removed possible extraneous sources of information: In a third experiment (36 months), we controlled for the effects of subtle sound cues in the room. We trained and tested Kelli as in Experiment 1. After half the testing session, however, Kelli was carried out of the room, and the array of objects was rotated 90° relative to the room: A was now placed at B's prior position in the room, B was now at C's prior position in the room, and so forth. Then, Kelli was carried back into the room and was placed at her prior position. If Kelli was moving by reference to subtle sound cues within the room, she should now make systematic errors, moving to the wrong landmarks. She did not make such errors; rather, she continued to move appropriately to the landmarks, performing at the same level as before her removal from the room. Further, her performance was not significantly different from that in Experiment 1.

A fourth experiment controlled for experimenter bias. Here, Kelli (53 months) was trained as before, but she was tested by an experimenter naive as to the correct identity of the target landmarks. That is, two identical landmarks were used, called by different names; the testing experimenter never heard the names and referents paired. When she gave Kelli commands to "find X," she did not know whether or not Kelli was moving in the correct direction. Kelli still performed at the same level as in previous experiments.

Finally, we studied Kelli's navigation in the absence of any training. Could Kelli (48 months) navigate to landmarks from various points in the room, without having had prior information about the landmarks' locations, but by using echolocation or some other sensory information? The answer here was clearly negative: in the 1 experiment out of 6 (1 additional not reported here), Kelli performed at chance on all measures. She was only able to navigate between

---

[2]The landmarks changed in each experiment, but the same initials are used here to allow the reader to locate the new landmarks in the array.

landmarks when she had received prior information about their spatial relationships.

The findings of these experiments provided evidence that Kelli had spatial knowledge: She was sensitive to spatial relationships among objects, and she could infer new relationships among those objects. We also replicated the effect with sighted but blindfolded 2- to 3-year-old children, who performed at roughly the same level as Kelli, and with sighted blindfolded adults, who performed better than the children. The comparability of blind and sighted children in this task suggested that the spatial knowledge system arises independently of the particular source of sensory experience.

Kelli's successes in the navigation tasks raised one final question: Were her abilities confined to these navigation tasks, or could they be seen as well in tasks involving maps? Starting at 54 months, Kelli was tested on her ability to use maps to guide her locomotion. These experiments provided evidence that Kelli understood two-object maps from her earliest exposure to them. She could use the maps to locate objects in a large space (10' × 10'); both when the maps were positioned directly in front of her, and when they were presented in several non-canonical positions: under vertical rotation, and sideways translation. Performance in this latter condition was particularly striking: when the map was to Kelli's left (hence both objects on the map were to her left), she was nevertheless able to find a target object located to her right in space (hence, to the right of the "Kelli-symbol" on the map). The experiments demonstrated, therefore, that Kelli understood the relationships displayed on the map to be independent of her own position relative to the map. Kelli's ability to systematically locate the target objects using only the information provided on these maps is testimony to an underlying system of knowledge that was sufficiently rich to make contact with a highly abstract form of experience—a real map.

Some Implications about the Nature of Spatial Knowledge

We suggest that the performances of Kelli and other children provide evidence for a spatial knowledge system with certain definite properties. In particular, solution of the navigation tasks requires a system in which one can record and manipulate metric properties of space. To see why this is so, consider again the navigation tasks. In these tasks, the children were walked along three paths relating four objects: One object served as the origin (A), and each of the three paths lay between A and one of the other three objects in the array. This spatial array could be encoded in a variety of ways. For example, the array could be encoded as a set of landmarks *connected* to each other by the experienced paths. From such a representation, the child would know that paths exist between the pairs of landmarks so encoded. However, if the representation contained only the notion *connectedness,* then one could make inferences only about further connectedness relationships. For example, the child might be able to infer that two other objects are also connected by some path, but he would not be able to differentiate among the infinite number of such paths. He would have no basis for differentiating between paths that lead him randomly around the room, ending up at the goal, and those that are directionally specified straight-line paths between start and goal.

In contrast, the array could be encoded as a set of objects that are connected to each other by paths holding distinct distance and direction relationships to each other. From such an encoding, the child could infer new distance and direction relationships between pairs of the objects. The children's inferences showed that they could determine the new angular relationships between pairs of objects, relationships among paths they had never traveled before. This solution can be described in simple geometric terms: given an angle and two distances (e.g., <BAC and distances AB, AC), one can compute the new angle-distance relationship between objects B and C. The significance of this description is that it suggests a much richer set of geometric properties manifest in early spatial knowledge than has heretofore been imagined (but see Huttenlocher & Newcombe, 1984; Mandler, 1983; for similar notions). Where Piaget (1954; Piaget & Inhelder, 1967; Piaget, Inhelder, & Szeminska, 1960) had envisioned development of spatial knowledge from Topological through Projective and finally Euclidean geometries, it appears from our evidence that Euclidean (or other metric) geometric properties are highly accessible early in life. Note that by this we do not mean that the child's knowledge can be described completely and exhaustively as a Euclidean geometry; this would be highly unlikely, for it would rule out spatial properties such as orientation, which we know to be extremely important in human spatial representations. Rather, we mean that the child's spatial knowledge system incorporates certain metric properties, notably, angles and distances, that can be used to solve navigation-type problems.

To summarize, the use of the navigation paradigm has revealed the presence of a spatial knowledge system that is intact early in life and that has arisen in children with different modalities of sensory experience. However, as we hinted in the beginning, children may not always show that knowledge; certain task demands may bias them toward failure even if they have spatial knowledge. The example we offer in this paper is a rotation task, requiring location of an object in a small array, over 180° rotations. We turn to the results of this paradigm with the blind child and with sighted controls.

2. MASKING OF SPATIAL KNOWLEDGE IN ROTATION TASKS

In these experiments, we sought to compare the spatial capacities uncovered by the navigation tasks to the capacities revealed by a traditional rotation task. We followed procedures similar to those used by Acredolo (1977, 1978) and

Bremner (1978), with the same subjects who had participated in our navigation tasks. To our great surprise, the blind subject who had shown competence in simple detour tasks systematically failed the rotation task. Moreover, we repeated the experiment at intervals spaced over 2 years and found repeated failures, with final success only when she reached 5 years of age. In contrast, most of the sighted blindfolded children succeeded in solving the rotation problem at the same ages at which they had solved the navigation inference task.

EXPERIMENT 1: REACHING OVER ROTATIONS

Subjects

Kelli participated in this experiment at 34 months of age. Four sighted subjects participated, all wearing opaque goggles to prevent vision. They ranged in age from 35 months to 47 months, mean age 37.5 months. These sighted subjects had all participated in the navigation studies reported above, at the same ages. Although Kelli was slightly younger than the sighted subjects at this session, replication over time allows comparison of blind versus sighted subjects at the same age.

Procedures

Each subject was seated in the middle of one side of a rectangular table, 30" × 18" in size. The experimenter sat across from the child, and a third and fourth person (the child's mother and a research assistant) sat at each of the shorter sides (see Fig. 2.3). The child was told she would be having a tea party, and that her task would be to give people cups, napkins, and cookies. To prevent the sighted children from seeing the array, they were equipped with opaque goggles before entering the room. Each child was guided to his or her chair, and allowed to explore the table. They were also told where each person was sitting, and each person confirmed this by saying "I'm here." All the children had met the experimenter and assistant before the experiment, and none had any difficulty recognizing each person's voice.

After the child was seated at the table, training began. The experimenter handed the child a cup and asked, "Would you please give this one to _____?" Each child reached in the appropriate direction (left, right, or straight ahead), and the target person took the cup, thanking the child aloud. The request was repeated, until everyone had a cup. Then, the child was asked to give each person a spoon, then a cookie, always in the following order: mother (A), assistant (B), experimenter, child. Each time a person received something, he or she thanked the child verbally, confirming their location. All children performed perfectly in this part of the task.

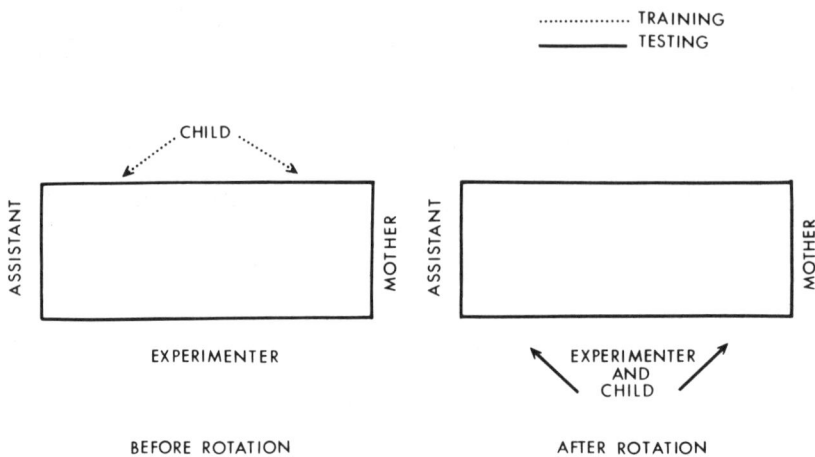

FIG. 2.3. Table layout for spatial rotation task. Children were trained in the position labeled "before rotation." They then moved around the table, and were tested in the position labeled "after rotation."

After training, the child was asked to move around the table to join the experimenter: "Would you please come around and help me?" Each child then walked around the table, past his or her mother, found the experimenter, and climbed up on her lap, to face the table (see Fig. 2.3). Testing then began.

In testing, the experimenter then repeated the same commands as above, asking the child to give persons A and B a cookie, twice in a row, A, B, A, B, yielding a total of 4 test trials in the rotated position. This time, however, no feedback was given about any person's whereabouts; the experimenter took each cookie from the child's extended hand, and said "OK," continuing with the next command. After these 4 trials, the child was asked to return to his or her seat. The original training procedure was then repeated, followed by a second rotation and testing. Thus there were 2 test trials each to A and B for each of two test series, in each of the two conditions—original position and rotated position. This yielded a total of 16 test trials per subject, 8 from the original position, and 8 from the rotated position.

Results

Performance from the original position was perfect, both for the first set of trials, and for later sets that followed testing from the rotated position. This indicates that without vision, both blind and sighted subjects were perfectly capable of determining the positions of all participants, and of holding those positions in memory, even after moving back and forth around the table several times.

The results from the rotated position are quite different and are shown in Table 2.1, as percentage correct, incorrect, and error type. The sighted but

TABLE 2.1
Kelli's and Sighted Controls' Performance in the Rotation Experiments

Experiment	Percent Correct	Percent Incorrect	Percent of Errors	
			Perseveration	Other[a]
Experiment 1				
Kelli (34 mos.)				
Rotation 1	0	100	100	0
Rotation 2	0	100	100	0
Sighted controls[b]				
Rotation 1	75	25	100	0
Rotation 2	75	25	100	0
Experiment 2[c]				
Kelli (35 mos.)				
Rotation 1	50	50	50	50
Rotation 2	67	33	100	0
Rotation 3	0	100	100	0
Experiment 3				
Kelli (37 mos.)				
Rotation 1	50	50	0	100
Rotation 2	0	100	100	0
Rotation 3	75	25	100	0
Experiment 4				
Kelli (51 mos.)				
Rotation 1	0	100	100	0
Rotation 2	0	100	100	0
Experiment 5				
Kelli (57 mos.)				
Rotation 1	25	75	100	0
Rotation 2	25	75	100	0
Experiment 6				
Kelli (60 mos.)				
Rotation 1	100	0	0	0
Rotation 2	100	0	0	0

[a]These responses were of one type only, where, although the child failed to reach to precisely the correct location, she nevertheless effected the proper right-left reversal, by reaching across from herself, to her original location. See text for discussion.

[b]Four sighted controls were all blindfolded before entering the room. Scores reported for these children are mean percent correct and incorrect.

[c]In all experiments, there were a total of 4 responses per subject for each rotation; but in Experiment 2, one test trial was inadvertently omitted for Rotation 2, hence the percents here are based on 3 responses for the rotation.

blindfolded subjects were correct on 75% of the trials, locating both A and B, even though this required a right-left reversal in response. The 25% errors were attributable to one child, who showed right-left perseveration on all these trials. Kelli also was systematically wrong, with all errors right-left perseverations. This initial finding raised two puzzles. First, why had Kelli and the one sighted child failed this task, when both had been so successful in the navigation task? Second, did blindness bias toward failure in this task, accounting for Kelli's failure in both this initial rotation task, and in later similar tasks (see below)?

If our analysis is correct of the requirements of the navigation task, then all of the children should have been able to solve the rotation task at the same time as they solved the navigation task. To be specific, we have argued that the children had a system of spatial knowledge, in our sense: They could detect the directional relationships among objects, and deduce new relationships among them as they moved through space. On initial inspection, the rotation task seems to require just this sort of ability: predicting new directional relationships after movement in space. In fact, an initial examination of the navigation and rotation tasks shows that the two are formally quite alike. First, both tasks use a four-object array, in a "baseball diamond" configuration. Second, both tasks include a training phase and a testing phase. The training phase in both tasks required the child to locate the three target objects, either by walking (navigation experiments) or by reaching (rotation experiment). Testing in both tasks required the child to walk to the landmark opposite his initial position, and then locate the objects from this new position. Both tasks seem to require a spatial inference, since the test routes were not experienced during training in either case. Yet, there must have been some task differences that caused Kelli and the one sighted child to fail the rotation task but succeed in the navigation task.

In the next sections, we propose three hypotheses about the relative difficulty of the two tasks, and evaluate them with some re-analyses of the navigation task data, and with data from later rotation studies with Kelli. In particular, we keep an eye toward answering the two puzzles raised above: Why would any child who succeeded in the navigation task then fail in the rotation task? And, why might a blind child be more likely than a sighted child to fail the rotation task?

The first hypothesis is that degree of rotation from the trained position at test time has an effect on the accuracy of one's inference: the greater the degree of rotation, the more difficult the inference. The second hypothesis is that tasks in which both training and testing require a left-right reaching response bias the subject toward perseveration. The third hypothesis is that lack of sufficient information about one's position in the array further biases toward a perseveration response. We argue that all three factors cooperate to make the 180° rotation task especially difficult for any child. We further suggest that the third factor may be particularly troublesome for a blind child. In discussion, we argue that these factors can help account for the numerous findings in the literature of failure by sighted infants and children in similar tasks. We conclude that the rotation task does not reveal spatial knowledge—not because such knowledge is lacking, but because systematic biases conspire to mask such knowledge.

Hypothesis 1: Increasing the Degree of Rotation Increases Task Difficulty

Intuitively, the two tasks seem to differ in the requirement to effect a significant mental rotation at test time. In the navigation task, the children were often given test commands from a position facing the target as in training ("canonical" position), or from a position slightly different from this; but they were rarely given a test command from a position that differed by 180° from their trained position (see Part I, p. 32). In contrast, in the rotation task, they were always given test commands from a position that was 180° rotated from the canonical position. We know that 180° rotations are difficult for adults and children alike, over different tasks (Acredolo, 1977, 1978; Cooper & Shepard, 1978; Huttenlocher & Presson, 1979). These facts would predict that the 180° rotation task should be significantly more difficult than the navigation task, simply because the degree of rotation at test time is more extreme. Furthermore, some investigators have suggested that blind children have particular difficulties performing such rotations. Specifically, it has been proposed that blind children's spatial representations are "kinesthetic" in nature, derived from their experience exploring an array; and that these kinesthetic representations are difficult to reverse or rotate, since they preserve the sequenced nature of the original experience. In contrast, vision-based representations are thought to be considerably easier to manipulate, since all parts of an array are available more or less simultaneously (Millar, 1975, 1976). This view would predict Kelli's failure in the rotation task, relative to the success of three of the sighted children; and if true, would suggest an important difference between blind and sighted children's spatial knowledge systems.

To evaluate the hypothesis that degree of rotation (a) affects performance in sighted subjects and (b) differentially affects performance in the blind subject, we returned to the navigation task data. First, we computed each child's position at the time each test command was given. The results are shown in Table 2.2, which displays the positions (canonical or non-canonical, by degrees) held by the children at the beginning of each test trial. Canonical positions were considered to be those experienced by the child at each landmark during training, i.e., facing forward into each landmark (see center arrowheads at each landmark, Fig. 2.1). Kelli was in canonical position on 5 of the 12 trials, and the sighted controls were in canonical position on 33 of the 48 trials. The sighted control who failed the rotation task is S4, whose pattern of positions at test time is not different from either Kelli's or the other sighted children's. The most frequent deviation from canonical position was by 46–90°; in fact, most of these were actually 90°

TABLE 2.2
Deviations from Canonical Position at Test Time (Number of Trials)

Subject	Canonical	Non-canonical (degrees)			
		5–45	46–90	91–135	136+
Kelli	5	0	4	3	0
Sighted subjects					
S1	11	1	0	0	0
S2	6	1	5	0	0
S3	9	0	1	1	1
S4	7	3	2	0	0

deviations. A child was in a non-canonical 180° rotated position on only 1 out of the 72 trials across all subjects. Thus, although in the navigation task a child was virtually never tested from a 180° rotated position, still, the children were tested from non-canonical positions that would have required mental alignment of the actual space with the represented space. If increasing the degree of rotation increased difficulty of response, performance from canonical positions should be better than from non-canonical positions.

To see whether or not this was true, we cross-classified each trial for each subject in terms of canonical versus non-canonical starting position, and success versus failure on that trial. For the latter, we used the strict criterion of success on both measures (initial turn, final 40° segment; see Part I). The results are presented for Kelli and the sighted controls in Table 2.3.

As can be seen, the children appear to do well with canonical starts, but less well with non-canonical starts. They clearly *can* perform inferences from non-canonical starts, although these tend to be less accurate than from canonical starts. Kelli's performances pattern the same way as the sighted children's. In addition, the single sighted subject who failed the rotation task showed the same pattern of performance here as both Kelli and the other sighted children; so failure in the rotation task does not appear to be related to a distinctive pattern of

TABLE 2.3
Canonical Position at Test Time and Success on Navigation Task

		Success	Failure
Canonical Start	Kelli	4	1
	Sighted	5.75	2.5
Non-Canonical Start	Kelli	4	3
	Sighted	1.75	2

performance in this analysis. Non-canonical starts produce worse performance than canonical starts for all subjects.

These results confirm the notion that increasing the degree of rotation from canonical position increases the difficulty of the response, and is in accord with other findings in the literature (see above). However, the second prediction—that of differential effect on the blind subject—is disconfirmed by the data: Kelli's performance patterns the same way as the sighted children's. This disconfirms the notion that blindness interacts with degree of rotation so as to produce poorer performance by the blind with increased rotation. Although our sample is too small to draw firm conclusions, it appears that inferences from non-canonical positions are less accurate than from canonical positions, but that degree of rotation does not differentially affect the blind child.

To summarize, degree of rotation does seem to affect performance, but similarly for Kelli and the sighted subjects. This suggests that although part of the rotation task difficulty can be attributed to the extreme degree of rotation required, it does not completely account for the difficulty some children experience in this task.

Hypothesis 2: Motor Interference Biases Toward Perseveration in 180° Rotation Tasks

The second hypothesis is that tasks requiring a left-right reaching response in both training and testing bias toward perseveration. The source of such a bias could be the normal tendency to use a body reference system within reaching spaces, coupled with motor interference after rotation. For example, we often encounter small (tabletop) arrays from a fixed position, hence we may be used to relying on fixed responses in such settings. Very often, such a bias will result in success, for instance, while searching for one's fork at the dinner table (always on one's left), or for one's stapler in the desk (always in the right-hand drawer), and so on. In contrast, for navigation tasks, such a bias would be successful only in very restricted circumstances in which the starting point is fixed, e.g., walking out the front door to go to the garage; walking into one's bedroom to go to the closet. In fact, anecdotal observations of Kelli in her home environment support the notion of a bias toward perseveration in reaching spaces, but not navigation spaces. For example, when Kelli was seated at a table, either to eat a meal or to do some work, the objects on the table were always in a fixed spatial relation relative to her. This was because her parents were quite careful to arrange them consistently: Her cup was always placed to the left of her plate during mealtime, her Braille slate was always placed to the right of her text during school work, etc. Kelli knew where to find these objects and where to replace them; and she also knew that they would always occupy these same positions. There were several occasions on which Kelli was unaware that she was in a new position at the table, and perseveration from previous responses was rampant. This rarely happened outside of these situations. Thus the in-principle difference in the utility of a body-reference system for reaching versus navigation tasks seemed to be a true difference in fact.

The utility of fixed responses in many small array reaching tasks introduces an important extra variable in tasks requiring reaching after movement. If fixed responses are normally used, then requiring a left-right reversal after movement may introduce interference from the motor system, independent of whether or not one *knows* where the objects are. If such interference exists, it should be possible to reduce or eliminate it either by omitting the trained responses, or by changing them relative to the tested responses. This logic can be seen in an experiment by Bremner (1978), who prevented 9-month-old infants from reaching before a 180° rotation, and found a significant reduction in perseverative responses after rotation. We used a similar method to evaluate the motor interference hypothesis with Kelli. Specifically, we tested Kelli in two modifications of the rotation task. These modifications were based on the logic that if reaching in both training and testing biases toward a self-reference system, then changing the response in either training or testing should improve performance. In Experiment 2, we trained Kelli on reaching, but tested her on walking; in Experiment 3, we trained Kelli on walking, but tested her on reaching. In both experiments Kelli's performance improved, although it was still not perfect.

EXPERIMENT 2: CHANGING THE TEST RESPONSE TO WALKING

The study was conducted when Kelli was 35 months old. We trained Kelli as before, and asked her to move around the table in a path resulting in a 180° rotation as before, but then tested her differently. We included three rotations: after each of the first two, we asked Kelli to *walk* to the target people; after a third rotation, we asked her to *reach,* as in Experiment 1. Thus, there were 12 trials from the original position and 12 trials from the rotated position (4 after each of three rotations).

As in Experiment 1, Kelli performed perfectly from the original position. The results from the rotated position are presented in Table 2.1. After the first rotation, Kelli got 50% correct, with half of the errors perseverations. The other half were errors in which she did not reach directly to the correct person (A), now on her right, but rather, reached across the table, in between B's and A's true positions. This response type was classified as an error, although it shows the proper left-right reversal. If this "error" is classified as correct on the basis of correct reversal, Kelli achieves 75% correct, with 25% perseveration. The results after the second rotation are similar. Here, Kelli got 67% correct, with 33% perseveration errors. These two sets of responses suggest that walking during testing does aid in breaking the set of perseverative responding. Further, the results after the third rotation reinforce this conclusion: When asked to reach during test, Kelli completely failed, with 100% of the responses perseverations. This is even though she had enjoyed some moderate success on the two previous rotations.

EXPERIMENT 3: CHANGING THE TRAINING TO WALKING

In this experiment, Kelli was 37 months old. We trained Kelli as in Experiment 1, except that she was asked to *walk* from her original position, directly to A and B. After the first and second rotation, Kelli was asked to *reach* to each of the participants; after a third rotation, she was asked to *walk* to them. As in the prior experiments, after each rotation, Kelli returned to her original position, and was re-trained—each time with walking.

As before, Kelli's performance from the original position was always perfect. Results from the rotated position are shown in Table 2.1. After the first rotation, Kelli was asked to reach, and was correct 50% of the time. The remaining 50% of the responses were errors of the sort described in Experiment 2: responses where Kelli reached across the table, achieving the proper left-right reversal, but without the precise accuracy required for a "correct" response. Collapsing these "errors" with the correct responses yields a total of 100% responses that were correct. After the second rotation, however, Kelli failed, with 100% of her responses perseverations, suggesting that whatever advantage had been gained by training her with walking was rather fragile. After the third rotation, Kelli walked to the targets correctly 75% of the time. This latter success may have been due to feedback on the initial trial: She erred by reversing left and right, reaching the assistant instead of her mother. She exclaimed "Kathy!" as if to say "What are you doing here?" Then, on the remaining trials, she reversed left and right correctly.

To summarize the results of Experiments 2 and 3, it seems that some improvement in responding was achieved by requiring a different response during training and testing. Kelli's performance was poorest in the condition in which she was trained by reaching and tested by reaching. Her performance improved somewhat when she was trained with reaching and tested with walking, trained with walking and tested with reaching, or trained and tested both with walking. The difference between reaching and walking tasks seems to reflect the greater likelihood of initially responding via a body reference system during training with reaching responses, coupled with the ensuing interference from the requirement to reverse this right-left response.

We should note that Kelli's improvement in Experiments 2 and 3 was not due to the mere fact that she was older at this time than in Experiment 1. Kelli continued to fail the original rotation task (train, reach; test, reach) two more times: once at 51 months and once at 57 months (Experiments 4 and 5, see Table 2.1), with all errors left-right perseverations. Finally, she was completely successful in the original task at 60 months (Experiment 6, Table 2.1). Thus, motor interference appears to account for part of Kelli's poor performance in the rotation task. However, it is not the only explanation: suspending the reach-reach requirement improved Kelli's performance, but did not make it perfect.

Hypothesis 3: Lack of Information About One's Current Position Leads to "Egocentric Localization" of Objects

An enormous body of literature attests to the fact that information about one's current position is crucial to making accurate spatial inferences. This fact was first discovered within the animal literature, in the context of the place-response debate (Tolman, 1948; Tolman, Ritchie, & Kalish, 1946; see O'Keefe & Nadel, 1978; and Restle, 1957, for reviews). The relevant paradigm here was one in which the animal is trained to run through a cross-maze, making either a right or left turn, to get to a goal box. After training, the maze is rotated, or the animal is started from a new location, and the experimenter observes whether the animal runs to the same *place* in the maze, or makes the same *response* as in training, running left if trained to the left, and right if trained to the right. The outcome of an enormous set of such studies suggests that animals are not constrained either to learn exclusively about their own actions or to learn exclusively about the layout of the environment. Rather, the particular behavior observed is a function of information provided in the environment. Rats will apparently take advantage of a variety of spatial cues in an environment, and their response depends on what cues are available. When very little information is available—especially when run in a homogeneous or poorly lit environment—the rats tend to be response learners. When rich extra-maze information is present, they tend to be place learners.

Surprising parallels have been found in developmental investigations of human spatial abilities. Infants and young children tend to learn to repeat actions that were previously successful when there is little information in the environment, and they tend to learn about places in space when there is more information available. For example, both infants and young children tend to behave like "response learners" in unfamiliar settings (Acredolo, 1977), with few or no landmarks (Acredolo, 1978), and when only parts of the background, not the objects themselves, are distinguishable (Bremner, 1978). In contrast, when there is more information, infants and young children learn about the locations of objects in the spatial layout (Acredolo, 1979; Bremner, 1978). For example, even 9-month-old infants can retrieve an object after they have undergone a 180° rotation when the objects are distinctively marked (Bremner, 1978). Moreover, an interesting developmental trend has been found: Infants seem predisposed to use landmark information that is proximate to target places, but toddlers and children increasingly use landmark information that is more distant from the targets (see Huttenlocher & Newcombe, 1984, for a review).

These findings are relevant for an analysis of Kelli's failure in the rotation task. In general, it appears likely that Kelli may have perseverated with trained left-right responses because she had no information available to indicate where she had moved. The argument has several parts, each of which predicts a differential difficulty in this task for a blind subject.

First, the pragmatic situation for the blind child is very often one of information deficit: Whereas the sighted infant, child, or adult can look around and observe landmarks, there are few sources of information about the surrounding spatial layout that the blind can normally use, even in principle. Thus, the blind child is often in the position of not knowing where she is. There are, of course, ways that the blind learn to compensate in part for this lack—by taking advantage of subtle cues in the environment, or by keeping mental track of where they have been, inferring where they must now be. However, the normal pragmatic lack of information might plausibly lead the blind to rely on a body reference coding whenever possible. We have already argued above that the reaching task was one that Kelli would have been biased to code in this way, through her normal experience.

Second, it would be possible for Kelli to break this set if there were some compelling information available that would enable her to locate herself in the array as she moved around it. For example, if some constantly sounding object had been in the room, she possibly would have been able to determine where she was in the array after the rotation. The table itself provided no such information, since it was straight-edged and wooden, identical from both sides. There was one source of information, in principle, however—the experimenter's position. Kelli apparently did not use this information—a fact to which we return below.

In contrast to the conditions of the rotation task, the navigation task provided rich information about the child's current position in the array. For example, the child always either reached the target landmark, or was guided to it after a failure, before starting on the next test trial (recall that the child always started a test trial from some landmark). Each landmark had a distinctive spatial configuration, hence could be used to mentally align one's mental map with one's current position. In contrast, in the rotation task no feedback was given: The children were to reach out toward each target person, but no feedback was given as to whether or not the direction of the reach was correct (the experimenter took each cookie from the child's outstretched hand, and said "OK"). This informational difference in itself would predict the increased difficulty for the rotation task over the navigation task. But why did three of the four sighted and blindfolded children succeed, while Kelli failed?

There was one source of information that the sighted children must have been using: the position of the experimenter herself. The successful children must have known that she was seated opposite them before rotation, and must have been able to determine that when they reached her lap, they were in a position 180° rotated from their original position. There is independent evidence that sighted infants can use their mothers as a landmark (Presson & Ihrig, 1982); hence it seems likely that our toddler subjects used the experimenter as a landmark. But why didn't Kelli use this information?

The key issue here seems to be the selection of only certain kinds of information as reliable guides to locating objects. Although Kelli could have succeeded if she had used the experimenter's position as a landmark, it is well known that young children are not always capable of using information that in principle seems sufficient for guiding search (DeLoache, 1984). In the present case, we speculate that while people and other animate objects are never very good landmarks for any spatial animal, they are particularly poor landmarks for the blind. In order to be useful landmark information, an object must be stably located and predictable. Clearly, people are neither, although for the sighted child, it is certainly easier to track a person's whereabouts than it is for the blind child, whose only source of information for tracking moving objects is sound. In fact, sound alone appears to be a rather poor guide to locating objects for the blind as well as the sighted. Fraiberg (1977) showed that blind infants could not use sound to guide search behavior until late in the first year; Freedman, Fox-Kolenda, Margileth, and Miller (1969) showed the same was true of sighted infants who were prevented from using vision. Recently, Bigelow (1984) has uncovered some intriguing and compelling facts about search in blind infants: Although the infants cannot locate a sounding object that has been taken from their grasp and moved along a simple trajectory, they *can* locate a *silent* object that they have dropped spontaneously. This strongly suggests that information one might assume would be useful for the blind (i.e., sound) will not always be useful in fact. It is possible that the key difference between information about sound and information derived from dropping an object has to do with its relative predictability: One can predict the trajectory of a dropped object if one implicitly has knowledge of some basic physics; but one cannot necessarily predict the exact location of a sounding object unless it is very familiar.

In sum, it seems likely that Kelli was not using the information about the experimenter's position simply because she did not entertain the possibility that the experimenter was a good source of information about the layout. Given the frequent occasions when Kelli must have assumed someone was in a stable position, only to find out they had (silently) moved, this would be sensible behavior.

Summary of the Rotation Task Results

We have proposed three hypotheses to account for Kelli's and the one sighted child's failure in the rotation task, relative to their success in the navigation task. First, we proposed that increasing the degree of rotation will inevitably increase the task difficulty for blind and sighted subjects alike. Second, we proposed that tasks requiring reaching in both training and testing might bias toward perseveration due to initial coding biases plus interference from the motor system when a right-left reversal is required during testing. Based on evidence from the infancy literature, we suggested that this bias might affect blind and sighted subjects alike. Finally, we proposed one serious difference between blind and sighted subjects, in the kinds of information they will use to guide their spatial behavior. Blind subjects may be less likely than sighted subjects to use people and other animate objects as spatial markers, because these potential markers are both unpredictable and often untrackable. It may well be more crucial for the blind child to select potential landmarks with extreme care, since the chances of getting lost increase tremendously if one cannot explore the world visually.

It should be clear that none of these differences alone will completely account for the difficulty of the 180° rotation task, nor for Kelli's failure relative to the three successful sighted children. However, each factor biases toward right-left response learning in this task, and the combination of factors must surely add up to a propensity to perseverate during testing. There may well be additional factors that have not been discussed here that contribute to the difficulty of this task. For example, recent evidence suggests that an important variable is the complexity of the movement the subject undergoes: When infants undergo a simple rotation (change of orientation, not location), or a simple translation (change of location, not orientation), they can account for 90° or 180° rotations, and simple translations. In contrast, if they undergo a combined rotation and translation—as in rotations around a table, changing both orientation and location—they tend to perseverate (Kramer, 1984; Landau, 1984). No doubt there are other factors as well that conspire to make the traditional rotation task extremely difficult. But we do not believe that any of these factors causes difficulty because of deficits in the spatial knowledge system.

3. CONCLUSIONS

In this chapter, we have presented evidence on the spatial abilities of young children, using two very different types of task. In a navigation task, a blind child and sighted but blindfolded children performed well, recording the spatial relationships among objects in a large array, and making inferences to predict new angle-distance relationships among those objects. These results suggested the existence of a spatial knowledge system that has arisen rather early in life, and independent of the modality of experience. In a rotation task, most of the sighted children at the same age were also seen to perform well; but the blind child systematically failed the task through age 5. The results of the rotation tasks suggested that it is not always possible for children to show their spatial knowledge. In particular, an analysis of the rotation task suggested several features that may conspire to bias children toward "egocentric localization" of objects, masking the expression of spatial knowledge that we have seen evidenced in the navigation task.

The results as a whole suggest that the basic elements of spatial knowledge may be intact rather early in life, but that the expression of this knowledge may require development of at least two kinds. One is the increasing coordination between knowledge and the systems that use this knowledge to act on the world. For example, in the case of the rotation task, a motor bias may result in the failure to locate an object after rotation, even if the child knows where the object is. As the child grows, increasingly precise coordinations between knowledge of space and the motor system will lead to increased success in locating objects under yet more demanding conditions. A second kind of development is the increasing coordination between knowledge and the markers that exist in the world and are used to address this knowledge. For example, children must learn that certain objects and not others make good landmarks. The blind child's difficulty in our rotation task may have been due partly to our provision of only a limited and rather ineffective kind of landmark—a person. Yet she, as well as sighted children, will come to recognize the existence of a much broader range of possible landmarks, and will no doubt become more flexible in her use of them.

Both kinds of development presuppose that the spatial knowledge system, even if present very early in life, must become aligned with devices that will allow its expression. One kind of alignment is with the action system that will enable the child to actually retrieve objects. Another kind of alignment is with the evidence provided in the real world—information that can be used to guide and address the knowledge system. For example, objects exist in the world, and they can be used as landmarks to mediate the interchange between the spatial knowledge system and the physical world. Children must discover which of these objects can and cannot be reliably used as landmarks, and which of these objects *typically* are or are not used as landmarks. These discoveries and alignments are part of the development of spatial abilities—but not part of the development of spatial knowledge itself.

ACKNOWLEDGMENTS

We wish to thank Henry Gleitman and Lila Gleitman for extensive conceptual support and collaboration in all phases of this project. This work was supported by a Social and Behavioral Sciences Research Grant from the National Foundation—March of Dimes to Lila R. Gleitman and Barbara Landau; a Biomedical Research Grant to Barbara Landau; and a NICHD award to Elizabeth Spelke.

REFERENCES

Acredolo, L. P. (1977). Developmental changes in the ability to coordinate perspectives of a large-scale space. *Developmental Psychology, 13,* 1–8.

Acredolo, L. P. (1978). Development of spatial orientation in infancy. *Developmental Psychology, 14*, 224–234.
Acredolo, L. P. (1979). Laboratory vs. home: The effect of environment on the 9 month-old infant's choice of spatial reference system. *Developmental Psychology, 15*, 666–667.
Berla, E. P. (1982). Haptic perception of tangible graphic displays. In W. Schiff & E. Foulke (Eds.), *Tactual perception: A sourcebook*. Cambridge: Cambridge University Press.
Bigelow, A. E. (1983). Development of the use of sound in the search behavior of infants. *Developmental Psychology, 19*, 317–321.
Bigelow, A. E. (1984, April). *The development of blind infants' search for dropped objects*. Paper presented at the International Conference on Infant Studies, New York.
Bremner, J. G. (1978). Egocentric vs. allocentric spatial coding in 9 month-old infants: Factors influencing the choice of code. *Developmental Psychology, 14*, 346–366.
Carpenter, P. A., & Eisenberg, P. (1978). Mental rotation and frame of reference in blind and sighted individuals. *Perception and Psychophysics, 23*, 117–124.
Cheng, K., & Gallistel, C. R. (1984). Testing the geometric power of an animal's spatial representation. In H. L. Roitblat, T. G. Bever, & H. S. Terrace (Eds.), *Animal cognition*. Hillsdale, NJ: Lawrence Erlbaum Associates.
Cooper, L. A., & Shepard, R. N. (1978). Transformations on representations of objects in space. In E. C. Carterette & M. P. Friedman, *Handbook of perception* (Vol. 8). New York: Academic Press.
DeLoache, J. S. (1984, April). *Toddlers' exploitation of cues to guide memory-based searching*. Paper presented at the International Conference on Infant Studies, New York.
Fraiberg, S. (1977). *Insights from the blind*. New York: Basic Books.
Freedman, D. A., Fox-Kolenda, B. J., Margileth, D. A., & Miller, D. H. (1969). The development of the use of sound as a guide to affective and cognitive behavior—a two-phase process. *Child Development, 40*, 1099–1105.
Hein, A., & Jeannerod, M. (Eds.) (1983). *Spatially oriented behavior*. New York: Springer-Verlag.
Huttenlocher, J., & Newcombe, N. (1984). The child's representation of information about location. In C. Sophian (Ed.), *The origins of cognitive skills*. Hillsdale, NJ: Lawrence Erlbaum Associates.
Huttenlocher, J. A., & Presson, C. (1979). The coding and transformation of spatial information. *Cognitive Psychology, 11*, 375–394.
James, G. A. (1982). Mobility maps. In W. Schiff & E. Foulke (Eds.), *Tactual perception: A sourcebook*. New York: Cambridge University Press.
Jones, B. (1975). Spatial perception in the blind. *British Journal of Psychology, 66*(4), 461–472.
Kramer, S. J. (1984, April). *Infant coding of spatial orientation as a function of different transformations*. Paper presented at the International Conference on Infant Studies, New York.
Landau, B. (1984, April). *Rotations and translations in infancy*. Paper presented at the International Conference on Infant Studies, New York.
Landau, B. (forthcoming). Early map use by a congenitally blind child.
Landau, B., & Gleitman, L. R. (in press). *The language of perception in a blind child*. Harvard University Press.
Landau, B., Gleitman, H., & Spelke, E. (1981). Spatial knowledge and geometric representation in a child blind from birth. *Science, 213*, 1275–1278.
Landau, B., Spelke, E., & Gleitman, H. (1984). Spatial knowledge in a young blind child. *Cognition, 16*, 225–260.
Leonard, J. A., & Newman, R. C. (1967). Spatial orientation in the blind. *Nature, 215*, 1413–1414.
Maier, N. R. F. (1929). Reasoning in white rats. *Comparative Psychology Monographs, 6* (29).
Mandler, J. M. (1983). Representation. In J. H. Flavell & E. M. Markman (Eds.), *Handbook of child psychology: Vol. 3. Cognitive Development*. New York: Wiley.
Marmor, G. S., & Zaback, L. A. (1976). Mental rotation by the blind. *Journal of Experimental Psychology: Human Perception and Performance, 2*, 515–521.

Menzel, E. W. (1973). Chimpanzee spatial memory organization. *Science, 213,* 943–945.
Millar, S. (1975). Spatial memory by blind and sighted children. *British Journal of Psychology, 66,* 449–459.
Millar, S. (1976). Spatial representation by blind and sighted children. *Journal of Experimental Child Psychology, 21,* 460–479.
Norris, M., Spaulding, P. J., & Brodie, F. H. (1957). *Blindness in children.* Chicago: University of Chicago Press.
O'Keefe, J., & Nadel, L. (1978). *The hippocampus as a cognitive map.* Oxford: Oxford University Press.
Piaget, J. (1954). *The child's construction of reality.* New York: Basic Books.
Piaget, J., & Inhelder, B. (1967). *The child's conception of space.* New York: Norton.
Piaget, J., Inhelder, B., & Szeminska, A. (1960). *The child's conception of geometry.* New York: Basic Books.
Potegal, M. (Ed.) (1982). *Spatial abilities: Development and physiological foundations.* New York: Academic Press.
Presson, C., & Ihrig, L. (1982). Using mother as a spatial landmark: Evidence against egocentric coding in infancy. *Developmental Psychology, 18* (5), 699–703.
Restle, F. (1957). Discrimination of cues in mazes: A resolution of the "place-vs-response" question. *Psychological Review, 64,* 217–228.
Tolman, E. C. (1948). Cognitive maps in rats and men. *Psychological Review, 55* (4), 189–208.
Tolman, E. C., Ritchie, B. F., & Kalish, D. (1946). Studies in spatial learning I. Orientation and the short-cut. *Journal of Experimental Psychology, 36,* 13–24.
Warren, D. H. (1977). *Blindness and early childhood development.* New York: American Foundation for the Blind.
Warren, D. H., Anooshian, L. J., & Bollinger, J. G. (1973). Early vs. late blindness: The role of early vision in spatial behavior. *Research Bulletin, American Foundation for the Blind, 26,* 151–170.

3 Active Movement and Development of Spatial Abilities in Infancy

J. Gavin Bremner
University of Lancaster

P. E. Bryant
University of Oxford

Problems about space are rarely static. Object search is probably the best example from everyday life that makes this point. When we put something away in a container, usually either we move or the container is moved before we look for it again. Thus relocating the object would be impossible unless we had some way of taking these sorts of movements into account. This raises an interesting question as far as infants are concerned, for during the first 9 months or so of life their movements are constrained. They certainly perceive and show interest in moving objects from very early on, and they are themselves moved around their environment. But it is not until the age of 9 months, when they begin to crawl, that they get active experience of moving around in space under their own control.

It is perhaps rather surprising that until recently (Bremner & Bryant, 1977; Campos, Svejda, Campos, & Bertenthal, 1982) the implications of this developmental change at 9 months have received very little attention. Although Piaget (1954) stressed the importance of walking for children's understanding of space, he seems to have laid very little stress on the effects of the earlier event of crawling. But it may very well be that there is a qualitative difference in the effect of information about the results of the passive movements that characterize very early infancy, and those of the active movements that predominate once the baby starts to crawl. Indeed, hypotheses about the greater significance of active movements over passive movements in perceptual development would lead to the suggestion that children's understanding of space, and particularly the role of their own movements, must be poorly developed until they begin to crawl (Held & Hein, 1963).

53

The most extreme possibility is that until infants make their own way around space, the way that they code positions of objects would take no account of subsequent changes in their own spatial position. Until recently such a possibility has not been discussed a great deal, but it is possible to extend Piaget's idea of egocentrism to the question of infants dealing with the results of their own movements around space, and to draw the implication from his theory that up to the age of 12 months or so they should pay little attention to the results of their own movements when recalling the spatial position of an object. In his hiding tasks, Piaget was not concerned with the movements of children, but with the movements of objects and containers that hid objects. However, his argument that children only remember the location of a hidden object in terms of its relationship to the child's body at the time it was first hidden is relevant to the question of children's understanding of the significance of their own movements. If they fail to take account of subsequent movements of the object, they may also fail to take account of their own movements between seeing an object hidden and trying to find it.

When one considers the question of the child's understanding of movement in relation to his memory for the locations of things in space, one can ask two related questions. Suppose that one hides an object in a container. One question is what happens when one moves the container, and another is what happens when one moves the baby between hiding the object and letting the baby look for it. If it can be shown that young children have difficulties with either of these kinds of movements, there is a subsidiary question of whether these difficulties can be traced to the distinction between active and passive movements which we made earlier.

KEEPING TRACK OF A HIDDEN OBJECT THAT MOVES

We know that quite young infants have no difficulty in keeping track of the movements of a continuously visible object (Bower, 1974), but we cannot say the same thing of their ability to keep track of the movements of a hidden object. Although Bower claims that infants can infer the movements of an object behind a screen from knowledge of its movements before disappearance, other workers have questioned this conclusion, either interpreting his findings in other ways (Goldberg, 1976; Moore, Borton, & Darby, 1978) or failing to replicate the findings altogether (Gratch, 1982; Meicler & Gratch, 1980; Muller & Aslin, 1978). On the other hand, we do know that up to around 8 months of age, infants have considerable difficulty dealing with the disappearance of an object, even if it does not move at all (Piaget, 1954). Once they solve that problem, they run into difficulties again if hiding is combined with movement to a new location.

The best known example of this difficulty is the task Piaget used to assess infants' ability to represent the movements of a hidden object. The object is placed in a container (often the experimenter's hand) and is then transported to a new hiding location and deposited there. He found that Stage V infants (12 to 18 months) searched in the first container, but on failing to find the object, did not go on to investigate the second location; he took this as evidence that they could not represent the movements of the hidden object. However, this is rather a complicated way of testing such an ability. From the infant's point of view, the object could be in either the original container or the second location, and he or she may not be able to deal with alternative possibilities like this.

Simpler tasks have been used though, and again there seems to be evidence that quite old infants have difficulties with invisible displacements. For instance, in one condition of a study incorporating a variety of object and infant movements, Wishart and Bower (1982) hid an object under one of two cups and let infants search after the table had been rotated through 180°. Although there are reasons to doubt whether some of the general conclusions reached by Wishart and Bower are actually suggested by the data, the one thing that seems clear is that at least a residual difficulty with this sort of task extends well into the second year of life. Even at 12–14 months, infants often made the error of searching in the cup that occupied the same self-referent location as the correct cup had before the movement of the table. The reason for questioning the generality of this difficulty is that Wishart and Bower administered a large series of different types of rotation, involving the array, the infant, or both. With so much going on, the errors by older infants (and maybe some by younger ones as well) may have been the result of confusion rather than anything else.

Admittedly, Neilson (1982) also obtained errors on a similar task from infants over a year old. In this study, the object was hidden in one of two cups that were transposed before the infant searched. Again, however, this task was one of a number presented in the same session. So infants may again have erred through confusion, maybe carrying over a solution that actually was appropriate in another task. Thus although simpler tasks have been devised to test the infant's ability to take account of invisible displacements, these have often been embedded in a series of variations, and so the advantages to be gained by simplifying the task may well have been lost by its being embedded in a series tasks requiring different solutions.

However, this sort of task on its own might still present particular difficulties to the infant, difficulties that are not connected with the invisible displacement of the object per se. Two containers are transposed in such a way that the infant might lose track of the one that the object was in. Hence the problem might be one of keeping track of one container during a somewhat confusing exchange of positions with another container, rather than in knowing what this manipulation does to the location of the hidden object.

One way of surmounting this problem is to make it easier for the infant to follow the movement. The simplest way of doing this is probably to make the two locations distinct in some way, so that they are unlikely to be confused with each other. Several workers have investigated the effects of position differentiation in a number of different types of search task (Acredolo, 1978; Acredolo & Evans, 1980; Bremner, 1978a, 1978b; Goldfield & Dickerson, 1981), one version of which is formally similar to the transposition task discussed above (Bremner, 1978b; Goldfield & Dickerson, 1981). It turns out that certain types of position differentiation are effective. This is clearly the sort of evidence we are looking for if we want to identify the beginnings of an ability to update the position of a moving hidden object, so we must look at these studies in some detail.

Bremner (1978b) set infants a task in which they had to relocate an object hidden at one of two fixed locations after the surface supporting them had been rotated. Infants were first given some familiarization experience, in which the object was partially hidden a few times. These trials alternated between two containers symmetrically placed to the infant's left and right, and were completed by one trial in which the object was totally hidden at a position halfway between the two containers. The point of this sequence was to ensure that infants understood the search component of the task, while at the same time avoiding establishment of a search bias to one side rather than the other. Five experimental trials then followed, in which the object was hidden in one container but search was prevented until the table on which the containers rested was rotated through 180°. After each trial, the table was rotated back, and hiding was repeated, always in the same container. As Fig. 3.1 shows, the locations were made distinct either by placing them against different backgrounds (one half of the table was black and the other half was white), or by making the covers for the two containers different (one cover black and the other white).

In the background differentiation condition most infants failed to update the object's position and searched at the side where they had seen the object go before the rotation. In contrast, those in the cover cue condition were more successful, but despite their significant superiority over the background cue group, their performance was by no means perfect; almost half of them searched at the wrong location on the first trial. This did not appear to be a case of random responding, since individuals did not distribute search randomly over the five trials. If they were correct on the first trial, they tended to stay correct for all five trials, whereas if they made an error they tended either to continue to err for all five trials or to shift at some point to consistently correct responding.

Goldfield and Dickerson (1981) included a similar task in a series of spatial displacement problems that they gave to 8- and 9-month-old infants. The only difference between their apparatus and Bremner's was in the form of position cueing provided. The positions were either identical or were covered by differently colored covers (yellow versus green), and the background was uniform in both cases. Again, they obtained evidence of a cue effect, but only in the case of 9-month-old infants. In this age group, the infants in the cue condition performed better than those in the undifferentiated condition. Overall, their 9-month-old

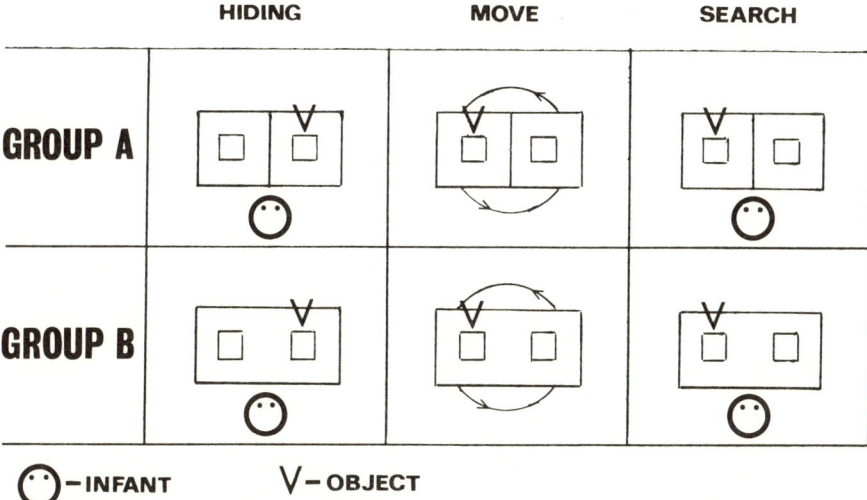

FIG. 3.1 The array rotation conditions of Bremner (1978b). Group A: background cues. Group B: cover cues.

infants managed this task better than the ones in Bremner's study. For example, in the cued condition most of Goldfield and Dickerson's infants (10/12) found the object successfully after array rotation. This may have been because the average age of infants in this group was slightly greater than in Bremner's study, or alternatively because color differentiation was a more effective spatial cue than black-white differentiation. On the other hand, 8-month-olds did not benefit from the provision of cues and performed slightly below chance level in both conditions. This points to the possibility that spatial cues of this sort are only effective in interaction with some basic grasp of the task by the infant. They may act as a useful prop during the formative stages of dealing with these sorts of displacements.

The results of another study complicate the picture and show that we need to take account of at least one other factor in interpreting the results of these sorts of tasks. Lucas and Uzgiris (1977) found that 8-month-old infants had greater difficulties with invisible displacements under particular circumstances. Their method was to place an object either in front of or to the side of a stationary screen, and then to transport it away behind a second moving screen that appeared from the side of the array (this second screen picked up the object as it moved in front of it). They found that infants tended to search behind the stationary screen if the object had formerly been placed in front of it, but that this was much less likely if it had initially been placed to the side of the screen.

Lucas and Uzgiris suggest that infants make quite basic topological codings of relationships between objects, so that when two objects overlap perceptually, one is coded as in the neighborhood of another, with no distinction made between "in front" and "behind." Consequently a response on the displacements task that would seem reasonable in the case of an object initially hidden behind the screen is also applied to the case when it is placed in front of it. Although precise interpretation need not concern us here, it is important that we keep this result in mind, since it indicates that the degree to which infants take account of an invisible displacement may be affected by the strength with which the object has been associated with an initial position. A strong association with an initial place may make the infant less likely to accept or appreciate that an object has moved to a new place.

This leads to the need for reevaluation of the assumptions underlying the simplified invisible displacement tasks. The possibility is that they do not really measure infants' abilities with invisible displacements at all. Infants may associate the object with a particular location and return to that location whatever manipulation takes place within the task. Hence, when they fail, they wrongly identify the position of the location with which the object is associated, failing to take account of the change in the array. When they succeed, they may do so by correctly identifying the location with which the object is associated, and cover cues may help this by allowing the place to be identified in a way that needs no updating during the transformation. Success interpreted this way says nothing about the infant's ability to infer things about the movements of an invisible object. On the other hand, failure on the more conventional Piagetian task need not indicate that the infant has no knowledge of invisible displacements, for the reason already given. They may search only at the first location because the object has become very strongly associated with it. Thus we may be faced with a difficult methodological problem, since it may be that neither type of task measures the infant's ability accurately. However, it is possible that the two factors cannot be theoretically separated either. If infants do adopt strong associations between objects and particular places, they may do so just because they lack the ability to understand what happens to objects when hiding and movement are combined.

KEEPING TRACK OF A LOCATION WHILE THE INFANT MOVES

One advantage of the array rotation tasks reported in the preceding section is that an equivalent change in the relationship between the infant and the array can be brought about by moving the infant instead of the array. Hence, the basic task is ideal for the purpose of comparing infants' ability to keep track of a hidden object that moves, with their ability to keep track of a stationary hidden object during a movement of self. Despite the similarity of the subject-array transformation in the two cases, there are a number of factors that might lead to different performance between one version and the other. For instance, we might expect the added distraction of the infant's movement to result in poorer performance on that form of the task. Or we might suggest that the added proprioceptive information about self-movement, along with the overall optical flow that accompanies movement, would provide more accurate information about the changing relationship between self and object. From this perspective, infants would be expected to perform better in the infant movement case.

A number of studies have investigated the infant's reorientation ability after a movement of self (Acredolo, 1978; Acredolo & Evans, 1980; Cornell & Heth, 1979), but only a few have directly compared infant movement with array movement (Bremner, 1978b; Goldfield & Dickerson, 1981). Wishart & Bower (1982) include both self and array movement tasks, but do not report the results separately. Bremner (1978b) included two infant movement conditions that were the equivalents of the two array rotation conditions described in the first section. The only difference was that instead of the array being rotated after the object was hidden, the infant was moved round to the opposite side of the table (the seat was on a turntable). Thus the full experiment had a two-by-two design, with array versus infant rotation as one factor, and cover versus background cues as the other factor (see Fig. 3.2).

Table 3.1 shows the frequency of correct responses on the first rotation trial, including the same data for the array rotation groups for comparison. Again, in the infant rotation task, infants in the cover cue group performed better than those in the background cue group. But the important point here is that the infants in both infant rotation groups performed better than those in the equivalent array rotation group. The cue effect is nothing new and simply adds to the generality of the effect, but the superior performance of the infant rotation groups is important, since it gives the first suggestion that infants are relatively good at taking account of their own movements. With strong cues present, they performed really quite well after they had been moved, with a significant majority locating the object correctly on the first attempt.

There are a number of possible reasons for the outstandingly high level of success after the infant has moved. The infants may be better at updating their own movement than the movement of the array. This could arise from the fact that more information specifies infant movement than array movement, or it could be due to the simpler possibility that infants are just more used to movements of themselves than they are to rotations of a table. However, attempts to interpret the cue effect raise another issue that complicates matters. Spatial cues could be helpful because they aid infants in making some sort of continuous updating of the object's position during their movement, or they could help just because they made continuous updating unnecessary. With strong cues present, infants may have coded the object's position as "under the black cover," or the cues may have helped them to locate the object within a wider spatial framework, and codings of this sort require no updating. If this is so, however, the problem of explaining superior performance by the infant movement groups becomes more tricky. It is not immediately clear why infants should switch to such a coding when they rather than the array are moved, unless for some reason they realize that such a switch is appropriate under these circumstances.

The cover cues had a powerful effect, but this effect interacts with the type of movement. It appears that this arises because infants pay more attention to what is happening following a movement of self than following a movement of the array. Evidence for this was obtained by Bremner (1978a) in a slightly different task based more on the Piagetian Stage IV object search task. In this case, infants searched for an object several times in one place, whereupon they were moved to the opposite side of the table, where they saw the object hidden again. When cover cues were present infants searched accurately no matter which of the two

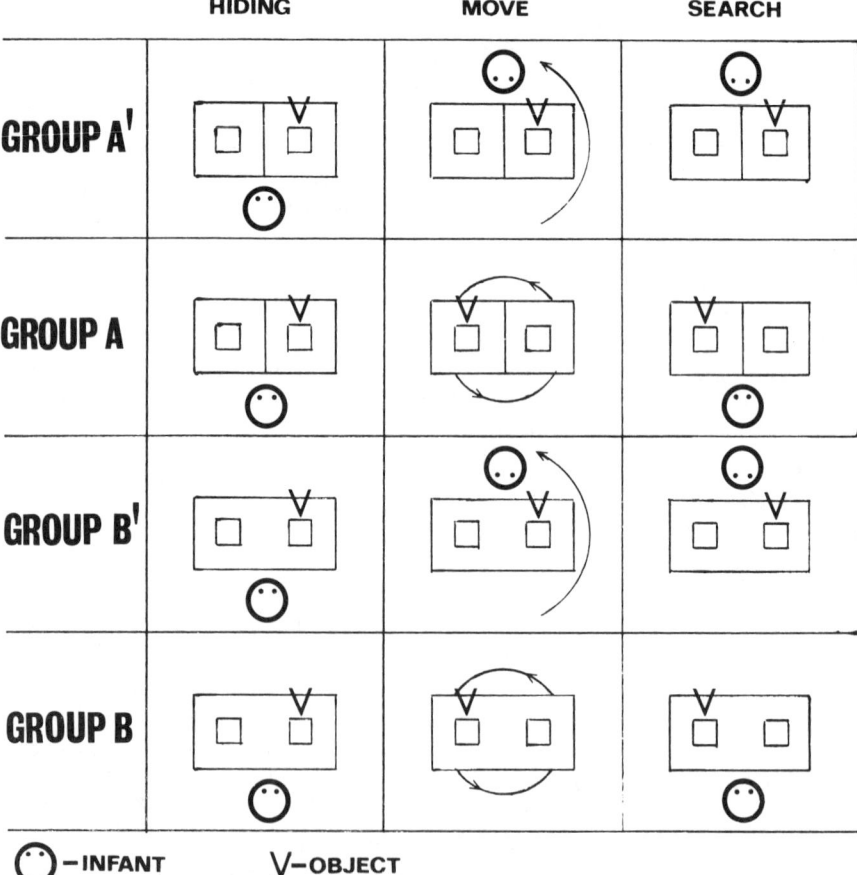

FIG. 3.2. Infant rotation and array rotation conditions from Bremner (1978b).

TABLE 3.1
Number of Infants (Out of 16) Making Errors on Each Trial, and Mean Error over Five Trials for Each Group in Bremner (1978b)

	trial 1	*2*	*Rotation trials 3*	*4*	*5*	*mean error*
Group A'	6	4	5	5	9	1.8
Group A	12	10	8	11	7	3.0
Group B'	3	4	5	5	4	1.3
Group B	6	9	8	9	8	2.5

places was chosen for hiding. This was surprising, since there was no evidence here for the sort of search perseveration characteristic of 9-month-old infants, and these results were in marked contrast to those of a study in which the only difference lay in the use of background cues instead of cover cues (Bremner & Bryant, 1977). When background cues were used, the majority of infants continued to search at the same place relative to self as had housed the object before their movement. Thus the cover cues had a powerful effect, but in interaction with the type of movement, since infants were not so successful when the movement involved the array rather than themselves.

The conclusion to be drawn from these results seems to be that infants are more attentive to an event if they are moved, and that the effect is so strong that in some cases they show no evidence of the usual Stage IV perseverative error. But this is not a general effect. Although strong cues do aid performance, it seems that really good use can only be made of them after the infant has moved. If this is the correct interpretation of all these results, our problem is to explain why this should be.

Unfortunately for the account being developed so far, Goldfield and Dickerson's (1981) comparison of performance on infant movement and array movement tasks yielded some contrary results. Their version of the array movement task was mentioned in Section 2, and their infant movement task followed the same pattern, apart of course from the form of movement. No difference between array and infant movement versions was obtained with the 8-month-old group, but at 9 months, infants were better at the array rotation than at the infant rotation. This comes as a surprise, since apart from their obtaining a similar cue effect (in this case, between no cues and cover cues), their results on the "movement type" dimension were very much the opposite of those obtained by Bremner (1978b).

Goldfield and Dickerson (1981) suggest that this reversal in results may have arisen from a subtle difference between the procedures adopted in the two studies. In Bremner's study, the infant's parent stayed in one place (normally behind the experimenter's initial position) throughout the session, whereas in theirs, the parent moved with the infant. They suggest that in the latter case, the mother could not have acted as an additional stable landmark that infants might have used to relocate a stable position, the requirement of the infant movement task. They are not alone in identifying the mother as a potential landmark. Presson and Ihrig (1982) have shown that the mother can be used as a landmark, and have suggested that many cases of "egocentric" responding arise because infants inappropriately use the mother as an objective but unstable landmark. However, there are serious difficulties with such a notion. First, stability of the mother is certainly not a guarantee of "objective" responding in tasks involving infant movement, as the results of Bremner's (1978b) background cue condition show. Second, whether the mother moved or not, she remained in the midline and hence, unlike the case in Presson and Ihrig's study, provided no direct cue to the object's location. Infants would have to be in possession of a very sophisticated spatial reference system before they could make use of an orthogonal cue of this type.

However, two other differences between the studies might explain the conflicting results. The first relates to a study done by Acredolo (1979), in which she compared performance on an infant rotation task done in the infant's home with performance on the same task done in a laboratory. She replicated Bremner's result (the cover cue condition) in the home, but obtained very low success rates from the group tested in the laboratory. This could explain the difference between Bremner's and Goldfield and Dickerson's versions of the infant movement task, since Bremner's work was done in the home, whereas Goldfield and Dickerson's was done in a laboratory. However, this does leave us with the difficulty of explaining why infants do perform better at home than in the lab. The attractive reason is that the home surroundings provide a better framework for orienting and would provide particularly good circumstances for infants to keep track of a stable position. However, the question here is why, if the surrounding framework was so helpful, was it necessary for strong immediate cues to be present as well (remember, infants were not so good at this task when no cues or background cues were presented). We could explain this by suggesting that strong immediate cues are useful only if they can be set in the context of a familiar stable framework, but this argument is more complex. The alternative is to argue that infants perform better at home simply because they are more relaxed, and hence more attentive to the task. However, this explanation will not do, since it does not explain why Goldfield and Dickerson's infants were better at the array movement task, despite being tested in the laboratory.

The second difference in procedure reduces explanation of the conflicting results to a more mundane level, and may actually be at the root of the matter. Whereas Bremner only gave infants one task, with the object always hidden in one place, Goldfield and Dickerson gave each infant six tasks, including infant movement, array movement, and object movement. Thus, in their task, object stability even within a task was by no means the rule, and under such circumstances there is the strong possibility that infants learned to deal with object movements (visible and invisible) better than self-movements with a stable object. Some supplementary evidence given by Goldfield and Dickerson accords with this interpretation. They found that very few infants in either age group made the Piagetian Stage IV search error, evidence that their infants were unusually good at dealing with visible movements of an object.

Other workers have investigated the infant's ability to take account of self-movement through use of a slightly different technique. Instead of adopting object search as the basis of the task, they have used anticipatory looking as the measure of the infant's ability to update the relation between self and a stable position in space. The procedure is to allow infants to learn that an event occurs consistently at one location (say to their left), and then to measure direction of looking once the infant has been moved to a different place.

This method has the advantage of being applicable to larger scale spatial tasks. For instance, Acredolo (1978) trained infants to anticipate an event at one of two windows in the walls of the test room to left and right of the infant, after which infants were moved to the opposite side of the room and direction of anticipation was measured when the cue to look was given. This task was presented to 6-, 11-, and 16-month-olds, under one of two conditions. In the "landmark" condition, the correct window was surrounded by a large star pattern, whereas in the "no-landmark" condition no such differentiation was provided. At 6 months, most infants anticipated at the window that occupied the same self-referent position as the correct one before movement. Hence, they failed to update their relation to the stable location, and this "egocentric" responding was prevalent even in the "landmark" condition. At 11 months, much the same thing happened with the "no-landmark" group, but more infants responded correctly when a landmark was present. Finally, at 16 months, the majority of infants responded objectively whether or not the landmark was present. Hence, the picture that emerges is an increasing ability to deal with a displacement of self, with a middle stage when direct spatial cues enhance performance.

Although there was clear evidence of improvement with age in this study, the 11-month-olds did not perform as well as 9-month-olds in Bremner's (1978b) study, even in the landmark group. This may in part be due to the laboratory home difference that we have discussed already. On this point, Acredolo found that preliminary familiarization with the experimental space did not improve the young infants' performance, so if a difference in familiarity between home and laboratory is at the root of things, this is not a difference that can be removed by a relatively short familiarization with novel surroundings. However, another factor may have increased "egocentric" responding in Acredolo's task. Infants were trained to anticipate an event that occurred consistently at one place, and this may have increased a tendency for response perseveration, and hence obscured any objective ability. In fact, Bremner (1978b) found that giving infants five preliminary search trials at one place led to a significantly higher incidence of "egocentric" responding on the rotation trials that followed. In addition, McKenzie, Day, & Ihsen (1984) found that "egocentric" responding was much reduced if infants were initially trained to anticipate events at both positions.

On the other hand, Acredolo and Evans (1980) found that an increase in the salience of the landmark led to good performance even at 9 months. But in this case the landmark consisted of a pattern of flashing lights, and there is the danger of objective responding being confused with capture of attention by this very noticeable sort of landmark. Acredolo and Evans argue that this was not the case, citing as evidence the fact that similar amounts of initial training were required with and without this landmark. They also claim that if correct responses were due to attention capture, such responding would have been just as noticeable at 6 months as at later ages. However, ruling out the attentional salience interpretation on these grounds alone may not be justified. The snag about using only one landmark rather than differentiating the surroundings in a more balanced manner is that it is always going to be difficult to rule out the possibility that at least some of the objective responses obtained under such circumstances may be due to the "attention getting" properties of the landmark. Thus, although Acredolo and Evans' results agree with those obtained by Bremner (1978b), we cannot be totally confident that their study gave an accurate measure of objective responding. So in the end, we may have to fall back on building our account of the development of objective responding from the general pattern that emerges from comparison of results from a number of studies.

Two other studies help us to work this pattern out. Rieser (1979) investigated younger infants' ability to take account of a different type of movement of self. In the conditions that we are concerned with, 6-month-old infants were placed on their backs facing a screen containing four windows, above, below, left, and right of central fixation. After infants had been trained to anticipate an event at one of these windows, they were rotated about their line of sight through 90°, so that windows formerly above and below were now left and right, and vice versa. Rieser found that infants responded egocentrically unless the correct window was marked by a pattern, in which case quite a number of their responses were correct. However, he argues that in this case "geocentric" (correct) responding is in part a matter of preferential looking at the patterned landmark, since if the "egocentric" window was marked in this way, "egocentric" responding was higher.

McKenzie, Day, and Ihsen (1984) investigated 6- and 8-month-old infants' ability to take account of body axis rotations. In their studies, infants sat upright in a chair, and a measure was taken of their ability to deal with body axis rotations of up to 60° (or in one study, 90°). They adopted a useful modification of the sort of training method used by Acredolo. Infants were trained to anticipate an event at a fixed position, but this training took place in three blocks, first of all with infants in one orientation, then with them in another orientation that required the opposite response to relocate the target, and finally with their orientation varying randomly between the two. This had the advantage of eliminating any tendency toward response perseveration that might have been a feature of performance in the more conventional training tasks. Infants had to learn a "place" response during training, and the test was whether they could generalize this response sufficiently to identify the correct event locus from a totally new orientation of self.

They found that both age groups performed this task well. The only difference was that 6-month-olds showed more gradual improvement over the training trials, and they suggest that younger infants need a fair amount of that type of training before they can acquire a place response. It would be nice if we could conclude that in comparison with "egocentric" responding obtained by Acredolo, they obtained objective responding with even younger infants because their training technique was superior. However, they also rotated the infant by a smaller amount, and they favor this as the main factor responsible for infants' high level of success, suggesting that infants may initially be able to deal only with changes in infant-environment relations that stay within the visual field.

McKenzie et al. (1984) conclude that this is evidence that objective responding develops early and does not wait upon the development of self-executed movements around the environment. However, this conclusion needs further analysis. Six-month-olds are probably in a position to control the sorts of movements that McKenzie et al. presented, since the sorts of change involved can be brought about purely by movement of head and trunk. Thus, as soon as infants have good control over head movements and can sit up, they should be able to produce such movements. From this point of view it becomes crucial to separate movements involving body rotation from movements involving body displacement plus rotation. If the argument is that active experience of these sorts of movements leads to competence in dealing with them, we would predict that competence with the rotation alone should precede competence with rotation and displacement together, since the former is achieved once the infant can sit up, whereas the latter only comes once the infant can crawl. In fact, the prediction could be tied even more closely to physical development, by pointing to the fact that early control over bodily rotation is limited in range; the infant can only turn as far as head and trunk movements allow. This appears to fit exactly with the developmental sequence that appears to be emerging. Infants sit unaided between 6 and 8 months, but only crawl by about 9 months. They are capable of taking account of limited body axis rotations at 6 months, but only take account of movements involving bodily displacement and rotation at 9 months, with evidence that they are still perfecting this more sophisticated skill for some time beyond that age. Hence, it looks as if we have a good starting point for building an account of the development of knowledge about the consequences of self-movement that is based in large part on consideration of the types of movement that the infant is capable of executing at different points in development.

SELF-PRODUCED MOVEMENT AND THE DEVELOPMENT OF SPATIAL AWARENESS

As we noted in the introduction, surprisingly little attention has been paid to the role of self-produced movement in development of spatial orientation. There is an abundance of evidence from animal work, pointing to the fact that the experience of the world arising from self-produced movement has more effect on development of spatial orientation than that arising from passive experience (e.g., Hein, 1972; Held & Hein, 1963). It would be no real surprise if we obtained similar findings in human developmental studies, since activity is a central factor in theories of development (e.g., Gibson, 1969; Piaget, 1954).

Although there is now a growing body of work on the active-passive issue in human development, the evidence is mainly concerned with the relation between depth perception and active locomotion. This work is well reviewed by Campos, Svejda, Campos, and Bertenthal (1982). The main finding seems to be that although infants perceive depth from an early age, wariness of vertical depth does not appear until shortly after infants have begun to crawl. If crawling and non-crawling infants of the same average age are tested for wariness of depth, it is typically only the ones who can crawl who show wariness. For instance, prelocomotor infants placed over a drop showed no cardiac acceleration, whereas locomotor infants treated in the same way do show acceleration (Schwartz, Campos, & Baisel, 1973). Second, it turns out that infants do not show wariness of depth as soon as they start to crawl. Newly crawling infants quite readily venture onto the deep side of a visual cliff, but within a month, an extreme reluctance to go onto the deep side indicates that wariness of depth has set in.

Of course, both of these studies confounded age and locomotor ability, but a further study showed the same relation between locomotor ability and wariness with age controlled. Svejda and Schmid (1979) measured heart rate as infants were lowered onto the deep and shallow sides of a visual cliff, and found that non-crawling infants showed no difference in response between deep and shallow sides, but that crawling infants of the same average age showed appreciable cardiac acceleration on the deep side alone. In addition, Campos, Svejda, Bertenthal, Benson, & Schmid (1981) have shown that infants provided with baby-walkers at 5½ months showed a clearer wariness response than comparable infants who had not had such an opportunity for early locomotion.

The inference drawn from these studies and other similar ones is that self-produced movement acts to enrich awareness of depth rather than to create the awareness in the first place. After all, infants can be shown to be responsive to depth information well before they can crawl (Bower, 1965; McKenzie, Tootle, & Day, 1980). Campos et al (1982) suggest that infants may be aware of relative depth information (e.g., that one object is further away than another) quite early, but that in order to develop a knowledge of depth in terms of absolute distances from the body, infants have to be able to move through the range of distances to be calibrated in this way. In other words, infants can only calibrate an absolute system for depth through action, and while action is limited to the range of the infant's reach, well-calibrated space is limited in the same way. In this, they adopt an argument that is very similar to Piaget's, and it brings us back again to puzzle over why Piaget laid so little stress on the onset of crawling as an important marker in the development of spatial awareness.

The evidence discussed above relates mainly to detection of vertical depth, and wariness about the dangers that accompany it. If anything, we should expect the beginning of crawling to have an even more marked effect on the infant's understanding of horizontal depth, since this is the plane in which crawling normally takes place. But in this case, as well as expecting to see an increased awareness of surrounding spatial relations, we would expect that the very activity of crawling would make the infant more aware of the dynamic relationship between self and the stable surroundings. This might explain why infants in Bremner's (1978b) study were better at taking account of their own movements than of the movements of the hidden object. Through crawling, infants may have developed an awareness of self-movement to a more advanced level than awareness of movements of other objects, or they may simply have learned that particular attention needs to be paid to changes in the surroundings when their body is moved. Once established, this sort of awareness need not accompany active movement alone, even if it was active movement that established it first.

In contrast to the work mentioned above, rotation-search tasks investigate the infant's ability to take account of dynamic information about space: information about changes in the spatial relationship between self and environment. Because of this, it is possible not only to look at the relation between infants' "mobility status" and their spatial awareness, but to compare performance on rotation tasks involving passive movement with performance on similar tasks in which the movement is effected by the infant. Hence the active-passive factor can become an experimental variable.

Although the methodological problems in doing this are considerable, a start has been made. Adopting the usual two-position rotation-search paradigm, Benson (1980) used an ingenious arrangement to make possible a comparison of active and passive movement. Although the two-position array was much the same as usual, it was set on the floor of the test room, and a plexiglass screen surrounded it on three sides (during familiarization, one panel was removed to allow the infant direct access to the array). The main test trials involved the hiding of the object in one of the two positions with the infant watching from the screened side. In the active condition, infants then crawled around to the opposite side of the array in order to gain access to it (they had previously been given some training in this). In the passive condition, they were carried round to the opposite side, facing the array as they went.

Benson's general finding was that infants were more likely to relocate the object correctly in the active condition than they were in the passive condition. This fits the general picture that is developing, but there is some need for caution with this sort of comparison. First of all, we need to know what the difference means. A significant improvement in performance could be due to a shift from predominantly incorrect responding to chance responding, and this possibility is not adequately ruled out in this case, since comparisons to chance are not made. In the active condition, infants were under no constraint to approach the accessible side of the array at its mid-point, and approaches off center along the shortest path from the opposite side could have led to a bias for the closest container that would have averaged out as a random error over different hiding sides. There is some reason to suspect that this might have been happening, since infants performed better in the active condition when the side of hiding was the same as the side around which they crawled. No such effect was obtained in the passive condition.

Fortunately, it seems that we can rule out this possibility, since Acredolo, Adams, and Goodwyn (in press) replicated and extended Benson's findings, using a method that equated infants' line of approach across active and passive conditions. They found a clear active-passive difference at 12 months, which seemed to be related in some way to tracking, since in addition to being more successful in search, the active infants were more likely to track the array as they moved round. Investigating this, they found that if tracking was prevented by insertion of opaque side screens, the active infants' superiority was removed. Thus, active movement seems to facilitate appropriate tracking, and tracking seems to be necessary for successful performance at this age. Finally, they found that by 18 months, infants performed well under active and passive conditions even if opaque side screens were present. So it may well turn out that active experience is only an important determinant of successful orientation during a particular phase in development of the skill.

But another methodological problem remains, although in this case it is a more interesting one from the point of view of theory. In the passive conditions of both studies, infants were picked up under the arms by a parent and moved around in a vertical posture. This sort of social intervention could have been taken as a break in the session. In fact, the whole question of how the infant responds to being picked up is important here. Campos et al. (1982) have suggested that infants "switch off" spatially when picked up. If they do, maybe it is because they realize that an adult has taken control, and that they need no longer attend to what is happening. This would be an interesting question for study in itself, but it needs to be separated from the pure active-passive question before we can proceed.

3. ACTIVE MOVEMENT AND SPATIAL ABILITIES   69

Although the growth in attention to the effects of active movement is welcome, it may be that we should not concentrate all our attention on locomotion. The infants may find out a good deal about the relationship between self and environment, and about the structure of the environment, through simpler types of active movement. As we pointed out in the previous section, infants engage in rotational movements of the head and trunk well before they can crawl, and the suggestion was that fairly unimpeded movements of this sort are possible once infants can sit up unaided. Thus, the sorts of change in relationship between self and environment that were brought about in McKenzie, Day, and Ihsen's study are effectively under infants' control before they begin to crawl. Once they can sit up and exercise fine control over head and trunk movements, they are in a position to make movements that change the positions of objects within the visual field, in much the same way as happens when they are rotated about the body axis passively. This sort of controlled movement may lead them to a clearer knowledge of the relationship between their own movements and the changes of position of stable objects within the visual field. In other words, some of the properties of spatial relations may be systematically disentangled once infants can sit up and explore the environment by controlled movements of head and body.

An interesting complication of the issue emerges here. Once infants can sit unaided, control over head movements precedes control over rotational movements of the trunk. This leads to the possibility that we may need to distinguish between position relative to the body (or manual response), position relative to the head, and position in the external world, since while the infant is only capable of head movements, the relation between body and the world remains relatively fixed (as far as actively brought about changes are concerned). Hence, the body-centered system is confounded with any stable external system. On the other hand, position relative to the head system is dissociated from position in the external system whenever head movements are made. If active movements of this sort have an important effect on the structuring of space, the prediction emerges that infants should quite early be able to dissociate position within a head-based system from position in the world, but that they should take longer to dissociate a body-centered system from stable external systems. The important point here is that manual responses are coordinated with the body system, so externally defined place and response are only dissociated if the body is moved.

If we accept the emphasis on active movement, the model we construct to account for development of early spatial awareness has to give a central place to physical maturation. We would expect that infants would gain information from active movements fairly early; in particular, as we have suggested, once they can sit unaided and move their heads. Hence, at around 6 months we might expect to find that they can deal with changes in the relation between environmental positions and the head in quite a sophisticated manner, but that dissociation of place and response might come later. There is a chance here that the place-response dissociation might actually be delayed, because infants who do not yet have trunk control know that although the relation between head and external place changes, the relation between place and response remains constant. Once they achieve control over trunk movements, the resultant visual changes only alter in degree, so there may be no direct evidence that the assumption of a constant relation between response and place is no longer valid.

Later, we would expect infants to gain knowledge relating to spatial changes resulting from bodily displacement. So far, all the studies investigating infant movement have also incorporated a rotation in addition to the displacement. It is important that we also investigate infants' ability to take account of simple linear movements of self, in particular comparing left-right linear movements with the type of forward movement achieved through crawling. The prediction here is that infants would be more likely to be able to cope with forward movements than left-right movements, since only the former result from crawling.

Physical maturation may have another less direct effect on the infant's spatial awareness. Before babies can sit up, their parents probably put them in relatively few places that are appropriately designed to give them support (e.g., the baby chair, cot, or changing mat). Other places are relatively inappropriate, and if used are unlikely to allow infants a clear view of the surroundings. So apart from the advantages in terms of visual exploration that come with the achievement of the sitting posture, there comes the added advantage that infants can be put in many more positions than before. They no longer need physical support structures other than a solid horizontal surface. Hence, we can supplement the developmental account in the following way. Infants may initially be limited to a few relatively static views of the world, and it is possible that they do not integrate these separate views into an overall scene. Although integration could happen as the infant is moved from one place to another by a parent, the argument is that such passive information is not sufficient to ensure full integration. However, once infants can sit up, the number of perspectives will increase dramatically; something that will be happening in parallel with the increased knowledge of the relation between infant and environment that results from the more sophisticated visual exploration afforded by the sitting posture. We assume that this progress in understanding space will still take place in relatively static settings, which will not be properly integrated until the infant has had time to learn from active bodily displacements.

In the end, we have said much more about infants' awareness of the consequences of their own movements than we have about their awareness of movements of the hidden object. From our point of view, this is probably appropriate, for although infants have to cope with movements of self very frequently, and may have to relocate objects and events from new perspectives, it is probable that they are not so often faced with objects that disappear and then move while out of sight. When objects disappear, they often do so at stable points (e.g., the toy in the toy box, or as may be more usual, under the sofa), and even the infant's parents frequently appear and disappear at the same points (typically doorways). Thus, theories that lay store on the importance of active experience as an amplifier of spatial awareness probably have rather little to say about object displacement tasks. But this is not to say that such tests are irrelevant. Even if early spatial abilities can to some extent be explained in terms of the infant's experience of everyday events, there is still the important question of the generality of the knowledge that is developed. Presumably, once spatial logic has advanced sufficiently, it can be applied to novel events. Hence, although the infant may not be faced with invisible displacements very often in everyday life, there should be a point at which the knowledge gleaned from experience of frequent events is sufficiently developed to be applied to the invisible displacements of objects. The evidence suggests that this ability does come somewhat later than infants' ability to take account of their own movements, but really only a start has been made on testing the range of spatial abilities that may be developing within the first year. Our suggestion is that this project will advance at a more rapid rate if future research is partly driven by consideration of the different types of spatial experience that face infants at different points in their development.

REFERENCES

Acredolo, L. P. (1978). Development of spatial orientation in infancy. *Developmental Psychology, 14*, 224–234.

Acredolo, L. P., Adams, A., & Goodwyn, S. W. (in press). The role of self-produced movement and visual tracking in infant spatial orientation. *Journal of Experimental Child Psychology.*

Acredolo, L. P., & Evans, D. (1980). Developmental changes in the effects of landmarks on infant spatial behavior. *Developmental Psychology, 16*, 312–318.

Benson, J. B. (1980). *Spatial understanding during object search in infancy: The influence of active and passive movement.* Unpublished masters' thesis, Clark University.

Bower, T. G. R. (1965). Stimulus variables determining space perception in infants. *Science, 149*, 88–89.

Bremner, J. G. (1978a). Spatial errors made by infants: inadequate spatial cues or evidence of egocentrism? *British Journal of Psychology, 69*, 77–84.

Bremner, J. G. (1978b). Egocentric versus allocentric spatial coding in nine-month-old infants: factors influencing the choice of code. *Developmental Psychology, 14*, 346–355.

Bremner, J. G., & Bryant, P. E. (1977). Place versus response as the basis of spatial errors made by young infants. *Journal of Experimental Child Psychology, 23*, 162–171.

Campos, J. J., Svejda, M. J., Campos, R. G., & Berthenthal, B. (1982). The emergence of self-produced locomotion: Its importance for psychological development in infancy. In D. Bricker (Ed.), *Intervention with at-risk and handicapped infants*, Baltimore, MD: University Park Press.

Campos, J., Svejda, M., Bertenthal, B., Benson, N., & Schmid, D. (1981). *Self-produced locomotion and wariness of heights: New evidence from training studies.* Paper presented at the meeting of the Society of Research in Child Development, Boston, MA.

Cornell, E. H., & Heth, C. D. (1979). Response versus place learning by human infants. *Journal of Experimental Psychology: Human Learning & Memory, 5*, 188–196.

Gibson, E. J. (1969). *Principles of perceptual learning and development.* New York: Appleton-Century-Crofts.

Goldberg, S. (1976). Visual tracking and existence constancy in 5-month-old infants. *Journal of Experimental Child Psychology, 22,* 478–491.
Goldfield, E. C., & Dickerson, D. J. (1981). Keeping track of locations during movement in 8- to 10-month-old infants. *Journal of Experimental Child Psychology, 32,* 48–64.
Gratch, G. (1982). Responses to hidden persons and things by 5-, 9-, and 16-month-old infants in a visual tracking situation, *Developmental Psychology, 18,* 232–237.
Hein, A. (1972). Acquiring components of visually guided behavior. In A. Pick (Ed.), *Minnesota Symposia on Child Psychology (Vol. 6).* Minneapolis: University of Minnesota Press.
Held, R., & Hein, A. (1963). Movement produced stimulation in the development of visually guided behavior. *Journal of Comparative and Physiological Psychology, 56,* 872–876.
Lucas, T. C., & Uzgiris, I. C. (1977). Spatial factors in the development of the object concept. *Developmental Psychology, 13,* 492–500.
McKenzie, B. E., Day, R. H., & Ihsen, E. (1984). Localization of events in space: Young infants are not always egocentric. *British Journal of Developmental Psychology, 1,* 1–10.
McKenzie, B. E., Tootle, H., & Day, R. H. (1980). Development of visual size consistancy during the 1st year of human infancy. *Developmental Psychology, 16,* 163–174.
Meicler, M., & Gratch, G. (1980). Do 5-month-olds show object conception in Piaget's sense? *Infant Behavior and Development, 3,* 265–282.
Moore, M. K., Borton, R., & Darby, B. L. (1978). Visual tracking in young infants: evidence for object identity or object permanence? *Journal of Experimental Child Psychology, 25,* 183–198.
Muller, A. A., & Aslin, R. N. (1978). Visual tracking as an index of the object concept. *Infant Behavior and Development, 1,* 309–319.
Neilson, I. (1982). An alternative explanation of the infant's difficulties in the stage III, IV and V object-concept tasks. *Perception, 11,* 577–588.
Piaget, J. (1954). *The construction of reality in the child* (M. Cook, Trans.). New York: Basic Books. (Original work published 1936).
Presson, C. C., & Ihrig, L. H. (1982). Using mother as a spatial landmark: Evidence against egocentric coding in infancy. *Developmental Psychology, 18,* 699–703.
Rieser, J. (1979). Reference systems and the spatial orientation of six month old infants. *Child Development, 50,* 1078–1087.
Schwartz, A., Campos, J., & Baisel, E. (1973). The visual cliff: Cardiac and behavioral correlates on the deep and shallow sides at five and nine months of age. *Journal of Experimental Child Psychology, 15,* 86–99.
Svejda, M., & Schmid, D. (1979). *The role of self-produced locomotion on the onset of fear of heights on the visual cliff.* Paper presented at the meeting of the Society for Research in Child Development, San Francisco, CA.
Wishart, J. G., & Bower, T. G. R. (1982). The development of spatial understanding in infancy. *Journal of Experimental Child Psychology, 33,* 363–385.

4 The Logical Search Skills of Infants and Young Children

Susan C. Somerville
Arizona State University

Robert J. Haake
University of Minnesota

Searching for something is an activity with which we are all quite familiar. Perhaps because the search itself is apt to seem a waste of time, there are a number of strategies that we adopt in order to minimize our efforts. Not all of these strategies are particularly logical or rational ones. For example, we may keep looking in the kitchen drawer for a pair of scissors, convinced that that is where they should be, long after there is sufficient evidence to show that they are not there. There may also be times when we choose an easy place to search for something, ignoring the fact that we did not lose or leave it there. An apocryphal example is the story of the professor who defended searching on the wrong side of the building for spectacles that fell out of the window by pointing out that the windows on the other side had thorny bushes growing underneath. In short, many of our searches have a rather frustrating, irrational quality to them.

On the other hand there are some very rational procedures for searching, which are at least understood if not always followed by adults. Sometimes information can be used to eliminate places that need not be searched and in these circumstances the searcher should know how to recognize and interpret this information. At other times there are no grounds for choosing between the members of a whole array of possible locations. Then the searcher must know how to conduct a series of searches covering every location, preferably involving only one visit to each. Different strategies, perhaps requiring different cognitive skills, are appropriate for different types of search problems.

Children's ability to search for hidden or missing items is of interest because it reveals their knowledge of general strategies such as the comprehensive and selective ones outlined above (Wellman & Somerville, 1982). It is also of interest because searching typically requires an understanding of spatial and temporal relations and may also require the child to estimate probabilities or make inferences. This chapter examines the performance of young children and infants on search problems requiring inferences, that is, problems in which it is logical to search only a subset of the total array of locations. The problems are logical ones because the selection of the locations to search depends on inferences about events that are not perceived directly, but that are implied by other events. There are, of course, many other grounds on which a subset of appropriate locations might be selected, not dependent on the making of inferences. For example, an object might be seen to disappear, directly, into a hiding place, or it might be possible to exclude certain locations from a search because they are visibly empty.

During the second 6 months of life, infants become adept at solving search problems in which they actually see an object disappear into a hiding place. Early in the second year infants begin to be able to infer that a hiding or displacement of an object has occurred, even when they do not see it occur (Piaget, 1954). They now understand that invisible displacements are implied by other events. For example, if an object is placed in a cup and the cup then disappears under a cloth and reemerges empty, the infant will search under the cloth. The logical search problems that we discuss resemble the invisible displacement tasks devised by Piaget (1954) and others (Corrigan, 1978, 1981; Kramer, Hill, & Cohen, 1975; Miller, Cohen, & Hill, 1970; Uzgiris & Hunt, 1975). Those tasks were designed primarily to investigate the latter stages of development of the object concept, in infants aged 1 to 2 years. In contrast, our problems are intended to reveal whether infants and young children understand logical implications about where an object must be. Our procedures differ from the traditional ones because they incorporate visible events designed to convey that some locations may, whereas others definitely do not, contain the object. As an example, suppose that an object is placed in a container which then travels into and out of four possible hiding places. We can convey that the object was not hidden at either of the first two places by showing the object still in the container after leaving those places. Then if we also show that the container is empty once the remaining two places have been visited, this implies that the object was hidden in one or the other of them.

It is possible to imagine a variety of problems in which the movements involved in the hiding of an object are not all visible. Some of the variations become apparent if we compare our logical problems in more detail with the classic tasks used by Piaget (1954) and others. In the traditional procedures the object to be hidden is placed visibly into a container such as a cup or a hand and the closed container is then moved into and out of a succession of hiding places (e.g., under a number of cloths). In this type of sequence the displacements of the object (e.g., from cloth to cloth) are not visible. More importantly, the movements of the container allow the possibility that the object may have been taken from the container and left in one of a number of places, out of view of the child. The fact that this second type of invisible displacement may have occurred is not implied directly by the movements of the container. Rather it is the initial disappearance of the object into the container and the subsequent discovery that it is no longer there that imply such a displacement.

Piaget (1954) claimed that infants at about 1 year of age were unable to infer that an invisible displacement of the object from the container had occurred and would search only in the container itself. Toward the middle of the second year infants began to search the possible hiding places implied by the movements of the container, but did so in a fashion that Piaget regarded as showing only limited understanding of the displacements. That is, they searched the hiding places in the same order as they had been visited by the container, perhaps basing their actions on those of the experimenter rather than on a symbolic representation of the sequence of displacements. Toward the end of the second year infants began to search locations in the reverse order, beginning with the one visited last, and Piaget argued that they were now basing their actions on a reversible representation of the implied sequence. Although this argument about representational skills is important and has been debated by a number of investigators (Corrigan, 1981; Fischer & Jennings, 1981), it is only of tangential relevance to the question of logical search skills. This is because, in the sequences of invisible displacements used by Piaget and others, every location in the array is visited by the container and they are all equally likely to contain the object. Thus it is no more *logical* to search the hiding places in the reverse than in the direct order. The only way in which it might be logical is if, in planning the search, the infant assumed that the container would stop visiting locations as soon as it had deposited the object. Then, strictly speaking, only the location visited last need be searched.

Our tasks were designed specifically to assess the ability of infants and young children to infer *where* in a sequence of movements an unseen event must have occurred. To investigate this we needed to provide information beyond that contained in the traditional invisible displacements tasks. This additional information, as indicated earlier, is a simple demonstration that the object is or is not still in the container at some point along the way. Once additional information like this is introduced into an invisible displacement sequence it becomes possible to create logical search tasks, and to create comparable tasks for both infants and young children, assessing the same logical skills.

Information about children's performance on problems of this sort can extend our knowledge of early cognitive development in three principal ways. In the first place the tasks assess children's ability to coordinate spatial movements with temporal orderings of events and do so in a more direct way than Piaget's (1954) original tasks were able to do. They also tell us about children's inferential skills, because they give children the opportunity to eliminate certain places from their searches on definite logical grounds. Finally, the tasks reveal children's developing knowledge of when to select certain locations from a larger array rather than searching the array comprehensively.

This chapter has two major sections. In the first we discuss the findings of a series of studies of children's logical search skills. In the next we consider the implications of these findings for the three issues outlined above: comprehension of spatial and temporal sequences; logical inferential abilities; and knowledge of selective search procedures.

LOGICAL SEARCH SKILLS

Logical inferences are essential to our everyday knowledge of the positions and movements of objects. We do not watch any object continuously, over long periods, and yet we know exactly or approximately where to find the things that we need at various points in time. This knowledge depends on the ability, given information about an object's whereabouts at a particular time and about its present or previous path of travel, to infer its position at another point in time. For example, before catching a train that stops at a platform, it is important to decide what its next or ultimate destination might be. Or, if a child fails to arrive home from school on time, the parent who wants to search must envisage and check the possible ports of call on the way. If someone or something becomes lost in the course of a journey, we are all familiar with the logical method of pinpointing his, her, or its whereabouts. What is required is information (a) about the place where the missing person or object was last seen and (b) about the path traveled after that place and up to the point where the loss or absence was discovered. Then, logically, the person or object must be somewhere on the path between the points of last known presence and first known absence.

We first became interested in young children's ability to infer the whereabouts of a missing item in the context of everyday event sequences such as those described above. We had anecdotal evidence, for example, that preschoolers seemed to infer that a friend down the road must be home because the car in which the friend had been traveling was now parked on the street; or because when they telephoned the friend's house the phone was answered by someone who was known to have just been out with the friend. By contrast, there was evidence from a laboratory task involving the points of last presence and first absence of an object that 5-year-olds were not capable of logical inferences about the whereabouts of a missing item (Drozdal & Flavell, 1975). We decided initially to devise naturalistic tasks, involving staged sequences of real-life events, in order to examine the logical search skills of young children.

Naturalistic Procedures

Wellman, Somerville, and Haake (1979) conducted a study in which seventy 3-, 4-, and 5-year-olds searched eight marked locations on a familiar preschool playground for a missing object, under two different conditions. Each child initially searched the locations under a control condition in which there was no information specifying that the missing item (a calculator) should be at some location(s) rather than others. Next the child participated in a series of eight games at the locations, arranged so that events occurring at two of them defined a critical search area. These events set the stage for a second, logical task, in which the child searched the same eight locations for a camera that had been used to take his or her picture at the third location and was subsequently discovered missing from the carrying bag at the seventh location.

Even the youngest children understood some implications of the events pertaining to the camera. In the control condition, only 20% of the children went first to a location in what was to become the critical region for the logical task. By contrast, in the logical condition 76% of the children searched first in this region. The central four of the eight locations constituted the critical area; therefore if a child searched end to end, or in a haphazard manner, two of the first four searches would fall in this area by chance. In the control condition the mean number of the children's first four searches in the critical area was 2.05. It rose to 2.84 in the logical condition. There were no differences between 3-, 4- and 5-year-olds on these measures of logical search ability.

However the 3-year-olds did differ from the older children in some respects. In the logical condition, the modal first search choice of every age group was the third location (where the picture was taken). When just those children whose first search was at this location were considered, it was found that the second searches of 3-year-olds were less likely to be in the critical area than those of 4- and 5-year-olds. After these inaccurate second searches, 3-year-olds tended to return to the critical area, but they also showed a greater tendency than older children to repeat a search of a location, in particular of the third location. These findings raised the possibility that the younger children's searches at this location were determined primarily by a strong association of the camera with that place, rather than by the knowledge that that place was the last point in the sequence of events where the camera was present.

To distinguish between these possibilities, Haake, Somerville, and Wellman (1980) conducted a second study, on a different playground, incorporating two logical search conditions. One condition was identical to that of the previous study, and the new condition differed only in that the child's picture was taken at each of the first, second, and third locations. This new condition was designed to establish associations of the camera with locations outside the critical area. If young children's searches were guided primarily by associations, they would be expected to do worse in the new condition than in the original one. The searches of forty 3- to 9-year-olds (approximately half in each condition) were not different under these two conditions and were comparable to the logical search scores in Wellman et al.'s (1979) study. There was also no difference between the performance of younger and older children. Haake et al. concluded that the children's searches were not guided by associations; that the children instead were making logical inferences about the location of the missing camera, on the basis of events occurring in the spatio-temporal sequence. This conclusion was supported by the results of a similar study by Anooshian, Hartman, and Scharf (1982). Their logical search task was based on a series of games played at seven indoor locations in a preschool, arranged so that the third, fourth and fifth locations became the critical search area. As in Haake et al.'s (1980) study, the missing item had been seen and used at each of the first three locations. For their twenty-six 3- to 6-year-olds, an average of 2.16 of the children's first three searches were in the critical area (i.e., approximately 70% of these searches were correct, a figure similar to those obtained by Wellman et al. (1979) and by Haake et al. (1980) for their children's first four searches).

The combined results of these studies suggested that children as young as 3 years of age could infer the location of an object specified only indirectly by perceived events. Children's performance was essentially the same on large preschool playgrounds, where the array of eight locations could be viewed from a single vantage point (Haake et al., 1980; Wellman et al., 1979) and indoors where the locations were distributed over several rooms and hallways and were never simultaneously in view (Anooshian et al., 1982). The comparability of findings obtained in different environments and conditions suggested that children's success on these logical tasks was not due to the idiosyncrasies or the familiarity of particular situations. It might have been a problem for the Wellman et al (1979) study, for example, that the third location (a sandbox) was such a "good" place to search. The children's success in a variety of conditions encouraged us to develop tasks that were similar to the naturalistic ones in the logical skills they required but that did not involve elaborate settings and the simulation of real-life events.

There were several reasons for developing these new tasks. The first reason was to replicate and extend the findings of the naturalistic studies, using a uniform set of locations and incorporating controls for factors such as the direction of travel across locations and the spatial position of the critical search area. The second aim was to investigate more adequately the subtle age differences in understanding of the critical area suggested by some of Wellman et al.'s (1979) results. An issue that seemed potentially relevant here was the fact that although the naturalistic tasks were presumably easy for young children to comprehend, the search problems were actually introduced incidentally to the child. Without forewarning of the need to monitor the movements of an object, the younger children may have been less able than the older ones to recall the information necessary to infer the correct area and search accordingly. Alternatively, the younger children may have been genuinely less able to understand that there was more than one location that might contain the object. To resolve this ambiguity we decided to use tasks in which the nature of the search problem could be explained explicitly, in advance. A further advantage of explicit tasks was that each child could be given repeated presentations of the same type of problem.

These repeated presentations enabled us to examine children's use of individual strategies (e.g., to search a particular spatial location) in addition to the overall performance of different age groups.

The tasks involved short sequences of events occurring in tabletop arrays of locations. The sequences consisted of ordered appearances and disappearances of a variety of objects that could be enclosed in the experimenter's hand.

Four-Location Tasks

Four white cloths were spaced evenly across a table, which was covered with a dark cloth. In the *Hiding* task, the experimenter initially showed a small toy (e.g., rubber doll) in an open hand to one side (left or right) of the cloth array. The hand was then closed and passed under each of the cloths in turn, with brief pauses underneath and between them. After the fourth cloth the hand was opened to show that the toy was absent. These events were common to all hiding sequences, but two different search conditions were established by introducing one further intermediate event into the sequence (see Fig. 4.1). In the *Object Present* condition, the hand was opened between cloths 2 and 3 to show that the toy was still present; in the *Object Absent* condition it was shown to be absent at the same point. In the context of the overall sequence, these intermediate events specified that the object must have been hidden at one of the first two locations in the absent condition and at one of the last two locations in the present condition. Since both directions of travel were used, the correct locations were equally often on the child's right and left, for both conditions. Across different trials in each condition the toy was hidden equally often in each of the two eligible locations, but no cues were given to the child to indicate which of these two locations contained the toy.

Experiment 1. In the first four-location study (Haake, 1982), eighty-nine 2-, 3½- and 5-year-olds were tested, each receiving eight *Object Present* and eight *Object Absent* trials. In all three age groups the mean percentage of correct first searches (i.e., searches at one of the two eligible locations) was above what would be expected by chance (50%) and there were no differences between the age groups in the percentages of correct first searches. However, the extent to which individual children were consistently correct, across 16 trials, did change with age. We adopted the criterion that 12 or more of a child's 16 first searches had to be correct for him or her to be classified as a "logical" searcher (the probability of such a pattern occurring by chance is .039). Sixty-eight percent of the 2-year-olds, 55% of the 3½-year-olds, and 75% of the 5-year-olds met this criterion.

When a correct first choice did not succeed in locating the object, the 2- and 3½-year-olds were less successful than the 5-year-olds in performing a correct second search. Only the oldest group was above chance in its choice of a second

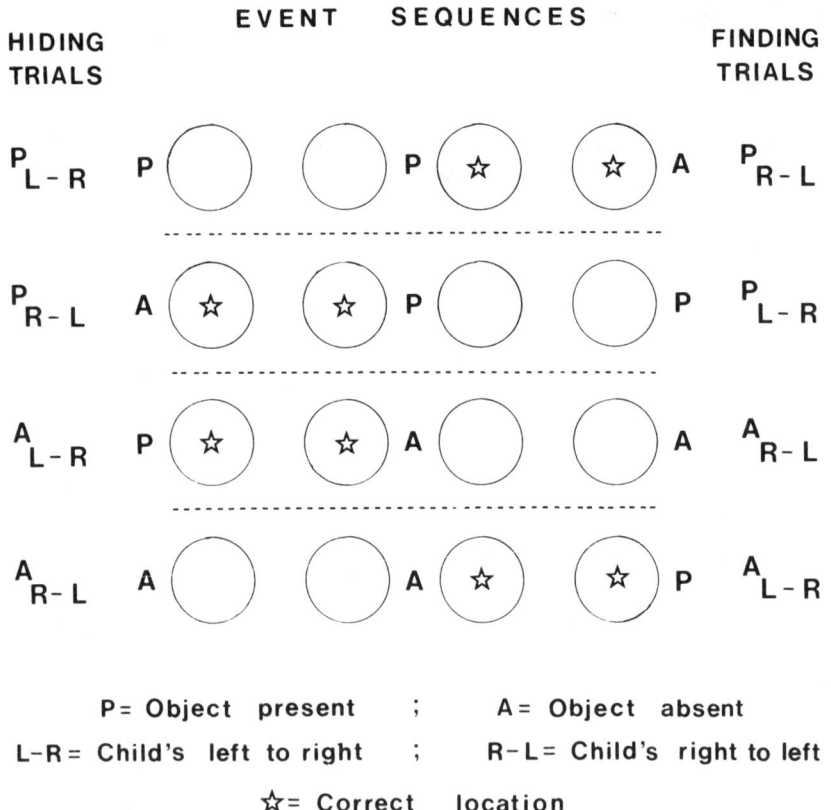

FIG. 4.1. Sequences of Events in the Four-Location Hiding and Finding Tasks. (Reprinted from Somerville and Capuani-Shumaker, in press, *British Journal of Developmental Psychology*).

place to search. This suggests that the youngest children understood less clearly that there were two equally plausible locations implied by each sequence of events.

Finally, for children in all three age groups the sequences in which the object was still present after two cloths had been visited were easier than those in which it was absent at the same point. There were no effects involving direction of travel (right-to-left versus left-to-right). Collapsed across direction of travel, the mean percentages of correct first searches for 2-, 3½- and 5-year-olds respectively were 85%, 86%, and 83% for the object present condition and 67%, 64% and 76% for the object absent condition. Two distinct types of explanation could account for this effect. First an intermediate present event might be more salient or memorable for the child, per se. That is, the child's attention might be caught more readily by the sight of the object than by the sight of an empty hand, or it might be easier to remember a place where the object was seen than a place where an empty hand was shown. Second, the higher success rates given an intermediate present event could be due not to the type of event per se, but to the search implications of this event in the context of the overall spatio-temporal sequence. The present event showed the child that the object had not been hidden at either of the first two places and made the last two places visited the correct ones to search. The intermediate absent event held the reverse implications for where to search. So sequences with a present event might have been easier because they implied that the two locations visited most recently should be searched.

Experiment 2. The first study did not allow us to distinguish between these two interpretations of why sequences with a present event were easier. A second four-location study was designed in part to do so. This second study (Somerville & Capuani-Shumaker, in press) included a new task, the *Finding* task, which was the inverse of the *Hiding* task in the sense that it created the opposite search implications for the same intermediate present and absent events. In fact it was a young child in the first four-location study (Haake, 1982) who inadvertently drew our attention to the possibility of using symmetrical hiding and finding procedures. This child was reliably wrong in her searches for objects hidden by the experimenter, always looking where the object could not possibly have been placed. One possible explanation of her systematic errors is the following. Whenever the experimenter showed her that the object was still present, which in the hiding procedure signified that it had not yet been hidden, she may have assumed instead that it had just been found. Similarly, when shown that the object was now absent (i.e., had already been hidden), she perhaps assumed that it had not yet been found. That is, she may have interpreted the events as though the experimenter were finding rather than hiding objects. Her errors led us to devise procedures for which those incorrect interpretations would have been correct. The finding sequences corresponding to each hiding sequence are shown in Fig. 4.1.

In the *Finding* task two identical toys (rubber dolls, e.g., Minnie Mouse and her "twin sister") were initially hidden together under one of the four cloths while the array was screened from the child's view. The screen was then removed and the child watched while the experimenter found one of the dolls. The finding sequence consisted of a hand initially shown empty at one end of the array, then closed and passed under each of the cloths, and finally opened after the fourth cloth to reveal that the toy was present. All finding sequences contained these events but, as in the hiding task, two different conditions were established by the inclusion of a further intermediate event between the second and third cloths. The intermediate object present event, in finding, implied that the toy had been found at one of the first two locations; the intermediate absent event that it was yet to be found at one of the last two locations.

The child's task, in finding, was to search for the duplicate of the toy that the experimenter had found, given that the two dolls were always hiding under the same cloth. The search implications of the intermediate present and absent events, in finding, were exactly the reverse of their respective implications in hiding. Thus to search correctly in both tasks a child had to interpret the same intermediate events differently, in the contexts of different overall event sequences. The finding task, although more complex in some ways, might possibly be expected to be easier than the hiding task since (a) the finding actions of the experimenter provided a more direct model of what the child was about to do and (b) the experimenter did not adopt the "hider" role with its possible implications of trying to trick the child (cf. Bertenthal & Fischer, 1983).

Sixty-four 3½- and 4½-year-olds were tested on a block of eight *Hiding* trials and a block of eight *Finding* trials, the order of the blocks being counterbalanced across children within each age group. These trial blocks contained four with an intermediate present event and four with an intermediate absent event. Overall the mean percentage of correct first searches was greater for 4½-year-olds (77%) than for 3½-year-olds (67%). There was no difference between performance on the hiding and finding tasks and no task by age interaction. However, there was an interaction of task with the type of intermediate event in the sequence (present versus absent); and this interaction was the same for both age groups. In the hiding task, as in the previous four-location study, performance was higher with an intermediate present event (79%) than with an intermediate absent event (69%). In the finding task, by contrast, performance was higher in the absent (78%) than in the present (60%) condition.

This interaction effect cannot be explained by a difference (e.g., in salience) between the present and absent events themselves. The differential performance is attributable instead to the implications of the events for searches in the two tasks. The easier event in each task was the one that rendered the last two locations (i.e., those visited most recently) the correct ones to search, which may indicate that children remembered the critical information better when it occurred at the end of the sequence of events. However, there is an additional factor that may also have been important. In the sequences with the more difficult intermediate event (absent in hiding, present in finding) there was a repetition of this event at the end of the sequence, which did not add any information about where the object was hidden. It may also have been difficult for the children to ignore this essentially redundant event.

An important question was whether children's first searches in these hiding and finding tasks were correct more often than would be expected by chance. Since two of the four locations were always correct the chance probability of choosing correctly was .5. Because of the task by event interaction, discussed above, and the overall difference between the two age groups, separate comparisons to chance were made for the distributions of first search scores of each age group in each task by event condition, using the Binomial theorem. In all but one case (the younger children in the finding task with an intermediate present event), performance was better than would be expected by chance.

It is useful to compare the overall performance of young children in the four-location tasks with that in the earlier, naturalistic studies. In the studies using playground and indoor environments (Anooshian et al., 1982; Haake et al., 1980; Wellman et al., 1979), preschoolers correctly allocated about 70%, on the average, of the number of searches that logically should have been allocated to the critical area. That is, although they chose correct locations more often than would be expected by chance, they fell short of the ideal strategy of searching all and only the correct locations. The same is true of the results obtained in the hiding and finding tasks. In the second study, the average percentage of trials on which children's first searches were correct, for both tasks combined, was 72% (77% overall for the 4½-year-olds and 67% for the 3½-year-olds). Similar overall figures were obtained for 2- to 5-year-olds on just the hiding task in the first study. Thus, although the overall success rates were estimated somewhat differently for the naturalistic and the four-location tasks, the estimates obtained were very comparable, indicating better-than-chance but less-than-perfect choice of the correct locations in each case.

Two conclusions follow from these results. The first is that preschoolers can make logical inferences about unseen displacements of an object. Children's searches were more accurate than would be expected if they searched randomly, systematically end to end, or according to particular spatial or temporal preferences and, in the naturalistic studies, were also different from searches under a control condition. However, the second point is that the children were not completely successful on these logical tasks. The younger children especially seemed to show less precise understanding of the implications of the event sequences than might have been expected. Two aspects of their performance on the hiding and finding tasks in the second study provided further evidence about just how precise and reliable their understanding was. Since the children were each given eight trials on each task, we were able to examine (a) their individual strategies and (b) the accuracy of their second searches following a first correct but unsuccessful search.

Individual Strategies in the Hiding and Finding Tasks

The hiding and finding tasks were considered separately to determine the individual strategies used in each. Since the probability of choosing a correct location on any trial by chance was .5, the probability that a child would make seven or eight correct first choices, by chance, on either task was .035 (Binomial theorem). Any child with seven or eight correct first searches on a task was therefore classified as using a logical strategy. Using the same criterion of seven or eight first searches conforming to the choices that a particular strategy would prescribe, children's conformity to seven other strategies was also assessed. These strategies all stipulated that either one of two locations should be searched first: (a) either location on the right hand side, (b) either location on the left hand side, (c) either of the first two locations visited, (d) either of the last two locations visited, (e) either of the incorrect (i.e., illogical) locations, (f) either of the end locations (defined spatially or temporally) and (g) either of the inner locations. It should be noted that a child's searches could conform to one of the last two strategies at the same time as conforming to any other strategy, including the logical strategy.

In the hiding task the percentages of 3½-year-olds (44%) and 4½-year-olds (59%) who adopted a logical strategy were not very different. In the finding task more of the older (47%) than of the younger (19%) children used a logical strategy. Three children were consistently illogical in the hiding task, two in the finding task, but there was no evidence that their misinterpretations of events were a result of carryover from the other task. Of the children who were not consistently logical or illogical, the younger ones did not have a greater tendency than older ones to adopt simple spatial or temporal strategies (i.e., strategies a, b, c, d, f, and g above), on either task. In the hiding task, 22% of the younger and 31% of the older children adopted one of these strategies; and 25% of the younger and 9% of the older children were not classifiable as users of any of the eight strategies investigated. In the finding task, 44% of the younger and 22% of the older children conformed to a spatial or temporal strategy, the most common being to search consistently in one of the last two places visited; 34% of the younger and 28% of the older children were not consistent users of any strategy.

In summary, although the younger children were less consistently logical than the older ones, the strategy analyses did not show that they were more prone to respond in a biased way toward particular spatial or temporal locations. It therefore seems reasonable to conclude that the 3½- and 4½-year-olds understood and attempted to draw inferences from the sequences of events in much the same way. This conclusion is also supported by the fact that the various task conditions showed the same pattern of difficulty for both age groups, as indicated by the task by event interaction discussed earlier. However, both the strategy analyses and the estimates of overall success rates were based just on children's first searches, summed across trials. Since there were always two locations consistent with the events in any trial, a child's first search, even though correct, did not necessarily locate the object. We were therefore able to examine a certain number of trials, for each child, in which the second searches were informative about his or her understanding of the sequences of events.

Second Searches in the Hiding and Finding Tasks

When children's first searches were correct and at an endpoint of the array of cloths, their second searches were correct on 92% of occasions (combined across tasks) for the 3½-year-olds and 97% for the 4½-year-olds. However this did not necessarily mean that children understood that the second location was correct, because they may simply have tended to move to an adjacent location. This possibility is supported by the fact that following first searches that were *incorrect* and at an endpoint, children of both ages also searched next in the adjacent location on more than 90% of occasions, overall. The most informative second searches were therefore those that occurred following first searches that were correct, unsuccessful, and at an inner location. The correct inner location always had a correct (end) location on one side and an incorrect (inner) location on the other. Following correct first searches of this type, children's second searches were by no means uniformly successful, being correct on 51% of occasions overall for the younger and 61% for the older children. When analyses were conducted for just those children with sufficient numbers of trials of this type to provide meaningful estimates, it was found that the success rate in second searches was higher for the older than for the younger children in the finding task, but that the age groups were not different in the hiding task. Further, assuming that a child would always search adjacently to the first choice and that the chance probability of a correct second search was therefore .5, the second searches of the older but not the younger children were correct more often than would be expected by chance.

These findings suggested, as had those of some of the earlier naturalistic studies, that younger children might be less aware than older ones that there was more than one correct location to search. Even the older children, despite being better than chance, were relatively unsuccessful in their second searches when the first correct search was at an inner location. The information obtained about second searches from these hiding and finding tasks was limited, however, because of the need to discount trials in which the first correct search was at an endpoint. Arguably, children might have searched deliberately at the endpoint first, as a means of remembering most easily where to go to next. However there was no direct evidence that this was the case.

One way to avoid the endpoint problem was to conduct the same hiding and finding procedures, using a nonlinear array of cloths. So, in an attempt to get more extensive data about children's second searches, we used four-location tasks in which the array was a square, oriented diagonally with respect to the experimenter and child. In these tasks, the experimenter's hand moved in a circular path under and between cloths, with the same sequences of object present and object absent events occurring between cloths as in the four-location tasks with linear arrays. The initial and final event of any given sequence, of course, occurred in exactly the same position. Each child was given eight hiding and eight finding trials, with the starting position and the position in which the toy was actually hidden counterbalanced across trials in a similar manner to that in the study with linear arrays. For half of the children the direction of travel was clockwise for the hiding task, counterclockwise for the finding task, and vice versa for the other half.

Sixteen 4½-year-olds participated in this study. In the hiding task, the percentages of correct first searches were comparable to those for the linear task: 75% overall; 80% for sequences with an intermediate present event and 70% for those with an absent event. Seven of the children were consistently correct (i.e., on 7 or 8 trials). The percentages of correct first searches were lower in the finding task: 57% overall; 47% with a present event, and 67% with an absent event. Only 1 of the 16 children made consistently correct first searches in the finding task with the square array. Since children's first searches were correct at a level above chance only for the hiding task, their second searches were examined for that task only. The total number of correct but unsuccessful first searches, summed across children and trials, was 48; and the first search was followed by a correct second search on only 28 of these occasions (58%). Even for the seven children who made consistently logical first choices, the second searches were correct on only 56% of relevant occasions. These data confirmed the evidence from the linear tasks that children were not able to choose the second correct location reliably when their first correct choice failed to locate the object.

There are a number of possible interpretations of children's failures in their second searches in both the linear and nonlinear tasks. One interpretation is that they failed because of the problem of remembering the second location after the first search had failed, at which point the child was presumably also trying to remember where the first search had been so as not to search there again. A second interpretation is that when a child's first search was correct but unsuccessful there was a tendency for the child to reject altogether his or her initial decision about both of the correct locations. This would amount to the child's using the information gained from the first search illogically, as evidence against the object's being in the other correct location. The third interpretation, like the second, postulates limitations in the child's logical ability. In this interpretation, the child is seen as mistakenly concluding that there is only one correct location (the one searched first), on the basis of the sequence of events. That is, the child treats his or her inference about one of the correct locations as necessarily true, when in fact it is merely consistent with the events. Since the second and third possibilities are related to other evidence about the development of inferential abilities in young children, they are discussed in more detail later.

Summary of Results from the Four-Location Tasks

Two- to 5-year-olds showed evidence of logical ability in the four-location tasks. At all ages, children were able to select an appropriate location to search initially, on the basis of a spatio-temporal series of events. Each study was designed so that a consistent tendency to choose a particular spatial location or locations (e.g., endpoints) would result overall in chance levels of performance. A tendency to choose locations visited (for example) late in the temporal sequence of events would also result in chance levels of success, overall. Children's better-than-chance success in their first searches therefore cannot be accounted for in terms of purely spatial or purely temporal strategies such as "look on the right hand side" or "look where the experimenter's hand went last" (cf. Fischer & Jennings, 1981). Instead, the children must have integrated and interpreted events at particular spatial locations in the context of a particular temporal sequence. Some sequences were more difficult than others because the children had to make and maintain an appropriate interpretation when there were uninformative events occurring late in the sequence (sequences with an intermediate absent event in the hiding task and an intermediate present event in the finding task). There was no overall indication, in the second study, that the experimenter's adoption of a "hider" (rather than a "finder") role affected the searches of either the 3½- or the 4½-year-olds, although fewer of the younger children were consistently logical in the finding task than in the hiding task. However, in the follow-up study with a circular path of travel the 4½-year-olds found the finding task more difficult overall than the hiding task.

The developmental changes in the percentage of correct first searches were small, in fact insignificant in the first experiment. Both younger and older children were able to interpret the sequences of events in ways that enhanced their initial success. However, the older children were apparently more aware than the younger ones that the sequences of events always defined two equally appropriate locations to search. This was indicated by their greater (although by no means complete) knowledge of where to search next on some of the trials, following a correct but unsuccessful first search. Since the search strategies of even the youngest children were merely imperfect, rather than completely erroneous, the next step was to find out whether the same logical search skills would be exhibited by toddlers and older infants. To this end the *Hiding* task was made as as simple as possible by reducing the array to just two locations, keeping all the other aspects of the task the same.

Two-Location Hiding Task

This task used the same sequences of events as the four-location hiding task, the intermediate present and absent events occurring between the two locations. Each hiding sequence specified one of the two locations as the correct place to search. In the first study (Haake & Somerville, in press) 12 hiding trials were presented to each of a total of 60 infants, comprising 9-, 12-, 15- and 18-month-olds. Eight trials were directly analogous to those in the four-location hiding task. Four of these trials contained an intermediate present event, four an intermediate absent event, and two of each type were conducted from left-to-right, two from right-to-left. The additional four trials were the same as the other trials with an intermediate present event, except that a short delay was introduced at the end of the sequence of events, before the infant was permitted to search.

These trials were included because there was a longer delay between the point where the object was shown to be absent and the point where search began in the standard object absent condition, than in the standard object present condition. Since the introduction of the delay had no effect on performance in the object present trials, the trials with and without a delay will be combined in what follows. The toy was hidden in the correct location on every trial, which was equally often on the child's left and right, and equally often the first and last location visited, across the block of 12 trials. If the child did not search when the hiding sequence was complete and the table placed within reach, a standard series of up to five prompts was given.

Even after prompting, the 9-month-olds searched for the object in the array on only half of the trials. Infants in the three older groups searched on almost every trial. With increasing age, fewer prompts were required to elicit search. When 9-month-olds did search, their first choice was correct, on the average, on 51% of trials in the object absent condition, 38% in the object present condition (neither figure deviating from chance level—50%). Similarly, the 12-month-olds did not search at levels better than chance in either the absent (39%) or the present (58%) condition. The performance of 15-month-olds was better than chance and better than that of 12-month-olds in both the absent (63%) and the present (67%) conditions; and the performance of 18-month-olds was better again (77% in the absent, 80% in the present condition).

These results established that children 15 months and older were capable of searching logically in a very simple array, guided by a sequence of events. The events in which the object appeared or was shown to have disappeared at particular positions were interpreted correctly, within the temporal sequence. It seemed likely that the high levels of performance of these young subjects would be disrupted if the experimenter's hand traveled in a less regular path across the array (thus destroying the direct correspondence of spatial and temporal orderings). In an additional study, twenty 18-month-olds were tested in two new hiding conditions, one in which the hand began in between the two cloths and traveled an essentially circular path, another in which the hand started outside the array at one end, moved next to the middle of the array before visiting the cloth at the other end, then back to the middle of the array, finally visiting the cloth next to the starting position (a crossed path). The same intermediate events of object presence and absence as in the previous study were incorporated into these irregular paths of movement. The 18-month-olds demonstrated the same high levels of success in their first searches under each of these new conditions: The overall percentages of correct searches were 81% for the circular path and 73% for the crossed path. Further, these infants were correct at levels above chance for sequences with each type of intermediate event in each movement pattern.

Haake and Somerville (in press) also examined individual 12-, 15- and 18-month-olds' conformity to five strategies, using the criterion that an infant's choice on 10 or more of the 12 trials had to be the choice prescribed by a strategy for the infant to qualify as a user of that strategy (Binomial $p = .019$). The five strategies prescribed choices of (a) the logical (correct) location, (b) the location on the left, (c) the location on the right, (d) the first location visited, and (e) the last location visited. One 12-month-old who refused to search on five trials was excluded, with the result that the conformity to these strategies was examined for fourteen 12-month-olds and 15 in each of the other two age groups. Sixty-seven percent of the 18-month-olds were consistently logical, by comparison with only 20% of the 15-month-olds and none of the 12-month-olds. Nine of the 15-month-olds were not classifiable as users of any of these five strategies and children in this age group were less likely to use non-logical strategies (rather than no strategy at all) than were the 12-month-olds. Fifty-seven percent of the 12-month-olds used a spatial strategy, 43% searching consistently on the right. Two of the 12-month-olds ($<2\%$) searched consistently in the last place visited.

Summary of Results from the Two-Location Task

There were quite dramatic changes with age in infants' ability to solve the two-location logical search task. The 9-month-olds' frequent refusals to search at all and their lack of success when they did search suggests that they had difficulty inferring that an invisible displacement of the object had occurred. Twelve-month-olds apparently inferred that the displacement had occurred, since they searched in the array on almost every trial, but were unable to decide which location contained the object at levels better than chance. Rather than coordinating the spatial and temporal information to make a correct inference, they seemed to search regularly in the same place, defined either spatially or temporally. Infants aged 15 and 18 months, in contrast, were able to interpret the events correctly and thus infer the position of the hidden object. The 15-month-olds did so at levels better than chance, but were much less consistently correct in their choices than the 18-month-olds. The success of older infants in this two-location task and of younger children in a variety of similar tasks involving greater numbers of locations has broader implications for development in three main areas. These are the understanding of spatio-temporal sequences of events, inferential abilities, and knowledge of selective and other search procedures. These areas are discussed in turn.

IMPLICATIONS OF LOGICAL SEARCH SKILLS FOR THREE AREAS OF DEVELOPMENT

The results of our logical search studies allow us to trace some connections between the skills of infants and those that develop in the next few years. As we have suggested above, a rather complex combination of cognitive skills is required to solve even a two-location logical search task. We examine three classes of skills separately, although this does not mean that we consider them to be independent of one another.

I. COMPREHENSION OF SPATIO-TEMPORAL SEQUENCES OF EVENTS

The original studies of children's understanding of spatio-temporal sequences were conducted by Piaget and his colleagues (Piaget, 1970; Piaget & Inhelder, 1967) using small-scale representations of activities involving a sequence of events (e.g., hanging items of washing on a line; recording the successive appearances of colored bands on a strip traveling behind a slit). Children aged between 2 and 8 years were asked to copy, predict, and transform an order of travel (Piaget, 1970) or to perform the actions necessary to produce a direct, reversed, or otherwise transformed copy of a stationary ordered array (Piaget & Inhelder, 1967).

According to Piaget and Inhelder, children's performance on these tasks indicated that up until about 6 or 7 years of age children did not understand the basis of a spatio-temporal ordering. These authors' central argument was that 3½- to 4-year-olds understood an ordered array only as a "pattern of uncoordinated proximities" (1967, p. 90), failing to grasp that the production of a complete ordering required a fixed direction of travel from one item to the next. They also suggested that older children (i.e., 4½- to 5-year-olds) were able to maintain a fixed direction of travel, but at first only when required to make a direct copy of an ordering that was perceptually available and aligned with the original. Finally, they found that children at about 6 or 7 years could succeed when a linear ordering had to be reversed, or a circular ordering transformed into a linear one. There have been relatively few subsequent studies of children's performance on these tasks. Braine (1959) and Pufall and Furth (1966) devised somewhat different tasks in which children were required to match an ordering and in each case obtained low levels of success among 3- to 5-year-olds.

By contrast, Brown and Murphy (1975) tested 3-, 4- and 5-year-olds on Piaget and Inhelder's (1967) washing-line task and found high levels of success, even among 3-year-olds, on direct linear copies of up to seven-item arrays. Brown and Murphy also investigated 4-year-olds' memory for orders that were no longer perceptually available. The same items of clothing were used, placed on a line, but now the child had to recall an order displayed earlier and construct his or her copy from memory. Again the children succeeded and there was no difference in their memory for orders that were randomly arranged and orders that reflected the familiar order in which clothes would be placed on a doll.

The hiding and finding tasks that we presented to infants and young children involved events occurring in sequences, much like the sequential hanging of items on a line. The child did not have to copy the sequences of events or reproduce them from memory; nevertheless, the order information had to be interpreted in certain ways. By contrast with Piaget and Inhelder's (1967) tasks, each event in the hiding and finding tasks did not result in an item (e.g., of washing) which remained visible in a spatial array. Instead the events occurred in relation to an existing array, whose appearance did not change. The events defined a sequence of movements (partially seen, partially unseen) of a single object, and the child's task was to infer the unseen from the seen parts of this sequence.

The child could not infer the movements of the object without taking into account the direction of travel with respect to the array. If the child had merely noted that the object appeared or disappeared near certain locations, it would not have been possible to discriminate the correct from the incorrect places to search. In other words, the hiding and finding tasks could not be solved using simple notions of spatial proximity. In the most general terms, the hiding task required an understanding that the current location of an object lies in a spatial domain defined by the point where the object last appeared and the path it traveled (invisibly) after that point and up to the point where it was known to have stopped traveling. For the finding task, the general rule is similar but defines a spatial domain where the object must have been before it began traveling. To the extent that infants and young children solved these logical tasks, they showed an ability to go beyond notions of simple proximity relations. In doing so, they incorporated information about an object's initial position and direction of travel.

The important point is that children's success in the hiding and finding tasks implies that they were able to comprehend and remember the temporal sequence in which several events occurred. Every sequence in both the two- and four-location tasks comprised three events, two of which were critical for the inference about the correct location(s). Because the implication that young children could retain the temporal ordering of a series of events was somewhat surprising, in the context of the traditional literature, we decided to investigate children's memory for temporal orders more directly. In particular, we wanted to discover whether their ability to retain a temporal order was dependent on some form of correspondence between that temporal order and a spatially ordered array. With the exception of the second two-location study, in which the paths of travel were irregular, our search tasks always involved a linear or square array of cloths and events occurring in a temporal sequence that corresponded directly (left-to-right, right-to-left, or in a circular manner) to the spatial arrangement.

Memory for Temporal Order

Somerville, Niedorowski, and Haake (1984) investigated children's memory for the order in which three events occurred. In preliminary explorations we discovered that it was quite difficult to devise a task in which children's attention could be directed solely or primarily toward the temporal ordering of events. For example, if we engaged a child in a series of simple actions such as pouring out some water, then banging with a hammer, and so on, and then asked the child to repeat the same actions in the same order, 3- and 4-year-olds showed no evidence of recalling the temporal order although they did repeat all the actions. However it seemed to be a lack of attention to the instruction to maintain the same order, or perhaps the fact that there was no particular point to recalling the order, that was leading to their failure.

We next devised a task in which the events consisted simply of the successive presentation of three everyday items to the child, for identification by touch without vision. The child had to feel each item as it was placed under a cover, in a constant spatial position, and to state the name of each item as soon as he or she had decided what it was. The objects used on a given trial came from a pool of 18 for each child, which that particular child had been able to name in a pretest when all the items were visible. Some of the objects typically included were a fork, a hairbrush, a shoe, a rock, and a set of keys. As the objects were presented, haptically, the child was told: "This is the first one, this is the next one, and this is the last one": and instructions were given to the child to remember which was first, next, and last so that he or she would be able to choose them later from a visible array. Since the haptic recognition of each item usually required several seconds, there was time to emphasize the position of each item in the temporal order.

Using this recognition task we tested whether various spatial arrangements of the three items affected children's recall of the order in which they had been presented haptically. On two control trials (the first and last of a series of six for each child), the three items were not spread out, but grouped together in the center of a long white board. On these trials there was no spatial arrangement that might either enhance or interfere with recall of the temporal order. The intermediate trials comprised four different linear arrangements, their order of presentation being counterbalanced across children: 1-2-3, in which the items which had been presented first, next, and last were arranged left-to-right in front of the child (with large gaps between them) on the white board; 3-2-1 in which they were arranged right-to-left; 3-1-2 in which the item presented first was in the center, the next on the right and the last on the left; and 2-3-1 in which the first was on the right, the next on the left, and the last in the center. These linear arrays were constructed out of the child's view, using the movable board, and were only shown to the child when completed (so that all items appeared simultaneously).

Ninety-six children were tested, including 3-, 4-, 5-, and 6-year-olds. The results can best be considered by grouping the six trials into three sets of two; (a) the two control trials in which there were was no spatial array, (b) the 1-2-3 and 3-2-1 trials in which there was a direct correspondence between the linear spatial array and the temporal order for which recall was tested, and (c) the 3-1-2 and 2-3-1 trials in which there was no direct correspondence between these spatial and temporal orders. Each child was given a score of 2, 1, or 0 on each of these three pairs of trials: 2 for correct recall of the complete three-item order on both trials, 1 for correct recall on one but not the other trial, and 0 for correct recall on neither trial. Because there are six possible orderings of three items, if a child guesses randomly the probability of a correct answer on any trial is .167. Using the Binomial theorem we calculated that of the 24 children in each age group, by chance one would expect 16.65 (69%) to score 0 on any pair of trials, 6.68 (28%) to score 1 and 0.67 (3%) to score 2.

There was no evidence that the 3-year-olds could recall the temporal order in which the three items had been presented, except when there was a linear spatial array that corresponded to that temporal order. On the control trials with no spatial array, 4% scored 2, 38% scored 1 and 58% scored 0 (the overall percentage of correct responses was 23%) and on the trials with noncorresponding spatial arrays, 12% scored 2, 21% scored 1, and 67% scored 0 (the overall percentage correct was again 23%). Neither of these distributions differed from that expected by chance. However, when either a left-to-right or a right-to-left spatial array corresponded to the temporal order, their performance was better than chance, with 25% of the children scoring 2, 42% scoring 1, and 33% scoring 0 (the overall percentage of correct responses was 46%). Half of those who scored 1 were correct on the right-to-left trial, half on the left-to-right trial.

The performance of older children was markedly different from that of the 3-year-olds. For the 4-, 5- and 6-year-olds, 92% or more of the children in each age group were correct (a) on one or both of the trials with no spatial array (the overall percentages correct being 75%, 81%, and 83%, respectively, for the age groups); and (b) on one or both of the trials with corresponding linear arrays (the overall percentages correct being 69%, 79%, and 83%, respectively). By contrast with the 3-year-olds, these children could recall the temporal order either with or without the support of a corresponding spatial ordering. Ninety-two percent of the 6-year-olds could also do so (i.e., scored either 1 or 2 correct) when there was a noncorresponding spatial array (i.e., on the 3-1-2 and 2-3-1 trials, the overall percentage correct being 71%). Thus for the oldest children there was no evidence that the lack of correspondence interfered with their recall of the temporal order. For the 4- and 5 year-olds this was not the case. Although both of these age groups were above chance on the 3-1-2 and 2-3-1 trials (54% of the 4-year-olds and 67% of the 5-year-olds had 1 or 2 correct), in each case their success rate was below that on the other types of trials. The overall percentages of correct responses on these trials, for these age groups, were 42% and 54%, respectively.

When children made errors on the noncorresponding trials, a great proportion of them were errors of going right-to-left across the spatial array; for 3-, 4-, 5- and 6-year-olds, respectively, the overall percentages of errors that were right-to-left were 42%, 75%, 68%, and 86%. Since there were five possible error patterns in each case, these proportions were indicative of a bias to respond right-to-left, particularly in the older children. This is not a surprising finding for the 231 trial, in which the first item in the temporal order was on the child's right, but the proportions of right-to-left errors were comparable on the 2-3-1 and 3-1-2 trials and the same explanation is not applicable in the latter case. For the 3-, 4- and 5-year-olds there was also a tendency to make right-to-left errors when the correct response was left-to-right (the 1-2-3 trial), the percentages of errors on this trial that were right-to-left being 69%, 56%, and 33%, respectively. Six-year-olds never made this type of error on this trial. The tendency to make the opposite type of error (left-to-right when the correct response was right-to-left) was about as strong as for right-to-left errors, for the 3-year-olds (54%), but, by contrast, was near zero for children in the three older groups.

In summary, only the 6-year-olds consistently recalled the temporal order in which three objects had been presented, whatever the spatial arrangement of the objects when recall was tested. However, although their performance did not differ across spatial arrays, they were not at ceiling on the task, their mean total number of correct responses being 4.75 out of 6 (79%). Although 4- and 5-year-olds did as well as the 6-year-olds when the temporal and spatial orders did not conflict, they were worse on the noncorresponding trials, resulting in mean total scores of 3.71 (62%) and 4.29 (72%) for the two age groups, respectively. In these two age groups children's erroneous responses indicated that they expected the temporal order to correspond to a right-to-left spatial order. Three-year-olds showed no such expectation and in fact were completely unable to recall the temporal order of presentation of three items, except when those items were arranged in either a right-to-left or left-to-right corresponding order. Overall the mean number of correct responses for 3-year-olds was only 1.79 (30%).

These results suggest that young children's notions of temporal succession might depend on, or be connected initially with, notions of spatial ordering. This is plausible, if for no other reason than that many events that are ordered in time also occur at different points in space. This is true, for example, of many of the tasks used by Piaget (1970; Piaget & Inhelder, 1967) and others (Brown & Murphy, 1975) to examine children's understanding of ordered sequences. In the washing-line task, for example, the child is instructed to hang a number of items on the line in the same (temporal and spatial) order as the experimenter. That is, the items that are placed, in turn, on the line also occupy different spatial positions (Piaget & Inhelder, 1967). Even in tasks that have no immediately obvious spatial component, such as one used by Piaget in which colored bands appear successively through a narrow slit, the temporal succession is achieved by arranging the items in some spatial order on a card (or a rotating drum). The child is shown this arrangement, beforehand, and asked to reconstruct the temporal order of appearance by constructing his or her own spatial array to correspond to it (Piaget & Inhelder, 1967).

The hiding and finding tasks that we presented to children also entailed events separated both in space and time. Furthermore, the correspondence between the spatial and temporal orderings in these tasks was, except in one two-location study, always simple and direct. Search problems, in common with many everyday events that young children experience, tend to involve coordinated spatial and temporal changes. In our logical search tasks, a correct interpretation of such coordinated changes allowed an inference about a hidden object's position to be drawn. The findings from the study of children's recall of temporal orders suggest that 3- to 5-year-olds would find these logical search tasks more difficult if the direct correspondence between the temporal and spatial ordering of events were destroyed. On the other hand, infants in their second year were able to make the same type of inference in the two-location hiding task and, furthermore, their performance was unaffected by changes in the path of travel across locations.

Overall our studies have revealed a sensitivity to temporal order information, extending to children younger than 3 years, which is impressive and has not been apparent in many previous studies. This suggests that search problems are particularly suited to the study of temporal concepts in and beyond infancy. The characteristics that make them useful include the fact that they depend on a single sequence of interconnected events, which the child watches and interprets. In these tasks it is also relatively easy for the child to focus on the temporal succession of events, since those events occur within a static, unchanging spatial array. In these respects the search tasks can be contrasted with the ordering tasks used by Piaget and Inhelder (1967), in which the sequences of events are arbitrary and in which the most obvious change occurring is the gradual construction of a spatial array. As we have shown, in order to reveal young children's understanding of a temporal ordering it is advisable to use a task in which the temporal information is not interfered with or overruled in importance by a spatial display. Logical search tasks are an obvious everyday example of problems in which the temporal ordering of events is crucial to a correct solution. We have shown that even infants can use this type of temporal information to solve a simple search task.

II. INFERENTIAL ABILITIES

When an inference is made about something for which there is only indirect evidence, an important cognitive skill involved is the application of general rules or knowledge to a particular instance. That is, an inference entails more than the joining of two items, or ideas, on the basis of contiguity or some other form of association. The grounds for connecting the items of information must be provided by some formal system or set of principles. There are a great many systems within which legitimate inferences can be made. Perhaps the best known area of developmental investigation has involved systems of asymmetrical relations such as length or height, within which transitive inferences can be made about the relative positions of items in a seriated array (e.g., Adams, 1978; Bryant & Trabasso, 1971; Piaget & Szeminska, 1952). It has been found that 4-, 5- and 6-year-olds are able to make such inferences, although there is a tendency for them to use noninferential methods of solving seriation problems if the task conditions permit (Adams, 1978).

Many problems concerning the spatial location of a person or object require inferences, sometimes inferences of a transitive nature. For example, if person A is known to be with person B and person B is known to be at the library, person A must be at the library. These inferences depend on an understanding of the general rules governing the movements and possible positions of objects in space. Somerville, Hadkinson, and Greenberg (1979) found that 5- and 6-year-olds were able to make inferences of this type, but that the younger children also showed a striking limitation in their logical ability. This limitation was revealed when more than one possible location was consistent with the information that children had been given, for example, when someone was known to live in a house with a blue table and two houses were presented each of which contained a blue table. Under these conditions 5- but not 6-year-olds tended to choose one of the two equally consistent possibilities, with no apparent awareness that their choice would not necessarily be correct. This suggested that there are two separable components to the making of an inference. The first involves the integration of information to draw a conclusion (e.g., that a house with a blue table is a correct choice). The second requires an assessment of whether the conclusion necessarily follows or is merely consistent with the information given. For a finite set of possibilities, the second component amounts to an awareness of which, if any, of the possibilities can be eliminated and which should be retained. The importance of retaining all of the consistent possibilities, rather than choosing between them, was apparently not clear to the 5-year-olds in Somerville et al.'s (1979) task.

The logical search studies add to our knowledge of children's ability to make inferences in several ways. Consistently correct first searches in either a two-location or a four-location task can only be made if the child applies general principles about the movements of objects to the events that are seen on any given trial. That is, the child cannot be consistently correct by making a particular learned response (e.g., to reach to the left) or by searching a particular type of location (e.g., the one visited last by the object's container). The fact that many 18-month-olds were consistently correct in the two-location hiding task and that 15-month-olds, while less consistent, did better than would be expected by chance establishes that these infants can make inferences based on an understanding of sequences of events. Thus the first conclusion to be drawn is that infants in their second year can infer the location of an unseen displacement of an object. In the two-location task, since there was only one location consistent with the event information, no assessment of infants' appreciation of logical necessity could be made.

However, in the naturalistic studies and in the four-location hiding and finding tasks presented to preschoolers the question of necessity was of considerable importance. In these tasks there was always more than one location consistent with the sequence of events, so that no necessary conclusions about a single correct location could be drawn. This was the aspect of these tasks that children of all ages seemed to understand least well. The most extensive data on this point were those provided by the four-location hiding and finding tasks (Somerville & Capuani-Shumaker, in press). In these tasks, although many 3½- and 4½-year-olds were consistently able to choose a first correct location (especially in hiding), they often made incorrect second searches on those occasions when the first search did not locate the object. These results reflected some form of uncertainty in the children's minds that there were two equally eligible locations to search. The younger children showed more uncertainty than the older ones because they were less successful in their second searches.

As we pointed out earlier, the second search failures could be attributed either to memory problems or to logical problems arising from the fact that no necessarily correct inference about a single location could be drawn. The younger children in particular may have arrived at one location that was consistent with the events, without understanding that the object would not necessarily be found there. There are a number of ways in which one might characterize reasoning processes leading to such a conclusion. For example, they might be processes incapable of making a distinction between a consistent and a necessary conclusion, similar to those suggested by Somerville et al. (1979) as an explanation for the performance of 5-year-olds on their spatial inferences task. They might also be thought of as processes derived from children's understanding of the regularities governing familiar events, rather than from an abstract understanding of possible event sequences. In order to assess whether a conclusion necessarily follows, a child must consider all of the possibilities and decide whether there is sufficient information to rule out all but one. If the child instead uses a strategy of selecting one possibility initially, on some grounds, and then asking whether this possibility is consistent with the information available, he or she will not be in a position to decide whether this possibility is the only one (supposing that it is consistent). It seems quite plausible that young children might proceed in this second way, in the logical search tasks. That is, they may tend to look for confirmation of a particular choice instead of making their choice by the elimination of other possibilities.

If our interpretation of children's failures in their second searches is correct, it follows that these limitations in logical awareness would lead young children to make errors on other kinds of selective search tasks. For example, if young children were given the task of looking through all of the red containers (in a set including some red, some blue, and some green) in order to discover all those with a particular item inside, we might find that they tended to stop searching as soon as one red container with the item had been found. Similarly, if the first red container they searched happened not to contain one of the designated items, children might tend not to search any other red containers, perhaps switching their attention to the blue or the green ones instead. Each of these types of error, if they occurred, would indicate that confirming evidence for a particular choice is something that children seek and tend to use in ways that are not strictly logical. The difficulties that these types of error suggest are difficulties in keeping a set of possibilities in mind and making sure that all of them have been considered or tested before drawing a general conclusion about the entire set. Concluding that one confirmed choice is the only correct one is one type of error. Concluding that other similar choices will not be confirmed, when the first is not, is the other type. As we argued earlier, children could have made either one or both of these errors of reasoning in the hiding and finding tasks. That is, their second searches could have been wrong either because they considered only one correct location in the first place, or because in face of a first failure they concluded wrongly that their initial idea about the other possibility must also be wrong.

In summary, the studies of logical search skills have contributed to our understanding of the development of inferential abilities in the following ways. First they have shown that infants in their second year can use knowledge of the rules governing sequences of events to make inferences about a particular unseen event. The developments occurring beyond infancy seem to be concerned not with the ability to make inferences per se, but with the ability to assess the logical status of the inference(s) that can be made. That is, these later developments have to do with children's understanding that the information provided by a sequence of events may or may not specify exactly where a hidden object will be found. In common with the results of other studies, the young children's failure to search both of the correct locations in the four-location tasks suggests that they may not see the importance of deciding whether a particular choice necessarily follows from the information given or is merely consistent with it. Alternatively, their problem could be one of still seeing the second possibility as potentially correct after the first possibility has been disconfirmed.

III. SELECTIVE SEARCH SKILLS

A selective strategy is appropriate for any search problem in which there is evidence that some locations within a total array are unlikely to contain the object, or, in the limit, could not possibly contain it. A very simple form of selective searching is to ignore any containers that are not large enough, or not the right shape, to hold the missing item. In this case, no information about the immediately preceding movements of the object is necessary to indicate where it is appropriate to search.

The problems with which we have been concerned belong to a category of selective search tasks in which an array of equally plausible hiding places is pointed out initially to the child. Then a sequence of actions is used to establish that an object has been hidden and, moreover, that not all of the hiding places should be searched for it. There are many tasks in this category in which the object only disappears from the child's view when it enters the eventual hiding place. That is, these tasks involve only visible displacements of the object (from place to place, and even into the hiding place itself). The sequences of actions in our hiding and finding tasks involved invisible displacements of the object, as did the events occurring in the earlier naturalistic studies of logical search skills. That is, the movements of the object from place to place and also the depositing (in hiding) or retrieval (in finding) of an object by the experimenter were not visible and had to be inferred from other events. Because they involved invisible displacements, these tasks might be expected to be more difficult than tasks involving visible displacements of an object.

If we argue in this way, it seems that the next question to ask is whether infants even younger than the ones we tested would show the same kind of logical skills in a task using visible rather than invisible displacements. However, when we consider the skills that can be tested using visible displacements, it becomes apparent that they are somewhat different from the logical skills that we investigated. In fact it would not be possible to test the same logical, inferential abilities using visible displacements because the child would always have direct perceptual evidence about where the object was last placed. In a logical search task, the position of the hidden object must only be implied and not given directly by the perceived events. It is possible to imagine logical search tasks suitable for younger infants, for example tasks that examine eye movements to discover whether infants look at the place where an object must have been displaced from a vehicle in which it was traveling. However, we are not aware of any studies of this kind, and as we pointed out earlier, the studies with younger infants that use sequences of visible displacements are not capable of providing information about the kind of logical skills with which we are concerned.

There are other kinds of selective search skills, in addition to the logical ones in which we were interested, and some studies using tasks with only visible displacements have demonstrated that infants have other selective search skills. One type of selective skill that might be expected to develop early is the ability to search only at locations visited by the object. Sophian and Sage (1983) presented 13- and 21-month-old infants with a visible non-displacement problem, in which the object was visibly hidden at one location, after which the experimenter's visibly empty hand was moved to a second location, as if to hide the object there. A third location in the array was never visited by either the hand or the object. Infants of both ages almost invariably avoided the third, unvisited, location in their first searches. However, errors of choosing the location visited second, by the empty hand, were quite often made by the younger but not the older children. Similarly, infants aged between 8 and 18 months have been shown to make frequent errors in their first searches when an object is visibly removed from its first hiding place and hidden at a second location (and, perhaps, at a third) before the infant is permitted to search at all (Kramer et al., 1975; Miller et al. 1970; Sophian & Sage, 1983). These results and others suggest that there is a gradual development of selective search skills appropriate to visible displacement tasks, tempered by tendencies to make perseverative and other types of errors, beginning at about 12 months of age or even earlier. For a review of this literature, the reader is referred to Sophian (1984).

Of most direct relevance to our studies of logical search skills are tasks in which at least some of the displacements and the hiding(s) of the object are not visible but must be inferred. We argued earlier that the traditional invisible displacement tasks used by Piaget (1954) and others (e.g., Corrigan, 1978, 1981; Kramer, Hill, & Cohen, 1975; Miller, Cohen & Hill, 1970; Uzgiris & Hunt, 1975) were not designed to examine selective search skills, since the displacement sequences were such that any of the visited locations could have contained the object (cf. Sophian & Sage, 1983). However, several recent studies using variations of the traditional invisible displacement sequences have established that infants in their second year show the same basic form of selective searching that we have already discussed for visible displacements. That is, infants will search first at or near locations visited by the object's container, in an invisible displacements task (Cummings & Bjork, 1981; Sophian & Sage, 1983). In these studies, the infants were found to avoid unvisited locations in their first searches even when the object's container had visited more than one location on a given trial (Sophian & Sage, 1983); and also when the location not visited on the current trial had been visited (and the object hidden and found there) on several previous trials (Cummings & Bjork, 1981).

These results establish that infants as young as 12 or 13 months (a) are able to infer the occurrence of an unseen hiding event from the movements of an object's container and (b) also understand that the unseen hiding must have occurred at a place visited by the container. This was evident from the locations the infants chose for their first searches. In Sophian and Sage's invisible displacements task, two of the three locations in an array were visited by the container and infants therefore had some opportunities to search a second time when their first searches, though correct, did not locate the object. Neither 13- nor 21-month-olds showed evidence of choosing the second visited location in preference to the remaining unvisited one, in their second searches.

In our studies using two- and four-location hiding and finding tasks (Haake, 1982; Haake & Somerville, in press; Somerville & Capuani-Shumaker, in press), all of the locations were visited by the object's container and the opportunity to search selectively was provided by incorporating critical events in which the object was seen to be in or out of the container. Our results showed that infants 9 and 12 months of age were unable to use this information to choose the correct location in a two-location array. However 15- and 18-month-olds were able to do so. In the four-location tasks, the first searches of 2- to 5-year-olds were correct at levels significantly above chance, demonstrating that they also understood that the sequences of events provided information enabling them to search selectively. This evidence of young children's use of selective strategies can be contrasted with the results obtained by Wellman et al. (1979) in a study that was parallel to their playground study, discussed earlier, but which used a set of eight connected cupboards. In this study, 3-, 4- and 5-year-olds were required to search for something which, according to a sequence of naturalistic events, must logically have been left in one of cupboards 3 to 6. Wellman et al. found that children of all three ages tended to search all of the cupboards, often from one end to the other, rather than selecting the logical subset. The children also searched the cupboards in this systematic, comprehensive fashion in a control condition in which no logical subset had been established.

Wellman et al. (1979) argued that the children did not search selectively in the cupboards task partly because it was easy to open all of the cupboard doors in quick succession. The cupboards were also hard to distinguish from one another, which may have made it difficult for children to recall exactly where the critical events that would enable them to search selectively had occurred. The hiding and finding tasks resembled the cupboards task in some respects but not in others. There was a small, uniform array of locations, but because the problem was explained explicitly to the child in advance and because the array had four locations rather than eight, it was presumably easier to remember and interpret the critical events in the hiding and finding tasks than it was in the cupboards task. The fact that 3- to 5-year-olds used a comprehensive strategy in the cupboards task and a selective one in the hiding and finding tasks suggests that they can assess the relative merits of different strategies in various circumstances. When it is difficult to recall the information necessary to solve an unforeseen logical problem, it may be best to search as though no information were available. However, with forewarning of the problem it becomes more efficient to extract the information required to search selectively.

There are many everyday circumstances in which a child needs to monitor the movements of people or of objects in order to be able to select the right place to search if they move out of sight. Often it will simply be a matter of keeping track of the person or object for long enough to follow in the path of disappearance. However, at other times the child will have to rely on only indirect information about where someone or something must have gone. Our studies of the logical search skills of infants and young children suggest that the step to making inferences about where to look, based on indirect information, occurs very early. The effect of drawing these inferences is to enhance the efficiency with which an object or a person can be found. An important additional question raised by some of the studies with older children is to what extent their choice of a selective search strategy implies an understanding of the efficiency with which they will be able to implement it to solve a particular problem.

SUMMARY AND CONCLUSIONS

The first studies of logical search skills that we conducted involved the simulation of sequences of real-life events. This was because we felt that young children might only exhibit their skills in a well-differentiated, familiar environment in which they experienced the critical events directly. It is now clear from the consistent evidence of logical searching, both in these tasks and in the laboratory tasks with tabletop arrays, that young children's ability to make logical inferences about where to search is quite robust. Moreover, the conditions under which they have been found to ignore logical information and search comprehensively are ones in which an adult might well decide to do the same thing. That is, there is some evidence to suggest that young children may be able to assess the relative efficiency of different strategies in different circumstances.

The second major outcome of the logical search studies is the link they have forged between the skills of infants and those of young children. Whereas the naturalistic tasks probably could not have been adapted for infants, the hiding and finding procedures (which were directly analogous to them in the logical skills they required) were readily adaptable, at least for infants in their second year. When the two-location hiding task was presented to these infants, we found that it was mastered by infants between 15 and 18 months of age. That infants have these logical search skills means not only that they can make inferences about an unseen event, but also that they can use temporal and spatial information to decide on the place where the event must have occurred.

The logical skills that older children displayed in the four-location tasks were similar to those of infants in the two-location task, as far as their first searches were concerned. That is, the older children showed the same ability to use logical inferences to guide their initial search of the array. However, there was an interesting limitation to the success of 2- to 5-year-old children in the four-location tasks, reminiscent of limitations revealed by tasks measuring other reasoning skills in this age group. This limitation was their inability to search both of the locations that were consistent with a given sequence of events. Either because they had difficulty in remembering both of the correct locations while performing their searches consecutively, or because they had logical problems with the notion that two locations could be equally correct, or both, children were relatively unsuccessful in their second searches when the first correct search did not locate the object.

We have argued that the logical first searches that the infants and young children made are indicative of several important cognitive skills. First, their understanding of the spatio-temporal sequences of events must have involved more than just simple notions of spatial proximity. That is, an ability to coordinate spatial and temporal information about the movements of an object was required. Second, this information about perceived events in a spatio-temporal sequence had to be used to infer the occurrence and the location of an unseen event. Finally, the children had to comprehend the usefulness of the perceived and inferred information as a guide to making an efficient search of a simple array. When the results of these studies are considered as a whole, at least two questions seem worthy of further investigation. The first is whether the development of selective search skills goes hand in hand with that of comprehensive search skills, the one being in some sense the negation of the other. Implied by this question is that of children's developing ability to assess the relative merits of the two strategies under various conditions (see Cross & Wellman, this volume). The second question is whether children can use the strategies that they exhibit in the tasks we concoct for them when they are faced with search problems of their own. It would be nice to know why young children seem to be no better or worse than we are at finding those scissors in the kitchen drawer.

REFERENCES

Adams, M. J. (1978). Logical competence and transitive inference in young children. *Journal of Experimental Child Psychology, 25,* 477–489.

Anooshian, L. J., Hartman, S. R., & Scharf, J. S. (1982). Determinants of young children's search strategies in a large-scale environment. *Developmental Psychology, 18,* 608–616.

Bertenthal, B. I., & Fischer, K. W. (1983). The development of representation in search: A social-cognitive analysis. *Child Development, 54,* 846–857.

Braine, M. D. S. (1959). The ontogeny of certain logical operations: Piaget's formulation examined by nonverbal methods. *Psychological Monographs, 73,* No. 5, Whole No. 475.

Brown, A. L., & Murphy, M. D. (1975). Reconstruction of arbitrary versus logical sequences by preschool children. *Journal of Experimental Child Psychology, 20,* 307–326.

Bryant, P. E., & Trabasso, T. (1971). Transitive inferences and memory in young children. *Nature, 232,* 456–458.

Corrigan, R. (1978). Language development as related to Stage 6 object permanence development. *Journal of Child Language, 5,* 173–189.

Corrigan, R. (1981). The effects of task and practice on search for invisibly displaced objects. *Developmental Review, 1,* 1–17.

Cummings, E. M., & Bjork, E. L. (1981). The search behavior of 12- to 14-month-old infants on a five-choice invisible displacement hiding task. *Infant Behavior and Development 4,* 47–60.

Drozdal, J. G., & Flavell, J. H. (1975). A developmental study of logical search behavior. *Child Development, 46,* 389–393.

Fischer, K. W., & Jennings, S. (1981). The emergence of representation in search: Understanding the hider as an independent agent. *Developmental Review, 1,* 18–30.

Haake, R. J. (1982). *Search by very young children for sequentially displaced objects.* Unpublished doctoral dissertation, Arizona State University.

Haake, R. J., & Somerville, S. C. (in press). The development of logical search skills in infancy. *Developmental Psychology.*

Haake, R. J., Somerville, S. C., & Wellman, H. M. (1980). Logical ability of young children in searching a large-scale environment. *Child Development, 51,* 1299–1302.

Kramer, J. A., Hill, K. T., & Cohen, L. B. (1975). Infants' development of object permanence: A refined methodology and new evidence for Piaget's hypothesized ordinality. *Child Development, 46*, 149–155.

Miller, D. J., Cohen, L. B., & Hill, K. T. (1970). A methodological investigation of Piaget's theory of object concept development in the sensory-motor period. *Journal of Experimental Child Psychology, 9*, 59–85.

Piaget, J. (1954). *The construction of reality in the child.* New York: Basic Books.

Piaget, J. (1970). *The child's conception of movement and speed.* London: Routledge & Kegan Paul.

Piaget, J., & Inhelder, B. (1967). *The child's conception of space.* London: Routledge & Kegan Paul.

Piaget, J., & Szeminska, A. (1952). *The child's conception of number.* London: Routledge & Kegan Paul.

Pufall, P. B., & Furth, H. G. (1966). Recognition and learning of visual sequences in young children. *Child Development, 37*, 827–836.

Somerville, S. C., & Capuani-Shumaker, A. (in press). Logical searches of young children in hiding and finding tasks. *British Journal of Developmental Psychology.*

Somerville, S. C., Hadkinson, B. A., & Greenberg, C. (1979). Two levels of inferential behavior in young children. *Child Development, 50*, 119–131.

Somerville, S. C., Niedorowski, L., & Haake, R. J. (1984). *Young children's recall of temporal orderings of three items.* Manuscript in preparation.

Sophian, C. (1984). Developing search skills in infancy and early childhood. In C. Sophian (Ed.), *Origins of cognitive skills* (pp. 27–56). Hillsdale, NJ: Lawrence Erlbaum Associates.

Sophian, C., & Sage, S. (1983). Developments in infants' search for displaced objects. *Journal of Experimental Child Psychology, 35*, 143–160.

Uzgiris, I. C., & Hunt, J. McV. (1975). *Assessment in infancy.* Urbana: University of Illinois.

Wellman, H. M., & Somerville, S. C. (1982). The development of human search ability. In M. E. Lamb & A. L. Brown (Eds.), *Advances in developmental psychology* (Vol. 2, pp. 41–84). Hillsdale, NJ: Lawrence Erlbaum Associates.

Wellman, H. M., Somerville, S. C., & Haake, R. J. (1979). Development of search procedures in real-life spatial environments. *Developmental Psychology, 15*, 530–542.

5 The Origins of Search and Number Skills

Paul L. Harris
University Of Oxford

THE CHILD'S GRASP OF NUMBER

> *Without being truly conceived as having several copies, the object may manifest itself to the child as assuming a limited number of distinct forms intermediate between unity and plurality. . . . When Lucienne looks for me at the window when she knows that I am beside her two behavior patterns are obviously involved, "papa-at-the-window" and "papa-in-front-of-oneself"; and if Lucienne does not hesitate to consider the two papas as being one and the same person, she nevertheless does not succeed in abstracting this person from the total pictures with which he is connected sufficiently to refrain from looking for him in two places simultaneously.*
>
> —Piaget, 1954, p. 69

In the above quotation, Piaget hints at the theme that I try to develop in this chapter. Although there is already a considerable body of research on the development of search during infancy, and there is also beginning to accumulate a robust set of findings on the infant's perception of number, developments in these two domains have not been related to one another either informally or systematically. Piaget's quotation above is perhaps one of the few hints available that this separation is ill-founded. I try to show that knowledge of how to search for an object and the ability to perceive number have a reciprocal influence upon one another. More specifically, I try to show that the development of search will frequently require the ability to count. For example, wherever more than one object is hidden, an exhaustive and systematic search requires that the infant note and remember how many objects have been hidden. In addition, the understanding of object displacement which the infant acquires in the course of searching for and retrieving objects is crucial to an understanding of number. Unless the nature of object displacement is understood, the infant will be unable to distinguish between an encounter with the same object in two different places and an encounter with two similar looking but distinct objects in two different places. Accurate counting depends upon such a distinction, because the first type of encounter involves one object only, whereas the second type of encounter involves two objects.

In summary, search depends upon insight into number, and insight into number depends on the search-related skill of keeping track of object-displacements. In the sections that follow, I weave back and forth between findings on number and findings on search. Although this sometimes involves a fairly detailed look at each domain, I draw attention, wherever possible, to those issues that bring the two domains together.

A THEORY OF SEARCH DEVELOPMENT

As this volume testifies, research on the development of search, especially during the period of infancy, has been extensive in the last 10–15 years. I believe that the gradual improvement in search skills during infancy is attributable to the infant's growing appreciation of the special regularities that pertain to the successive positions of a single object. This account echoes the quotation from Piaget (1954) given above in stressing that the infant does not think of these successive positions as forming a set of mutually exclusive positions. Unlike Piaget, however, I attribute the infant's difficulties not to the absence of a belief in permanence or a tendency toward egocentricity, but to the difficulties facing the infant in discovering exactly when such regularities obtain (Harris, 1983, in press).

The young infant will frequently encounter an object that looks more or less identical to an object seen elsewhere. This can come about in two quite different ways. The infant may simply have come across another instance of a given class of objects, another egg, for example, or another spoon. Alternatively, the infant may have had two successive encounters with the same object, which has moved, or been moved, from the first location to the second. What distinguishes these two types of encounter? If the infant sees two eggs side by side at the same time, there need, in principle, be little doubt that more than one egg is involved. However, if the two encounters are successive, it is much more difficult to specify whether one or two objects are involved. The conclusion that one object is involved depends ultimately upon an appreciation of the way in which the movements of an object, be they visible or invisible, can connect up its appearances at particular positions. The conclusion that two separate objects are involved is probably the safest assumption unless there are strong grounds for postulating such connecting movements.

What are the characteristics of such connecting movements? Although the various positions of different instances of a class of objects are independent of one another, the various positions of a single object are causally connected. The current position or trajectory of an object can be used to anticipate its future position or trajectory, insofar as the latter will be adjacent to or an extension of the former. Second, the present position of an object provides information about its past positions, insofar as it indicates that all past positions should be deleted as candidates for finding the object.

The evidence that is currently available on infant search strongly suggests that infants do not appreciate either of these lawful regularities in the movements of a single object. They do not use an object's current position to anticipate its future position nor to exclude past positions. There are two sources of evidence that speak directly to these claims. First, young infants aged 3–9 months who can track an object that moves visibly from place to place are nevertheless poor at predicting its future position along the same trajectory, if it should briefly disappear behind a screen (Meicler & Gratch, 1980; Nelson, 1971).

Second, infants who can search manually for a hidden object are prone to error when it is moved from a previous hiding place (A) to a new hiding place (B). They fail to treat A and B as mutually exclusive. They search at the previous hiding place (A) instead of, or as well as, searching at its current hiding place (B), their selection between these hiding places being determined by irrelevant factors such as the delay between hiding and search (Gratch, Appel, Evans, Le Compte, & Wright, 1974; Harris, 1973), or the distinctiveness of the hiding places (Bremner, 1978), rather than by the crucial information that the movement of the object from A to B excludes A as a potential hiding place (Harris, 1983, in press).

When do infants come to grasp the lawful nature of a single object's successive positions? The process appears to be a gradual one in which the infant adopts various useful but potentially misleading heuristics. In particular, infants of 6 months and upwards discover that salient landmarks offer a convenient guide that connects an object's past position with its future position: If they see an object positioned on, under, or near a landmark, they use it as a guide to the object's later location (Acredolo, 1978; Acredolo & Evans, 1980; Cornell & Heth, 1979; DeLoache & Brown, 1983; Rieser, 1979). This heuristic is often a useful one, since it successfully predicts the location of a static object, and it can do so even if the infant moves or is moved relative to the landmark (Harris, 1984). However, it is a fallible guide under other circumstances. If the object is visibly moved away from such a landmark, as in the Stage IV task of Piaget's sequence of search tasks, the landmark should be deleted; as I noted earlier, infants of 9 months and even older (Diamond, 1983; Harris, 1974; Webb, Massar, & Nadolny, 1972) return to an earlier location, even when clear indications are available that they have encoded and can still remember a later position of the object. They behave as if the object they saw disappearing at A, and the object they have just seen disappearing at B, are unconnected with one another.

The landmark heuristic will also break down if the landmark can be readily confused with other similar landmarks. For example, if the object is hidden under a container, which is then moved so as to exchange places with another similar looking container, the infant is prone to search as if no such exchange had occurred. On the other hand, if the target container is distinctive (Bremner, Experiment 2; 1978; Cornell, 1981; Goldfield & Dickerson, 1981), infants keep track of its movements fairly successfully, and avoid returning to the location that would have been correct had no movement occurred. If the containers are not distinctive, but are nevertheless two familiar objects moved in their standard upright orientation rather than inverted, then 12- and 15-month-old infants still produce above-chance performance when the containers are first transposed (Freeman, Lloyd, & Sinha, 1980; Lloyd, Sinha, & Freeman, 1981). When three identical containers are used, and a succession of trials, performance even at 18 months and beyond is still well below 100% (Sophian, 1984; Wishart & Bower, 1982).

At about 15–18 months, infants begin to treat the movements of an object inside a distinctive container such as the experimenter's hand as a set of causally related positions. This has been recently demonstrated by Haake and Somerville (in press). The infants saw an object placed in the experimenter's hand, which then moved under first one cloth and then a second cloth. After visiting each cloth, the infant was shown whether or not the experimenter was still holding the object or (by implication) had left it under one of the two cloths. By 15 months and even more clearly at 18 months, infants grasped the import of these two types of information. They realized, for example, that if the experimenter still held the object after visiting the first cloth, the latter should be deleted as a candidate for finding the object. Conversely, if the experimenter's hand was empty after visiting the first cloth and had been full before visiting it then search should be confined to the first cloth. These findings provide a clear demonstration of the way in which the infant is beginning to grasp the mutually exclusive nature of earlier and later positions: Presence at some intermediate point along a trajectory excludes presence from earlier positions, and absence from that intermediate point prevents presence at later positions.

Adopting the terminology associated with Stage IV, we can say that the experimenter's hand is temporarily located at a point intermediate between the first cloth A and the second cloth B. The object's brief visible presence in that hand when it is opened up deletes A as a candidate location. Stated in this way, we can see that the infant has made enormous progress since the age of 9–12 months when he or she is most prone to the AB̄ error. At that point, even when the object is continuously visible as it moves from A to B, the infant does not treat that information as excluding A. Indeed, even if the object is stationary and visible at B, residual errors to A still occur (Harris, 1974).

This review reveals two general conclusions. First, if my argument is correct, young infants who reach inaccurately do so in part because they do not appreciate how many objects they are dealing with. They are not aware that they are being presented with a single object rather than a pair or set of unrelated objects. Lacking this insight, they do not treat movement from A to B as canceling prior information about the presence of the object at A. For them, the object hidden at B, being a separate object, does not preclude the presence of the previously found object at A.

A second conclusion, and one which is pertinent to the next section, is that the successive appearances of a single object, be it static or mobile, can gradually be predicted on a lawful basis. Landmarks, including cloths and containers, can be used as intervening variables to connect the earlier and later positions of an object, be it visible or invisible. At first, however, infants treat such intervening variables as overly stable, continuing to use them as predictors of an object's location even when the object has visibly moved elsewhere. Eventually, in the middle of the infant's second year, he or she becomes able to use a brief visible presence or absence from an intermediate location as a cue for searching at an earlier or later landmark. Successive locations are connected in a coherent causal chain, such that earlier positions serve as preconditions and predictors of later positions, and later positions serve as consequences and cancellations of earlier positions.

I eventually try to show that this slowly developing insight into the movements of a single object is crucial for an appreciation of number.

THE ORIGINS OF COUNTING

Recent work with infants has suggested that they can distinguish between displays bearing a different number of objects, provided the number of items is quite small. It is also clear that children's verbal counting is usually much more accurate for small numbers up to three than for bigger numbers. What is the connection between these phenomena? I shall argue that there are important differences between the perception of numerosity, of which the newborn appears to be capable, and the counting of small sets, which young children can manage. Despite these differences, the earlier capacity is a precursor of the later, and it is the development of search skill that serves as a crucial link between number detection and verbal counting.

Identifying Small Set Sizes

One of the earliest investigators to suggest that children may be especially good at identifying very small numbers was Descoeudres (1921). She noticed that children's ability to identify a particular set size shows a marked drop in accuracy when a set size of three items is exceeded. She called this the "un, deux, trois, beaucoup" phenomenon, the implication being that young children's estimates of number are accurate up to three items but undifferentiated beyond that. This turns out to be something of a simplification but not far from the truth.

Some recent experiments by Gelman and her colleagues provide illustrative data (Gelman & Gallistel, 1978). They showed 3- to 5-year-old children cards that displayed a given number of items ranging from 2 to 19. Sometimes the items were all the same, for example red circles, sometimes they were a mixture, for example red and blue stars and circles. The card was shown for 1 second or 5 seconds or 60 seconds, and the child's task was simply to say how many items there were.

Whereas there was little difference in accuracy for three as compared to two items, there was a clear drop-off for four items. Moreover, the children were quite accurate even when they were given only 1 second to look at the card, suggesting that they did not necessarily engage in sequential counting but identified the display at a glance. Gelman and Gallistel (1978) note that although children did make a lot of mistakes with the larger set sizes, they were not always as indiscriminate in their answers as Descoeudres' characterization would suggest. They tended to offer an ascending series of numbers for the larger quantities. Thus, for the set sizes of one to seven items, they might offer the numbers "one," "two," "three," "four," "seven," "eleven" and "nineteen" respectively, suggesting that they did realize that the quantities were getting bigger, rather than being an undifferentiated "beaucoup." We need to look further therefore at two issues. How is it that children are so good at quantifying sets of up to three items? Second, what do they need to know in order to count larger numbers?

There have been two different answers to the question of how children identify small set sizes. Klahr and Wallace (1973) suggest that in common with other species, children and adults can see at a glance how many items there are in a small set. This perceptual process of subitizing, as it is often called, does not require the child to attach a number name sequentially to each item, and could conceivably be found in infants who have not yet learned to talk or count in the conventional manner. Gelman and Gallistel (1978) propose, on the other hand, that subitizing is probably the result of conventional counting. When a child has encountered a variety of different displays that can all be counted up to three, for example, the child will eventually be able to assign the label "three" to these various displays without having to go through the counting process. They will simply recognize the display as one that in the past they have counted and that contains three items. This hypothesis, unlike that of Klahr and Wallace (1973), implies that infants who cannot count will not be able to subitize. So, it becomes important to ask whether or not preverbal infants show any sensitivity to number. There have been several recent experiments with infants that provide a very consistent picture. Starkey and Cooper (1980) presented 22-week-old infants with displays containing 2, 3, 4, or 6 items. A display bearing a constant number of items, but varying in line length and density, was repeatedly presented until the infant's attention waned. A display bearing a different number of items was then introduced and the experimenters checked to see whether attention would recover. Whenever a shift from two to three items or the reverse occurred, attention did recover. On the other hand, when a shift from four to six items or the reverse occurred, there was no recovery—the infants treated the novel display as equivalent to the preceding display. Similar results were obtained by Strauss and Curtis (1981). They tested older infants aged 10–12 months. Again, the infants paid more attention when a shift occurred from two to three items or the reverse, whereas a shift from four to five items or the reverse produced no recovery.

At what point in infancy does this discrimination emerge? Antell and Keating (1983) carried out a replication of Starkey and Cooper's (1980) experiment, but with newborn infants who were on average just over 2 days old. They obtained essentially the same results: shifts from two to three items or from three to two items provoked a recovery of attention, but shifts from four to six items or the reverse produced no recovery.

It is possible that although the above experiments appear to demonstrate number discrimination, they are actually indicating something else. The displays of two and three items might differ in some subtle way, such as the total area of the figures, or background brightness. One way to reduce the likelihood of such alternative discriminations is to check for number discrimination across rather than within a particular sensory modality. For example, if infants treat two dots in the same way as they treat a sequence of two sounds, variables like figure area and background brightness are ruled out. Starkey, Spelke, and Gelman (in press) have carried out this check with infants of 6–8 months. The infants were presented with two displays side-by-side, one bearing two items and the other three items. A sequence of two or three drum beats was then played. The infants appeared to seek out the display that matched the sound, since they spent more time looking at the three-item display when they heard three drum beats and more time looking at the two-item display when they heard two drum beats.

Taken together, these results strongly suggest that infants show the Descoeudres effect; they possess a perceptual mechanism for registering small numbers; they possess it at birth; and it is not tied to any specific modality. This clearly demonstrates that the registration of small numbers does not depend on learning to talk or count in the conventional manner. Rather, the results suggest that the young child's accuracy in identifying displays of up to three items may be a product of perceptual subitizing rather than sequential counting.

Verbal Counting

Counting proper, as opposed to identifying a display that is small enough to subitize, requires the recognition of various principles. These have been spelled out clearly by Gelman and Galistel (1978). Three are especially important.

1. The one-to-one principle: Every item should be tagged with one and only one unique tag.
2. The stable-order principle: The tags must be stably ordered across trials.
3. The cardinal principle: The last tag used in the count represents the number in the set.

Gelman and Gallistel (1978) argue that although children sometimes make mistakes, for example by inadvertently counting the same object twice or by using an idiosyncratic sequence such as "one, two, three, five," children do grasp these three principles. They make mistakes but these are often attributable to inattention during execution rather than ignorance of the basic principles. In support of this argument, Gelman and Meck (1983) have shown that young children's errors with large numbers can be attributed to errors in performance rather than any failure to appreciate that the basic principles apply to large as well as small numbers. They asked children aged 3-4 years to watch a puppet count and to tell him whether he had counted properly or not. The children typically spotted the various errors. For example, when the puppet violated the one-to-one rule, by counting the same item twice or by missing an item, they corrected him. Similarly, when the puppet produced a set of numbers that were not ordered conventionally or violated the cardinal principle by offering a number different from the last one mentioned in the count sequence, the children spotted the error. Finally, Gelman and Meck (1983) demonstrated that counting was a lot easier if the children could touch or move the objects rather than count them under a plexiglass cover. In sum, the results reinforce Gelman and Gallistel's (1978) claim that when children make a mistake in counting it is not because they are unaware of the basic principles of counting, but because they make mistakes in applying those principles.

From Perceptual Discrimination to Verbal Counting

So far, we have seen that children begin life with some ability to register the number of items in an array, and by about 3 years they know some of the fundamental principles that underlie counting, even if they occasionally err in the execution of those principles. What is the developmental link between these two abilities? How does the infant's ability to register numerosity get converted into sequential counting? Two important insights are vital before genuine counting can occur. First, the infant must appreciate that the various displays of one, two, and three items that he or she can distinguish do actually imply different absolute numbers of objects, that number remaining constant even if the display is altered by moving one of the objects, and remaining constant even if all the objects forming the display are removed from view. For all we know from the data currently available, the infant might register the various displays as being perceptually different but without realizing, for example, that in order to retrieve two objects, two separate searches must typically be made even when the perceptual appearance of the display they compose is altered. This issue is reminiscent of the young infant's capacity to discriminate depth cues. The ability to distinguish various depths might be present with no appreciation of their consequences for action (Bower, 1972; Yonas & Pick, 1975). One way to look at the infant's ability to translate numerosity into action is to present the infant with displays of objects that vary in number, and to see whether the infant reaches an appropriate number of times for the objects displayed. However, such tasks could probably be solved without any appreciation of number: the infant need only use a simple rule such as "keep reaching out until there is nothing left to pick up." Such tasks would only demonstrate, therefore, the ability to distinguish some objects from no objects.

Consider, however, an infant who has seen each of two or three objects moved to separate hiding places. As the infant retrieves the objects from their various hiding places, there is no cue available to indicate whether search should be brought to a halt, because all the objects have been found, or whether there are still more objects to be found. Such a task can show whether the infant appreciates how many objects compose a particular display even when the display itself has been decomposed. Indeed, it seems highly likely that everyday experience of such search tasks will teach the infant not only about the fact that the displacements of a single object form a coherent causal chain, but more generally, that the movements of several objects form such a chain so that the original number of objects can always be restored to view provided one follows their displacements and carries out the corresponding number of searches. At first, no doubt, there will be occasions when the infant will undershoot or overshoot (i.e., will execute fewer or more searches than the original number of objects), as well as occasions when the infant successfully, albeit inadvertently, matches the number of objects with the number of searches. Such experiences will unremittingly instruct the infant that the original number can be restored, but never more. Such experiences seem highly likely to eventually produce an admittedly limited, but nevertheless crucial, form of number conservation: the insight that 0–3 objects can be moved around, and hidden in all sorts of ways, but will remain 0–3 objects. This is not number conservation in any full sense since it is limited to a small number of items, pertains to a single set rather than two sets, involves the absence of perceptual cues rather than the presence of misleading cues, and does not involve language, but it is an important kernel of number knowledge. Below, I discuss some evidence that suggests that infants can translate numerosity into search appropriately, although the evidence is tantalizingly limited.

The second insight is related to the first. On the one hand, a perceptual display of two or three items indicates an absolute number of items that remains constant even when the display is altered in appearance. On the other hand, the display itself can be altered by the addition of a new item or the removal of one already in the display. Indeed, the various displays can be shown to be related to one another by the operation of addition and subtraction. They form part of a chain of numbers, with one-step increments between adjacent values. For example, by adding one item to another item, a set of two items will result; if another item is added, a set of three items will result, and so forth. For genuine counting to occur, the child must appreciate that the number sequence constitutes an extended chain in which adjacent numbers are located with one-step increments.

So far, we have no indication from research with young infants that they do, in fact, appreciate that the displays of one, two, and three items, which they can register as distinct, are nevertheless related to one another in this fashion. For all we know, the infant might register these numerosities as being distinct and unrelated to one another—as unrelated as the color red is to the color blue, or as unrelated as a circle and a triangle. How then would a child discover the intimate relationships between adjacent numbers? One plausible answer has been proposed by Cooper (1984) based on ideas initially proposed by Klahr and Wallace (1973). Suppose the infant looks at an array of two toys, and begins to play with them. The infant picks up one of the toys leaving the other on the floor. Then the infant picks up the second toy, in addition. This type of experience is likely to be repeated often. What could it teach the infant? Provided the infant can register the initial array of two toys, the presence of one toy on the floor after one of them has been picked up, and the eventual restoration of the array of two when the other is retrieved, it could teach the infant that two can be reduced to one by displacement, but that one can be increased to two by retrieval of the displaced object. In short, such experiences can teach the infant that displays of one, two, and three items have a systematic set of relationships: Displays of one and two are related to one another by the removal and retrieval of one item, as are displays of two and three items. Armed with this knowledge, the child would be in a much better position to appreciate that the number tags applied to those displays (i.e., "one," "two," and "three") are an ordered and interrelated set, since the object(s) they are applied to (i.e., groups of one, two, and three items, respectively) are themselves an ordered and interrelated set. Each adjacent pair of items is related to one another by the operation of removing (subtracting) and adding (retrieving) a single object. Indeed, knowledge of the interrelations among sets of objects would be particularly useful for the execution of sequential counting. Sequential counting involves the identification or isolation of one item, the "addition" of a second to that one item, the "addition" of a third to those two and so forth. This is of course what young children do when they start counting: They typically identify or isolate one item by touching it, and then they "add" a second item by moving it closer to the first, and then "add" a third, by moving it closer to the first two. Their counting is much less accurate if they are prevented from touching and moving objects, as we have seen (Gelman & Meck, 1983).

In sum, we can tentatively hypothesize the following stages. First, infants begin their lives with a perceptual mechanism for registering small numerosities. Second, during a transitional period, infants begin to make a crucial distinction between number-preserving and number-transforming operations. They discover that the various set sizes that they can register specify a constant number even when each item in the set is displaced. Thus when a set of objects is hidden so that its remembered cardinal value must be used as a stop rule, infants learn to adjust their actions to that value. In other words, if one object is hidden, they search once. If two objects are hidden, in two different places, they search twice, and so forth. During the same transitional period, they also discover that the operations of addition and subtraction transform the original set size but in an orderly and predictable fashion. These two operations can convert one discriminable display of, say, two items, into an equally discriminable display of one item or three items.

These insights into the role of cardinal values and the interrelations among different set sizes of objects serve as a context for understanding the meaning of the number terms "one," "two" and "three": They are not names for distinct and unrelated perceptual displays, they are an ordered set of tags, for an ordered set of displays, and in the same way that a display of one object can be increased by addition to a display of two objects, the execution of sequential counting involves the isolation of an initial item, labeled "one," and the implicit or actual addition of a second item to the first, such that the label "two" applies simultaneously to that second object, and also constitutes the cardinal value of the display considered as a group of two distinct items.

Infants' developing search skills, and more specifically, their growing insight into the lawful displacements of a single object, provide a crucial foundation for distinguishing number-preserving from number-transforming displacements. When they can keep track of the displacements of a moving object, and search for it, they are in a position to discover that whenever a set of items disappears, be it one, two, or three items, keeping track of each displaced object and executing the appropriate number of searches are sufficient to restore the original set size. Second, the ability to keep track of the displacements of a single object allows them to discover that some operations do not conserve set size: The displacement of a single object away from an existing set reduces that set by one; conversely the retrieval of that displaced object and its placement alongside the reduced set increase it by one.

This story succeeds in positing a plausible transition mechanism from perceptual numerosity detection in infancy to sequential counting in early childhood. However, plausibility is one thing and evidence is another. Two implications, in particular, appear to go well beyond the currently available evidence. First, I have suggested that infants will come to search systematically for a given number of objects well before they can count in any conventional sense. Second, I have implied that infants who cannot count will nevertheless be able to understand the effects of addition and subtraction. Indeed, I have implied that each of these two insights is a prerequisite for the insightful counting of young children. In the next section, I return again to a discussion of infant search in the hope of finding evidence relevant to both of these proposals.

SEARCH, REVISITED

In the section on search, I argued that infants only gradually show a systematic understanding of the displacements of a single object. By 15–18 months, they appear to grasp that such displacements form part of a coherent causal chain, even if they take place within a container. Insight into the displacements of a single object ought to set the stage for the child to grasp the two fundamental facts about number outlined earlier: First, perceptual displays can be decomposed into an absolute number of discrete and independently moving single objects, be it one, two, or three objects. Second, perceptual displays can be transformed into one another by the addition and subtraction of a single object. Is there any evidence that infants possess either of these insights into number?

Search for More than One Object

Although as we have seen, infants can distinguish between displays of one, two, and three items, this does not show that they realize that a particular display is composed of a given number of items. It is quite possible that an infant could see a display of two items as different from a display of one or three items, without realizing that it was actually composed of two independently moving objects. How could we demonstrate such a realization? If we show the infant a display of two objects and then hide them, either in the same place or in separate places, an infant who registers the number of items accurately should continue searching until two objects have been retrieved, or should be surprised if more or less objects are revealed when he or she does search.

Regrettably, very few investigators have explicitly used the search task as a diagnostic tool for the infant's number concepts, but there are some suggestive pieces of evidence. Cornell and Heth (1983) tested infants aged 15–16 months with two hiding places. Instead of hiding a single object, they hid two treats, one at each of the hiding places. Once infants had found the first treat, Cornell and Heth (1983) gave two different prompts to infants who hesitated to search for the second treat; a weak prompt consisted of saying "Is that all the candies you can find?" A stronger prompt consisted in briefly exposing the second treat, and then covering it. Infants rarely needed the stronger prompt. Unfortunately, Cornell and Heth do not report how often infants needed the weaker prompt, so we cannot tell how many babies had noted and spontaneously recalled the fact that two treats had been hidden. However, they do report that in general, children gathered both treats, and repetitive search at one location, after the treat had been retrieved from it, was exceedingly rare (4 out of 240 trials). These results are very suggestive: It looks as if 15- to 16-month-old infants can keep track of the number of objects that have been hidden, even if they have been hidden in separate hiding places, and the infants can distribute their searches appropriately. It would be interesting to know whether this systematicity can be extended to three objects and breaks down thereafter.

However, to be sure that infants really do appreciate how many objects have been hidden, we need to build additional controls into the search task devised by Cornell and Heth (1983). First, so long as there are as many treats as there are cups, we cannot tell whether the infants are really keeping track of the number of treats, or adopting a simple rule of searching all cups, whether baited or not. This can be readily checked by having fewer treats than the number of cups, and noting whether infants cease to search when they have found all the treats, by looking at the appropriate number of baited cups. Even correct performance on this task, however, would only indicate whether infants could keep track of the number of hidings, as opposed to the number of objects. Recall that infants sometimes search in more than one place even if only one object has actually been hidden. An infant who searches at two out of three cups, having seen two of them baited may not appreciate whether the same object "intermediate between unity and plurality," to use Piaget's (1954) phrase, has been hidden in each or whether two distinct objects have been hidden in each. An additional control procedure is needed in which a single treat is hidden first in one cup, and then visibly moved on to a second; but in the experimental procedure two separate treats are employed, one being hidden at one cup, and one being hidden at a second. If the infant successfully searches in both cups in the experimental procedure, but at only one cup in the control procedure, we can safely conclude that the infant is able to keep track of the number of objects and translate that number into appropriate action.

Addition and Subtraction

Is there any evidence that older infants do eventually grasp the interrelationships among small numbers, and more specifically, the effects of addition and subtraction before they can count? We know that insight into addition and subtraction does not have to be taught to young children because even preschool children can solve simple problems involving concrete objects rather than written numbers. Two studies of 3 to 5-year-olds provide illustrative data. In a study carried out by Starkey and Gelman (1982), children watched the experimenter pick up a small number of pennies in her hand, and were asked how many there were. The experimenter then closed her hand so that the pennies could no longer be seen and either removed some and showed them to the child or placed an additional number in her hand. The child's job was to figure out how many pennies were in the experimenter's hand. Children were quite accurate provided the numbers involved were small. Even at 3 years of age most children were correct if the numbers involved did not exceed three. For example, 87% of the children were correct on the problems: $1 + 1 = ?$ and $2 - 1 = ?$ Similar results were obtained by Hughes (1981). The children were again asked to solve problems concerning concrete objects: They watched while bricks were put into a box or taken out of it, and they did very well provided the problems involved numbers less than four.

How were the children solving the problem? In particular, was the ability to count a precondition for solving the task? I argued earlier that insight into the effects of addition and subtraction is a precondition for insightful counting. Accordingly, we would expect at least some of the younger children to solve the problems without counting. Starkey and Gelman (1982) report that among the older children aged 4 and 5, there was good evidence for the use of counting strategies. They sometimes counted aloud or used their fingers. However, in line with the hypothesis put forward earlier, such strategies were less noticeable among the 3-year-olds. On the other hand, this evidence is not conclusive because the 3-year-olds probably did have the ability to count up to three. The fact that a counting strategy was not obviously noticeable does not necessarily mean it was never used.

Given these doubts, a recent study by Starkey (1983) is especially interesting, since it does strongly suggest that counting is not necessary for the solution of very simple addition and subtraction problems. He looked at still younger children aged 2 to 3 years using an ingenious search task that did not involve the use of number words by the children. The children first put a set of two to four identical objects one by one into a container. The experimenter either added another object to the ones already in the container, took one away, or did nothing. The children were then asked to remove all the objects from the container. They could only be removed one at a time and only one object was visible on any given retrieval. Accordingly, Starkey could infer from the number of times that the infants searched how many objects they thought were in the container. Just as Starkey and Gelman (1982) and Hughes (1981) found with somewhat older subjects, the children did well so long as the numbers involved were three or less. For example, on the problems $2 + 1 = ?$ and $3 - 1 = ?$ the children were right about two thirds of the time. On the other hand, for problems involving four items such as 3 + 1 = ? and 4 − 1 = ? only about one third of the responses were correct.

Starkey (1983) noted that although one child did use some conventional number names, none of the other children did. How, then, did children reach the right answer? The most plausible explanation is that children have discovered in the past that sets of one, two, and three objects are interrelated by the operations of addition and subtraction. Thus, even though they cannot count forwards or backwards, and have not learned any number facts on a rote basis, they have observed and can remember, for example, what happens when one item is added to another two, or one item is removed from a set of three. This past experience is extended to new situations provided they involve numbers that do not exceed three.

To be absolutely sure that a counting strategy is not being used, and indeed to study the actual emergence of addition and subtraction skills, it may be necessary to adapt Starkey's procedures. A hybrid procedure, borrowing elements from recent research on both number and search, might suit. Imagine an infant habituated as in the standard paradigm (Starkey & Cooper, 1980; Strauss & Curtis, 1981) to a display of two items. The standard posttest involves the presentation of a novel display of, for example, one or two items. Suppose, however, that instead of being repeatedly presented with displays of dots or shapes, the infants are shown a display of one object that is repeatedly screened and unscreened. It is now possible to introduce the type of displacement that is used in search tasks in the interval between the habituation trials and the posttest. More specifically, the infant can be presented with an addition (the movement of a second object) into the visual field and its eventual disappearance behind the screen so that there are two objects in total behind the screen.

The infant who understands the effects of addition should now behave quite differently on posttest trials. In the standard procedure, a display of one item should be expected and familiar, and a display of two items should be unexpected and novel. For the addition procedure, however, precisely the opposite is true: A display of one item should be unexpected and presumably novel, whereas a display of two items should be expected, and presumably familiar. A control procedure, namely a display of three items, should indicate whether subjects can figure out the exact results following an addition of 1 + 1, or whether they simply expect an increment beyond what they have seen hitherto.

The same procedures could obviously be used, mutatis mutandis, to check the infant's insight into subtraction. If the above analysis is correct, there should be a period in which, despite being able to distinguish displays of one, two, and three items, infants have no definite expectations about the effect of addition and subtraction, and in all probability react as if such operations had not occurred. On the other hand, when search tasks indicate that the displacements of a single object from one place to another are quite well understood, infants should begin to manifest appropriate expectations, provided the operation involves the displacement of a single object and a total of one to three objects. The above procedure, of course, also permits an assessment of whether operations that result in zero are more difficult to grasp than those involving positive integers.

Conclusions

An examination of early number skills shows that infants can distinguish between displays of one, two, and three items. By the age of 3 years, they have considerable insight into the basic principles of counting, even though they do not always apply those principles accurately especially in the case of large numbers. Given their ability to distinguish between displays of one, two, and three items, it would seem, at first glance, a trivial task for the infant to appreciate the transformations among sets of objects that the displacements of a single object can produce. However, the last decade of research on the development of object permanence has confirmed that although there may be flaws in Piaget's account of object permanence, one fundamental claim—namely, that infants even in the second 6 months of life do not fully comprehend the displacements of a single object from one place to another—has been endorsed by most investigators. Lacking insight into such displacements, and more specifically failing to act as if an object moved to place B has necessarily been removed from place A, the infant is unable to grasp the effects of number preserving and number-transforming displacements. Thus, the infant does not appreciate that an entire set of objects that has been removed one by one can be restored by searching an appropriate number of times, nor that the removal of one object necessarily reduces it by one, whereas its addition necessarily increases it by one.

These insights are important for several reasons. They enable the infant to appreciate that the discriminable numerosity of a display amounts to its cardinal value, which remains constant even if the display is decomposed by moving and/or hiding all the objects. Second, they enable the infant to understand the relationship among the various numerosities that he or she can detect, to appreciate, for example, that a set of two items is one more than a single item and that a set of three items is one more than a set of two. This insight effectively constitutes an appreciation of the operations of addition and subtraction. It allows the infant to grasp that the various perceptual displays that he or she can discriminate constitute an ordered series, in which there is an increment of one step at a time. Such an insight is potentially important for the child in understanding how to count: The names for the displays that can be discriminated (i.e., "one," "two," and "three") refer to an interrelated and ordered series. Hence, the child is prepared through an understanding of concrete objects to appreciate that the number words themselves constitute an ordered series, and the final tag in that ordered series identifies the cardinal value of a set, a value that remains constant if the objects are moved or hidden.

Finally, it is worth stressing that the infant's discoveries about number are likely to have an impact upon the process of search itself. In particular, the young infant must gradually extend the ability to keep track of and search for more than one object, into a very general persist/stop rule. Thus, having seen a certain number of objects located in a given place, infants must eventually appreciate that the same number of objects can be retrieved, even if they have not witnessed or cannot remember the movements that led to the disappearance of any or all of the objects. For example, if two objects have been hidden, but they can only find one, this is a signal that a fresh sampling of the environment is required, so that the remaining object can be found. More generally, a consideration of the role of number makes it clear that one should distinguish carefully between two types of exhaustive search. One type of exhaustive search is a systematic examination of all possible hiding places with no foreknowledge of the number of objects to be found. The other type of exhaustive search does involve number; indeed it involves number conservation, albeit without the misleading cue of length. It involves foreknowledge of the number of objects hidden and the ability to search exhaustively until they are recovered.

REFERENCES

Acredolo, L. P. (1978). Development of spatial orientation in infancy. *Developmental Psychology, 14*, 224–234.

Acredolo, L. P., & Evans, D. (1980). Developmental changes in the effects of landmarks on infant spatial behaviour. *Developmental Psychology, 16*, 312–318.

Antell, S. E., & Keating, D. P. (1983). Perception of numerical invariance in neonates. *Child Development, 54*, 695–701.

Bower, T. G. R. (1972). Object perception in infants. *Perception, 1*, 15–31.

Bremner, J. G. (1978). Egocentric versus allocentric spatial coding in nine-month old infants: Factors influencing the choice of code. *Developmental Psychology, 14*, 346–355.

Cooper, R. G., Jr. (1984). Early number development: Discovering number space with addition and subtraction. In C. Sophian (Ed.), *Origins of cognitive skills*. Hillsdale, NJ: Lawrence Erlbaum Associates.

Cornell, E., & Heth, C. D. (1979). Response versus place learning by human infants. *Journal of Experimental Psychology: Human Learning and Memory, 5*, 188–196.

Cornell, E. H. (1981). The effects of cue distinctiveness on infants' manual search. *Journal of Experimental Child Psychology, 32*, 330–342.

Cornell, E. H., & Heth, C. D. (1983). Spatial cognition: Gathering strategies used by preschool children. *Journal of Experimental Child Psychology, 35*, 93–110.

DeLoache, J. S., & Brown, A. L. (1983). Very young children's memory for the location of objects in a large scale environment. *Child Development, 54*, 888–897.

Descoeudres, A. (1921). *La développement de l'enfant de deux à sept ans*. Paris: Delachaux & Niestle.

Diamond, A. (1983). *The development of recall memory from 7 to 12 months*. Paper presented at the meeting of the Society for Research in Child Development, Detroit, Michigan.

Freeman, N., Lloyd, S., & Sinha, C. G. (1980). Infant search tasks reveal early concepts of containment and canonical usage of objects. *Cognition, 8*, 243–262.

Gelman, R., & Gallistel, C. R. (1978). *The child's understanding of number*. Cambridge, MA: Harvard University Press.

Gelman, R., & Meck, E. (1983). Preschoolers' counting: Principles before skill. *Cognition, 13*, 343–359.

Goldfield, E. C., & Dickerson, D. J. (1981). Keeping track of locations during movement in 8- to 10-month-old infants. *Journal of Experimental Child Psychology, 32,* 48–64.

Gratch, G., Appel, K. J., Evans, W. F., LeCompte, G. K., & Wright, N. A. (1974). Piaget's Stage IV object concept error: Evidence of forgetting or object conception? *Child Development, 45,* 71–77.

Haake, R. J., & Somerville, S. C. (in press). The development of logical search skills in infancy. *Developmental Psychology.*

Harris, P. L. (1973). Perseverative errors in young infants. *Child Development, 44,* 28–33.

Harris, P. L. (1974). Perseverative search at a visibly empty place by young infants. *Journal of Experimental Child Psychology, 18,* 535–542.

Harris, P. L. (1983). Infant cognition. In M. M. Haith & J. J. Campos (Eds.), *Handbook of child psychology: Vol. 2. Infancy and developmental psychobiology.* New York: Wiley.

Harris, P. L. (in press). The development of search. In P. Salapatek & L. B. Cohen (Eds.), *Handbook of infant perception.* New York: Academic Press.

Harris, P. L. (1984). Landmarks and movement: Commentary on papers on the origins of search skills. In C. Sophian (Ed.), *Origins of cognitive skills.* Hillsdale, NJ: Lawrence Erlbaum Associates.

Hughes, M. (1981). Can preschool children add and subtract? *Educational Psychology, 3,* 207–219.

Klahr, D., & Wallace, J. G. (1973). The role of quantification operators in the development of conservation of quantity. *Cognitive Psychology, 4,* 301–327.

Lloyd, S. E., Sinha, C. G., & Freeman, N. H. (1981). Spatial reference systems and the canonicality effect in infant search. *Journal of Experimental Child Psychology, 32,* 1–10.

Meicler, M., & Gratch, G. (1980). Do 5-month olds show object conception in Piaget's sense? *Infant Behavior and Development, 3,* 265–282.

Nelson, K. E. (1971). Accommodation of visual-tracking patterns in human infants to object movement patterns. *Journal of Experimental Child Psychology, 12,* 182–196.

Piaget, J. (1954). *The construction of reality in the child.* New York: Basic Books.

Rieser, J. (1979). Spatial orientation of six-month-old infants. *Child Development, 50,* 1078–1087.

Sophian, C. (1984). Spatial transpositions and the early development of search. *Developmental Psychology, 20,* 21–28.

Starkey, P. (1983). *Some precursors of early arithmetic competencies.* Paper presented at the meeting of the Society for Research in Child Development, Detroit.

Starkey, P., & Cooper, R. G. Jr. (1980). Perception of numbers by human infants. *Science, 210,* 1003–1035.

Starkey, P., & Gelman, R. (1982). The development of addition and subtraction abilities prior to formal schooling in arithmetic. In T. C. Carpenter, J. M. Moser, & T. A. Romberg (Eds.), *Addition and subtraction: A cognitive perspective.* Hillsdale, NJ: Lawrence Erlbaum Associates.

Starkey, P., Spelke, E., & Gelman, R. (in press). Detection of intermodal numerical correspondences by human infants. *Science.*

Strauss, M. S., & Curtis, L. E. (1981). Infant perception of numerosity. *Child Development, 52,* 1146–1152.

Webb, R. A., Massar, B. M., & Nadolny, T. (1972). Information and strategy in the young child's search for hidden objects. *Child Development, 43,* 91–104.

Wishart, J. G., & Bower, T. G. R. (1982). The development of spatial understanding in infancy. *Journal of Experimental Child Psychology, 33,* 363–385.

Yonas, A., & Pick, H. L. Jr. (1975). An approach to the study of infant space perception. In L. B. Cohen & P. Salapatek (Eds.), *Infant perception: Vol 2. From sensation to cognition.* New York: Academic Press.

6 The Early Development of Planning

Henry M. Wellman
William V. Fabricius
The University of Michigan

Catherine Sophian
Carnegie-Mellon University

It is a common observation that humans engage in planning. Pure examples abound: constructing a vacation itinerary, outlining a class lecture, planning a construction project by making a set of blueprints. Indeed, there are even occupations where the person's primary vocation is planning, for example, city planners. In addition, many problem-solving endeavors require planning at some point along the way: solving a complex algebra problem, preparing one's chess moves, collecting various items at the grocery store. In this chapter we consider the early development of the ability to plan ahead as revealed in children's problem solving. We do so by focusing primarily on our research investigating the development of children's plans for finding objects.

Searching for hidden or missing objects is a common problem-solving endeavor. Objects we want are seldom immediately at hand; they are often missing or out of sight and must be found or retrieved. This dilemma confronts the young as well as the old. As a result, searching for missing objects is a problem-solving task understood even by very young children (Wellman & Somerville, 1982). Solving search problems can require considerable planning, as when one must plan a route in order to search all possible hiding locations, or plan to search the most likely locations first.

Although our own research has investigated planning as revealed in children's solution of search problems, we also wish to consider the development of planning more generally. To do so, in the first section of this chapter we consider definitional issues, such as what is planning and how could one assess its presence in young children? We then turn to our research on preschoolers' planning in search problems. This is followed by a section addressing the possibility of early planning skills in infants. Finally we present some preliminary thoughts on how planning, once acquired, develops further.

DEFINITIONS AND DIAGNOSIS

The term *planning* has come into considerable vogue lately in the literature on problem solving (e.g., Hayes-Roth & Hayes-Roth, 1979); the term *plan* has a long history of psychological use (e.g., Miller, Galanter, & Pribram, 1960); and in developmental psychology the term *planful* has often been employed as a descriptor for a variety of intelligent, deliberate acts (e.g., Flavell, 1970). These terms and traditions, while related, do not refer to precisely the same things. Planning, like many important psychological constructs, denotes a fuzzy or ill-defined concept that encompasses a variety of more or less prototypic activities; different investigators have thus focused on varying uses of the term.

At least three different senses of planning can be distinguished in the psychological literature. One equates a plan with an intention to do or avoid doing something in the future (e.g., Patterson & Mischel, 1975). This is common in everyday usage, where a statement such as "I plan to go to the party" often means roughly the same thing as the statement that "I intend to go to the party." The second sense equates the term planful with any deliberate means-end activity. The early means-end behavior of infants—e.g., removing a barrier to retrieve an object (Piaget, 1953)—would qualify as planful here. Likewise, it is in this sense that deliberate use of simple memory strategies has been called planful (e.g., Wellman, 1977). Finally, the third sense of planning is a subset of the second and refers to formulating an extended sequence of steps in advance in order to reach a goal or solve a problem. For this sort of planning, one must look ahead beyond the results of any single step to determine what subsequent steps should follow. This sense of the term planning is often invoked in the problem-solving literature. Witness the often-cited definition by Hayes-Roth and Hayes-Roth (1979) that planning requires the "predetermination of a course of action aimed at achieving some goal." This definition emphasizes predetermination of a *course of action,* that is, a sequence of acts, steps, or choices. Planning a course of action is also what most of us probably understand as distinctly planful behavior, in contrast to the more generic categories of deliberate or means-end behavior. Thus, this sense is also common in everyday usage, such as "I am planning my vacation." Planning a course of action is the sense of planning on which we focus in this chapter.

Having distinguished several senses of the term planning, we must next ask how this ability, and especially how planning a course of action, can be researched empirically. A crucial distinction here is that between research tasks that require formulation of a plan alone, versus those that require planning as a component of some other larger task. Many often-cited studies on planning involve the former. In this sort of research, for example, the subject's job is to determine a sequence of errands (Hayes-Roth & Hayes-Roth, 1979), to schedule a series of classroom activities (Pea, 1982), or to plan a sequence of moves in a game (Klahr & Robinson, 1981), and to do so without actually running the errands, conducting the activities, or playing the game. Indeed, in the Klahr and Robinson (1981) research, the authors were careful to run the experiment in a "pure planning mode," where the result was a verbal plan, *not* playing the game. We refer to such research as studies of plan formulation. Studies of this sort often aim to generate models of the component cognitive processes required to formulate relatively complex plans. The best known example here is the Hayes-Roth and Hayes-Roth (1979) Opportunistic Planning Model. In general, research modeling plan formulation derives some of its flavor from computer programs that are specifically designed to tackle such tasks (e.g., to schedule rooms in a hospital, routes for a bus company).

A strength of this approach to researching planning is that it avoids problems of diagnosis. The question of whether some subject has actually engaged in planning or not hardly ever arises. Since an overt plan is produced, planning is therefore obvious.

In many situations, however, planning can also be inferred from subjects' problem-solving behavior itself. Imagine yourself setting out to drive across country from New York to Los Angeles. You might start with a general plan to go directly, avoiding side trips, to use the freeways, and to stop for the night in large towns. Such planning would obviously influence your behavior on the trip, e.g., deciding to go around St. Louis on the beltway rather than through the middle of town. The resulting character of your performance could thus provide evidence of your planning even though you never overtly produce a concrete plan, e.g., an itinerary. Studies that focus on planning as exhibited in the execution of a relevant task goal we term studies of planned action.

There are several advantages to studying planned actions, at least for the developmental psychologist. Of foremost importance is that studying planning in this fashion may be necessary if one wants to look at the origins of planning in young children. Getting the young child to adopt a "pure planning mode" or to formulate an independent plan is itself a difficult endeavor. In addition, such a requirement may often obscure rather than reveal the young child's planning ability. Except for some everyday plan formulation tasks—e.g., making a Christmas card list, constructing an itinerary—planning even for adults most often goes on in context. For young children, planning may go on *only* in this fashion. Plans may be made by the child only, or especially, as required to execute some immediate action.

Attempting to study planning by investigating planned action, however, confronts the researcher with definite diagnostic obstacles. Since planning in this case is not isolated in a relatively unambiguous plan formulation task, it becomes nontrivial to determine whether a series of acts was planned or not. This problem looms especially large when the focus is on early development. Since in this chapter we focus on young children's early development of planning skills, and do so by studying planned actions, there are several diagnostic issues that require advance discussion.

First, as argued previously, establishing that a course of action has been planned requires evidence of a goal-directed *sequence* of acts. Yet, as we demonstrate shortly, evidence of a goal-directed sequence, although necessary, does not constitute sufficient evidence of planning. A positive assessment of planned action essentially requires evidence of looking ahead. The sequence of actions taken must be formulated in advance in order to achieve the goal and/or goal constraints; it cannot be simply an incidental consequence of approaching the goal one step at a time. This, in turn, requires careful construction of tasks and conditions so that it is clear when the child has adopted a sequence of actions for the "right" reasons (adherence to a formulated plan), and it requires ruling out the possibility that the child's behavior resulted from some other, nonplanful approach to the task.

Second, it is important to note that when other confounding factors are controlled, execution by the child of a planned sequence of actions demonstrates a number of abilities. It demonstrates that the child (a) appreciates the goal and/or goal-constraints that makes that sequence desirable, (b) can formulate a plan to achieve such a goal-constrained sequence, and (c) has the ability and desire to carry out the plan, in action. It follows that planned action studies can provide evidence, which plan formulation studies cannot provide, of the child's sensitivity to the need to plan his or her actions as well as the child's execution of plans in action. It also follows that if children do not demonstrate planned action, it may not be for lack of planning; it may instead by the result of faulty sensitivity to the need for a plan or of unsuccessful or suspended execution of the plan. Diagnostically, positive demonstrations of planned action on the part of young children are relatively revealing whereas failures often are not.

PLANNING IN PRESCHOOLERS

Our studies of planning in preschoolers have focused on children's use of plans to solve comprehensive search problems. These are problems where, in order to find the desired object or objects, the child must search all of a number of locations (Wellman & Somerville, 1982). The question is whether children plan their search paths between the different locations in advance, and especially whether they plan their searches so as to minimize the distance they have to travel. In our work we contrast planned search sequences with sequences generated by an alternate process we call "sighting." By doing so we aim to rigorously diagnose the presence of plans encompassing an extended sequence of steps. In sighting, one proceeds toward the goal, but does so by thinking of only one step at a time. The solution path is thus determined by what step "looks good" at each successive point in time rather than by an overall plan constructed in advance. Newell and Simon (1972) describe this general sort of approach when they discuss direct problem-solving attempts. In general, sighting seems likely to be an earlier developing problem-solving approach than is planning, since it requires less future orientation and less comprehensive consideration of solution options. However, the relative developmental histories of these approaches have not previously been studied.

The importance of distinguishing between sighting and planning became clear to us from the first study we conducted of planning in children's searches (Wellman, Somerville, Revelle, Haake, & Sophian, 1984). In this study children were required to collect five Easter eggs which were hidden, while they watched, on their school's playground. The hiding places used fell roughly into two large irregular clusters (on opposite sides of the playground). The hider used a clearly non-optimal path to hide the eggs, zig-zagging across the playground.

Originally, we thought that planning might be straightforwardly revealed in children's tendencies to minimize the total distance they traveled in order to find all the eggs. That is, we assumed (a) that optimal performance would be based on total distance traveled, and (b) that optimal performance would reveal planning, since an optimal path required selecting or constructing a short sequence of searches from among many possible sequences. As it turned out, both of these assumptions required revision. First, the results showed no tendency to minimize total distance in 3-, 4- or 5-year-olds. Search routes were not significantly shorter than expected by chance alone. However, consider not distance as measured in feet and inches but instead a salient distance-related aspect of these arrays. Since the hiding places were in clusters on opposite sides of the playground, it required a long traverse of the playground to go from cluster to cluster. Hence, children could minimize long traverses of the playground even if they were not sensitive to distance in a more metric sense. Four- and 5-year-olds used fewer traverses (about 1.75) than 3-year-olds (who averaged 2 traverses), but at all three ages children required fewer traverses than expected by chance (about 2.4 traverses). That is, children's search sequences minimized traverses.

Having discovered this, however, it became obvious that such optimal behavior did not necessarily imply predetermination of a course of action since two different processes might have yielded minimal traverse searches. Children could have planned to search the locations on one side of the playground first, before traversing the playground to search the locations on the other side. Alternately, children could have chosen their first location to search because it was most obvious, closest, or salient in some other respect. Subsequent searches could likewise have been made, one at a time, by this same process, which would clearly be an instance of sighting. Given the arrays used, sighting from closest to next closest location might incidentally produce minimal traverse routes just as planning to minimize traverses would.

To distinguish between the sighting and planning explanations for children's minimal traverse search paths, we looked at other measures of how much children sighted, such as whether their first searches were determined by salient perceptual features of the search locations themselves. This evidence suggested that 3-year-olds' minimal traverse searches were produced by sighting processes, but that 4- and 5-year-olds' were more likely to have been deliberately planned.

In our current work (Fabricius, Wellman, & Sophian, in preparation), we have distinguished between planning and sighting more directly and definitively, by using search tasks especially constructed to contrast planned paths with those possible by sighting alone. To see how these search tasks work, consider the problems depicted in Fig. 6.1. Suppose the searcher, in the tasks depicted, is at the starting point "S," has to retrieve an object from each of the locations marked "X," and eventually has to end up at the endpoint "E." Further, suppose the searcher's goal is to minimize distance while collecting all the objects. In the left hand portion of Fig. 6.1, the goal of minimizing distance puts no constraints on the searcher since both possible routes are the same length. However, in the right hand portion of the figure, where the endpoint is adjacent to one of the search locations, the goal of minimizing distance now makes clear planning demands on the searcher. Our current research on spatial planning has exploited considerations and experimental manipulations of this sort.

Notice that in spatial arrays such as the right hand of Fig. 6.1, planning the shortest route can be accomplished with or without having to estimate and compare the exact lengths of alternate routes. One possible route in that array involves having to retrace one's steps in going from the last searched location to the endpoint. The other route involves no such backtracking. Thus, the shortest route can be planned without having to estimate and compare the metric lengths of the two routes, by simply discovering that one route requires backtracking. Planning to avoid backtracking is quite similar to avoiding multiple traverses in the Wellman et al. (1984) study; using more than one traverse there required the searcher to backtrack across the playground. For this reason, arrays such as those in Fig. 6.1 potentially provide a sensitive measure of young children's ability to plan to take the shortest route, because the child does not necessarily have to represent and compare exact distances. Less detailed or powerful representations of the search space will still afford planning a shorter route. Presson and Somerville (this volume) and Landau and Spelke (this volume) demonstrate that young children possess spatial representations adequate for the planning we seek to reveal.

In our first study in this series we used the five contrastive search arrays shown in Fig. 6.2. The child's task in each Array was to begin at a start point (S), to search at each of three clearly visible white buckets (A,B,C) collecting an Easter egg at each location, and at the end, to deposit all the items in a nearby, larger, red bucket, the endpoint (E). The red bucket is shown by a circle, and the three white buckets to be searched are indicated by Xs. The short arrow at S

6. PLANNING   129

```
              E


X           X        E  X              X


            S                          S
```

FIG. 6.1. Hypothetical search arrays that would and would not require planning in order to achieve minimal distance search routes.

indicates the child's initial orientation, which was controlled by having the child stand on a set of footprints. We had 3-, 4-, and 5-year-olds make comprehensive searches of these arrays. These were large-scale searches; the average distance between adjacent locations was 28 feet.

In these arrays, various sighting approaches could conflict with planning to take the shortest route. To illustrate, in Array 1 a searcher planning to minimize distance would take path CBA. In Array 3, two such routes are available, CBA and BCA. These routes require simple *distance planning* based on avoiding backtracks. In contrast, each array includes a number of possible sighting "cues," or different types of salient visual features associated with certain locations. For example, in each array a searcher influenced by *line of vision* sighting would search first by going to location B, that location straight ahead and therefore central in the line of vision. Alternately, in Arrays 2, 4, and 5 one location has a *proximity* cue since it is clearly closer to the start point than all the rest. Sighting based on going to closest locations first is thus possible in these cases. Finally, in all arrays the presence of the red bucket close to location A may serve as a distinctive *marker* cue. Two different sighting approaches could be based on this cue: it could be attractive and thus induce children to search location A first, or it could be aversive, in which case either location B or C would be searched first. The table at the bottom of the figure shows the first searches in each array that would result from planning versus the four possible sighting approaches.

In order for planning to be revealed in this task context, a searcher must be trying to be efficient. That is, part of the subject's goal must involve a desire to avoid wasting effort. If there was no sensitivity to this larger goal then long paths would not necessarily reveal a lack of planning (only adoption of some different goal). Thus, is there any sense in which young children strive to be efficient on these tasks? The need to be efficient on these tasks, while implicit, was compelling. Children searched each array four times over a period of 2 days, resulting in at least one quarter mile of walking. One measure of the child's understanding of

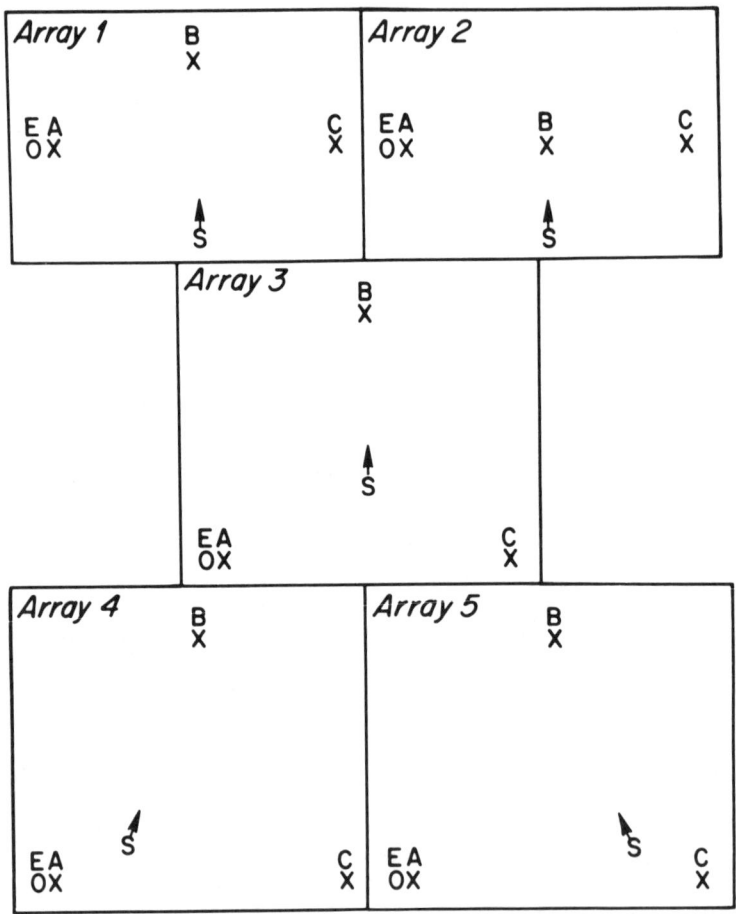

FIG. 6.2. Five three-location search arrays used to contrast various sighting and planning approaches.

some need to be efficient, comparable across all children whether they planned or not, would be whether they took efficient straight line paths *between* locations, whatever their chosen sequence of locations was. Wandering from straight line paths was infrequent (only 7% of the time) and did not differ by age. A different measure of efficiency would involve how often children searched a location more than once, since redundant searches can add a considerable proportion to the total effort required. Three-year-olds searched redundantly more often than older children, but even they required an average of only 3.3 searches to get the three items. Thus on approximately three out of every four trials they avoided any redundant searches at all. The redundancy rate of children at each age level can be shown to be well below that expected by chance. Children may or may not plan to minimize distance, but failure to do so was not simply a result of failure to be efficient at all.

Given this evidence of children's recognition of the need to be efficient, did children plan or sight? There were no age differences in first searches. At each age and in each array the first searches were most likely to be of the location straight ahead in the line of vision, that is, location B in Fig. 6.2. On the average, 66% of all first searches were at location B. In terms of first search, then, sighting on the basis of line of vision was clearly predominant. There was evidence that proximity sighting was also at work, but there was no evidence for marker sighting. In neither their individual patterns nor group performances did children show any evidence that the visually distinctive location next to the marker was either attractive or aversive. Thus, line of vision and proximity sighting accounted for first searches.

Planning, however, was evident on children's second searches. In spite of nonplanful first searches, planning to avoid backtracking could be evident in all arrays on second searches, especially second searches from location B. If the child first searched the line of vision location (B), he or she still faced a two-location search problem, just like that in the right hand portion of Fig. 6.1. Two locations remain, one to either side of the child, neither straight ahead and neither closer than the other. Across all five arrays, 3-year-olds avoided backtracking in this situation only 51% of the time (in other words, at chance level). Four-year-olds did so 69%, and 5-year-olds 77% of the time, both well above chance. That is, 4- and 5-, but not 3-year-olds, evidenced an ability to plan ahead, based on avoiding backtracks.

A possible objection to this conclusion might be that since they were given several trials on each problem type, children might simply have learned to take short paths, much like rats in a maze, without ever planning to do so. Like sighting, simply learning a complex response over trials represents a nonplanful approach to the task. However, analysis of children's searches yielded no trial effects. Thus first trial performance alone, where learning could not yet be operable, yields the same pattern of results as that reported above.

It might also be argued that line of vision sighting is not as important in preschoolers' search as these data lead one to believe. Instead, the results might have been due to the specific method used to control line of vision. That is, the footprints used to align the children might have strongly suggested a first path. However, in a subsequent study in the same series, we contrasted a condition that employed footprints, as in the first study, with a condition in which children were asked simply to position their toes on a line that was perpendicular to their intended line of vision. In addition, a third condition was included to ensure that children saw and took into account the location of the endpoint before beginning their searches. This was done by asking the child to point out the location of the red bucket, and the adult reminded the child, "That's where you have to go at the end to dump all your eggs." Three- and 5-year-olds were tested. These different conditions did not alter children's tendency, at either age, to search the line-of-vision location first.

To summarize, these results confirm much of what was hypothesized in the Wellman et al. (1984) study. First, sighting seems to play a strong and early role in the search solutions of preschoolers. Second, some type of planning ability in this domain develops during the preschool years. In short, "young children's search processes represent a mixture of sighting and planning, with planning growing in dominance over the preschool years" (Wellman et al., 1984).

The hypothesized mix of sighting and planning in young children's search having been established, an important issue becomes the relative developmental histories of sighting and planning tendencies. At what point does planning first appear? What are the relative weightings of sighting and planning, and how might they change with age? Further, is there a point when children become able to rely exclusively on planning in their searches?

We addressed these issues in a further study in this series (Fabricius et al., in preparation), using two-location search arrays, with 3-, 4- and 5-year-old children. The search arrays that were used are shown in Fig. 6.3. Notice that the two locations to be searched are set at equal angles from the child's line of vision so that neither is straight ahead in the line of vision. Thus, line-of-vision sighting was controlled. The sighting cue that we manipulated instead was proximity to the starting point. Both of these simplifications—use of only two locations and ruling out line-of-vision sighting—were instituted to yield a sensitive measure of early planning abilities. Otherwise the child's task was similar to the previous study, finding items at each location and taking them to the endpoint. In this case it was finding a baby animal at each location and taking the two babies to their mother, at the endpoint. Although large search arrays were again used, the distances involved here were somewhat smaller than the first study; the average distance between locations was 18 feet.

The four different arrays were designed to allow us to accurately estimate a child's tendency to search on the basis of proximity sighting, distance planning, or some mix of these two. In general, a complete assessment of the relative

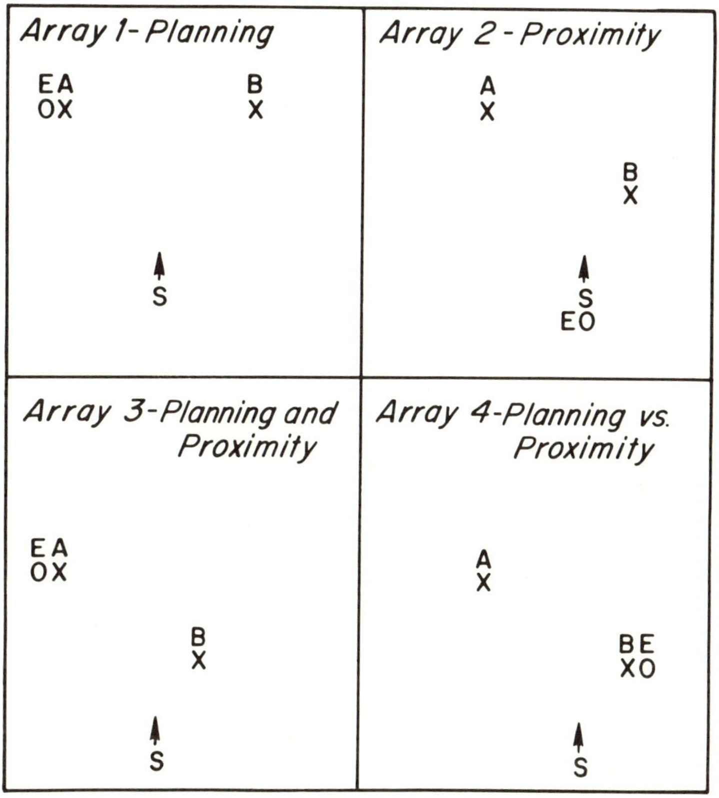

Array 1- Planning	Array 2 - Proximity

E A   B
O X   X
 	
↑
S
	A
	X
	
	           B
	           X
	
	↑
	S
	E O

Array 3-Planning and Proximity	Array 4-Planning vs. Proximity

E A
O X
 	
      B
      X
 	
↑
S
	A
	X
	
	           B E
	           X O
	
	↑
	S

FIG. 6.3. Four two-location search arrays used to estimate the independent and joint effects of sighting and planning.

weightings given to sighting and planning requires estimating the independent effects of each, and then examining performance when both sighting and planning approaches might be possible. For example, if search decisions represent a mix of planning and sighting, then choice of the shortest route should be more frequent when planning and sighting cues both indicate a first search of the same location. Conversely, planning should decrease in another situation if sighting indicates a choice of the opposite location. However, at some age the child might rely exclusively on planning when it conflicts with sighting.

Array 1 was designed to provide an estimate of the child's tendency to plan in a situation where proximity sighting was not a factor, that is, neither location was closest to the start point. In Array 2 the endpoint is at the same place as the start point so this yields the opposite estimate—a measure of the tendency to first search at the closest location (B) when planning was not a factor, since searching either A or B first would yield equal distances. Array 3 represents the condition in which sighting and planning might add together to determine search. Finally, Array 4 is the conflict situation—on the basis of distance planning one would first search A, yet on the basis of proximity one would first search B. Using these arrays, we were able to estimate the strength of planning and sighting tendencies separately (Arrays 1 and 2) as well as their relative strength when they might sum together (Array 3) and when they might compete (Array 4).

The full experiment included four age groups: 3-, 3½-, 4½- and 5½-year-olds. We were uncertain whether best performance would occur if we simply presented the problems with their implicit demands to the child, or if we provided specific instructions to take the shortest route. This was especially problematic for the youngest subjects, where the added instructions might either aid or confuse. Therefore two groups of 3- and two groups of 4½-year-olds were run initially. One group was told to go the ''quick way'' to retrieve the animals; the second group simply confronted the problems and retrieved the animals. In regard to planning, the instructions to go the quick way were sometimes helpful and never harmful. For example in Array 1 (see Fig. 6.3)—the situation where planning, if present, might be most obvious—3-year-olds were planful (searched A then B, not the reverse) 50% of the time in both conditions. This is exactly as expected by chance alone. The 4½-year-olds were similarly at chance when receiving no instructions, but searched planfully 73% of the time when instructed to go the quick way.

For these reasons the main experiment included four age groups all told to go the quick way. These data are presented in Table 6.1. Consider first the left-most column in the table. This presents the percentage of first searches of the planful

TABLE 6.1
Proportion of First Searches in Each Direction
Under Instructions to Go the "Quick Way"

AGE	ARRAYS			
	PLANNING	PROXIMITY	PLANNING and PROXIMITY	PLANNING vs. PROXIMITY
3.0	.50 .50	.42 .58	.47 .53	.47 .53
3.6	.42 .58	.42 .58	.30 .70	.52 .48
4.6	.27 .73	.27 .73	.17 .83	.47 .53
5.6	.08 .92	.62 .38	.08 .92	.88 .12

location in Array 1, the condition where planning alone is relevant. The first indication of planning (choice of the planful location greater than .50) is for 3½-year-olds and this increases steadily for 4½- and 5½-year-olds. Consider next the rows of the table. Looking across a single row gives a picture of how much children used both sighting and planning separately and in combination. Take for example the 4½-year-olds. The 4½-year-olds planned in Array 1 at a rate of 73%. This was comparable to that observed in the 4- and 5-year-olds of the original three-location study (69% and 77%, respectively) when they were faced with a similar problem (namely, a choice between two locations, A and C, on their second searches). In Array 2 the 4½-year-olds were influenced by proximity sighting, when it alone was relevant, to the same extent (73%) as they were influenced by planning in Array 1. Consequently their performance improved in Array 3 (83%), and furthermore they showed essentially no preference for sighting or planning when they were in conflict in Array 4. Thus the 4½-year-olds showed a pattern of performance where sighting and planning simultaneously and equally influenced the child's search decisions. Note in contrast that for 5½-year-olds, planning was essentially as high in the conflict situation of Array 4 as it was in the planning-only situation of Array 1. This provides evidence that they relied on planning alone in this situation, whereas 4½-year-olds were still inappropriately influenced by sighting.

Again, simple learning does not account for the data. There were no trial effects; first trial data are essentially identical to that in Table 6.1.

We have analyzed the data using log linear modeling techniques. This approach has the advantage of providing separate quantitative estimates of sighting and planning tendencies and testing whether performances in mixed situations—Arrays 3 and 4—can be predicted on the basis of these tendencies. Two parameters were incorporated in the model for each age group, one for planning and one for proximity sighting. The parameters are used to predict the observed frequencies in a contingency table. In this case, the contingency table was defined by the four arrays crossed with the two choices for the first search in each array. The model specified that both parameters would indicate the same choice in Array 3 but different choices in Array 4, while of course only planning was relevant in Array 1 and only proximity was relevant in Array 2. Thus the log linear model specified that the effects of sighting and planning would combine to determine performance in Array 3 and would compete, with neither being given priority over the other, in Array 4.

The results are shown in Fig. 6.4. Since the log linear model is multiplicative, a value of 1.0 means that the parameter has no effect in predicting cell frequencies, whereas values greater than 1.0 indicate increasingly positive effects. The values of the parameters indicate the following. Take the value of 2.32 for planning for the 4½-year-olds. That means that a location is 2.32 times more likely to be searched first if it is the planful location than if it is not (which translates to a predicted frequency of planning in Array 1 of 70%). The value

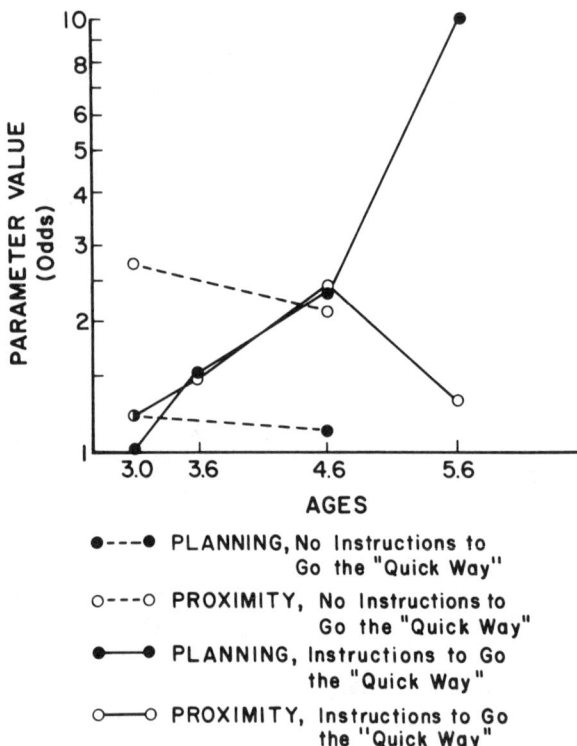

FIG. 6.4. Values of the estimated parameters for planning and sighting at four age levels.

2.53 for sighting for the 4½-year-olds means that a location is 2.53 times more likely to be searched first if it is the closest location rather than the farthest from the starting point (which translates to a predicted frequency of use of proximity in Array 2 of 72%). These values multiply to predict the odds of planning in Array 3 to be 5.87 (or 85% of first searches) and in Array 4 to be .92 (or 48% of first searches). It is clear from these results how closely children's searches can be predicted in different situations on the basis of their tendencies to plan ahead to minimize distance and to follow certain sighting cues.

The pattern of the parameters in Fig. 6.4 is thus very informative. Three-year-olds, although often influenced by sighting (e.g., in the no instruction condition), appear to never plan in these tasks. In contrast, 5½-year-olds essentially show only planning. The value of 1.5 for sighting for 5½-year-olds indicates that sighting has greatly decreased and, indeed, for 5½-year-olds a model excluding the parameter for sighting, including only planning, fits their data as well as a model with both. The intermediate groups —3½- and 4½-year-olds—show a mixture of sighting and planning.

In summary, by 3½ years of age planning is clearly evident in children's search sequences; its impact continues to increase whereas that of sighting decreases over the rest of the preschool years. Planning to minimize distance (or more specifically such distance-related spatial features as backtracks) can be validly assessed from children's patterns of search, because these patterns can be distinguished from those resulting from other possible determinants of performance. Specifically, we have carefully distinguished planning from several forms of sighting (e.g., line-of-vision sighting, proximity sighting, and attraction to or avoidance of single distinct locations) and from simply learning to do the task over repeated trials. At the same time, sighting does clearly co-exist with planning in the searches of preschoolers. Early in this age range, sighting is either the dominant search approach or equal in strength to planning; later planning becomes the principal if not the sole determinant of behavior in simple search tasks of this sort.

A further demonstration of these same conclusions is provided in recent research by Sophian (1984) on young children's abilities to conduct indirect searches. An example of indirect searching occurs in finding a book in the library. One typically does not search directly for the book (begin a systematic search of all the shelves) but searches first for information about its location in the card catalog. Search of this sort is indirect because it requires searching elsewhere before directly searching for the object. Such search requires a plan since one must predetermine an indirect course of action—looking in the card catalogue, and then looking on the shelves. An important similarity exists between direct versus indirect searches and searches based on sighting versus distance planning. Sighted search is like direct search in that it involves a direct approach to the target items, e.g., going to those directly straight ahead. Choosing a minimal distance path is typically indirect in the sense that one must often avoid the closest, "direct" location as the first place to search in order to achieve a short path overall.

In Sophian's task, 3- and 5-year-olds searched for a baby animal that could be in any one of several toy houses arranged on a tabletop. Each house had several baby rooms (obvious because of their small doors). Each house also had one grownup room (with a bigger door). The children were told that the baby could never be left by itself, so that it could only be in a house with a grownup. Direct search for the baby, in this context, would involve systematically searching the baby doors. Indirect search would involve searching the grownup doors, house by house, until a grownup was found at home. Only when a house with a grownup was found would one then search the baby doors for the baby.

Sophian contrasted first searching the grownup doors in this Indirect Search condition with two control conditions. The first of these, Baby Search, involved searching for a baby when there was no connection between the baby's location and the grownup's. That is, the child was simply told that the baby could be in any baby room, and then was directed to search for the bably. The other,

Grownup Search, involved searching for the grownup again when there was no connection between its location and the baby's. Across trials, a perfect indirect searcher would thus first search equally many grownup doors in the Indirect Search and the Grownup Search conditions and would search grownup doors in these conditions more often than in the Baby Search condition. A direct searcher, on the other hand, would first search equally *few* grownup doors in the Indirect and Baby Search conditions.

The results indicated that both 3- and 5-year-olds were more likely to first search grownup doors in the Indirect Search condition than the control Baby Search condition. This reveals an ability at avoiding direct search and planning an indirect search instead, where appropriate. However, this ability was far from perfect since first search of grownup doors was not as high as that evident in the Grownup Search condition, for both 3- and 5-year-olds. In short, once again overall performance represented a mix of planning and direct search tendencies.

In sum, these studies demonstrate early prowess at planning on the part of young preschoolers, albeit one not fully liberated from sighting or direct search tendencies. The sort of planning revealed is a fairly sophisticated one, planning an extended course of action as rigorously distinguished from deliberate but more direct solution attempts. The rigor and strictness of our efforts firmly establishes the phenomenon. The strength and sophistication of planning thus revealed further provokes interest in still younger children. What are the planning capabilities of infants and toddlers, if any?

PLANNING IN INFANTS AND TODDLERS

Although it is informative to consider the planning abilities of still younger children, this is a difficult task, for two reasons. First, since planning is a fuzzy construct, there is not one thing to look for. One could posit a single definition of planning and then look for its behavioral indications. However, the information yielded would be incomplete and the conclusions arbitrary. More fruitfully, one could examine many different sorts of performances that appear more or less planful and weave together a tapestry of the child's developing early abilities. This approach confronts the second difficulty, however. Many activities of the young child suggest a certain planfulness, but research carefully ruling out nonplanful interpretations of the child's actions—e.g., random search, direct search, sighting, learning over trials, or their analogs—is typically unavailable.

It is clear that planfulness, in the widest sense of simple, deliberate behavior, is demonstrable in infants late in the first year of life. Nine-month-old infants can deliberately employ an independent action—e.g., removing an obstacle, pulling on a support—to achieve their intended goals—e.g., retrieving an attractive object. In a search situation for example (Piaget, 1954), infants of this age remove a covering container to get the object. In a limited sense they plan to get the object from the start.

An informative demonstration of this was recently provided by Willats (1984). Children retrieved toys hidden under a single cup when they were 6, 7, and 8 months of age. Their searches were videotaped and the child's intentionality was scored from three aspects of his or her behavior. If the child lifted the covering cup away without playing with it, that was one possible index of planning to get the toy (rather than incidentally playing with the cup). Ambiguous behavior such as knocking the cup away (which may have occurred accidentally) was not considered clearly intentional. If, as the child removed the cup, his gaze went immediately to the uncovered toy (instead of wandering elsewhere or following the cup's movement) that was another potential index of intentionality. Finally, if the infant quickly retrieved the toy after removing the cup (rather than playing with the cup, or touching but not retrieving the toy) this was a possible third index of planning to get the toy all along. The results on these measures converged nicely. Intending to retrieve the toy increased over the 2 months. By the time they were 8 months old, children typically searched intentionally on all three measures. That is, they lifted the cup away without playing with it, immediately gazed at the toy, and picked it up. In a second study, comparing infants in a condition like the above with a condition where the cup was still present but contained no toy, it was clear that 7- and especially 8-month-olds were indeed deliberately acting on the cup to get at the hidden toy.

Such deliberate acts are "planful" in one sense but do not provide clear evidence of planning a course of action. In these cases it is possible to argue that only a single intervening act, removing the cup, is required to accomplish the goal. Lack of planning in the narrower, but informative sense of planning an extended course of action is clear when you consider that Willats' infants probably were engaging in simple direct search. The obstacle was removed as encountered; several steps were not planned in advance.

Studies of infants' search in invisible displacement tasks (Corrigan, 1981; Piaget, 1954; Uzgiris & Hunt, 1975), where the item is invisibly hidden in one of several locations, seem potentially more enlightening about planning a sequence of acts. Here, the infant must search a number of locations until the item is found. However, the arrangement of hiding locations in such tasks has, to date, been linear. Therefore, even when the infant searches sequentially (e.g., by reversing the hider's route through the locations) such behavior could be based simply on sighting (e.g., starting at an obvious endpoint and then going from one location to the next closest location) rather than planning a course of action. Indeed, in a recent study Bertenthal and Fischer (1983) have persuasively analyzed infants' systematic search in such tasks as involving only a first search of an endpoint followed by linear search persistence.

Another potentially informative set of studies on planning a course of action is that on shortest route behavior in toddlers (Cornell & Heth, 1983; Lockman &

Pick, 1984; Riesser & Heiman, 1982). Since here young children find a set of objects or visit a set of locations plus honor a shortest route constraint, such behavior could be a fertile ground for research on planning. As yet, however, these studies have not been designed to address issues of planning an overall route. As a result, shortest route behavior in toddlers seems parsimoniously explained as instances of sighting.

For example, Cornell and Heth (1983) had 1- and 3-year-olds retrieve two objects placed in cups in front of the child. The child was positioned to the right or to the left of the point halfway between the cups. The shortest route to find both items would then involve going to the nearest cup first, before going to the further one. There was evidence, for both the 1- and 3-year-olds, that children did this, but in this situation such behavior could represent simply sighting the nearest location first and going there. Similarly, in a study by Lockman (reported in Lockman & Pick, 1984) a child and its mother stood together behind a long, low partition—a short wall. The pair's starting point was clearly to one side or the other of the midline of the wall. Then the mother stepped *over* the partition calling to the child to come to her. Since the child could not step over, he or she had to go around. Eighteen-month-olds consistently chose the shortest route to get to mother and 12-month-olds gave some indication of doing so. Again, however, the child could have achieved the shortest route without planning a course of action, simply by sighting the nearer corner and going there.

Can nothing be said about the possible origins of planning a course of action in infants and toddlers? A recent study by Willats (1984) suggests that planning of this sort may also be demonstrable in 9-month-olds. Willats was interested in the early development of problem solving. The problem confronting the child was to retrieve a visible but out-of-reach object by means of pulling a support (a cloth) on which the item rested. Thus Willats was interested in the young child's notion of support and his or her ability to exploit support relations in order to solve a simple problem. In general, most studies on problem solving of this sort in infants (e.g., Piaget, 1954) fall prey to the same limitation as infant search studies when it comes to considering planning a course of action. That is, only a single goal-directed act (e.g., pulling a support, or removing a barrier) seems required to retrieve the goal-item rather than a more obvious sequence of such acts. In the second of his two studies, however, Willats (1984) presented 9-month-olds a task requiring removal of a barrier *and* pulling on a support in order to retrieve an object. Infants were confronted with a barrier (a low block of foam) behind which was visible a towel, on which rested a toy which the infant desired. Behavior in this support condition contrasted with a control condition where the infant was confronted with a barrier, behind which was visible a towel, right *beside* which rested a toy which the infant desired.

The first group of infants, those in the support condition, essentially reached for and removed the barrier then pulled the cloth and retrieved the toy. Such behavior could have resulted from planning—formulating the appropriate sequence of actions in advance—or from several other approaches. For example, the children could have simply reached for the barrier because of an interest in it, then having done so seen the cloth and become interested in it, and so on. That is, they could have retrieved the toy on the basis on an approach analogous to sighting. If so, however, then children in the control condition, where the toy was beside not on the cloth, should show the same behavior (except that pulling the towel would not bring the toy within grasp). Some infants in the control condition did reach for the barrier and then the towel. But, infants in the support condition made contact with the toy (on the average at 10.3 sec) long before the control group had even touched the cloth (23.3 sec). In addition, infants in the control condition essentially played with the foam when they first encountered it, whereas those in the control condition removed it, that is, put it aside. Thus infants might have retrieved the toy in the support condition via a sighting approach, but the character of their behavior, in contrast to the control group, suggests that they did not.

Another possibility is that infants in the support condition might have simply reached toward the toy itself. That is, they might have been reaching directly, in analogy to direct search. If so, they might incidentally have pushed the barrier aside, and then when their reach fell short of the toy it would have landed on the cloth, which was then pulled toward them. If this accounts for behavior in the support condition, however, then similar direct reaching should occur in the control condition. Yet as shown above, time to reach the barrier was greatly different between groups, as was treatment of the barrier once it was encountered. In addition, in the support condition very few infants failed to contact the cloth (this occurred on only 7 of 100 trials), yet in the control condition many did (61 of 100 trials).

Finally, suppose the infants in the support group started out as "sighters" or "direct reachers" and their behavior of this sort was reinforced over trials, since they would indeed retrieve the item. In this case the infants, because of these reinforced trials, might be quicker than those in the control condition, but they would only be showing learning over trials, not planning. However, differences of the sort described above were apparent examining just first-trial behavior, and further, infants' behavior in the support condition essentially stayed the same across trials.

In short, infants in this experiment may well have perceived the arrangement and figured out the sequence of actions required, in advance, rather than on the basis of sighting, direct reaching, or learning over trials. We conclude that infants *may* have planned, rather than that they did plan, because of the following possibility. What if the children in the experimental condition saw the toy on the towel as a "towel-toy" not caring that the two items were also separable? On this account, the child simply does one action (removes the barrier) in order to reach the goal (the towel-toy), i.e., he or she acts deliberately but does not plan a sequence of acts. The same toy-towel concept would not necessarily arise in the control condition since that condition might define only a relatively uninteresting towel and a separate unreachable toy.

At a minimum, Willats' study shows a plausible research method for the investigation of early abilities at planning, including planning a course of action. Shortest route studies could also yield information about planning a course of action in infants and toddlers, if tasks were carefully controlled to contrast planful and nonplanful behavior. In conclusion, we think it likely that ability to plan a course of action is acquired sometime in late infancy or only slightly later, and continued clever research might reveal this. In the next section we offer some reasons for why this should be so, in spite of the fact that planning on our own tasks appears at a somewhat later age.

THE DEVELOPMENT OF PLANNING

Understanding cognitive development requires a constant interplay between recognizing, on the one hand, the similarities in abilities or performances between children of different ages and, on the other hand, the differences. Various theories emphasize one or the other of these two perspectives; e.g., stage theorists seem to weight differences over similarities, whereas claims asserting the early competence of infants or young children often weight similarities over differences. A comprehensive understanding of cognitive development, however, requires attention to and appreciation of both these aspects.

Thus far we have emphasized early competence, and hence the similarities in planning abilities between younger and older children and adults. Specifically, we concluded that a fundamental ability to plan a course of action is acquired early in development; surely by 3 or 3½ years of age, possibly by 1 or 2 years. Thus, a wide range of ages are quite similar in that they can be characterized as able to plan ahead to formulate a course of action. Since the evidence for this planning ability comes from studies of planned action, it also provides evidence that humans across a wide age range can spontaneously make and successfully carry out such plans once formulated. Planfulness seems both an earlier and more generally apparent feature of human behavior than previously thought.

We now wish to briefly consider some of the age differences in early planning. Initial planning abilities, although demonstrably similar in certain ways to the accomplishments of older children, clearly differ as well. To organize this discussion, we distinguish between two sorts of developmental changes. The first sort are "inter-plan developments": developmental changes in the kinds of different plans children can generate and/or use. It seems likely that there is an expansion with age in the range of different plans that children can formulate. The second sort are "intra-plan developments": changes in how well the child is able to generate or use a given kind of plan. Even when a child has shown some ability to do a particular type of planning from an early age, there are likely to be continuing changes over an extended period of time in how systematically or effectively he or she does that planning.

Inter-plan Developments

Inter-plan developments can be thought of either in terms of the different sorts of *plans* a child can generate and use, or in terms of the different sorts of planning *tasks* the child can handle. Differences between plans are often obviously related to differences in the problem-solving tasks; different tasks require or afford different courses of action. Of course, the relation between plan and task is not straightforward—a single task may afford several different effective plans. Plans exist within the subject as cognitive products; their features are dependent on, but not determined by, task features themselves. Nonetheless, a discussion of inter-plan developments requires considering certain task features and differences as well as plan differences.

A discussion of inter-plan developments requires comparisons across quite different studies, since these issues have not been addressed in a single investigation. Our ideas here are thus preliminary. In addition, as discussed earlier, the planner's ability to achieve a planned action of a certain sort depends not just on the type of plan required but also on his or her sensitivity to the need to plan at all, the need for plans of a certain sort, and on his or her ability to execute the plan once formulated. All of these factors influence any evidence of inter-plan developments.

Given these qualifications, what inter-plan developments might occur in children's ability to plan a course of action? One development of this sort would be increases in the child's sensitivity to, and ability to take account of, various sorts of task constraints that influence the task outcome and therefore necessitate a plan of a particular type. A critical constraint is that of success. Some childhood activities such as finger painting or swinging can proceed with little or no planning; others, such as building a structure or baking a cake, will fall apart or misfire without a plan. Certainly, many things that adults do *are* thought-out and planned (or once were and are now only routine). However, the life of a young child is much less planned, and when planning is necessary it is often supplied and orchestrated by others, e.g., parents and teachers (Wertsch, McNamee, McLane, & Budwig, 1980). One crucial aspect in the development of planning, then, must be development of sensitivity to the need for planning in an increasing variety of task situations.

Although some tasks must be planned in order to succeed, some tasks require planning only in order to meet other solution constraints. Note that in the Willats (1984) study success itself was often dependent on formulating the correct sequence of acts in advance. On the other hand, note that in our studies with young preschoolers, a nonplanful sighting or direct search approach could indeed eventually solve the problem—i.e., find the items. A plan was needed there in order to find the objects while honoring constraints of efficiency. It may very well be that planning a course of action occurs first on tasks where planning is required in order to succeed at all, and only later on tasks where planning is needed to honor other constraints like those of efficiency. At the least, our studies demonstrate the presence of this later expanded sort of ability in 3-year-olds.

Although planning can be based on success alone, planning in order to be efficient is a central asect of planning, at least for older children and adults. Thus, what constraints must plans honor, or do good plans typically honor? Many such constraints will depend on, and therefore vary with, specific properties of specific goals or problems. However, given a human problem-solver, certain features of the organism itself place general constraints on most practical problem solutions. Specifically, the human problem solver is limited in time and space, and in respect to the resources he or she commands. In general, solutions that minimize time to success, number of acts required, and/or distance traveled are desirable, since these features regularly correlate with effort required. Success should be maximized and effort expended minimized; children must developmentally acquire sensitivity to and ability at formulating plans focusing on these indirect task features. In many problems these three aspects of a solution—time, number of acts, and distance—covary. In our studies, for example, a long rather than short path involved greater distance and hence more steps to be walked and longer time to travel. It may be that tasks involving redundant specification of effort to be minimized, such as these, would be the sorts where a need to honor constraints of efficiency or effort is first realized.

Beyond these general plan features or constraints involving effort are other important and often desirable planning constraints—things such as monetary expenses, or intangibles such as solution elegance or parsimony. One particularly important constraint of this sort would be boredom; among older children and adults planning is often sensitive to the need to avoid a boring or tedious solution. We would expect evidence of formulating plans involving these sorts of constraints—boredom, elegance, parsimony—to appear later in development than plans involving external constraints like distance.

In sum, one crucial feature of different plans that is related to the development of planning a course of action concerns the costs taken into account—what the plan is meant to conserve or enhance. A possible developmental progression here is from sensitivity to the need for and ability at formulating plans (a) designed to ensure success, to (b) those designed to ensure efficiency—in terms of the general constraints of effort—to (c) those designed to minimize cognitive costs, such as boredom. Such a progression, if verified, would help explain quite a few developmental differences in problem solving.

Note that in our research we have taken care, by using large spaces and hence extreme values of distance and time, to make constraints of efficiency salient for the young child. We believe that care in this regard is an important requirement for researching planning in young children. Only with increasing age would we expect children to be aware of the conventional value of minimizing these aspects of problem solution and thus to plan even when the costs avoided on these currencies are quite small—as for example, in minimizing distance on tabletop arrays or maps.

Several other plan types seem potentially later developments, in the sense that they would be added to the child's planning repertory only with increasing development. For example, in all the problem-solving situations reviewed in this chapter there was a single goal (e.g., finding all the items while using a short total distance to do so). Such situations can be contrasted with those where the problem solver must plan a course of action that balances a number of partly conflicting goals. Consider, for example, a typical college student's task in planning his or her course schedule so as to fulfill certain distribution requirements, specialize in a major, include subjects of interest, and avoid certain undesirable class times or teachers. Planning solutions that achieve a satisfactory or efficient mix of goals seems a likely candidate for later development. This sort of planning has been researched with adults by Wilensky (1981).

Finally, consider again our distinction between plan formulation tasks and planned action tasks. The converse of our argument that planning would be first revealed in action is that ability to formulate plans as an independent task can be expected to develop later. That is, learning to construct plans in the abstract, solving isolated plan formulation tasks, should be an "advanced" developmental acquisition and milestone. The Klahr & Robinson (1981) research shows that some form of such an ability is apparent in older preschoolers. However, the task situation there was quite supportive, involving much experimenter prompting and problem translation. An interesting research question remains concerning children's understanding of a need to formulate plans, separate from executing problem solutions, e.g., making a budget, making a map, making an outline.

Intra-plan Developments

In addition to developmental changes in the kinds of planning children can do, there are likely to be changes in how ably they handle the same kind of planning at different ages. Indeed we have evidence for these sorts of developments in our studies of planning search sequences. In particular, two interwoven developments of this sort are evident: increases in the strength of planning itself and decreases in the presence of competing nonplanful task tendencies. Figure 6.4 captures both these general developments, since it charts the independent courses of planning and sighting.

Changes in the strength of planning reflect a number of factors, including, at the very least, changes in the consistency or reliability with which children will plan, given the same task conditions. In general, younger children, although planful, are less consistently so. For example, in Array 1 of the two-location search study reported above (see Fig. 6.3) 13% of the 3-year-olds, 25% of the 3½-year-olds, 50% of the 4½-year-olds, and 69% of the 5½-year-olds searched planfully on all four of their four trials. In addition, changes in the strength of planning are evident in the increases in the difficulty of the plans that can be successfully formulated. Plans of the same "kind," e.g., planning a sequence of moves in a search route, can still differ in difficulty. Plan difficulty is an imprecise, complicated notion but an important one. Fortunately, one aspect of plan difficulty seems relatively obvious. This involves simply the number of moves or steps or alternatives that must be sequenced in the plan. Klahr and Robinson (1981) showed the influence of problem length or number of moves to be planned on planning performance in older preschoolers. Successful planning was first obvious only on problems requiring fewer moves, even though plans of the same type were involved. Similarly, our research shows effects of whether the child had only two or three locations to consider (A,B or A,B,and C). With same-age children, on tasks requiring the same plan type, solution of two-location problems were more likely to be planful than those of three-location problems.

In addition to performances indicating more strongly planful approaches to the task, there is evidence that children are at first also or even exclusively influenced by less appropriate aspects of the problem (e.g., sighting cues) and perform on the basis of irrelevant (e.g., left-right biases) or only partly relevant response tendencies. Again, the presence and nature of these competing tendencies are clear in the studies we have conducted, as evident in the data on sighting and direct search.

Notice that these two developments—strength of planning per se and presence of other response tendencies—are separable, and can be separated with appropriate tasks, since they yield different developmental patterns in our research. This is again evident in Fig. 6.4. In that figure, up until a certain age sighting increases or at least maintains its presence while planning is increasing in strength. Later, sighting becomes distinctly less influential while planning increases.

In general, the age differences in intra-plan performance should be captured by a model employing an appropriate mix of *task-adapted* responses (i.e., planning) and *task-irrelevant* response tendencies. Sophian, Larkin, and Kadane (this volume) propose a general model of this sort, which could apply to intra-plan age differences as well.

SUMMARY AND CONCLUSIONS

The primary aim of this chapter has been to establish the early presence of planning, in the strict sense of planning a course of action. We have done so primarily by focusing on children's plans for solving search problems as revealed in their planned actions. We have claimed, first and foremost, that a fundamental ability to plan a course of action is acquired quite early in development and is applied spontaneously to several sorts of problems. Second, we have argued that the development of planning beyond its early acquisition is an extended, multifaceted process. We characterized this process by distinguishing between (a) increases in the scope of children's planning abilities, or the range of different types of planning they can do, and (b) increases in the reliability and effectiveness with which they perform any one type of planning. The first of these factors includes changes in children's sensitivity to the need for plans as well as changes in their ability to do the planning required. The second includes changes in the strength of children's planning efforts and in the influence of competing response tendencies, which together enable children to produce increasingly consistent planning performances even in the face of increasingly difficult planning tasks. Both of these components, strength of planning and competing response tendencies, are summary terms subsuming a variety of related developmental influences on planning.

The support for our primary claim, that a basic ability to plan an extended course of action emerges quite early, comes most strongly and directly from our studies of planned searches in 3-, 4-, and 5-year-olds. In these studies, the first signs of planning appeared in 3-year-olds' performance. Suggestive evidence from younger age groups in other studies, however, raises the possibility that the origins of planning competence possibly lie with 1- and 2-year-olds.

Given that an initial ability to plan ahead is evident so young, then much of the development of planning consists of further modifications, perfections, and additions to this initial skill. Thus in the last part of the paper we turned briefly to consideration of age differences in planning. Support for our claims about age differences is of varying sorts and quality. That increasing planfulness combines with task irrelevant response tendencies to determine children's performance in planned action tasks is apparent from the developmental changes in sighting as well as in planning that we observed in our research. That plan difficulty, as measured by the number of steps or moves to be planned, influences planning performances has also been demonstrated empirically (e.g., Klahr & Robinson, 1981). That children become more generally able to formulate a variety of plan types seems irrefutable, but the specific developmental sequences of this sort that we discuss, while plausible, are admittedly speculative. Much research remains to be done on the early as well as later development of planning.

The research we have presented sheds light on the development of search and spatial problem solving specifically, as well as on the development of planning more generally. The early achievements revealed here elaborate and confirm our growing picture of the young child as an especially logical, deliberate, intelligent searcher (Somerville & Haake, this volume; Sophian & Wellman, 1983; Wellman & Somerville, 1982). These data also confirm previous evidence that even very young children often select the shortest route among a set of locations, and help to clarify the basis for this performance. Specifically, early exhibitions of shortest route behavior are likely to be the incidental products of sighting processes on the part of the child. Later, but still within the preschool years, shortest routes are planned as an extended course of action taking into account the overall distances of competing routes. However, the data strongly suggest that the conception of distance and representation of space that the child uses in this planning may not be a Euclidean, metric one but one based on more qualitative distance-related aspects of routes, such as the occurrence of backtracks.

The findings and the conclusions arrived at here also have implications for the development of problem solving more generally. Again, search performances have revealed the early problem-solving achievements and capabilities of quite young children (Wellman & Somerville, 1982). More specifically, young children can competently plan a course of action to solve certain problems. Why is this an important conclusion? Why is researching the early development of planning an important task for understanding cognitive development? In the introduction to this chapter we suggested that planning is ubiquitous in adult human behavior. This is so, we believe, because the motivation for planning ahead is essentially to ensure success while using an efficient course of action. In short, planning allows the allocation of scarce resources to important tasks. Given a human organism with (a) scarce cognitive resources, (b) an array of behavioral goals that require extended courses of action, and (c) a flexible problem-solving apparatus instead of a preprogrammed repertoire of behavior, then efficient problem solving is a central concern. Planning is instrumental to meeting this concern.

The conclusion that planning is present from an early age, then, suggests that very young children already have a powerful cognitive tool that may play a substantial role in their subsequent development. This is an implication of our primary claim, which has sizable theoretical import. The acquisition of many cognitive skills—memory, communication, enumeration, world knowledge—even very early developments in these domains, may be significantly shaped by the young child's *planful* efforts (see Wellman, 1984). At the same time, the limitations on early planning and the developmental changes we have identified suggest that developmental relationships between planning and other aspects of cognitive development are likely to be bidirectional and to extend over a wide age range.

ACKNOWLEDGMENT

Research reported in this chapter was supported by research grants from NICHD to the first and third authors.

REFERENCES

Bertenthal, B., & Fischer, K. (1983). The development of representation in search: A social-cognitive analysis. *Child Development, 54,* 846–857.

Cornell, E. H., & Heth, C. D. (1983). Spatial cognition: Gathering strategies used by preschool children. *Journal of Experimental Child Psychology, 35,* 93–110.
Corrigan, R. (1981). The effects of task and practice on search for invisibly displaced objects. *Developmental Review, 4,* 65–67.
Fabricius, W. V., Wellman, H M., & Sophian, C. (in preparation). The development of planning.
Flavell, J. H. (1970). Developmental studies of mediated memory. In H. Reese & L. Lipsitt (Eds.), *Advances in child development and behavior.* New York: Academic Press.
Hayes-Roth, B., & Hayes-Roth, F. (1979). A cognitive model of planning. *Cognitive Science, 3,* 275–310.
Klahr, D., & Robinson, M. (1981). Formal assessment of problem-solving and planning processes in children. *Cognitive Psychology, 13,* 113–148.
Lockman, J. J., & Pick, H. L. (1984). Problems of scale in spatial development. In C. Sophian (Ed.), *Origins of cognitive skills.* Hillsdale, NJ: Lawrence Erlbaum Associates.
Miller, G. A., Galanter, E., & Pribram, K. H. (1960). *Plans and the structure of behavior.* New York: Holt, Rinehart & Winston.
Newell, A., & Simon, H. (1972). *Human problem solving.* Englewood Cliffs, NJ: Prentice-Hall.
Patterson, C. J., & Mischel, W. (1975). Plans to resist distraction. *Developmental Psychology, 11,* 369–378.
Pea, R. D. (1982). What is planning development the development of? In D. Forbes & M. Greenburg (Eds.), *New directions for child development: Children's planning strategies.* San Francisco: Jossey-Bass.
Piaget, J. (1953). *The origin of intelligence in the child.* London: Routledge & Kegan Paul.
Piaget, J. (1954). *The construction of reality in the child.* New York: Basic Books.
Riesser, J. J., & Heiman, M. L. (1982). Spatial self-reference systems and shortest route behavior in toddlers. *Child Development, 53,* 524–533.
Sophian, C. (1984). *The development of indirect search strategies.* Carnegie-Mellon University.
Sophian, C., & Wellman, H. M. (1983). Selective information use and perseveration in the search behavior of infants and young children. *Journal of Experimental Child Psychology, 35,* 369–390.
Uzgiris, I. C., & Hunt, J. McV. (1975). *Assessment in infancy.* Urbana: University of Illinois.
Wertsch, J. V., McNamee, G. D., McLane, J. B., & Budwig, N. A. (1980). The adult-child dyad as a problem-solving system. *Child Development, 51,* 1215–1221.
Wellman, H. M. (1977). The early development of intentional memory. *Human Development, 20,* 86–101.
Wellman, H. M. (1984). *The early development of memory strategies.* Paper presented at the conference, Memory Development, Munich, Germany.
Wellman, H. M., & Somerville, S. C. (1982). The development of human search ability. In M. E. Lamb & A. L. Brown (Eds.), *Advances in developmental psychology* (Vol. 2, pp. 41–84). Hillsdale, NJ: Lawrence Erlbaum Associates.
Wellman, H. M , Somerville, S. C., Revelle, G. L., Haake, R. J., & Sophian, C. (1984). The development of comprehensive search skills. *Child Development, 55,* 471 481.
Wilensky, R. Meta-planning: Representing and using knowledge about planning in problem solving and natural language understanding. *Cognitive Science,* 1981, *5,* 197–233.
Willats, P. (1984a). The stage IV infant's solution of problems requiring the use of supports. *Infant Behavior and Development, 7,* 125–134.
Willats, P. (1984b). Stages in the development of intentional search by young infants. *Developmental Psychology, 20,* 389–396.

7 Memory-Based Searching by Very Young Children

Judy S. DeLoache
University of Illinois

"Get your shoes on."
"I don't know where they are."
"Where did you leave them yesterday?"
"I don't know."
"What did you do when you came home yesterday?"
"I don't remember."
"Think!"
(shrug)
"Come on. I'll help you find them."

This is a hypothetical dialogue between a mother and her preschool child, but it represents a common everyday interaction in which a parent attempts to prompt a child to search for something. This example involves "memory-based searching" (DeLoache, 1984a), in which the basis for deciding where to search for an object is one's memory for where it was last seen. My choice of this example to begin this chapter was stimulated by a comment I have often received after discussing my research on memory-based searching. After hearing about my work, which reveals surprisingly high levels of performance by very young children, some practical-minded person often says: "Well, that's all very nice, but why can't my child find his shoes?" An informal analysis of this example of everyday search behavior (or non-search behavior) provides a starting point for discussing the early development of memory-based searching.

If interactions like the above one (involving countless lost mittens, jackets, and toys) were the only source of information that parents of young children had about the memory abilities of their progeny, they might infer that young children have virtually no capability for remembering the location of objects. Parents are unlikely to reach such a conclusion, however, because they are likely to have observed numerous counterexamples of remarkable location memory by the same child. Recent diary studies testify to the prominence of location in early mnemonic activities. Nearly a quarter of all identified memory episodes in parental diary records of 7- to 11-month-old infants involve remembering the location of an object or a person (Ashmead & Perlmutter, 1980). Half the recall episodes in the diary records kept by mothers of 20- to 30-month-olds were stimulated or cued by the location where the remembered object had been experienced (Nelson & Ross, 1980). Many of these accounts were quite impressive, some of them involving memories for events several months old. The fact that spatial location serves as such a potent retrieval cue suggests that part of what is remembered about an event, even by very young children, is where that event occurred.

Why then, in the case of the missing shoes, does the child in the example fail to remember the location of his shoes? Attentional factors may play an important role. It is probably rare for a preschool child to pay close attention to the removal of his shoes or to the fact that the shoes will have to be retrieved at some later time. To put it another way, retrieving his shoes may not be a very salient goal of the child's, in part because it may not be something that the child must do himself. (In my experience with missing shoes, the parent is usually recruited to help search for them.) Thus, even though very young children tend to encode and remember the spatial location of events, this may be true only for events that are attended to.

It may be instructive to contrast the hypothetical child in this example with a hypothetical adult. Like the child, the adult may not be terribly interested in the event of shoe removal but, unlike the child, may be aware of the need to be able to find the shoes in the future. As a consequence, the adult may employ various standard strategies to facilitate future retrieval. For example, the adult might exploit the organization available in the environment and put the removed shoes in the closet. As Wellman and Somerville (1982) have pointed out, much of the organization we impose upon our environment enables us to avoid having to remember the location of specific objects. The adult might also plan ahead for future retrieval by making a mental note that he has left his shoes next to the back door. In the event that the adult failed to behave planfully, that is, failed to notice where he was leaving his shoes, he could employ various systematic retrieval strategies to organize his search efforts. For example, he could trace backwards, either mentally or physically, to discover the last point at which the shoes were present.

Analysis of this everyday example raises two sets of questions about early location memory and memory-based searching that are addressed in this chapter:

(1) What are the capabilities of very young children for remembering spatial location, and what is the basis for location memory? (2) Are young children able in any way to apply deliberate strategies to the task of remembering? If so, what is the nature of their early strategies, and how do they relate to memory performance? (3) How do they develop into more mature forms of mnemonic strategies? The first question is considered briefly and returned to later in this paper. The second set of questions, those concerning early memory strategies, is the main focus of the chapter. Finally, some speculations are offered concerning the third question about further refinement of earlier strategies.

It is no accident that a chapter in which the primary concern is early memory and memory strategies should appear in a volume on the development of search behavior. Much of what is known about memory in older infants and toddlers comes from object permanence and other memory-based search tasks (Harris, 1983). Young children are more enthusiastic participants (Wellman & Somerville, 1982) and exhibit mnemonic competence earlier (Brown & DeLoache, 1978; DeLoache, 1980) in external memory tasks that require the retrieval of objects from the environment than in tasks that involve purely internal retrieval. Remembering the location of an event or a currently invisible object is facilitated by the wealth of information generally available in the physical environment. The presence of external cues (Wellman & Somerville, 1982), or external cognitive support (Reeve, 1983), is especially important in young children's memory activity, since they have great difficulty generating and using internal memory cues. Further, it is essential to have a basic task that young children can understand, are motivated to participate fully in, and can perform competently. Only under these circumstances is a very young child likely to exercise any higher level cognitive skills that he may possess (DeLoache, 1980), since nascent skills tend to be fragile and domain specific (Brown, Bransford, Ferrara, & Campione, 1983; Gelman, 1978) and require greater cognitive effort.

MEMORY FOR SPATIAL LOCATION

The first question that was posed above concerned the capabilities of very young children to remember spatial location. My colleagues and I have conducted several studies investigating the ability of children between 18 and 30 months of age to remember the location of an object hidden in the large-scale environment (DeLoache & Brown, 1979, 1983, 1984; DeLoache, Cassidy, & Brown, in press). The data from this research reveal very robust memory performance that is immune to a number of variables that might reasonably be expected to influence it.

The memory task is presented to the child as a game of hide-and-seek that will be played with a small stuffed animal (Big Bird, Mickey Mouse). The children are told that Big Bird is going to hide and that they should remember where Big

Bird is so they can find him later. The child then watches while the toy is hidden in some natural location in the large-scale environment, often in the child's own home. The hiding locations consist of places common to almost any living room, such as under a couch or chair cushion, behind a door, inside a cabinet, and so forth. A timer is set for a specified interval, and the child is told that when the bell rings, he can go find the toy. During the interval, the children are usually engaged in talking or playing with the experimenter. The children readily apprehend the goal and the rules of the game, and most of them greatly enjoy playing it.

Children between 1½ and 2½ years of age have exhibited excellent memory for the location of a single object hidden in the large-scale environment. The level of performance across studies is quite high, averaging over 80% errorless retrievals. (An errorless retrieval is defined as the child searching *first* at the correct location.) We have, in fact, often obtained ceiling-level memory performance from 2-year-old children.

Within the age range of children tested, age has not been reliably related to memory performance in the basic hide-and-seek task. In some studies we have found significant age differences, with older subjects between 24 and 30 months outperforming younger 18- to 24-month-olds. In other experiments, no age effects have appeared. Thus, there may be a small degree of developmental change in memory for simple spatial location over this age period (that is, memory for the location of a single object in a distinctive location), but even 1½-year-olds generally perform quite competently in the basic task.

I have recently collected preliminary data that suggest that individual differences of another sort may also have minimal impact on simple location memory. A small sample of young Down's Syndrome children (ranging in age from 29 to 53 months) has been observed in the basic hide-and-seek task. Their mean level of errorless retrievals was 75%, a figure that is equivalent to that of the normal, albeit younger, children we have studied.

Performance in the hide-and-seek game does not vary with the amount of practice or experience in the game; children given pre-training on the task do not do better than children participating in it for the first time, and performance generally remains stable over days. It also does not matter whether the children are verbally instructed to remember the toy's location or not; subjects told to "be sure to remember where Big Bird is so you can find him" do not do better than children who receive no memory orientation.

In summary, the data from studies using the hide-and-seek task reveal robust memory performance as early as 18 months of age. Minimal age differences occur, and practice and instructions do not make any difference. Memory for location thus seems to emerge as a natural consequence of the meaningful events that constitute the hide-and-seek game. Later in this chapter I consider the issue of whether location is encoded *automatically*, as Hasher and Zacks (1979) and others (Mandler, Seegmiller, & Day, 1977; von Wright, Gebhard, & Karttunen, 1975) have claimed.

EARLY STRATEGIES FOR REMEMBERING LOCATION

The second set of questions posed in the beginning of this chapter concerned mnemonic strategies. Are very young children in any way able to apply deliberate strategies to the task of remembering spatial location? If so, in what ways do their early strategies resemble mature memory strategies, and in what ways are they different?

A very large body of research exists concerning the use of mnemonic strategies by school-age children and adults. When presented with challenging material to be remembered, a mature learner is likely to interact spontaneously with the material to make it more memorable, for example, by rehearsing, organizing, or elaborating upon it. A subject's decision to invoke a strategy and the selection of which particular one to use may be fully conscious and reasoned (an extreme example being a professional mnemonist's selection of the method of loci to enable him to impress his audience), or the subject may be only dimly aware that he is doing anything special to learn or retain information. Whether or not a mnemonic strategy is used depends upon, among other things, the subject's estimate of the task difficulty: Problems that are too easy or too difficult are less likely to elicit strategic behavior than problems that present a moderate degree of challenge. Which particular strategy is selected depends upon the nature of the task; for example, one is more likely to use rehearsal than semantic elaboration to remember a string of digits. Finally, the adoption of an appropriate strategy typically improves memory performance.

The developmental literature indicates that mnemonic strategies are commonly employed by school-age children in a variety of situations, and that the sophistication of the strategies and their application increases steadily with age (Brown, et al., 1983). Much less is known about their origins and very early development—the "early competencies that serve as building blocks for subsequent" mnemonic achievements (Flavell, 1979, p. 909).

The received view is that 2-year-old or younger children are not capable of behaving strategically. They are seen as non-planful and non-strategic (Brown & DeLoache, 1978) and are assumed to be capable of involuntary, but not voluntary, memory activity (Smirnov & Zinchenko, 1969). In other words, young children are generally believed to be incapable of subordinating another activity in the service of a memory goal. The data from memory studies using verbal recall measures do nothing to dispel this view (Myers & Perlmutter, 1978).

The data from the basic hide-and-seek task that were reviewed earlier might also lead one to be skeptical about the possibility that 2-year-olds might exert any effort to facilitate remembering the location of the hidden toy: Their excellent memory for the location of the hidden object appears to emerge as a natural consequence of the meaningful game. Furthermore, manipulations that might be expected to elicit strategic behavior do not affect memory performance. For example, as mentioned previously, the level of errorless retrievals is the same regardless of whether or not the child is instructed to remember the toy's location.

In spite of the above, data from several experiments suggest that 2-year-old and even younger children do seem to exhibit some very simple forms or precursors of strategic behavior. The evidence consists of two main types: (1) Direct observation of simple strategy-like behaviors that occur differentially as a function of memory demands and some other variables; and (2) indirect evidence in the form of age differences in location memory tasks that require effortful processing (Hasher & Zacks, 1979) (that is, more effortful processing than is required for the basic hide-and-seek task). These two types of supporting evidence reflect two distinct approaches that are common in studies of the development of mnemonic strategies in older children and adults.

Direct Observation of Mnemonic Activity

The direct approach to the study of memory strategies involves direct observation of mnemonic activity and is exemplified by the classic study by Flavell, Beach, and Chinsky (1966). They observed the delay interval behavior of kindergarten and school-age children who were supposed to memorize a list of words. During the interval between the presentation of the items and the recall test, some children spontaneously rehearsed the words by silently mouthing them; and subsequent recall was improved by such rehearsal.

For younger children, there are actually two separate questions that must be addressed: Are very young children capable of deliberate or voluntary memory, and if so, do they employ any kinds of strategic measures to facilitate memory? A study by Somerville, Wellman, and Cultice (1983) seems to answer the first question in the affirmative. Mothers of 2- to 4-year-olds asked their children to remind them to do something at a later time. Even the 2-year-olds were quite successful at remembering to remind their mothers, as long as the message concerned something of high interest to the child (such as buying candy at the grocery store).

There is also some evidence of deliberate strategy use by 3- and 4-year-old children. Istomina (1975) observed the use of mnemonic techniques by preschool children in a naturalistic situation (but not in a standard laboratory memory task). Some preschool children who were supposed to remember a list of items to "purchase" at a pretend store were observed repeating the items over and over to themselves (i.e., rehearsing) as they traveled to the "store."

In my own laboratory, we have made similar observations of 3-year-old children. The children waited while an object was hidden in one room, and they then went to a different room to retrieve a similar object from a model of the original. As they moved from one room to the next, several children have been observed whispering to themselves phrases like, "under the couch, under the couch."

Further evidence of strategic activity by preschoolers comes from a study by Ornstein and Baker-Ward (1983). They presented 4- to 6-year-old children with a set of common objects. One group of children was instructed to remember a subset of the items, and another group was simply told to play with the objects. The children who had been told to remember, including the 4-year-olds in the group, behaved differently from the children just told to play. The remember group more often verbally labeled the objects they were supposed to remember, they inspected them more, but they played with them less.

One interesting result of this study was that even though the 4-year-olds' behavior differed as a function of memory instructions, there was no effect on their subsequent recall; that is, the remember group did not recall more items than the play group. Ornstein and Baker-Ward (1983) suggest that these children may be at "a point at which children have a clear awareness that something special is required in memorization situations, but that these special activities may not yield mnemonic dividends" (p. 5).

The strongest evidence of very early deliberate mnemonic activity comes from a clever experiment by Wellman, Ritter, and Flavell (1975) that used a nonverbal memory task. Three- and 4-year-old children watched while an experimenter hid a small toy dog under one of three cups. The experimenter then left the room for 40 seconds, instructing the children either to "remember where the dog is" or simply to "wait here with the dog." The children in the memory condition engaged in several simple behaviors that appeared to serve a mnemonic function. They looked at, pointed to, and touched the baited cup more often during the delay period than did the subjects in the wait condition. One child provided an especially clear example of visual rehearsal: She looked at the baited cup and nodded her head yes, turned to the unbaited cups and shook her head no, then looked at the correct cup again nodding affirmatively. Another child ensured a successful retrieval by keeping his hand on the relevant cup during the entire delay interval. These simple behavioral strategies correlated positively with memory performance; children who exhibited more of them more often succeeded in retrieving the toy dog at the end of the interval.

A group of 2-year-olds observed by Wellman et al. (1975) in the same task gave no evidence of the deliberate behaviors described for the 3- and 4-year-olds. However, this negative result is inconclusive because, as the authors point out, the task was not appropriate for the 2-year-olds: Fully a third of them failed to complete even three trials, often because they were unwilling to remain alone in the testing room. We are left with the question of whether children younger than 3 years of age might be capable of some kind of mnemonic effort.

Our first positive evidence in this regard came from a study that had actually been designed for a different purpose. Cassify (1980) compared 22-month-old children's performance in the hide-and-seek task in two different settings—their own homes and a laboratory playroom. This experiment was designed to see if the excellent performance obtained in previous work with the hide-and-seek game (DeLoache & Brown, 1979, 1983, 1984) might be in part attributable to the fact that the children had always been tested in a highly familiar environment. Contrary to this hypothesis, the rate of errorless retrievals did not differ for the two environments. However, Cassidy observed two things—that her young subjects engaged in several behaviors similar to those reported by Wellman et al. (1975), and that they seemed to do so more often in the unfamiliar laboratory than in their own homes. We have since conducted two additional experiments investigating this phenomenon.

In those experiments (DeLoache, Cassidy, & Brown, in press), two observers recorded the behavior of 22-month-old children (18 to 24 months in age) during the interval between when they saw the toy hidden and when they were allowed to search for it. We found that the children often interrupted their play with a set of attractive toys to return their attention to the ongoing memory task, engaging in a variety of target behaviors that indicated they were still preoccupied with the memory task. One such target behavior was relevant vocalization. The children frequently talked about the toy ("Big Bird"), the fact that it was hidden ("Big Bird hide"), where it was hidden ("Big Bird chair"), or about their plan to retrieve it later ("Me find Big Bird"). Other target behaviors included looking or pointing to the hiding place, hovering near it, and peeking at the toy or attempting to retrieve it early. For example, on a given trial, the child might stop coloring a picture and look toward the pillow under which the toy was hidden, saying, "Big Bird." After returning his attention to his coloring, he might later get up and walk over near the pillow and even peek at the toy or try to retrieve it.

These behaviors bear a striking resemblance to some of the more complex mnemonic strategies displayed by older subjects, especially to rehearsal and self-monitoring or checking. The subject who talks about Big Bird or its hiding place, or who looks or points at the hiding location, is bringing the to-be-remembered information to mind and keeping it activated, just as in rehearsal. Similarly, the child who hovers in the general area seems to be trying to keep in touch (literally or figuratively) with the correct location. Peeking at the toy may be a way of checking one's recollection or seeking reassurance that the toy is still there. Early retrieval attempts could help the child escape the memory demands altogether.

These data thus suggest that children younger than 2 years of age may in some rudimentary way be sensitive to the memory demands of the task. However, additional evidence would be needed before one could conclude that these target behaviors represent mnemonic strategies or even precursors of strategies. Several forms of supportive evidence have been obtained.

For one thing, the target behaviors occurred differentially as a function of the familiarity of the environment in which the task was embedded, as well as the familiarity of the task itself. In both studies we compared the behavior of children playing the hide-and-seek game in their own homes versus in a laboratory playroom. One study used a between-subjects design, and the other was a within-subjects design in which each child was observed in both settings, with the order of the settings counterbalanced. As Fig. 7.1 shows, the settings effect was consistent: In both experiments, significantly more target behaviors occurred in the laboratory than in the home.

Why should very young children be more oriented to a hidden object in an unfamiliar laboratory than in their own homes, especially since there was no evidence that embedding the hide-and-seek task in the laboratory increased its actual difficulty? (Recall that the level of errorless retrievals was the same in both settings.) One hypothesis is that the unfamiliarity of the laboratory may diminish the children's confidence that they will be able to remember where the toy is hidden. Their uncertainty induces them to engage in a variety of activities to keep alive their memory for the location of the toy until they are permitted to retrieve

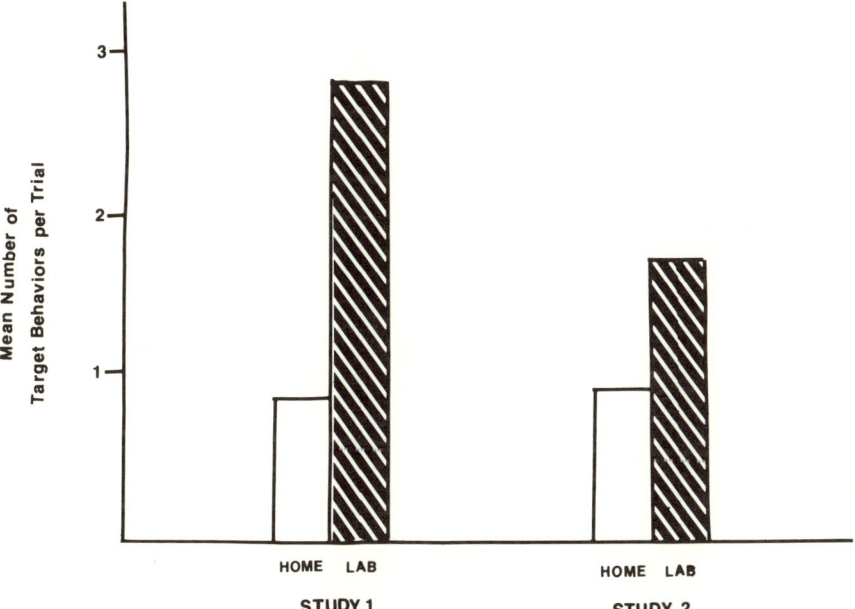

FIG. 7.1. The incidence of target behaviors as a function of setting. Significantly more occurred in the laboratory setting in both studies. (Study 1 used a between-subjects design, and Study 2 was within-subjects.) (DeLoache, Cassidy, & Brown, in press)

it. This suggestion is supported by the fact that Ceci and Bronfenbrenner (1983) reported a similar effect of more frequent monitoring activity in an unfamiliar laboratory than in the home. Ten- to 14-year-old children were given a prospective memory task (Meacham, 1982): They had to remember to take some cupcakes out of the oven in 30 minutes. The children observed in the laboratory were more vigilant: They more often monitored the passage of time by checking a clock than did the children tested in their own homes.

Our interpretation of the target behaviors is strengthened by the fact that in the within-subjects study significantly more target behaviors occurred on the first day of observation, during the children's initial exposure to the memory task, than on the second. The overall mean number of target behaviors for the two groups (lab-home and home-lab) combined dropped substantially and significantly from Day 1 to Day 2, as shown in Fig. 7.2. The day's effect was especially clear in an additional group of subjects tested only in the laboratory on two successive days (the lab-lab group). Thus, the target behaviors were prominent in two different situations where very young children might be expected to feel less confident—being tested in an unfamiliar setting or participating in an unfamiliar task. These two familiarity effects combined so that the condition that produced by far the most target behaviors was when the child's first exposure to the hide-and-seek game was in the laboratory (lab-lab and lab-home groups, Day

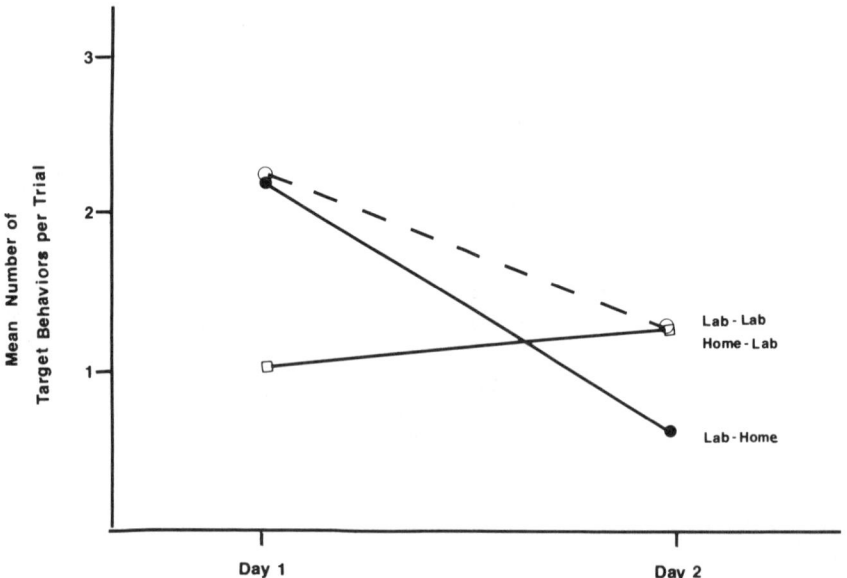

FIG. 7.2. The incidence of target behaviors over days. (DeLoache, Cassidy, & Brown, in press)

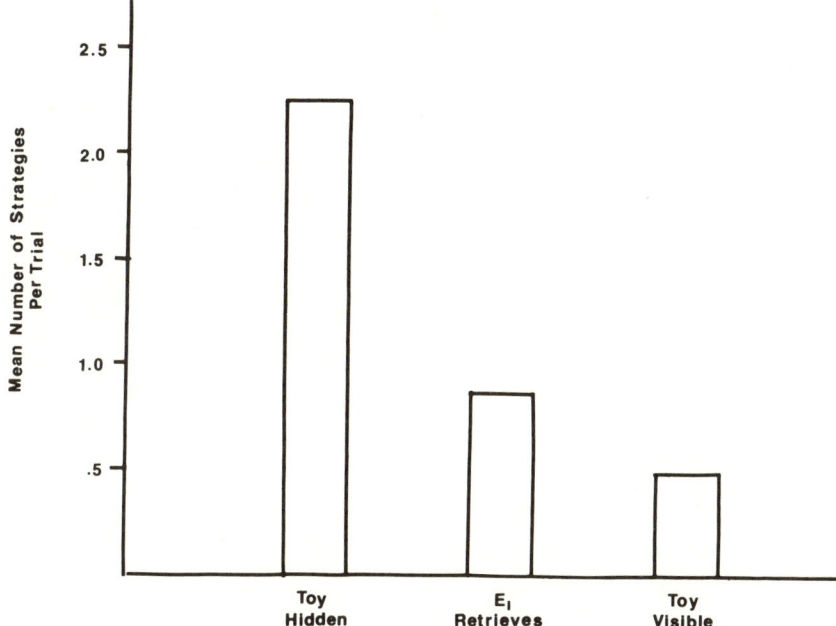

FIG. 7.3. Comparison of the level of target behaviors as a function of whether the child must remember the toy's location (Toy Hidden) or not (E retrieves and Toy Visible). (DeLoache, Cassidy, & Brown, in press)

1), while the least occurred when the familiar game was played in the child's own home on the second day (lab-home group, Day 2).

The question remains whether these target behaviors are exercised specifically in the service of memory. We assumed that if they are memory-related behaviors, they should only occur when the child is required to remember something, but not when there are no memory demands. Therefore, we tested two more groups of 22-month-old children in variations of the hide-and-seek game that removed the memory requirement. For one group (Toy Visible), the main modification to the task was that the toy remained in sight throughout the interval. At the time of hiding, the experimenter said to the child, "Big Bird needs to take a nap now, and when the bell rings, you can go and get him up." The toy was then placed so that it remained visible; for example, instead of hiding the toy under a cushion, the experimenter placed it on top of the cushion. For the second group (E Retrieves), the memory burden was removed from the children in a different way. For these subjects, everything was the same as in the standard hide-and-seek game except that instead of the child retrieving the toy at the end of the interval, the experimenter retrieved it. At the time of hiding, the experimenter said, "Let's hide Big Bird. When the bell rings, I'll go and find him." Figure

7.3 shows the number of target behaviors for these two non-memory conditions compared to the data for the standard memory task in which the toy is hidden and the child retrieves it. (These data are from the lab-lab group on Day 1.) In both of the non-memory conditions, very few target behaviors appeared, significantly fewer than in the standard memory task. Thus, when the toy was invisible and the children were supposed to retain its location in memory, they remained preoccupied with it during the interval. However, the children seemed unconcerned with the whereabouts of the toy when they did not have the responsibility for retrieving it themselves, and when the toy was visible during the interval. To rephrase a familiar term used for the pre-object permanence child, we might characterize the behavior of our subjects as, "in sight, out of mind."

The target behaviors thus appear to reflect a very early natural propensity to keep alive what must be remembered. These behaviors seem to arise spontaneously in the course of a memory task as a function of the child's uncertainty about the outcome of the task.

There was one additional and especially interesting behavior that we observed a few times in the regular hide-and-seek task. After watching the experimenter hide the toy, some children briefly checked a hiding place that had been used on a previous trial (most often the immediately preceding trial). Although this behavior was fairly rare (only six or seven subjects ever did it), it is intriguing in light of the fact that the most common error made by young children in memory for location tasks is searching a location that was correct on an earlier trial. It is possible that this behavior reflects mnemonic intent; perhaps these children were reassuring themselves of the irrelevance of the old location, eliminating it as a potential distractor.

Although the target behaviors are reminiscent of the mature strategies of rehearsal and monitoring and are similar to the deliberate mnemonic behaviors reported by Wellman et al. (1975) for preschool children, there is another impediment to interpreting them as strategies. In neither of the first two studies did they seem to facilitate memory performance: In both studies, the correlations between target behaviors and errorless retrievals did not approach significance. This result is reminiscent of the non-relationship between the strategy-like behaviors and memory performance reported by Ornstein and Baker-Ward (1983) for 4-year-old children. Thus, it would not be completely surprising if there was no relationship between the target behaviors we have observed in even younger children and their memory performance. However, more than half of the children in our experiments had perfect performance, and a majority of the remainder committed only one error. It could be that the target behaviors do facilitate remembering an object's location, but that the ceiling effects on performance obscured the relationship.

Another experiment was conducted to investigate this possibility, that is, to examine the relationship between the target behaviors and memory for location in the absence of ceiling effects. A multiple-hiding task was used that was expected to produce a substantially lower rate of errorless retrievals than the standard hide-and-seek task (DeLoache & Brown, 1979). On each trial, three attractive toys were sequentially hidden, each in a different natural hiding place. After the delay interval, the child was encouraged to find all the toys.

The multiple-hiding task did result in a lower rate of errorless retrievals— 53%, or 1.6 toys per trial. A detailed assessment of the relation between target behaviors and subsequent retrievals revealed a relationship between the incidence of strategy-like behaviors and memory performance. For each child, the mean number of target behaviors directed toward those toys that the child later retrieved was compared to the number directed toward toys that the child failed to retrieve. Toys that were subsequently retrieved had had more target behaviors directed toward them during the delay interval than had toys that were not retrieved. Thus, for any given child, the toys that he or she attended to during the interval were more often retrieved than were the toys the child ignored. This result is consistent with the expected effect of mnemonic strategies, namely, that engaging in them facilitates remembering.

What then can we conclude about the status of these target behaviors? A very liberal interpretation would be that they represent full-blown mnemonic strategies. A very conservative interpretation would be that they are simply by-products of the adoption of a memory goal, that they are just components of the "terminal responses" that the child plans or envisages making (Harris, 1984). For example, the child imagines going to the hiding place to retrieve the toy at the end of the interval, so he or she approaches the hiding place during the interval and maybe even hovers there or tries to retrieve the toy early. By this view, the target behaviors may in part reflect the young child's inability to inhibit the anticipated goal behaviors.

We suspect that the truth lies somewhere in between the extreme views of the young child's behavior as mere anticipatory goal responses versus fully conscious and planful strategies. On the one hand, we think that these target behaviors are more than simple anticipatory goal responses for at least three reasons. First, it is not clear to us why "terminal responses" should occur more frequently in unfamiliar than in familiar settings. Second is the fact that the most common target behavior is verbalization about the toy or the game. Unlike some of the other behaviors, verbalization is not one of the components of the terminal or retrieval response. Finally, it does not seem totally reasonable to require that to be considered strategic, a given behavior should not resemble the behavior that is to be carried out at the conclusion of the interval. If this requirement were enforced, the whole congregation of verbal rehearsal studies, from Flavell, Beach, and Chinsky (1966) on, would have to be rejected as evidence of mnemonic strategies.

On the other hand, we do not wish to interpret the target behaviors as full-fledged memory strategies for several reasons. First, their occurrence is probably limited to memory tasks in which there is considerable external support for the young child's mnemonic efforts. It is doubtful that the target behaviors we observed would have any contemporaneous counterparts in internal (i.e., verbal) memory tasks (Perlmutter & Myers, 1979). Second, these strategy-like behaviors are imperfectly tuned to task demands. The differentiation between the presence and absence of memory demands seems to be made quite early, but more experience may be required before the child is capable of accurately judging task difficulty and adjusting his or her behavior accordingly. The child has to learn what is and what is not relevant to determining the type and amount of effort required. To the extent that young children's task analysis is imperfect, then the use of strategies may not be perfectly adaptive. Finally, although our data establish that the target behaviors are memory-related, it seems to us unlikely that such young children consciously adopt them with the expectation that doing so will make future retrieval more probable.

In summary, the target behaviors described here can be interpreted as evidence of a very early natural propensity to keep alive what must be remembered. These memory-related behaviors occur spontaneously in the context of a memory-based search task in which the child has adopted the goal of retrieving a hidden object. They are appropriately sensitive to the presence of memory demands, but not yet finely tuned to task difficulty. It seems eminently reasonable that the young child's fledgling mnemonic efforts would meet some, but not all, of the criteria for mature strategies. In particular, it is not surprising that these early efforts would be elicited by the immediate situation, rather than emitted in a more planful fashion, and that they would require further modulation to be highly adaptive. Ornstein and Baker-Ward (1983) have made a similar argument about the early development of mnemonic skills. They suggest that memory development should be seen "as a broad continuum of mnemonic skill rather than a dichotomy of production or nonproduction of specific mnemonic mediators. . . . The picture suggested is that of a continuum from the first tentative application of various strategies (perhaps without mnemonic advantage) in certain highly salient stimulus situations to the efficient use of many mnemonic skills in a quite broad range of mnemonic contexts" (pp. 9–10). Waters and Andreassen (1983) also point out that strategies continue to develop after their initial acquisition. Later more elaborate mnemonic strategies may harness and build upon the spontaneous activities we observed, transforming these simple precursors into increasingly deliberate and planful behaviors in the service of memory.

The preceding studies thus show that children as young as 22 months of age exert some effort in the service of a memory goal. As I discussed above, the target behaviors occurred even in the absence of any apparent need for them. What would happen in a more complex task in which it would be difficult to remember the location of an object without engaging in active processing? We turn next to some studies that provide additional evidence of deliberate mnemonic behavior by very young children. In this case, strategic activity is inferred from the pattern of age differences that appear as a function of the level of effortful processing demanded by the tasks.

Indirect Evidence of Mnemonic Activity

Deliberate mnemonic effort is often not directly observable. Instead, strategic activity must be inferred from the comparison of performance in tasks that are judged to be amenable to strategic intervention and tasks in which strategic intervention should be impossible or unnecessary. In the developmental literature, a very common approach has been to compare the performance of different age groups in strategy-relevant and strategy-irrelevant tasks. The typical pattern of results (Brown, 1975) in such studies is that age differences tend to be smaller or nonexistent if strategies are impossible or not helpful. When more strategic effort is required, older children tend to be more likely than younger ones to spontaneously adopt relevant strategies, and hence significant age differences appear. For example, in a recognition memory task requiring recency judgments for a series of pictures, Brown (1975) and Brown, Campione, and Gilliard (1974) found no age differences between second- and fourth-grade subjects when no supplementary cues were available. When contextual, spatial, or color background cues were provided, the older children outperformed the younger ones, who failed to take advantage of the additional cues. Training the younger children to use these cues eliminated the developmental differences. This pattern of results was interpreted in terms of mnemonic strategy development: The older children strategically exploited the available cues to enhance memory, and they did so spontaneously; the less mature children did not use the cues on their own, although they could do so after training.

Two experiments based on this approach have been conducted with very young children. In both of these studies (DeLoache, 1984a; DeLoache & Brown, 1983), very young children were observed in conditions in which we assumed that stimulus intervention was (1) possible and likely to facilitate performance, (2) possible but unnecessary for excellent performance, or (3) quite difficult or impossible to apply. Our reasoning was that if we found the pattern of developmental differences described above (no age differences if stimuli are unnecessary or impossible, but significant age differences when strategies are applicable), this would constitute indirect evidence that very young children were behaving strategically. In this case, the form of the strategic intervention would be the active integration of available stimulus information when that was required for remembering.

In the first of these two studies (DeLoache & Brown, 1983), we compared the performance of two age groups of young children (21 and 26 months) in memory tasks that varied in terms of the amount of effortful processing required (that is, the tasks demanded different levels of cognitive effort for success). The least effortful task, the Natural condition, was the basic hide-and-seek task we have described in which an attractive toy was hidden on each trial in a different natural location in the child's home—in, under, or behind pieces of furniture. In the more effortful Landmark condition, the toy was hidden in one of four identical boxes, each of which was located on or near a piece of furniture. The nearby item of furniture was thus a landmark, a potential cue denoting which of the four boxes was correct. Note that the information that specified the location of the hidden toy—the piece of furniture—was the same in the Natural and Landmark conditions. However, the item of furniture was itself the hiding place in the Natural condition; whereas in the Landmark condition, the *relation* between the piece of furniture (the landmark) and the relevant box was what the child had to notice and remember. The child himself had to link or integrate the potential cue with the hidden object for it to be a functional cue. In a third condition, No Landmark, the toy was always hidden in one of four boxes that were arranged in the center of the room so that they were not near any potential landmarks. Since the boxes were all identical, their relative position was thus the only cue to the correct one.

These three conditions were assumed to vary in terms of the possibility and need for strategic intervention. In the Natural condition (the basic hide-and-seek task), strategic effort should not be necessary for excellent performance. In the No Landmark condition, there is no obvious strategy to be applied. In the Landmark condition, however, active processing of the relation between the landmark cue and the hidden object could facilitate, and indeed is probably necessary for, successful retrieval.

Figure 7.4 shows the level of errorless retrievals for the three conditions. In the No Landmark condition, where the toy was hidden in one of four boxes in the center of the room, the old and young groups were at the same relatively low level. Both age groups did substantially better in the Natural condition—the standard hide-and-seek task—and again there was no difference between them. The large difference in the performance of the two age groups in the Landmark condition indicated that the older children exploited the available landmarks, but the younger ones did not. The younger subjects may have failed to encode the relationship between the Landmark and the hidden object in the first place or they may have neglected to draw on that information for retrieval.

Based on this experiment and other literature on very young children's memory for location, DeLoache and Brown (1983) proposed that a crucial factor in young children's use of cue information has to do with the extent to which the child must actively integrate the available information with the hidden object. The precise nature of the stimuli should be of less importance. If this analysis is correct, then the pattern of age differences that occurred in the Natural and Landmark conditions should occur for any two sets of hiding places in which the relevant information is intrinsic to the actual hiding place in one condition, but must be integrated with the hidden object in the other. Although the existing

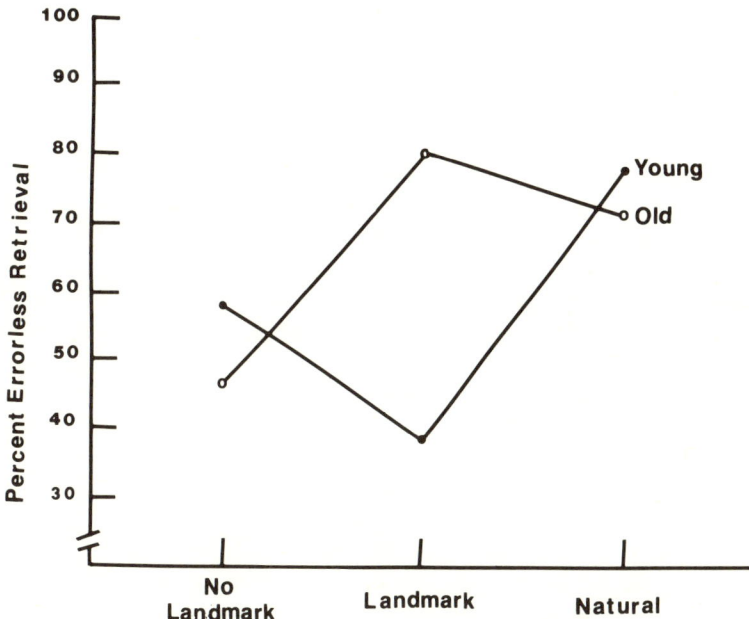

FIG. 7.4. Errorless retrievals as a function of the type of hiding place. (The apparent age × condition interaction is significant.) (DeLoache & Brown, 1983)

literature is not inconsistent with this hypothesis, it does not offer strong support for it, because the relevant comparisons must be made across several different studies that vary in many ways, including differing experimental procedures and non-comparable age groups. A rigorous test of this prediction would require a systematic comparison of young children's memory performance in conditions that are structurally analogous to DeLoache and Brown's (1983) Natural and Landmark conditions, but that involve very different types of hiding places and cues.

Accordingly, a study was conducted (DeLoache, 1984b; described in DeLoache, 1984a) in which two of the conditions had the same structural relationship to each other as the Natural and Landmark conditions. In one of the conditions, four visually distinctive containers (a tin can, a round woven basket, a plastic flowerpot, and a box covered with patterned paper) were used as hiding places for a small object (a piece of candy). The containers were analogous to the natural locations in that they were visually distinctive, but they differed from them in numerous other ways, including overall size (they all fit on a tabletop), spatial arrangement, and familiarity. In the second condition, the same containers were attached to the tops of four identical boxes, and the object was hidden in one of the boxes. This condition resembled the Landmark condition in that there was distinctive information available that could be integrated with the actual hiding places, but differed from it in other ways.

Effortfulness was also manipulated by including a third cue condition that was exactly like the second one (in which containers served as cues) except that photographs of the four containers were attached to the tops of the boxes. It was assumed that pictures would be less salient cues than the real objects (Daehler, Lonardo, & Bukatko, 1979). It was hypothesized that the ease of integrating an unrelated cue with a hidden object might depend in part on the salience of that cue, with more salient cues requiring less effortful processing.

In all three cue conditions, the containers or boxes either remained stationary after the object had been hidden, or they were rearranged. Moving the stimuli eliminated relative spatial position as a cue and left the visual information (the containers or pictures) as the only reliable cues for retrieval. Thus, only if a subject had fully integrated the available cue with the hidden object would he or she be able to retrieve the object.

The results of this study are shown in Fig. 7.5. The most important comparison is between the Container = Location and Container = Cue conditions, that is, between the two conditions that are structurally analogous to the DeLoache and Brown (1983) Natural and Landmark conditions. As can be clearly seen in the figure, there were no developmental differences in the least effortful

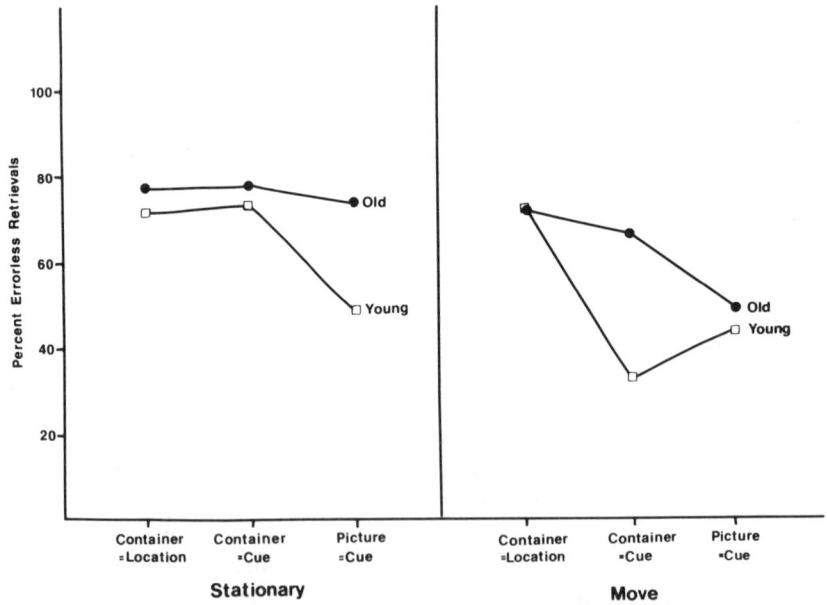

FIG. 7.5. Errorless retrievals as a function of different kinds of cues. (DeLoache, 1984a)

condition, but there were substantial age differences in the more effortful ones. In the least effortful condition, in which all of the hiding places were visually distinctive (Container = Location), both the older and younger children achieved a high level of errorless retrievals, and the two groups did not differ, even when the stimuli were rearranged. When the same distinctive visual information was available as a cue but had to be integrated by the child with the hidden object (Container = Cue), the two age groups were equivalent so long as the stimuli remained stationary, but a significant age difference appeared when the boxes were moved. The older children readily exploited the container cues, but the younger children's performance suffered when these cues were the only reliable source of information about the location of the hidden object (Container = Cue/Move). These results, like those obtained by DeLoache and Brown (1983), reveal the presence or absence of age differences as a function of the extent of effortful processing required by the task. If very little cognitive effort is required, old and young children do equally well; but if more effortful activity is necessary for success, the younger subjects have difficulty.

Cue salience, which was hypothesized to be related to the ease of processing, also affected the children's exploitation of the potential cues. All aspects of the Container = Cue and Picture = Cue conditions were identical, except that the available cues differed in salience (i.e., two-dimensional pictures vs. three-dimensional objects). The older children effectively exploited the real object cues (Container = Cues). They also benefited from picture cues that supplemented spatial position information (Picture = Cue/Stationary), but not from pictures that were the sole reliable cues to the location of the hidden object. The younger subjects profited to some extent from the stationary object cues, but not at all from the picture cues or from the rearranged object cues. Note that the pattern of results for the older children in the Container = Cue and Picture = Cue conditions is exactly the same as that for the younger children in the Container = Location and Container = Cue conditions.

The reason for the age differences obtained here and in DeLoache and Brown's (1983) Landmark condition becomes clearer when we examine the younger children's performance in the Container = Cue/Stationary condition. The absolute level of errorless retrievals in this condition (73%) suggests that the available container cues did in fact assist the younger subjects. For one thing, their performance was at the same high level as that of the younger children in the Container = Location condition. Second, it was significantly higher than the level achieved by the young group in either of the Picture = Cue conditions. In addition, we can assume that the young children in the Container = Cue/Stationary condition performed better than they would have done had no visual cues been available. Their level of errorless retrievals was substantially higher than the approximately 50% that has been frequently reported for 2-year-olds in similar tasks when only spatial position information is available, that is, when an object is hidden in one of a stationary set of identical containers (Blair, Perlmutter, & Myers, 1978; Daehler, Bukatko, Benson, & Myers, 1976; DeLoache & Brown, 1983; Horn & Myers, 1978; Perlmutter et al., 1981).

These data indicate that the younger children did notice and even profited from the available container cues when those cues remained stationary. This rules out one account of their failure to exploit the same cues in the move condition; their poor performance was not due to a simple failure to notice the available cues in the first place. The younger children's problem may be that even though they noticed and encoded the container cues, they did not fully integrate them with the hidden object so that when the boxes were rearranged, the link between the cue and the object was not firm enough to support retrieval. Or they may have adequately encoded the relation between the cue and the object, but then failed to draw on that information to guide their retrieval efforts. Thus, this study does not enable us to definitively situate the observed age differences in either encoding or retrieval processes, but it does provide additional evidence that those differences have to do with the extent of active, effortful processing performed by the children in the service of the memory goal.

There is one discrepancy between the results of the present study and the DeLoache and Brown (1983) landmark study: The younger children in the Container = Cue/Stationary condition did extremely well, whereas the same age group in the structurally similar Landmark condition performed quite poorly. A possible reason for this difference has to do with the ease of using relative spatial position information. In the Container = Cue condition, the boxes were close together and were arranged in a regular configuration on top of a table. They could all be seen at once, and each bore a constant relation to the child's body when he or she faced them. In contrast, the boxes in the Landmark condition were spread out irregularly around the child's living room so that the child was less likely to see all four at one time and may have needed to turn his or her body to orient from one to another. Thus, it is possible that relative spatial position was salient and an easily exploitable cue in the present study, but not in the landmark one.

The landmark and container cues studies provide indirect evidence of strategic intervention. This conclusion is based on several aspects of the data. (1) The pattern of age differences that was found in both experiments is the same pattern that has been taken as evidence of strategy development in older children (Brown, 1975; Brown et al., 1974). The case would, of course, be strengthened if we could provide some kind of training to the 22-month-old subjects and elevate their performance to the level of the 26-month-olds. (2) The age difference does not seem to be attributable to simple differences in attentional capacity or deployment. The younger children profited from the presence of a visual cue when the containers remained stationary (Container = Cue/Stationary), showing that they were not unaware of the cues. However, they did not exploit them in the active, effective way the older children did. Very strong evidence that the older children's advantage in these studies is the result of strategic intervention would be if they do well in the Landmark and Container = Cue conditions when they know they have to remember the location of the object, but not when no memory orientation is given. (3) The direct observation of mnemonic effort by very young children described in the preceding section lends credence to the interpretation of the indirect evidence presented here as reflecting strategic activity. The convergence of these two sources of data suggests that very young children are capable of simple deliberate effort in the service of a memory goal.

It is clear that an important next step will be to investigate the development of mnemonic strategies from the rudimentary forms observed in our 2-year-old subjects' memory for location to the variety of elaborate, effective strategies evidenced by older children. In the final section of this chapter, I offer some speculations about some of the factors that may contribute to early mnemonic development. Before doing so, however, it may be useful to relate the research described in this chapter to other literature on memory for location. In particular, I would like to consider this research in light of Hasher and Zacks' (1979) theory of automatic cognitive processes. The question that concerns us in this section is whether, or under what circumstances, spatial location is encoded automatically.

IS SPATIAL LOCATION ENCODED AUTOMATICALLY?

Children, as well as adults, frequently remember spatial information without intending to, such as the location on the page of something they have read (e.g., Rothkopf, 1971; Zechmeister, McKillup, Pasko & Bespalec, 1975) or the spatial positions of items whose identity (but not location) they have been instructed to remember (Mandler, Seegmiller, & Day, 1977; von Wright, et al., 1975). These and other phenomena have led some researchers to conclude that spatial location information is encoded "routinely" (Schulman, 1973) or "automatically" (Hasher & Zacks, 1979; Mandler et al., 1977; von Wright et al., 1975).

The most explicit and comprehensive position relevant to the encoding of spatial location is that of Hasher and Zacks (1979). They propose that there is a "continuum of attentional requirements among encoding processes" (p. 358), with the processes at one end being fully automatic and the processes at the other end requiring the expenditure of considerable attention and cognitive effort. "When a person attends to an input, some of its attributes are automatically encoded into long-term memory whereas others require more or less effortful processing to be encoded into a permanent memory trace" (p. 358). According to Hasher and Zacks, spatial location is one of the attributes that is encoded automatically for any event that is the focus of attention. (Other automatically encoded attributes include the time and frequency of occurrence of events.)

Awareness or intention is not required for automatic encoding, nor can the process be willfully inhibited. Little or no cognitive effort is expended.

In contrast to automatic processes, Hasher and Zacks (1979) propose that effortful processes do require cognitive effort, their use is voluntary and is usually conscious, and they limit one's ability to simultaneously perform other effortful processes. Prototypical examples of effortful processes include mnemonic strategies such as rehearsal, organization, and others.

With respect to the *origin* of these processes, Hasher and Zacks (1979) suggest that automatic processes (encoding spatial location, frequency, and time of events) are innate. (Other processes can become automatic through extensive practice; LaBerge, 1973; Schneider & Shiffrin, 1977; Shiffrin & Schneider, 1977.) These genetically programmed automatic processes are assumed to be "minimally influenced by differences in age, culture, education, early experience, and intelligence" (p. 360). Because they are innate, little or no developmental change should occur. By contrast, effortful processes become more efficient with practice, and they should show substantial developmental change. Hasher and Zacks (1979) thus predict that there should be minimal age differences in remembering the simple location of an event or object. However, if a memory for location task is modified to require more effortful processing, then age differences should appear in the more effortful task.

Hasher and Zacks' (1979) position regarding the automaticity of the processing of spatial location has been disputed on empirical grounds. One source of negative evidence is research on age differences in location memory. Although Hasher and Zacks (1979) assert that age differences should not be found for automatic processes, several researchers have reported significantly better location memory performance by young or middle-age adults than by elderly subjects (Light & Zelinsky, 1983; Park, Puglisi, & Lutz, 1982; Pezdek, 1983). Age differences in location memory have also appeared in research with children (e.g., Acredolo, Pick, & Olsen, 1975), including some studies that have generally been taken as evidence for automatic processing of location because of equivalent performance for intentional and incidental memory conditions (Mandler et al., 1977; von Wright et al., 1975).

One problem with accepting these reports of age differences as negative evidence regarding automatic encoding of spatial location is that the age differences could originate in the retrieval demands rather than the encoding process. As Hasher and Zacks (1979) explicitly state, if effortful retrieval is required by a task, then age differences may appear, even if the spatial information had been encoded automatically. This is an important consideration, especially in light of data indicating that retrieving information from memory is more problematic for younger children than storing it (Brainerd, Howe, & Kingma, & Brainerd, in press).

Another source of negative evidence for Hasher and Zacks' formulation comes from studies contrasting memory under intentional versus incidental memory orientations. If location is encoded automatically, then memory for location should not be affected by the presence or absence of instructions to remember location information. However, some studies have found better memory for location under intentional than incidental conditions (e.g., Light & Zelinsky, 1983; Park et al., 1982). There are even some reports of significantly *poorer* performance by some subjects under instructions to remember location information than with no orientation (Park et al., 1982).

The results of my own research that have been summarized in this chapter are for the most part consistent with Hasher and Zacks' position. We have found minimal developmental differences in young children's memory for location in the basic, relatively non-effortful hide-and-seek task, but substantial age differences in the more effortful ones. The high level of performance by both age groups in the least effortful conditions in the DeLoache (1984b) and DeLoache and Brown (1983) studies is consistent with Hasher and Zacks' (1979) contention that memory for spatial location should emerge early and that minimal age differences should occur in it. (It should be noted that although these data are consistent with Hasher and Zacks' predictions, they do not provide unequivocal support for innate automatic processes. The same pattern of results would be expected if the abilities were not innate, but simply early developing.) Furthermore, as they hypothesized, we have found no effects for type of instructions, extent of experience, and individual differences in intelligence (although these last data are quite preliminary). On empirical grounds, then, the research summarized here on very young children's memory for the location of a hidden object lends some support to Hasher and Zacks' argument that spatial location information is automatically encoded.

Other aspects of our research, however, raise conceptual questions about automatic processing of spatial location. One of them has to do with the specification of the meaning of spatial location. What counts as a spatial location? In the Container = Location condition (DeLoache, 1984b), the object was hidden in one of four containers in a spatial array in front of the child. Each container occupied a unique spatial position, and it seems appropriate to think of the task as a memory for location problems. It seems clear that Hasher and Zacks would predict that the spatial location of the hidden object should be automatically encoded, and the very high performance in the Container = Location condition could reflect such automatic processing.

In the same study (DeLoache, 1984b), the containers were sometimes rearranged after the object had been hidden. Can we still think of them as representing spatial locations? What results would now be predicted by the theory? That is, what happens when part or all of the information specifying location is removed after the spatial location of the event has been encoded automatically? It seems to me that one would have to predict that memory performance should be disrupted to some extent in this situation. Surely any conceptualization of spatial location would have to include relative position as part of the relevant information; since that information is no longer available, performance should suffer. However, the data are at variance with this prediction. In the Container = Location condition, rearranging the containers had no effect; memory performance was the same regardless of whether the distinctive containers remained in the same spatial locations or not.

These results suggest that automatic encoding of spatial location may not be the most appropriate characterization of the process involved. It seems that what was encoded was not so much spatial location per se, but rather something about the relation between the hidden object and the container in which it was hidden. In the Container = Location condition, there was a direct relation between the two; the object was in immediate interaction with the container. Thus, the robust performance that was observed in this condition may have more to do with the directness or immediacy of the relation between the available information and the memory object than with automatically processed spatial information.

The data from the other two conditions in this study (DeLoache, 1984b) are consistent with this interpretation. The relation between the hidden object and the container in the Container = Cue and Picture = Cue conditions was only indirect. The object was in direct interaction with the box in which it was placed, but it was less directly related to the cue situated on top of the box. The subject had to provide the link between the container cue or picture cue and the invisible object. As we have seen, memory performance was poorer and age differences appeared in these conditions. Perhaps memory for location tends to be so robust precisely because there typically is a direct relation between a memory item or event and its spatial location.

WHAT ACCOUNTS FOR THE DEVELOPMENT OF MNEMONIC STRATEGIES?

The research described here has provided evidence of active mnemonic effort at a very early age. The behavior of the 1½- to 3-year-old children in the hide-and-seek studies revealed a sensitivity to memory demands: The children adopted the goal of retrieving the hidden toy, they engaged in simple actions that were directed toward the memory object during the interval, and their behavior differed as a function of the presence or absence of memory demands. The work of Wellman and his colleagues also shows deliberate remembering and strategic activity in young children (Somerville et al., 1983; Wellman et al., 1975). These data force a revision of the standard view of the very young child as incapable of voluntary remembering and as wholly nonstrategic. And they raise questions about development. How do the simple, context-specific, not-necessarily-effective strategies of the very young child evolve into the array of complex, flexible, and effective strategies available to the older child? What spurs the further development of strategic activity? In what domains does early development occur?

I have some intuitions about these questions. I suspect that an important impetus for further mnemonic development is provided by the young child's social interactions with adults, most notably his parents. Many theorists (e.g., Flavell & Wellman, 1977) have made similar conjectures. In summarizing the Soviet view of memory development, Ratner (1980) states: "Acquisition of mnemonic skills, then, is thought to be rooted in the social activities of daily life and parents are seen, at least in part, as instrumental in bringing about the shift from involuntary to voluntary memory" (p. 52). I would guess that a likely domain for the refinement of early strategies is external memory—remembering where things are. I use the terms *intuition, suspect, guess,* advisedly. I am speculating in the almost complete absence of relevant data. The existing evidence concerning parental effects on early memory is disappointingly small, and one of the most positive conclusions that can be drawn from it at this time is that a great deal of potentially exciting research needs to be done.

There are a number of ways that parents, or other adults such as preschool teachers, might influence the development of the young child's memory skills. Three possible avenues are considered here: memory demands, direct instruction, and joint problem solving.

Parental Memory Demands

A substantial proportion of the utterances addressed to infants and young children consists of questions of many different types (Newport, Gleitman, & Gleitman, 1977). Among the most demanding are queries about events in the remote past, that is, requests that the child remember and/or report on some previous experience. It seems possible that parental demands for recall and remembering might increase the child's awareness of memory goals, give him practice at attempting retrieval, and lead to the development of voluntary remembering and specific strategies. In the missing shoes dialogue, the mother's questions contain a great deal of memory-related information. Her questions about where the child last took off his shoes and what he did when he came home can be seen as attempts to establish a critical search area. Experience responding to questions such as these might help the child develop some understanding of the relevance of what he can remember to what he should do next. The mother's command, "Think!" serves as an instruction to the child to be persistent in his internal retrieval efforts.

In a study designed to address these issues, Ratner (1980) recorded everyday conversations of pairs of mothers and their 30- or 42-month-old children. Approximately one fourth of the mothers' utterances to the children were questions, which were classified as asking about general knowledge or about specific events, either past, present, or future. Only a minority of the mothers' questions concerned past events. Of the total number of event questions that were asked, only 14% concerned events that occurred in the remote past, that is, events prior to the beginning of the observations. Sachs (1983) and Lucariello (1983), who have examined mother-child conversations in some detail, also report a low incidence for conversations about past events.

This maternal bias toward talking about the present occurs in other, more specialized interactional contexts as well. For example, in research that I have conducted on joint picture book reading by mothers and toddlers, the majority of the mothers' statements and questions were in the present tense (DeLoache, in press). Some mothers, however, occasionally expanded the focus of the interaction to discuss past events, explicitly relating the material in the book to the child's own previous experience. Hoping to get more data on mothers' questioning about past events and their children's responses to those questions, we observed pairs of mothers and 24- to 36-month-old children looking at family photograph albums together. Here, a large proportion of the material in the "books" has to do with the child's own past experience; indeed, the child himself is often the focus of the photographs. We expected that with this contextual support, the mother would be substantially more likely to ask the child to recall past events. To our surprise, however, the vast majority of the mothers' queries were still in the present tense. For over three fourths of the pictures, the mother asked the child to describe, but not to recall, the content of the pictures: The child was asked to name the people present (Who's that?"), to tell where they are located ("Whose house is that?"), or to describe what is happening. Obviously, the child's response is based on memory for the relevant information, but it is not memory for specific past events. Generally, the mothers of the young children in this research have shown a strong bias to ask their children to report general knowledge rather than to recount specific events from personal past experience.

Ratner's data on everyday mother-child conversations and our own work on joint picture book interactions do not appear to offer much support for the idea that parental memory demands are an important force in early mnemonic development. Both studies reveal a low baseline of maternal demands for event memory. Another finding that was reported by both investigators was the fact that the word *remember* was used infrequently by the mothers. Other evidence that might be taken as negative is the low level of correct responding by the children. More often than not, the young subjects in these studies did not answer their mothers' memory questions (often they did not respond at all).

Overall, then, mothers of young children infrequently request that their children recall past events or experiences. However, it may be incorrect to infer from this that parental memory demands do not play a role in the development of the child's mnemonic skills. Ratner (1980) reported that even though the overall baseline level of memory demands for past events was low, individual mothers differed widely in their proclivity to question the child about the past: "Even though all mothers tended to talk primarily about present events with their children, some mothers were consistently more likely than others to introduce discussions of the past into their dialogues" (p. 58).

This finding takes on added significance when the children's performance in a subsequent laboratory memory task is examined. For the older children (the 42-month-olds), there was a significant positive correlation between maternal questions about past events and the child's memory performance: "Children whose mothers asked many questions about past events which required retrieval of information about events removed from the present were best able to retrieve information from long-term memory" (p. 61). These data thus provide some tentative support for the suggestion that parental memory demands may constitute an impetus for continued development of the child's memory skills during the preschool period. It should be noted, however, that Ratner's data are correlational. They could reflect a tendency for the mothers of more advanced or verbally capable children to ask more questions about past events. This direction of influence is quite possible, given the tendency of mothers to demand from their children the maximal level of performance of which they think the child is capable (DeLoache, in press). More research is needed to clarify this relationship, and to discover more about the nature of parental memory demands and their role in the young child's memory development.

Direct Instruction

A second possible source of parental influence is direct instruction. It is conceivable that parents of young children give them explicit directions concerning the existence and appropriate use of mnemonic strategies. Again, the available data are quite sparse, and the data that do exist do not offer much support for this idea.

Ratner (1980) reported that the mothers in her study "provided little knowledge about memory directly to their children" (p. 59). As noted above, use of the word *remember* was infrequent and, more generally, only a few utterances directly concerned memory. However, maternal use of the term *remember* was positively and significantly correlated with the children's performance on the laboratory memory test. Thus, Ratner's data indicate that mnemonic instruction is not a common activity by parents, but it may still be an important one.

A recent study by Justice (1983) examined strategy instruction by parents of 3½-year-old children. The mother-child pairs were observed playing a memory game ("Memory") that requires remembering the identities and locations of picture cards that are face down. Justice reported that the mothers made few attempts to instruct their children in the use of mnemonic strategies, in spite of the fact that there are simple, nonverbal strategies that are applicable to the game. No relationship was found between any maternal behaviors and the children's performance in a subsequent memory task. However, Justice reported that most of the mothers' effort was directed toward getting the children to follow the rules of the game. I have argued before (DeLoache, 1980) that a child is unlikely to display any higher level regulatory skills (such as memory strategies) in tasks that he does not understand. Similarly, it is not clear how a parent could instruct a child in strategies to apply to a game that the child does not understand in the first place. The rudiments of a task must be mastered before the task can be carried out in a sophisticated manner.

Although there is little positive evidence of parental strategy instruction, it may still be premature to conclude that this is a negligible factor in early mnemonic development. One thing that suggests caution in this regard is the fact that parents claim that they do try to teach memory skills. Justice (1983) interviewed the mothers in her study, and all of them reported encouraging their children to engage in various behaviors to enhance memory. Unfortunately, the exact nature of the mothers' behavior is not clear from this brief report. Griffith and Lange (1984) have also collected interview data in which parents (of kindergarten to second-grade children) reported engaging in some strategy teaching. Obviously, more research is needed to resolve this issue.

Joint Problem Solving

A third possible source of parental influence on young children's mnemonic development is the modeling of mnemonic strategies. There are numerous everyday problems in which parents may model memory strategies. A number of common examples that probably occur in almost all homes involve setting up external cues to provoke appropriate remembering or to eliminate the need for it. Every young child has probably seen his mother setting a kitchen timer to indicate when a cake should be taken from the oven (thereby eliminating the need to remember when to take it out), making and using shopping lists, and writing notes or calendar entries to jog her memory to do something at a future time (prospective memory—Meacham, 1982).

Possibly more important, and more instructive, is parental modeling of mnemonic strategies in the context of joint memory activity. May we consider for the last time the missing shoes dialogue at the beginning of the chapter. After asking a series of unsuccessful questions, the mother volunteers to help the child find the shoes. In the process of the ensuing joint search, the mother probably continues to try to get the child to recall relevant pieces of information. At the same time, she is likely to model systematic search skills, possibly verbalizing the basis for her actions, thereby communicating to the child that some locations are better places to search than others. For example, the mother might lead the child first to the door through which the child generally enters the house, pointing out that the child *must* have been wearing his shoes at that point. (Notice that this would define one end of a critical search space, a la Wellman & Somerville,

1982.) The mother might next proceed to lead the child to other likely locations, such as the child's room and favorite play areas.

In this hypothetical example, what was posed as a memory problem for the child alone is converted into a problem to be solved through joint effort. The mother structures the actual search, and in many ways she also structures the child's memory retrieval efforts. She asks the child to recall important relevant information, and she repeatedly prompts the child to persist in his recall attempts. She exposes him to potentially useful cues, both external (taking the child to the door) and internal (asking what the child did when he got home). The mother thus provides external, or other, regulation (Vygotsky, 1978; Wertsch, 1979; Wertsch, McNamee, McLane, & Budwig, 1980) for the child's mnemonic activity. Presumably, as the child's capabilities grow, the mother will take an increasingly less active and directive role, and the child will assume more and more of the responsibility for organizing and directing his own behavior. According to this formulation, the precise nature and the frequency of the memory demands and questions asked of the child might be less informative than the process that follows the child's non-response to those demands. How the parent assists the child to manage at least a minimal response would be our main concern. Is there any evidence that memory strategy development is assisted by such joint mnemonic effort? None that I know of; however, as far as I am aware, no one has directly examined this sort of activity by parent and child, so it is an open question.

This section has made it abundantly clear that very little is known about the everyday menmonic activities of young children and the role of their parents in such activities. Although some interesting data have been collected, the existing research is limited to a small number of subjects from a restricted age range: Ratner (1980) observed ten 30- and ten 42-month-olds, and Justice's (1983) sample comprised ten 42-month-old children. Additional research is needed concerning the social context of young children's memory activities, and obviously the prime target for such research will be further studies of parent-child interaction.

A second target for research on the social context of early memory would be the preschool classroom—another arena in which young children may receive mnemonic training. I am not aware of any research on this subject, but informal observation of preschool teachers' behavior has suggested to me that a number of simple mnemonic strategies are trained in this setting ("Put your artwork in your cubby so you will remember to take it home"). In conversations with teachers about this topic, some of them are quite aware of providing mnemonic training and may even have this as an explicit teaching objective. Others do not report having specific mnemonic goals and do not think they engage in such training. However, when queried about precise mnemonic techniques, they often respond, "Oh, of course, I do *that*."

In summary, there is really very little basis for evaluating the often-made suggestion that social interaction constitutes an important force in mnemonic development. As I stated earlier, I suspect that this hypothesis is correct, and I am currently making plans to investigate naturally occurring mnemonic activity between preschool children and their parents and teachers.

A very recent event demonstrated to me the impact of the parental instruction in mnemonic techniques and strategies that goes on in at least one home I am familiar with—my own. This example, by the way, took place *after* I had already written the beginning of this chapter around the missing shoes problem. Our family was at a friend's house. My 5-year-old wanted to take off his shoes so he could do gymnastics on our friend's living room couch. Apparently realizing that they would have to be retrieved when it was time to go home, he called me over, pointed at his shoes on the floor in a corner, and very sternly instructed me: "Look, Mom. I'm leaving my shoes right here, and it's your responsibility to remember where they are." This example testifies to the potential efficacy of training mnemonic strategies in young children, but somehow I'm not sure this is quite the effect I had in mind.

ACKNOWLEDGMENT

This research was supported by Grant HD-05951 from the National Institute of Child Health and Human Development.

REFERENCES

Acredolo, L. P., Pick, L. L., & Olsen, M. G. (1975). Environmental differentiation and familiarity as determinants of children's memory for spatial location. *Developmental Psychology, 11,* 495–501.

Ashmead, D. H., & Perlmutter, M. (1980). Infant memory in every day life. In M. Perlmutter (Ed.), *New directions for child development: Children's memory.* San Francisco: Jossey-Bass.

Blair, R., Perlmutter, M., & Myers, N. A. (1978). The effects of unlabeled and labeled picture cues on very young children's memory for location. *Bulletin of the Psychonomics Society, 11,* 46–48.

Brainerd, C. J., Howe, M. L., Kingma, J., & Brainerd, S. H. (in press). On the measurement of storage and retrieval contributions to memory development. *Journal of Experimental Child Psychology.*

Brown, A. L. (1975). The development of memory: Knowing, knowing about knowing, and knowing how to know. In H. W. Reese (Ed.), *Advances in child development and behavior* (Vol. 10). New York: Academic Press.

Brown, A. L., Bransford, J. D., Ferrara, R. A., & Campione, J. C. (1983). Learning, remembering, and understanding. In J. H. Flavell & E. M. Markman (Eds.), *Handbook of child psychology: Vol. 3. Cognitive development.* New York: Wiley.

Brown, A. L., Campione, J. C., & Gilliard, D. M. (1974). Recency judgments in children: A production deficiency in the use of redundant background cues. *Developmental Psychology, 10*, 303.

Brown, A. L., & DeLoache, J. S. (1978). Skills, plans, and self-regulation. In R. Siegler (Ed.), *Children's thinking: What develops?* Hillsdale, NJ: Lawrence Erlbaum Associates.

Cassidy, D. J. (1980). *The effects of environmental familiarity on very young children's memory for object location.* Unpublished master's thesis, University of Illinois at Urbana-Champaign.

Ceci, S. J., & Bronfenbrenner, U. (1983). *"Don't forget to take the cupcakes out of the oven": Prospective memory and context.* Paper presented at the meeting of the Society for Research in Child Development, Detroit.

Daehler, M., Bukatko, D., Benson, K., & Myers, N. (1976). The effects of size and color cues on the delayed response of very young children. *Bulletin of the Psychonomic Society, 7*, 65–68.

Daehler, M. W., Lonardo, R., & Bukatko, D. (1979). Matching and equivalence judgments in very young children. *Child Development, 50*, 170–179.

DeLoache, J. S. (1980). Naturalistic studies of memory for object location in very young children. In M. Perlmutter (Ed.), *New directions for child development: Children's memory*, San Francisco: Jossey-Bass.

DeLoache, J. S. (1984a). Oh where, oh where: Memory-based searching by very young children. In C. Sophian (Ed.), *Origins of cognitive skills.* Hillsdale, NJ: Lawrence Erlbaum Associates.

DeLoache, J. S. (1984b). *Toddlers' exploitation of cues in remembering the location of a hidden object.* Unpublished manuscript.

DeLoache, J. S. (in press). What's this? Maternal questions in joint picture book reading with toddlers. *Quarterly Newsletter of the Laboratory of Comparative Human Cognition.*

Deloache, J. S., & Brown, A. L. (1979). Looking for Big Bird: Studies of memory in very young children. *Quarterly Newsletter of the Laboratory of Comparative Human Cognition, 1*(4), 53–57.

DeLoache, J. S., & Brown, A. L. (1983). Very young children's memory for the location of objects in a large-scale environment. *Child Development, 54*, 888–891.

DeLoache, J. S., & Brown, A. L. (1984). Intelligent searching by very young children. *Developmental Psychology, 20*, 37–44.

DeLoache, J. S., Cassidy, D. J., & Brown, A. L. (in press). Precursors of mnemonic strategies in very young children's memory for the location of hidden objects. *Child Development.*

Flavell, J. H. (1979). Metacognition and cognitive monitoring. *American Psychologist, 34*, 906–911.

Flavell, J. H., Beach, D. H., & Chinsky, J. M. (1966). Spontaneous verbal rehearsal in memory tasks as a function of age. *Child Development, 37*, 283–299.

Flavell, J. H., & Wellman, H. M. (1977). Metamemory. In R. V. Kail, Jr., & J. W. Hagen (Eds.), *Perspectives on the development of memory and cognition.* Hillsdale, NJ: Lawrence Erlbaum Associates.

Gelman, R. (1978). Cognitive development. *Annual Review of Psychology, 29*, 297–332.

Griffith, S. B., & Lange, G. (1984). *Children's learning and memorization experiences at home and at school: Parents', teachers', and children's perceptions.* Unpublished manuscript.

Harris, P. L. (1983). Infant cognition. In M. M. Haith & J. J. Campos (Eds.), *Handbook of child psychology: Vol. 2. Infancy and developmental psychobiology.* New York: Wiley.

Harris, P. L. (1984). Commentary on papers on origins of spatial skills. In C. Sopnian (Ed.), *Origins of cognitive skills.* Hillsdale, NJ: Lawrence Erlbaum Associates.

Hasher, L., & Zacks, R. T. (1979). Automatic and effortful processes in memory. *Journal of Experimental Psychology: General, 108*, 356–388.

Horn, H., & Myers, N. A. (1978). Memory for location and picture cues at ages two and three. *Child Development, 49*, 845–856.

Istomina, Z. M. (1975). The development of voluntary memory in preschool-age children. *Soviet Psychology, 13*, 5–64.

Justice, E. M. (1983). *Parental behaviors in a memory relevant setting: How parents "teach" children to remember.* Paper presented at the meeting of the Society for Research in Child Development, Detroit.

LaBerge, D. (1973). Attention and the measurement of perceptual learning. *Memory & Cognition, 1*, 268–276.

Light, L. L., & Zelinsky, E. M. (1983). Memory for spatial information in young and old adults. *Developmental Psychology, 19*, 901–906.

Lucariello, J. (1983). *Context and conversation.* Paper presented at the meeting of the Society for Research on Child Development, Detroit.

Mandler, J. M., Seegmiller, D., & Day, J. (1977). On the coding of spatial information. *Memory and Cognition, 5*, 10–16.

Meacham, J. A. (1982). A note on remembering to execute planned actions. *Journal of Applied Developmental Psychology, 3*, 121–133.

Myers, N. A., & Perlmutter, M. (1978). Memory in the years from two to five. In P. A. Ornstein (Ed.), *Memory development in children.* Hillsdale, NJ: Lawrence Erlbaum Associates.

Nelson, K., & Ross, G. (1980). The generalities and specifics of long-term memory in infants and young children. In M. Perlmutter (Ed.), *New directions for child development: Children's memory.* San Francisco: Jossey-Bass.

Newport, E., Gleitman, L., & Gleitman, H. (1977). Mother, I'd rather do it myself: Some effects and non-effects of motherese. In C. Snow & C. Ferguson (Eds.), *Talking to children: Language input and acquisition.* Cambridge: Cambridge University Press.

Ornstein, P. A., & Baker-Ward, L. (1983). *The development of mnemonic skill.* Paper presented at the meeting of the Society for Research in Child Development, Detroit.

Park, D. C., Puglisi, J. T., & Lutz, R. (1982). Spatial memory in older adults: Effects of intentionality. *Journal of Gerontology, 37*, 330–335.

Perlmutter, M., Hazen, N., Mitchell, D. B., Grady, J. C., Cavanaugh, J. C., & Flook, J. P. (1981). Picture cues and exhaustive search facilitate very young children's memory for location. *Developmental Psychology, 17*, 109–110.

Perlmutter, M., & Myers, N. A. (1979). Development of recall in two to four-year-old children. *Developmental Psychology, 15*, 73–83.

Pezdek, K. (1983). Memory for items and their spatial locations by young and elderly adults. *Developmental Psychology, 19*, 389–390.

Ratner, H. H. (1980). The role of social context in memory development. In M. Perlmutter (Ed.), *New directions for child development: Children's memory, 10.* San Francisco: Jossey-Bass.

Reeve, R. A. (1983). *Factors affecting age differences in performance on the game of concentration: A study of location memory.* Doctoral dissertation, Macquarie University.

Rothkopf, E. Z. (1971). Incidental memory for location of information in text. *Journal of Verbal Learning and Verbal Behavior, 10*, 608–613.

Sachs, J. (1983). Talking about the there and then: The emergence of displaced reference in parent-child discourse. In K. E. Nelson (Ed.), *Children's language* (Vol. 4). Hillsdale, NJ: Lawrence Erlbaum Associates.

Schneider, W., & Shiffrin, R. M. (1977). Controlled and automatic human information processing: I. Detection, search, and attention. *Psychological Review, 84*, 1–66.

Schulman, A. T. (1973). Recognition memory and the recall of spatial location. *Memory and Cognition, 1*, 256–260.

Shiffrin, R. M., & Schneider, W. (1977). Controlled and automatic human information processing: II. Perceptual learning, automatic attending, and a general theory. *Psychological Review, 84*, 127–190.

Smirnov, A. A., & Zinchenko, P. I. (1969). Problems in the psychology of memory. In M. Cole & I. Maltzman (Eds.), *A handbook of contemporary Soviet psychology.* New York: Basic Books.

Somerville, S. C., Wellman, H. M., & Cultice, J. C. (1983). Young children's deliberate reminding. *Journal of Genetic Psychology, 143,* 87–96.

von Wright, J. M., Gebhard, P., & Karttunen, M. (1975). A developmental study of the recall of spatial location. *Journal of Experimental Child Psychology, 20,* 181–190.

Vygotsky, L. S. (1978). *Mind and society: The development of higher psychological processes.* (M. Cole, V. John-Steiner, S. Scribner, & E. Souberman, Eds. and Trans.). Cambridge: Harvard University Press.

Waters, H. S., & Andreassen, C. (1983). Children's use of memory strategies under strategies under instruction. In M. Pressley & J. R. Levin (Eds.), *Cognitive strategy research.* New York: Springer-Verlag.

Wellman, H. M., Ritter, R., & Flavell, J. H. (1975). Deliberate memory behavior in the delayed reactions of very young children. *Developmental Psychology, 11,* 780–787.

Wellman, H. M., & Somerville, S. C. (1982). The development of human search ability. In M. E. Lamb & A. L. Brown (Eds.), *Advances in developmental psychology* (Vol. 2). Hillsdale, NJ: Lawrence Erlbaum Associates.

Wertsch, J. V. (1979). From social interaction to higher psychological process: A clarification and application of Vygotsky's theory. *Human Development, 22,* 1–22.

Wertsch, J. V., McNamee, G. D., McLane, J. B., & Budwig, N. A. (1980). The adult-child dyad as a problem-solving system. *Child Development, 51,* 1215–1221.

Zechmeister, E. B., McKillip, J., Pasko, S., & Bespalec, D. (1975). Visual memory for place on the page. *The Journal of Genetic Psychology, 92,* 43–52.

8 A Developmental Model of Search: Stochastic Estimation of Children's Rule Use

Catherine Sophian
Jill H. Larkin
Joseph B. Kadane
Carnegie-Mellon University

What is the relation between the cognitive skills of infants and cognitive development in early and middle childhood? Despite research in both areas, we lack a coherent continuous picture of how an infant develops into a child. In this chapter, we present a line of research that begins to bridge that gap by looking at search for hidden objects in both infancy and early childhood.

The need for a more coherent picture of development from infancy into childhood is apparent both from the current empirical literature and from theoretical accounts of cognitive development. In empirical work, the behaviors investigated with infants and older children have differed substantially. Perceptual and discriminative abilities predominate in the infancy literature, whereas Piagetian logical abilities, such as conservation and class inclusion, and school-related skills, such as arithmetic and reading, are the focus of much of the work with older children. In theoretical work, likewise, there has been a fundamental division between infancy and childhood. Piaget characterized infant intelligence as sensorimotor—operating only through action—in contrast to the representational intelligence of older children, which enables them to think as well as act intelligently. This notion of qualitatively different levels of cognition in infancy and later childhood prevails in several more recent accounts of cognitive development as well (e.g., Case, 1980; Fischer, 1980), despite efforts to move away from some of Piaget's claims about developmental stages.

The limitations of this approach are evident from recent work revealing impressive cognitive abilities in infancy: for instance, the ability to make numerical discriminations (Starkey & Cooper, 1980; Strauss & Curtis, 1981), to detect categorical relationships (Strauss, 1979), and to make simple spatial inferences (Rieser & Heiman, 1982; Sophian, 1984a,b). It may still be possible to maintain that these early abilities are qualitatively different from the corresponding arithmetic, conceptual, and inferential skills of older children. Nonetheless, we would like to have a better understanding of how the initial cognitive skills of infants develop into the richer and more powerful cognitive skills of older children.

For this purpose, we need to look not only at whether infants and children succeed on various tasks but at *how* they perform these tasks, and we need to look at the same or closely related tasks across age groups. In both respects search tasks are promising. Studies of search provide information not only about children's level of performance but also about specific kinds of errors which may be important clues to the cognitive processes underlying performance. Moreover, recent studies have succeeded in using the same search task or closely related tasks to study both infants and young children (cf. Somerville & Haake, this volume; Sophian, 1984a; Sophian & Wellman, 1983). In the first part of this chapter, we briefly review recent research on infants and young children, highlighting the correspondences between age groups that have begun to emerge from this work.

The discovery of these close correspondences between age groups raises the problem of how best to characterize the age differences that are so widely observed. We need a theory of development that can accommodate the correspondences across different age groups and yet can also account for how patterns of performance change with age. In the second part of this chapter, we present a rule-based model that meets these complementary goals. According to this model, as children get older they acquire increasingly differentiated rules that incorporate the kinds of information their earlier rules were based on along with new information that enables them to handle a wider range of problems appropriately. Stochastic estimation procedures enable us to estimate the prevalence of each of the rules hypothesized in this model across a set of age groups. As an illustration, we apply the model to a set of data on 20-, 30-, and 42-month-old children's search for hidden objects on a spatial transposition task.

RESEARCH ON EARLY SEARCH: EVIDENCE FOR CONTINUITY

Much of the recent interest in studying young children's search for hidden objects has stemmed from the opportunity it provides to look at infants and young children in comparable ways. Search tasks are meaningful even to infants, and yet they can tap aspects of cognitive development that continue to be important well into childhood. Thus, by using appropriately designed sets of search tasks, researchers can begin to look at infants and children in a common framework and to identify possible correspondences as well as contrasts between them. Several lines of research carried out over the past few years have demonstrated the value of this approach. This research has demonstrated that although there are widespread age differences in early search, there are also important continuities. Continuities are evident in the cognitive abilities infants and young children show in their searches, in the kinds of systematic errors they make, and in the relationship between children's errors and the correct search patterns that become increasingly prevalent with age.[1]

Cognitive Abilities in Early Search

Several kinds of cognitive abilities underlie search both in infancy and in early childhood. The most fundamental ones involve understanding the nature of objects and of search: realizing that an object still exists when it is out of sight, that it can be recovered by searching for it, and that information about where it disappeared can be used to guide search. These competencies are generally thought to be acquired sometime in infancy, and it is no surprise that, once they are acquired, they persist into later periods of development. Hence, correspondences in these basic abilities are not very interesting evidence for continuity between infants' and older children's cognition. Other, more complex, abilities present a stronger and more interesting picture of continuity, since they may still be developing well into childhood but at the same time are already present in rudimentary form in infants' searches. Here we consider just one illustrative example—the ability to make inferences about movements of an object that were not directly visible.

Inferring Unseen Movements

The ability to infer unseen movements of an object was considered by Piaget a hallmark of the child's transition from sensorimotor to representational intelligence at the end of infancy. Several recent studies, however, have provided evidence that infants do make various kinds of inferences about unseen movements well before the close of the infancy period. Although some kinds of inferences, such as inferences about the effects of rotational transformations, continue to pose difficulty well into the elementary school years (cf. Huttenlocher & Newcombe, 1984; Huttenlocher & Presson, 1973, 1979; Lasky, Romano, & Wenters, 1980), some can be made as early as 1 year of age. Thus, despite substantial developments in the kinds of inferences children can make, infants do appear to be able to conceive of an object moving to a different place while it is out of view and to make at least some simple inferences about those movements.

Two lines of research have provided evidence that infants can make inferences about unseen movements of an object. The first is based on a variant of

---

[1]The case for continuity presented here borrows heavily from a more extended analysis of cross-age correspondences presented in Sophian (1984a).

the invisible displacement task Piaget used to assess the advent of representational intelligence at the end of infancy. The second focuses on search on spatial transposition problems.

On Piaget's invisible displacement task, an object is concealed within a container (or the experimenter's hand), which is then moved to several locations in turn. In the traditional Piagetian task, the object is usually left in the last location in the displacement sequence, and a child is considered to pass the task if she searches first at that location and then, if the object is not there, continues searching in the reverse order of the displacement sequence. It is not clear, however, why children should show this search pattern, since logically the object could be in any of the displacement locations. Therefore, Sophian and Sage (1983a) focused on a different aspect of invisible displacement performance: the ability to differentiate displacement locations, where the object could have been left, from control locations, where it could not be. Although performance improved with age, even 13-month-old infants showed some success here. They directed an average of .80 of their searches to one of the two displacement locations and only .20 to a control location, which represents significantly above-chance performance.

On spatial transposition problems, an object is hidden in one of several identical cups and then one or more cups are moved before the child is allowed to search. The object, of course, moves invisibly with its cup when that cup is moved. This task is like the invisible displacement task in that the object moves while it is concealed from view, but it is unlike the invisible displacement task in that the object's location can always be determined from the movements observed. In initial work with a version of this task in which two cups are simultaneously interchanged, 13-month-olds performed at chance (Sophian & Sage, 1983) and even 3½-year-olds continued to make systematic errors (Sophian, 1984c). However, a subsequent study (Sophian, 1984b) produced above-chance performance as early as 13 months.

Thus, two different lines of evidence indicate that some ability to make inferences about invisible movements is present as early as 13 months, well before the close of the infancy period. Although developments in the particular kinds of movements children can comprehend extend well into childhood, the basic ability to consider possible movements of objects while they are hidden from view is one that infants as well as older children possess. This is one indication that there are important continuities as well as age differences in early cognitive development.

Error Patterns in Early Search

The continuity between infancy and early childhood that emerges from looking at the cognitive abilities children show in their searches is even more striking in children's error patterns. There may be many ways of achieving partially correct performance, and so the fact that infants as well as older children succeed on various tasks does not in itself provide strong assurance that they are doing the same thing on those tasks. If they are alike, however, not only in achieving some degree of correct performance but also in making the same kinds of systematic errors, then there is more reason to believe that common processes underlie performance across ages. In fact, there are marked correspondences in the error patterns of infants and young children.

Two kinds of systematic errors that occur in both infants' and preschoolers' searches are discussed here. The first is the perseverative error pattern that has long been central to research on infants' search (cf Piaget, 1954). Perseverative errors are not restricted to infants but have been observed in older children's searches as well. A second, related, error pattern is the initial-location error children make on transposition problems when two cups are interposed after an object has been hidden in one of them. The initial-location error here consists of searching where the object was hidden initially rather than at the place it ended up after the transposition. Like perseverative errors, these errors persist long after infancy.

Perseverative Errors

Perseverative errors have received most attention in the context of infants' searches, where they have been viewed as an indication of the infant's egocentric conception of objects (e.g., Gratch, 1975; Piaget, 1954). Two recent lines of evidence, however, strongly suggest that they are neither as representative of infants' searches, nor as unique to that age group, as the Piagetian account implies. First, when appropriate methodological controls are included, perseverative errors appear to be much less pervasive in infants' searches than initially thought (Bjork & Cummings, 1984; Sophian, in press; Sophian & Wellman, 1983; Sophian & Yengo, 1984). Second, perseverative errors are by no means restricted to infants. Although older children make fewer errors than infants, the errors they do make often involve going to the place where the object was found on the preceding trial (e.g., DeLoache & Brown, 1983; Horn & Myers, 1978; Loughlin & Daehler, 1973; Sophian & Wellman, 1980).

A basic methodological issue in the study of perseveration concerns what is an appropriate measure of perseveration. The original studies used infants' relative frequency of searching at the first hiding place, A, versus at the correct place, B, to index perseveration. A problem with this measure, however, is that there is no way to identify systematic perseveration unless errors to A are significantly more frequent than correct responses. If searches at A are less frequent, they could reflect merely random responding rather than a systematic return to the prior location. A related problem, from a developmental perspective, is that there is no way to distinguish between decreases in perseveration with age and increases in correct performance that might occur for other reasons.

An alternative measure, characteristic of studies with older children and of a few recent infant studies, is one that measures perseverative errors relative to errors to one or more control locations, which we will call C. This measure permits the detection of systematic perseveration even when the level of correct performance is quite high, since as long as errors to A are more frequent than errors to C they cannot be due to random responding. Moreover, since this measure is based solely on the distribution of children's errors, it is independent of changes in their overall level of performance. However, this measure can only be calculated when the search task includes at least one control location in addition to the A and B locations.

Studies that have included such a control location have produced much less evidence of perseveration in infancy than the original object permanence studies, which did not control for random responses. For instance, Sophian and Wellman (1983) replicated many key findings from earlier, two-location, perseveration studies and yet found no evidence of systematic perseveration when errors to A were evaluated relative to errors to a control location. As in previous studies of perseveration, they found that (1) the proportion of infants' searches that were to the A location declined between 9 months of age and the later part of the infancy period; (2) 9-month-olds searched about equally often at A and at B; and (3) when 9-month-olds made errors to the A location they tended to repeat them on successive trials in non-random error runs. Analyses comparing searches at A with searches at the control location, however, did not support the conclusion that 9-month-olds were perseverating. Error runs to C were as long as error runs to A. Moreover, infants made just as many errors to C as errors to A. Thus, comparisons to a control location provided no evidence of perseveration at 9 months although previous findings thought to indicate perseveration were replicated. Other recent studies likewise have failed to document significant perseveration when controls for random responding were included (Bjork & Cummings, 1984; Sophian, in press).

These negative results clearly indicate the danger of inferring perseveration from two-location studies that do not control for random responses. At the same time, though, it is important to note that not all findings from two-location studies can be attributed to random search. In particular, a few studies have reported errors to A by a large majority of infants (e.g., Bremner & Bryant, 1977; Gratch, Appel, Evans, LeCompte, & Wright, 1974; Landers, 1971), and these above-chance errors clearly do not reflect merely random search. Likewise, significant perseveration has been observed in a few very recent three-location studies (Sophian & Sage, in press; Sophian & Yengo, 1984). These results indicate that perseveration does sometimes occur in infants' search, although it is much less prevalent than early reports suggested.

In addition to being less prevalent among 9-month-olds than initially thought, perseverative errors are not unique to that age group. In one study, perseverative errors continued to occur as late as 4½ years of age (Sophian & Wellman, 1983). Among these children, perseverative responses are characteristically much less frequent than correct searches, but they still account for a substantial proportion of children's errors.

The combined findings that perseveration is a fairly limited phenomenon in 9-month-olds' searches, and that it continues to occur even through the preschool years, considerably strengthen the picture of continuity between infancy and early childhood that emerged from the findings on cognitive abilities in early search. Here is an error pattern that was initially taken to reveal the fundamentally different way in which infants conceptualize objects, and it turns out to be in fact a pattern of searching that infants hold in common with much older children. Other kinds of errors show the same developmental pattern.

Initial-Location Errors

The initial-location errors children make on transposition problems are analogous to perseverative errors in that they involve returning to a place where the object was hidden earlier without taking into account displacements that have occurred since then. Transposition problems differ from the AB task, however, in that information about the object's initial location is in fact relevant to determining its final hiding place, whereas in the AB task it is of no value at all. Perhaps for this reason, the transposition task appears to be much more difficult and later to be mastered than the AB task.

As in the case of the AB task, the earliest studies of transposition problems used a two-location task on which it was difficult to distinguish between systematic errors to the initial location and merely random errors (Bower, 1977; Cornell, 1979; Freeman, Lloyd, & Sinha, 1980; Gratch, 1980). More recent studies, however, have added a third location, making it possible to evaluate the systematicity of children's errors by looking at the relative frequency of errors to the initial hiding place and errors to a control location (Sophian, 1984b,c; Sophian & Sage, 1983).

The developmental patterns in children's errors in these studies again provide strong evidence of continuity across infancy and early childhood. In one study, comparing 13-, 20-, and 30-month-olds, the total proportion of searches at the initial hiding place declined with age, but the proportion of children's errors that were to the initial hiding place was comparable at all ages (Sophian, 1984b). The same pattern also occurred in another study, which compared 20-, 30-, and 42-month-olds (Sophian, 1984c). Thus, while children make fewer errors on the transposition task as they get older, the errors they do make continue to be quite systematic and of the same form from 13 months of age until well into the preschool years.

Age Differences

Despite the correspondences across age groups in both the cognitive abilities children show and the errors they make, there is no question but that search performance improves with age. Within the very studies we have reviewed to support correspondences, there is recurrent evidence of developmental increases in correct performance and decreases in systematic errors. The question for a continuity theory, then, is how to account for the developmental shift from relatively error-prone to predominantly correct search patterns?

An important clue to the resolution of this problem emerges from a consideration of the relationship between early error patterns and correct performance. Characteristically, the systematic errors children make are based on part of the information needed for correct performance, in fact on partial information that is in itself sufficient to solve a subset of problems correctly. Thus, for example, perseverative errors involve using information about where a toy was hidden and/or found on a set of previous trials. This information is not useful on perseveration problems, because it has been superseded by other information (about the current hiding), but it is relevant for effective search across a wider range of situations. In particular, it can be a helpful cue to an object's location when more current information is not available (cf. Sophian & Wellman, 1983). Similarly, the initial-location errors children make on transposition problems are based on information about where the toy was hidden at the beginning of the problem. This information is in fact essential (although not sufficient) for correct performance on these problems. Moreover, although it leads to errors on transpositions where the container in which the object was initially hidden is moved to a new location, it is sufficient to solve a large number of other search problems correctly (any problem in which the object's location is not altered once it has been hidden).

This observation suggests that error patterns are linked to correct performance by a process of differentiation: Children's earliest searches are based on only a limited amount of information, which is sufficient to solve the simplest (and probably most common) search problems they encounter, but leads to systematic errors on other problems. With development, they gradually take into account additional information about the search problems that enables them to distinguish between types of problems that they had previously treated equivalently. Thus, they come to understand, for instance, that although objects are often where you have seen them hidden, certain classes of subsequent events may indicate that they have been moved to a different place. In this way, children acquire increasingly complex and differentiated search rules that are nevertheless continuous with their earlier, error-prone, rules in that they incorporate the same information the earlier rules were based on into a more complete decision process.

Conclusions

In summary, we have found considerable continuity between infancy and early childhood in looking at how children search for hidden objects. Continuity is evident in the cognitive abilities children show in their searches, in the kinds of errors they make, and also in the relationship between early errors and the correct search patterns that become prevalent later. Although there are certainly widespread age differences, still infants seem to approach search problems in much the same way as older children do. Our findings suggest that infants differ from older children primarily in that they take into account only part of the information that older children use to search intelligently. Thus, infants' early search patterns are linked to later ones by a process of differentiation, which enables children to incorporate more information into their search rules and so to respond appropriately to a wider range of situations.

The importance of differentiation in the early development of search implies that developmental changes may be seen most clearly by looking at children's search patterns across several interrelated problem types. Increases in differentiation should be reflected in findings that older age groups show distinct search patterns across problem types that younger children treat equivalently. A focus on search patterns raises special methodological problems, however. Often, a "pattern of search" is only vaguely defined. Further, even when a rigorous specification of a search pattern is available, traditional methods of data analysis cannot test the hypothesized search pattern directly. Instead, it is usually necessary to use separate analyses to look at several complementary aspects of the hypothesized search pattern (e.g., levels of correct performance and the distribution of children's errors) and then to integrate the results of those analyses subjectively. In the remainder of this chapter, we describe an alternative approach to studying children's search patterns. In this approach, we develop a model of early search based on hypothesized mental rules. Within this model, we can define precisely the search patterns we want to look for. We then use stochastic modeling techniques to directly estimate how prevalent those search patterns are from children's responses to a set of problems.

MODELING EARLY SEARCH

We characterize early search in terms of children's use of a set of hypothesized rules, which specify how they will respond to each of a set of related problems. In postulating rules, we are claiming that children respond in systematic ways, based on identifiable kinds of information, even when they do not perform correctly. Children may not be able to state the rules they are using explicitly, or even to pinpoint the information on which their rules are based, but nevertheless their use of a rule may be inferred from their pattern of responses across a set of appropriately constructed problems. Rules are a useful theoretical construct because they are both precise and potentially general. They make detailed, testable, predictions about both how well children should perform on a given task and what types of errors they should make. In addition, they capture patterns in the way information is used to solve a problem that may appear on many different tasks, so that the same types of rules can be used to provide a coherent analysis across a variety of tasks (see Siegler, 1981). This feature of rule-based analyses is crucial to developing a coherent model of cognitive development over a wide range of ages and tasks.

Although rule-based models have been fairly common in work on cognitive development during the elementary school years, they have not been used much in work with younger children. Development of a rule-based model of very early phases of cognitive development thus would be useful in linking our understanding of cognitive development in infancy and early childhood with what is known about later phases of cognitive development. However, identification of the rules used by very young children poses special difficulties because data from these age groups are characteristically limited in quantity and high in variability.

An influential approach to identifying cognitive rules in work with older children has been the rule assessment methodology developed by Siegler (Siegler, 1976, 1978, 1981). Here, each individual child is classified as using one of several hypothesized rules if his or her response patterns correspond (most of the time) to those predicted by the rule. Siegler and his associates have applied this methodology to such diverse tasks as balance scale problems, judgments of proportionality, and conservation problems. Across many domains they have found that young children use rules that focus on a single aspect or dimension of the problem, whereas older children use rules that take into account variations along more than one dimension at once (Siegler, 1981). Rule assessment methodology has not been able to capture what children below 4 or 5 years of age do on these tasks, however, as these children do not appear to use even the simplest rules consistently (Siegler, 1978).

The rule-assessment methodology, as used by Siegler and his colleagues, may be inappropriate to very young children for several reasons. First, the hypothesized rules typically do not include irrelevant bases of responding (e.g., position preferences or response biases of other kinds) that may be an important factor in very young children's performance (cf. Sophian, 1982; Sophian & Sage, 1983). Second, young children may not adopt a single coherent rule but may be influenced by several considerations simultaneously. For instance, infants may show correct search in looking for an object where they have seen it hidden on most trials, and yet may simultaneously show position preferences in their errors. More generally, very young children may simply be less consistent than older children in using a hypothesized rule, even though their performance as a group may reflect sensitivity to the information captured in the rule (e.g., Sophian, 1984a; Sophian & Wellman, 1983).

The modeling techniques we have been developing provide an alternative way of estimating children's rule use from their responses to a set of problems. They differ from the rule assessment approach in that they incorporate a wider range of types of rules, they allow for the coexistence of multiple bases of responding in an individual child's performance, and they incorporate stochastic processes to accommodate inconsistencies in young children's behavior. At the same time, there is a close correspondence between our work and the earlier rule assessment work in the form of the more task-appropriate rules we hypothesize, in the relationships between the more primitive and the more advanced of those rules, and in the kinds of interrelated problems we present to children in order to distinguish among the hypothesized rules. In the remainder of this chapter, we outline our modeling techniques and present a specific application of them, using data on 20-, 30- and 42-month-old children's search patterns on a spatial transposition task (Sophian, 1984). We begin with a model that incorporates the same assumptions about children's rule use that underlie Siegler's rule assessment work (Model 1). Further consideration of one theoretically important assumption, however, leads us to compare this model with a contrasting one (Model 2). Although both models support the same general developmental conclusions, differences between them are useful in developing a more precise picture of early search.

Model 1: A Stochastic Rule-Based Model

Our initial model is basically an extension of the rule assessment work of Siegler and his associates (see, e.g., Siegler, 1976, 1981) designed to cope with inconsistent response patterns. Like Siegler, we assume that each child has just one rule that corresponds to his or her understanding of a class of problems. Unlike Siegler, however, we do not assume that the child will necessarily use his or her rule on all or nearly all problems. Instead, we allow that on some proportion of trials the child may respond randomly or on the basis of irrelevant considerations like position preferences. As a result, we estimate rule use even when individual children do not respond consistently across a whole set of problems.

General Form of the Model

The model consists of rules and assumptions about how those rules are used. We assume that each child has a single *task-adapted* rule. This rule reflects the child's understanding of the task and characteristically makes use of at least part of the information needed for correct performance. The set of task-adapted rules we postulate are thus related to each other in that the most advanced rule(s) characteristically incorporate several kinds of information, which only occur separately in the simpler, less differentiated, rules.

In addition to the task-adapted rules, we also postulate a set of *fallback* rules. These rules are typically simpler than the task-adapted rules and can be used even when the child has not encoded crucial information from the task. We assume that on each trial there is some probability that the child will fail to use his or her task-adapted rule and instead use one of the fallback rules. The probability of a child using his or her task-adapted rule may vary across problem types, reflecting differences in problem difficulty. However, given that a child is *not* using his or her task-adapted rule, the conditional probability of using each fallback rule does not depend on problem type. The assumption is that the child is missing some crucial information and is selecting probabilistically among several strategies that do not relate directly to the problem situation.

The classification of a rule as task-adapted or fallback is always relative to the tasks considered; the same rule may be task-adapted on some problems and not on others. For example, searching the closest location would be a fallback rule on selective search problems, where children have some kind of information that could enable them to identify the correct location (which is not necessarily the closest one); at the same time, it would be a task-adapted rule on comprehensive search problems, where children do not have information about the object's location and thus must determine where to search on the basis of characteristics of the locations themselves. The key determinant of whether a rule is considered task-adapted or fallback is whether it makes use of at least part of the relevant information in the problem.

Both task-adapted and fallback rules may make probabilistic rather than deterministic predictions about a child's responses. For example, the random-choice fallback rule says that the child chooses each response with equal probability. Task-adapted rules too can specify that the child "muddles through" (Siegler, 1976) and chooses with specified probabilities between two or more possibilities.

The premise that the child uses just one task-adapted rule across problem types, although he or she may use several fallback rules with varying probabilities, is based on several considerations. First, as already noted, this assumption corresponds to the usual assumption in rule-based work with older children. Thus in making this assumption even for younger children, we are asking to what extent a common model can account for performance across age groups. Second, on a more pragmatic level, the major source of information about what rule a child is using is his or her pattern of performance across different problem types. If children were presumed to use different task-adapted rules on different problem types, it would not be possible to distinguish among many possible combinations of rules. In the extreme case, one could infer that a child simply used on each problem a single rule that produces the observed response on that problem.

Clearly, the most parsimonious assumption about rule use is the assumption of one task-adapted rule used on all problem types.

In short, Model 1 postulates, for a task and a group of children, two sets of rules. Task-adapted rules make use of relevant information from the task. Each child's performance is characterized by just one of these rules. Fallback rules are largely independent of information in the problem. We assume that on some fraction of trials (which may vary by problem type) a child fails to use his or her task-adapted rule and instead uses one of the fallback rules.

We estimate four sets of parameters characterizing the model:

- γ_v: the probabilities of using a task-adapted rule on each problem variety.
- α_i: the probabilities of each hypothesized task-adapted rule being the rule used by an individual child.
- β_j: the conditional probabilities of using each fallback rule when a child is not using his or her task-adapted rule.
- δ_r: the probabilities of each possible response being a child's favorite response. For any individual child, the favorite response, r, like the task-adapted rule used, i, is assumed to be constant over the entire set of problems.

The first two sets of parameters here provide the primary information about cognitive-developmental changes. Changes in the probabilities of the alternative task-adapted rules would reflect changes in rule use like those that have been focal in rule assessment work with older children. Increases in the probabilities of a child using his or her task-adapted rule (for different problem varieties) would reflect improvements in the child's attention to the task and in the degree to which his or her performance consistently reflects his or her best understanding of the problems.

The other two sets of parameters reflect children's responding when they are not making use of the available information and hence are not responding in accordance with their best understanding of the problems. Changes in the conditional probabilities of using each fallback rule would reflect changes in the kinds of extraneous considerations children rely on when they are not attending to the relevant information. Changes in the probability of a particular favorite response would indicate changes in response bias. These parameters capture what children are doing when they are not on task, performance that may constitute a considerable portion of children's responding at very young ages.

The total number of parameters estimated is $V + I + J + R$, where V is the number of problem varieties considered, I is the number of hypothesized task-adapted rules, J is the number of hypothesized fallback rules, and R is the number of possible responses. The degrees of freedom involved in fitting the parameters to data are actually three less than the total number of parameters estimated, because the α_i's, the β_j's, and the δ_r's must each sum to 1.0, resulting in a loss of one degree of freedom in each case. To estimate these parameters, we maximize the likelihood of an observed set of responses on the different problem varieties. The parameters that produce the greatest likelihood of the observed data are taken as the best estimates of the values of the corresponding probabilities for a population of children.

Any particular response x on trial t for a problem of variety v could occur either through the use of a task-adapted rule, with probability γ_v, or through the use of a fallback rule, with probability $(1 - \gamma_v)$. The probability of the response x thus is given by:

$$\gamma_v p(x|t,v,i) + (1 - \gamma_v) \sum_{j=1}^{J} \beta_j q(x|t,v,j) \qquad (1)$$

where $p(x|t,v,i)$ and $q(x|t,v,j)$ are respectively the probabilities of response x according to the task-adapted rule i and the fallback rule j. The summation runs over the J fallback rules.

Given a child with a specified task-adapted rule i and favorite response r, we assume that each trial's outcome is independent of the others. Thus, the probability of the child's set of responses to all trials from all problem varieties is:

$$\prod_{v=1}^{V} \prod_{t=1}^{T(v)} \{\gamma_v \, p(x|t,v,i) + (1 - \gamma_v) \sum_{j=1}^{J} \beta_j \, q(x|t,v,j)\} \qquad (2)$$

where the products run over the $T(v)$ trials for each problem variety v and over the V problem varieties.

We assume that a child's task-adapted rule i and favorite response r are independent. Then our probability of his or her set of responses is:

$$\sum_{i=1}^{I} \alpha_i \sum_{r=1}^{R} \delta_r \prod_{v=1}^{V} \prod_{t=1}^{T(v)} \{\gamma_v \, p(x|t,v,i) + (1 - \gamma_v) \sum_{j=1}^{J} \beta_j \, q(x|t,v,j)\} \qquad (3)$$

To estimate parameters for an entire population of children (e.g., a particular age group), we use data from C children whose responses are assumed independent (once the α's, β's, δ's, and γ's are known). The probability of an entire set of responses from C children is:

$$\prod_{c=1}^{C} \sum_{i=1}^{I} \alpha_i \sum_{r=1}^{R} \delta_r \prod_{v=1}^{V} \prod_{t=1}^{T(v)} \{\gamma_v \, p(x|t,v,i) + (1 - \gamma_v) \sum_{j=1}^{J} \beta_j \, q(x|t,v,j)\} \qquad (4)$$

This expression is the likelihood function, the probability of the observed data as a function of the parameters α_i, β_j, δ_r, and γ_v. By maximizing this function over these parameters, we estimate their values.

This maximization is not trivial. Packaged hill-climbing programs (e.g., minpack; More, Burton, & Hillstrom, 1980) were not effective, probably because the likelihood changes at very different rates as a function of the different parameters. Thus we developed methods we call global likelihood analysis (Larkin & Kadane, 1983). In this technique we view likelihood function as a general normal distribution. Therefore, if we use the vector Θ to represent the parameters (the α's, β's, and γ's), the likelihood can be expressed as:

$$\Lambda = K \exp[(-\tfrac{1}{2})(\Theta-\Theta_0)'V^{-1}(\Theta-\Theta_0)], \tag{5}$$

where K is a constant, Θ_0 is the estimated value of the parameters Θ, and V is the associated covariance matrix. Thus

$$-2 \log \Lambda = (\Theta-\Theta_0)'V^{-1}(\Theta-\Theta_0) - 2 \log K. \tag{6}$$

This function for $-2 \log \Lambda$ is a quadratic. We evaluate it at a grid of points, and fit a multidimensional parabola using ordinary regression techniques. This initial parabola tells us where the likelihood function is likely to be largest. Then we constrain our next grid of points to that region, which is elliptical in shape. The parabola is refit, and this process is repeated until we obtain stable estimates of the parameters and their covariance matrix.

Implementation

We have applied our model to data from a recent study of very young children's search on spatial transposition problems (Sophian, 1984c). In this study, twenty-two 20-month-olds, twenty 30-month-olds, and twenty-two 42-month-olds were tested on a set of 18 transposition problems. All the problems involved hiding an object in one of three cups placed in front of the child and then interchanging two of the cups before allowing the child to search. There were two varieties of problem, as depicted in Fig. 8.1: relevant transpositions, in which the cup containing the object was interchanged with another, and irrelevant transpositions, in which the two empty cups were interchanged, leaving the object in its original location. There were 12 relevant transposition problems and 6 irrelevant transposition problems, representing all possible combinations of where the object was hidden initially and which cups were interchanged.

On the relevant transpositions, three distinctive kinds of searches are possible: (1) searches at the correct location, which would be the middle cup in the problem shown in Fig. 8.1; (2) searches at the initial location, which is the leftmost cup in Fig. 8.1; and (3) searches at the control location, the rightmost cup in Fig. 8.1. Children's search patterns on these problems are summarized in Table 8.1. Basically, correct responding increased with age; searches at the initial location decreased; and searches at the control location were infrequent at all ages.

PROBLEM VARIETIES IN TRANSPOSITION STUDY

I. Relevant Transpositions

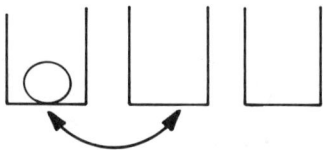

II. Irrelevant Transpositions

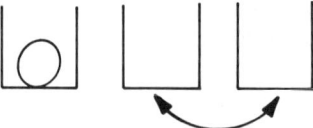

FIG. 8.1. Relevant and irrelevant transpositions used in Sophian (1984c) study.

On irrelevant transpositions, only two distinct kinds of searches are possible: (1) searches at the correct location, which is also the initial location—that's the left cup in Fig. 8.1—and (2) searches at one of the two transposed locations. Table 8.1 also summarizes children's searches on these problems. All three age groups generally searched the correct location, and there were no significant age differences.

TABLE 8.1
Search Patterns on Transposition Problems

Problem Type/Search Pattern	Age (in Months)		
	20	30	42
Relevant transpositions			
Search at correct location	.34	.47	.71
Search at initial location	.56	.48	.26
Search at control location	.10	.05	.04
Irrelevant transpositions			
Search at correct (initial) location	.66	.76	.79
Search at one transposed location + Search at other transposed location	.34	.24	.21

In modeling children's performance on this task, we postulated three task-adapted rules and two fallback rules. The first task-adapted rule was an *initial-cup* rule, which called for looking for the object where it was hidden initially, without regard for the transposition that was performed. This rule produces correct performance on irrelevant transpositions but systematic errors on relevant transpositions. The second task-adapted rule was a *moved-cup* rule, which specified that the child searches for the object in one of the two cups that were moved after the object was hidden, choosing randomly between them. This rule produces partially correct performance on relevant transpositions but consistent errors on irrelevant transpositions. Finally, the third task-adapted rule was a *combination* rule, which specified looking for an object in its initial location unless that cup was moved, in which case the child should search at that cup's new location. This rule, of course, produces correct performance on all problems. Note that all three of these rules take into account either where the object was hidden, or what cups were moved, or both. These are the relevant sources of

TABLE 8.2
Parameter Estimates for Model I[a]

Probabilities	Age (in Months)		
	20	30	42
Probabilities of each task-adapted rule being a child's rule			
initial location rule	.908	.464	.047
	(.181)	(.134)	(.097)
moved-cup rule	.036	.067	.130
	(.085)	(.084)	(.121)
combination rule	.056	.469	.823
	(.138)	(.126)	(.115)
Probabilities of using task-adapted rule			
on relevant transpositions	.351	.468	.655
	(.073)	(.049)	(.041)
on irrelevant transpositions	.513	.655	.805
	(.056)	(.058)	(.047)
Conditional probabilities of each fallback rule			
favorite box rule	.292	.260	.072
	(.067)	(.101)	(.214)
random search rule	.708	.740	.928
	(.067)	(.101)	(.214)

[a]Standard deviations for each estimate are given in parentheses.

information in transposition problems, and it is because these rules make use of them that we consider them task-adapted.

The two hypothesized fallback rules were, first, a *favorite-location* rule saying that the child searches at a favorite location, and second, a *random-choice* rule saying that the child chooses randomly among the locations. Neither of these rules takes into account either where the object was hidden or what cups were moved.

To estimate each parameter in the model and its standard error, we used the procedures briefly outlined earlier and described in more detail in Larkin and Kadane (1983). Numerical difficulties prevented our estimating the parameters δ_r, the probabilities of each location being a child's favorite location. Changes in these parameters did not produce enough change in the likelihood function to allow estimation. The reason is that the favorite-location rule is used relatively seldom, as we shall see, and, if each location is the favorite for only about one third of a 20-child sample, then there are not enough data relevant to these parameters to allow estimation. We therefore simply set all parameters δ_r equal to ⅓, postulating that each location is the favorite of roughly one-third of the children.

The estimates for each parameter in the model, and the corresponding error terms, are presented in Table 8.2. These estimates provide a fairly coherent picture of early developmental changes in search.

Consider first the estimated probabilities that each hypothesized task-adapted rule was a child's rule. As in previous rule-based work with older children, we find systematic changes with age in the kinds of rules children use. Basically, there is a shift from simpler to more complex rules. The most likely rule for 20-month-olds to use was the initial-location rule, which reflects only one of the two crucial sources of information. In contrast, the most probable rule at 42 months was the combination rule, which takes account of both kinds of information.

Developmental changes also occurred in how frequently children used their task-adapted rule rather than one of the fallback rules. The estimated probabilities of using the task-adapted rule increased with age on both relevant and irrelevant transpositions. In addition, they were lower on relevant than on irrelevant transpositions, reflecting differences in problem difficulty.

Finally, there is also some evidence of developmental change in the conditional probabilities of the two fallback rules, although this conclusion is somewhat less certain than the others because of the high standard error (0.214) associated with the favorite-box estimate for the 42-month-olds.[2] At all ages, there were relatively high probabilities associated with the random rule. These high probabilities suggest that the model is still not capturing much of what

---

[2]The estimation phenomenon is the following. There are few data supporting 42-month-olds' use of fallback rules. Hence we cannot estimate accurately which fallback rule they would use if they used one.

TABLE 8.3
Posterior Probabilities of Each Task-Adapted Rule for Each Subject

Age		Subject	Initial Rule	Moved-cup Rule	Combination Rule
20 Months		1	0.972	0.000	0.028
		2	1.000	0.000	0.000
		3	0.999	0.000	0.000
		4	0.957	0.022	0.022
		5	1.000	0.000	0.000
		6	0.997	0.003	0.000
		7	0.991	0.000	0.009
	*	8	0.425	0.000	0.575
		9	0.942	0.000	0.058
		10	0.896	0.049	0.055
	*	11	0.583	0.176	0.240
		12	0.846	0.034	0.120
		13	1.000	0.000	0.000
		14	0.943	0.003	0.054
		15	0.932	0.062	0.006
		16	0.998	0.000	0.001
		17	0.990	0.001	0.008
		18	0.992	0.000	0.008
		19	0.999	0.000	0.000
		20	1.000	0.001	0.000
		21	0.995	0.001	0.004
	*	22	0.422	0.575	0.003
30 Months					
	*	23	0.559	0.000	0.441
	*	24	0.559	0.001	0.441
		25	0.024	0.140	0.836
		26	0.918	0.082	0.000
		27	0.118	0.000	0.882
		28	0.028	0.000	0.972
		29	0.989	0.002	0.009
		30	0.003	0.000	0.997
		31	1.000	0.000	0.000
		32	0.000	0.000	1.000

children do when they are not using their task-adapted rules.

Although these results present quite a coherent and plausible account of developmental patterns in children's performance, the estimates of rule use we have obtained are only as good as the model they are based on. A particularly important assumption in the model is that each child has only one task-adapted rule. This assumption was quite plausible in the earlier rule assessment studies with elementary school children, where individual children responded highly

TABLE 8.3 (*Continued*)

Age		Subject	Initial Rule	Moved-cup Rule	Combination Rule
	*	33	0.224	0.000	0.776
		34	0.945	0.010	0.046
		35	1.000	0.000	0.000
		36	0.997	0.000	0.003
	*	37	0.431	0.000	0.569
		38	0.000	0.000	1.000
		39	0.998	0.000	0.002
		40	0.016	0.000	0.984
		41	1.000	0.000	0.000
		42	0.000	0.000	1.000
42 Months					
		43	0.013	0.986	0.001
		44	0.000	0.000	1.000
		45	0.000	0.000	1.000
		46	0.000	0.004	0.995
		47	0.000	0.000	1.000
		48	0.000	0.000	1.000
		49	0.000	1.000	0.000
		50	0.000	0.000	1.000
	*	51	0.462	0.103	0.435
		52	0.000	0.000	1.000
		53	0.000	0.000	1.000
		54	0.000	0.000	1.000
		55	0.000	0.000	1.000
		56	0.024	0.019	0.957
		57	0.000	0.000	1.000
		58	0.000	0.000	1.000
		59	0.000	0.000	1.000
		60	0.000	0.000	1.000
		61	0.000	0.000	1.000
		62	0.000	0.000	1.000
		63	0.000	1.000	0.000
		64	0.020	0.000	0.980

consistently, but it is more controversial in the present context, where individual children's response patterns are not very consistent and so might plausibly reflect use of a mixture of rules. Therefore, we made special efforts to examine the justifiability of this assumption.

If the one-rule assumption is correct here, it should be possible to determine which of the rules each individual child is most likely to be using. The probability that the child is using strategy i, given his or her set of responses x, is:

$$s(x|i)\alpha_i / \left[\sum_{j=1}^{I} s(x|j)\alpha_j \right], \tag{7}$$

given our model and the parameter estimates we obtained for it.[3] This posterior probability should be large for one of the task-adapted rules but small for the other two. Table 8.3 presents posterior probabilities for each of the task-adapted rules for each child. All but three of the twenty-two 20-month-olds, all but four of the twenty 30-month-olds, and all but one of the twenty-two 42-month-olds do fit a single identifiable rule. Those few children who do not fit any one rule well are marked by asterisks in the table. In general, they seem to be using a mixture of two rules, usually the initial-cup rule and the combination rule. One reasonable interpretation of these cases is that they may represent transitional children who are just in the process of changing from an early rule to a more advanced one. In any case, they represent only about 13% of the sample and the rest of the children fit our assumption of one task-adapted rule per child quite well.

A Contrasting Model

To further evaluate the controversial assumption that each child has just one task-adapted rule, and to determine its importance for the developmental conclusions we arrived at through the use of Model 1, we also considered a contrasting model without that assumption. This model, Model 2, instead assumes that the child chooses, independently on each trial, among the alternative rules. These choices are governed by a set of probabilities that reflect the prevalence of the alternative rules among children at that age level. The same mix of rules thus is assumed to characterize all children in an age group.

As in Model 1, children are not assumed to use a task-adapted rule on all trials but may sometimes use a fallback rule instead. The probability of a child using some task-adapted rule may vary across problem types, but the conditional probabilities of specific rules are assumed to be the same across problem types. This assumption precludes postulating entirely different rules for different problem types. Instead, a mixture of rules must be found that provides a reasonable fit to children's patterns of performance across both the relevant and the irrelevant transpositions.

The likelihood function for Model 2 is:

---

[3]The probability of the responses given the strategy $s(x/i)$ is an approximation to the posterior probability of the strategy i given the responses x. These posterior distributions would, in a more exact analysis, come from application of Bayes theorem to the data and some prior distribution through an integration of Equation 7. For our purposes of comparing rough orders of magnitude, this approximation is almost certainly adequate.

TABLE 8.4
Parameter Estimates for Model II[a]
(Model I Estimates Repeated for Comparison)

	20 Month		30 Month		42 Month	
	Model 1	Model 2	Model 1	Model 2	Model 1	Model 2
Probabilities of each task-adapted rule being a child's rule						
Initial location	.908	.592	.464	.456	.047	.237
	(.181)	(.113)	(.134)	(.057)	(.097)	(.033)
Moved-cup	.036	.097	.067	.137	.130	.025
	(.085)	(.356)	(.084)	(.063)	(.121)	(.036)
Combination	.056	.311	.469	.374	.823	.738
	(.138)	(.165)	(.126)	(.068)	(.115)	(.036)
Probabilities of using task-adapted rule						
On relevant transpositions	.351	.707	.468	.859	.655	.881
	(.073)	(.054)	(.049)	(.092)	(.041)	(.022)
On irrelevant transpositions	.513	.566	.655	.766	.805	.667
	(.056)	(.207)	(.058)	(.070)	(.047)	(.030)
Conditional probabilities of each fallback rule						
Favorite box	.292	.476	.260	.029	.072	.036
	(.067)	(.150)	(.101)	(.066)	(.214)	(.022)
Random	.708	.524	.740	.971	.928	.964
	(.067)	(.150)	(.101)	(.066)	(.214)	(.022)
$-2 \log \Lambda$	724.132	685.197	621.229	586.552	542.665	546.032

[a]Standard deviations for each estimate are given in parentheses.

$$\prod_{c=1}^{C} \sum_{r=1}^{R} \delta_r \prod_{v=1}^{V} \prod_{t=1}^{T(v)} \{\gamma_v \sum_{i=1}^{I} \alpha_i \, p(x|t,v,i) + (1 - \gamma_v) \sum_{j=1}^{J} \beta_j \, q(x|t,v,j)\} \quad (8)$$

In this likelihood function, unlike that for Model 1 (see Equations 4 and 7), the total likelihood of a child's responses is *not* the sum of terms $s(x|i)$ which are the likelihood of an entire set of responses conditional on the single rule i. Instead, for each child, Equation 8 is the sum of separate terms for each problem.

Thus, unlike Model 1, Model 2 is not particularly sensitive to a child consistently using one rule but estimates the rule-use parameters to best characterize the responses of all children in an age group. Estimates of the parameters for this model and their standard deviations are obtained just as they were for Model 1, using maximum likelihood estimation techniques.

Although Equation 8 looks very similar to Equation 4 for Model 1, and the symbols for parameters are the same, the meanings of all these parameters are different. First, the parameters α_i in Model 2 are the probabilities of any child using task-adapted rule i on any trial, whereas in Model 1, they are the probabilities that rule i is a child's sole task-adapted rule. Moreover, as we shall see in the following discussion, these changes in the meaning of α_i imply that the remaining parameters also differ between the two models.

Table 8.4 shows the parameter estimates and their standard deviations for Model 2. Estimates for Model 1 are repeated for ease in comparison. The global picture of development is much the same for both models. There are changes in the kinds of task-adapted rules children use (toward more complex rules), in the probabilities that children will use a task-adapted rule rather than a fallback rule (which generally increase with age), and in the conditional probability of the favorite-cup fallback rule (which decreases with age). The correspondence in the basic developmental conclusions that emerge from both models provides some assurance that those conclusions in fact reflect regularities in the way children of different ages respond to the task and are not just a result of the particular model we have chosen to use to assess children's search patterns.

Comparing the Two Models

Although Models 1 and 2 produce essentially the same developmental picture, they do differ considerably in how they characterize children's searches. Comparisons between the two models may be useful for determining which of these characterizations is more accurate or how a new model might be formulated that would do better than either of these. Any such comparison, however, must take into account differences in the specificity of the models as well as differences in how well they account for the data we have on children's searches.

Under Model 1, each child uses only one task-adapted strategy, which is used throughout the trials. There are three of these; consequently each child is, under this model, doing one of three things (to the extent that she is using a task-adapted strategy). Under Model 2, however, each child chooses, at random as if from an urn, a task-adapted strategy anew on each trial. Since there are 3 possibilities on each trial, and 18 trials, there are 3^{18} possibilities for each child under Model 2. (Although some of these possibilities are extremely unlikely relative to others, the total number of reasonable possibilities is still enormously greater than 3.) Thus Model 2 allows many more possibilities (i.e., is much less specific) than Model 1.

Comparing the estimates in Table 8.4, we see a pattern of less dramatic developmental change under Model 2 than under Model 1. The use of the initial-location rule is estimated to be less for the youngest children and more for the oldest children in Model 2 than in Model 1. Similarly, the use of the combination strategy is estimated to be greater for the youngest children but less for the oldest children under Model 2 than under Model 1. This result is to be expected for the following reason. Suppose a 20-month-old has many responses consistent with the initial-location rule, but some responses consistent with the combination rule. Under Model 1, this child and others like her are viewed as most likely to be users of the initial-location rule, leading to a high estimate of the parameter characterizing this rule. In contrast, under Model 2, these children are viewed as often using the initial-location rule, but sometimes using the combination rule; thus some appreciable value is obtained for the parameter associated with the combination rule as well as for the parameter associated with the initial-location rule. The result is less change in the rule-use parameters in Model 2.

Model 2 also differs from Model 1 in that the estimates of the probabilities of children using a task-adapted rule are consistently higher in Model 2, and the estimated frequency of random search is correspondingly lower. This result again appears to be a consequence of the difference in the specificity of the two models. Consider trials, on both relevant and irrelevant transpositions, on which a child responds randomly. Under Model 1, few of these responses will match the child's one task-adapted rule; hence, these trials contribute to the estimate of use of the random rule. Under Model 2, however, these responses can be classified as instances of the use of any of the three task-adapted rules, at least to the extent that corresponding search patterns occur on both relevant and irrelevant problems. Thus estimates of task-adapted rule use will tend to be higher under Model 2 than under Model 1, and correspondingly estimates of random rule use will be lower.

The estimates of children's probabilities of using a task-adapted rule on the relevant versus irrelevant problem types present a puzzle for Model 2. Each age group is estimated, under Model 2, to be more likely to use a task-adapted rule on relevant problems than on irrelevant problems. This is the opposite of the pattern obtained for Model 1; it is also the opposite of what we would expect since the irrelevant problems are intuitively simpler and in fact correct performance is much higher on them. The higher estimates for relevant problems under Model 2 appear to result from a difference between the two problem types, which Model 2 is able to capitalize upon because of its lack of specificity. On relevant transpositions, two of the three possible responses are to locations that correspond to one of the two frequently used task-adapted rules, whereas on irrelevant transpositions only one possible response—search at the initial location—fits these rules. Thus, in Model 2, where more than one rule can be invoked to explain a set of responses, more responses to relevant transpositions than to irrelevant transpositions can be taken as evidence of task-adapted rules. This difference between the two problem types does not affect the estimates of task-adapted rule use for Model 1 in the same way, since estimates of task-adapted rule use in that model are based on the entire set of responses from a child and not on individual responses.

The likelihood, Λ, maximized in estimating the parameters, provides a measure of how well a model captures a set of data. Λ is the probability of the data, given the model with the parameters as estimated. Table 8.4 shows values of $-2 \log \Lambda$ for the two models and three age groups. This value is lower (i.e., Λ is higher) for Model 2 than for Model 1 for the younger two ages. Λ is slightly higher for Model 1 for the oldest age group. Again the greater specificity of Model 1, compared to Model 2, makes its generally lower likelihoods unsurprising. Thus, while we regard the likelihoods reported here as relevant, they are by no means the full story in model comparison.

In sum, then, the assumption that each child has just one task-adapted rule seems to provide a fairly good characterization of children's performance, but there do appear to be some limitations on its validity. On the one hand, it received considerable support from the analyses of posterior probabilities for individual children, which showed that the specific rule a child was using could be identified in almost every case. On the other hand, however, comparisons between Models 1 and 2 show that the one-rule assumption in Model 1 leads the model to invoke random search more often than Model 2 and, at least for the two younger groups, also reduces the maximum likelihood the model can achieve, or the probability of the data given the best estimates of the parameters in the model. The better fit of Model 2 to the data, however, is to a large extent to be expected since it is so much less specific than Model 1. Thus, we think the better performance of Model 2 is not sufficient reason to abandon the notion that each child generally has just one task-adapted rule, but it does suggest that Model 1 may need to be elaborated to allow for some circumstances under which children may use more than one task-adapted rule. We are just beginning to develop such an elaborated model.

One circumstance that might lead to some deviations from the pure single-rule model is the occurrence of encoding or memory difficulties with respect to some information the child needs for her principal task-adapted rule. For instance, a child who typically uses the combination rule might be distracted on some trial and fail to notice where the object was hidden initially. When this kind of difficulty occurs, the child might well revert to an alternative task-adapted rule for which she does have the requisite information (in this case, presumably, the moved-cup rule) rather than using a fallback rule that does not take into account any of the available information. In general, such memory difficulties will lead to occurrences of only those task-adapted rules that are degraded or simplified forms of the child's primary rule, in the sense that they require only a subset of the information that the primary rule requires. (Thus, for example, a child whose primary rule is the moved-cup rule would *not* be expected to use the initial-cup rule when memory problems occurred.) In addition, since memory problems ought to be infrequent, they may not seriously compromise the fit of individual children's data to single rules. However, they may occur often enough, across children, to account for at least some of the advantage of the multiple-rule model in fitting children's search patterns.

To take into account this type of deviation from a single-rule model, we need to elaborate Model 1 into a more detailed information-processing model, specifying what kinds of information the child encodes and what she does with it as she chooses a place to search. The probabilities of specific responses according to the model would then depend on encoding and memory parameters as well as on the probabilities of alternative task-adapted rules being a child's primary rule.

A second circumstance under which children might use more than one rule is when they are in transition from a relatively primitive rule to a more advanced rule. This possibility was raised earlier in discussing the posterior probabilities for individual children under Model 1. We know that children tend to use different rules as they get older, and presumably they do not switch from one rule to another instantaneously. Instead, there is likely to be a transition period during which the two rules coexist until the new rule has eclipsed the old. As long as these transition periods are relatively brief, they may not seriously compromise the assumption that children generally have just a single task-adapted rule. The incorporation of developmental transitions in the model, however, would allow for a small proportion of children dividing their searches between two rules. (Note, though, that children would still not be expected to mix all three rules together.)

A fully satisfactory model incorporating developmental transitions would have to be based on children's patterns of behavior across different points in time, since it is only their relation to earlier and later rules that defines mixed-rule response patterns as transitional. Such a model would in turn require longitudinal data to be properly evaluated. Where only cross-sectional data are available, the best approximation may be an elaboration of Model 1 incorporating new task-adapted rules that are mixtures of two of the original rules. For each such mixed rule added to the model, one additional parameter would be needed to estimate the probability of children using that rule, and another to estimate the balance between the two component rules in the mixed rule for that population of children (although for simplicity this second set of parameters might be arbitrarily set to .50). If the assumption that children spend relatively little time in transitions and usually have a single predominant task-adapted rule is correct, then the probabilities estimated for these mixed rules should be low relative to those for the pure rules in our original model.

These proposals for elaborating Model 1 suggest that two kinds of data would be useful that we did not collect in our initial study. First, experimental data providing independent measures of children's encoding and retention of each of the key forms of information in a problem, and perhaps directly manipulating the memory demands of the search problems in some way, would be useful in testing to what extent memory problems contribute to deviations from a pure single-rule model. Second, longitudinal data would be useful in evaluating the hypothesis that mixed-rule children are in transition from one rule to another. Clearly, if that hypothesis is correct, we should see a predominance of one of the two rules in sessions preceding the mixed-rule observations, and a predominance of the other rule in subsequent sessions, and presumably a monotonic shift in the relative probabilities of the two rules in between. Research along both lines is currently planned.

In addition to new kinds of data, we may need more data. Even in our current model we do not have enough data to estimate some parameters (the probabilities of each location being a child's favorite). As we attempt to estimate more detailed models, an adequate quantity of data will be crucial.

SUMMARY AND CONCLUSIONS

The principal goal of the present work was to clarify the relationship between infants' initial cognitive skills and later phases of cognitive development by looking at early developments in children's search for hidden objects. A review of recent research on search spanning infancy and early childhood produced strong evidence of continuity in early cognitive development and suggested that differentiation may play a central role in the early development of search. This conclusion highlighted the importance of looking at children's search patterns across a whole set of related problems, which in turn required the development of new data-analytic techniques. We accordingly developed a stochastic modeling procedure that characterizes children's changing patterns of performance in terms of their use of hypothesized rules. This modeling effort produced three important results. First, it established that children's performance is in fact rule-governed from an early age. Second, it produced a coherent picture of developmental changes in rule use. And third, it helped to refine our understanding of the cognitive processes underlying early search.

The success of our modeling technique in characterizing rule use as early as 20 months of age, and indeed in identifying which specific rule individual children were most likely to be using, is important both methodologically and theoretically. Methodologically, it indicates the power of our stochastic estimation procedures for identifying rules despite inconsistencies in children's responses. Whereas the non-stochastic rule assessment procedures of Siegler and his associates were unable to identify rules below 4 or 5 years of age, the present procedures were able to identify rule use even in children less than 2 years of age. Theoretically, this result is important because it further strengthens the picture of continuity between infancy and childhood that emerged from earlier search work. Very young children not only respond in a rule-governed fashion, but they use rules based on the same kinds of information that contribute to correct performance. Moreover, despite inconsistencies in their responses, they appear to be like older children in having a single primary rule that represents some coherent understanding of the problems, rather than sampling among a set of different rules of more or less equivalent status.

By estimating the prevalence of a set of hypothesized rules at three different ages, we were able to characterize developmental changes in performance in terms of changing patterns of rule use. Two distinct kinds of developmental change emerged from this work. First, there were changes in which task-adapted rules were most prevalent, with older children tending to use rules that took into account more information about the problems than the rules the youngest children used most often. And second, there were changes in how often children used their task-adapted rules, reflecting improvements in how often children were "on task" and responded in accordance with their best understanding of the problems. Although both of these changes lead to improvements in correct performance, it is useful to distinguish between them because they suggest different developmental mechanisms. The first kind of change clearly corresponds to the increase in differentiation discussed earlier, with older children incorporating the same kinds of information younger children used into more complete search rules. The second kind of change, however, seems to have more to do with memory or attentional limitations that become less problematic with increasing age.

While our primary interest in this work was in estimating children's rule use, consideration of what particular model to use to get the estimates we wanted proved to be interesting in its own right. Although neither of the models we examined was completely satisfactory, comparisons between them were useful in giving us a better idea of what a more complete model might look like. Perhaps the most valuable characteristic of this kind of work is its utility in identifying directions for further work. We began with the relatively simple questions "Is early search rule-governed, and if so how do the rules children use change with age?", and we ended up with some preliminary answers to those questions but also with a whole set of new questions about when children use different rules and how they get from earlier rules to more advanced ones. These new questions, in turn, suggest some promising lines of empirical research as well as some new theoretical models to explore.

ACKNOWLEDGMENTS

An earlier version of this paper was presented as part of a symposium entitled "Development of Search Ability" at the biennial Meeting of the Society for Research and Child Development, Detroit, April 1983. The authors gratefully acknowledge the contributions of Wesley Wilson to the large amount of computer programming involved in this work. This work was supported in part by NICHHD grant #1R01 HD1695-01 and by NSF grant number 1-55035.

REFERENCES

Bjork, E. J., & Cummings, E. M. (1984). Infant search errors: Stage of concept development or stage of memory development. *Memory and Cognition, 12,* 1–19.

Bower, T. G. (1977). *A primer of infant development.* San Francisco: Freeman.

Bremner, J. G., & Bryant, P. E. (1977). Place versus response as the basis of spatial errors made by young infants. *Journal of Experimental Child Psychology, 23,* 162–171.

Case, R. (1980). Intellectual development: A systematic reinterpretation. In F. H. Farley & N. J. Gordon (Eds.), *New perspectives in educational psychology.* Canada: National Society for the Study of Education.

Cornell, E. H. (1979). The effects of cue reliability on infants' manual search. *Journal of Experimental Child Psychology, 28,* 81–91.

DeLoache, J. S., & Brown, A. L. (1983). Very young children's memory for the location of objects in a large scale environment. *Child Development, 54,* 888–897.

Fischer, K. W. (1980). A theory of cognitive development: The control and construction of hierarchies of skills. *Psychological Review, 87,* 477–531.

Freeman, N. H., Lloyd, S., & Sinha, C. G. (1980). Infant search tasks reveal early concepts of containment and canonical usage of objects. *Cognition, 8,* 243–262.

Gratch, G. (1975). Recent studies based on Piaget's view of object concept development. In L. B. Cohen & P. Salapatek (Eds.), *Infant perception: From sensation to cognition.* New York: Academic Press.

Gratch, G. (1980). Some thoughts on cognitive development and language development. In A. P. Reilly (Ed.), *The communication game: Perspectives on the development of speech, language, and non-verbal communication skills.* Johnson & Johnson Baby Products Company.

Gratch, G., Appel, K. J., Evans, W. F., LeCompte, G. K., & Wright, N. A. (1974). Piaget's Stage IV object concept error: Evidence of forgetting or object conceptualization? *Child Development, 45,* 71–77.

Horn, H. A., & Myers, N. A. (1978). Memory for location and picture cues at ages two and three. *Child Development, 49,* 845–856.

Huttenlocher, J., & Newcombe, N. (1984). The child's representation of information about location. In C. Sophian (Ed.), *Origins of cognitive skills.* Hillsdale, NJ: Lawrence Erlbaum Associates.

Huttenlocher, J., & Presson, C. C. (1973). Mental rotation and the perspective problem. *Cognitive Psychology, 4,* 279–299.

Huttenlocher, J., & Presson, C. C. (1979). The coding and transformation of spatial information. *Cognitive Psychology, 11,* 375–394.

Landers, W. F. (1971). The effect of differential experience on infants' performance in a Piagetian Stage IV object-concept task. *Developmental Psychology, 5,* 48–54.

Larkin, J. H. & Kadane, J. B. (1983). *A global maximization method for likelihood functions* (Tech. Rep.). Departments of Psychology and Statistics, Carnegie-Mellon University. Manuscript submitted for publication.

Lasky, R. E., Romano, N., & Wenters, J. (1980). Spatial localization in children after changes in position. *Journal of Experimental Child Psychology, 29,* 225–248.

Loughlin, K. A., & Daehler, M. W. (1973). The effects of distraction and added perceptual cues on the delayed reaction of very young children. *Child Development, 44,* 384–388.
More, J. J., Burton, S. G., & Hillstrom, K. E. (1980). *Users' guide for minpack-1.* National Technical Information Service, U.S. Department of Commerce.
Piaget, J. (1954). *The construction of reality in the child.* New York: Basic Books.
Rieser, J. J., & Heiman, M. L. (1982). Spatial self-reference systems and shortest-route behavior in toddlers. *Child Development, 53,* 524–533.
Siegler, R. S. (1976). Three aspects of cognitive development. *Cognitive Psychology, 8,* 481–520.
Siegler, R. S. (1978). The origins of scientific reasoning. In R. S. Siegler (Ed.), *Children's thinking: What develops?* Hillsdale, NJ: Lawrence Erlbaum Associates.
Siegler, R. S. (1981). Developmental sequences within and between concepts. *Society for Research in Child Development Monographs, 46,* (Whole number 189).
Sophian, C. (1982). Selectivity and strategy in early search. *Journal of Experimental Child Psychology, 34,* 342–349.
Sophian, C. (1984a). Developing search skills in infancy and early childhood. In C. Sophian (Ed.), *Origins of Cognitive Skills.* Hillsdale, NJ: Lawrence Erlbaum Associates.
Sophian, C. (1984b). *Understanding the movements of objects: Early developments in spatial cognition.* Manuscript submitted for publication.
Sophian, C. (1984c). Spatial transpositions and the early development of search. *Developmental Psychology, 20,* 21–28.
Sophian, C. (in press). Perseveration and infants' search: A comparison of 2- and 3-location tasks. *Developmental Psychology.*
Sophian, C., & Sage, S. (1983). Developments in infants' search for displaced objects. *Journal of Experimental Child Psychology, 35,* 143–160.
Sophian, C., & Sage, S. (in press). Infants' search for hidden objects: Developing skills for using information selectively. *Infant Behavior and Development.*
Sophian, C., & Wellman, H. M. (1980). Selective information use in the development of search behavior. *Developmental Psychology, 16,* 323–331.
Sophian, C., & Wellman, H. M. (1983). Selective information use and perseveration in the search behavior of infants and young children. *Journal of Experimental Child Psychology, 35,* 369–390.
Sophian, C., & Yengo, L. (1984). *Infants' search for visible objects: Implications for the interpretation of early search errors.* Submitted for publication.
Starkey, P., & Cooper, R. G. (1980). Perception of numbers by human infants. *Science, 210,* 1033–1035.
Strauss, M. S. (1979). The abstraction of prototypical information by adults and 10-month-old infants. *Journal of Experimental Psychology: Human Learning and Memory, 5,* 618–632.
Strauss, M. S., & Curtis, L. (1981). Infant perception of numerosity. *Child Development, 52,* 1146–1152.

9 A Comparative Description of Representation and Processing During Search

C. Donald Heth
Edward H. Cornell
University of Alberta

INTRODUCTION

By "search," we typically mean the delineation and choice of alternatives toward some ultimate goal. Search invariably entails a series of responses; these may range from the repetition of simple motor sequences to deliberate acts of mental planning. As the chapters in this volume illustrate, the analyses of human approaches to search involve memory, problem solving, and other cognitive capacities. Because search is so basic to these topics, it behooves us to consider some natural manifestations of search behavior. Beyond its metaphorical usage (as in "memory search," or "search of a problem space"), search, and associated processes of spatial orientation, play a fundamental role in the life of any organism.

This is not a new perspective. Early in the history of the comparative study of psychological processes it was recognized that all ambulatory species are concerned with finding lunch. Although it was obvious that different organisms had different solutions to this problem, students of animal behavior sought general laws to characterize the localization and utilization of resources. Learning and motivation were the theoretical processes of adaptive functioning, and the maze was one laboratory prototype for spatial problem solving. For example, Tolman (1932) suggested that the organization and purposiveness of behavior could be revealed by considering where the organism was. In other words, locations of activities and patterns of movement were seen as an indication of the drives and plans of the organism.

Historically, then, aspects of search were viewed as reflecting both motivation and cognition. However, the most fundamental point is that search is an adaptive process within the context of finding and using resources (Collier, 1981). That is, for many organisms, organized search behaviors may be automatic response algorithms, independent of planning or cognitive effort. And, as the initial and often most extensive part of a long and interdependent behavioral sequence, the outcome of search determines to a large extent the outcome of the entire sequence. For example, Collier divides the chain of events involved in feeding behavior into subcomponents of foraging, ingestion, and utilization. In nature, foraging animals are selective, and a nutritious and preferred menu requires search, identification, procurement, handling, and sometimes storage of foodstuffs prior to consumption and digestion. Clearly, it is advantageous that the organism not lose more in finding the resource than would be gained by assimilating it. Hence, we would expect that evolutionary factors would act so as to select those mechanisms that would make search efficient; that is, optimize the ratio of benefits to costs of localization.

Indeed, it is just those mechanisms that psychologists regard as "intelligent" in search performance. A child who searches in several places when only one would have sufficed is regarded as exhibiting less "planful" or less "strategic" behaviors. Even in the metaphorical sense, we regard computer searches that inefficiently examine every possibility as "brute strength" or "dumb" algorithms. The concept of efficiency seems built into our own connotation of intelligent search, and it seems reasonable to regard natural selection as placing a similar emphasis on it.

However, the attribution of intelligence to an efficient searcher raises the question of whether planfulness is necessary for efficiency. In this review we will see many cases of efficient search and behavioral organization in species that might not exhibit anticipation of outcomes. We should recognize that natural selection would favor searchers that are efficient regardless of how their behavior is mediated.

To develop this perspective, we review some of the ecological and anthropological observations made on how animals and people search for and exploit spatially defined resources in their own environment. Presented first are examples of search as a component of foraging by animals. A variety of applications of search are apparent; each can be evaluated in relation to the organism's niche.

In our second major section, we present an economic analysis of the natural problem of localizing resources. In comparative and ethological theory the approach is known as the optimal foraging analysis of search. The analysis provides a useful heuristic for understanding how different types of search are efficient for particular ecologies. For example, the analysis stipulates how travel between areas is optimal in environments with heterogeneous distributions of resources.

The third and last major section of this chapter is intended to suggest analogies between animal and human solutions to the requirements of search. We describe methods of spatial representation that are still used by certain hunting and gathering cultures. We then indicate how children may organize their search behaviors in a laboratory task that simulates several aspects of hiding and recovery of gathered resources. We see that children can choose locations according to grouping strategies that make the overall result highly efficient. We interpret this efficiency in the context of biological and social considerations of the role that spatial behaviors play in adapting an organism to its environment.

FORAGING BY ANIMALS

Within this topic we describe behaviors that indicate the representation of spatial information, and then consider how the organization of search activities may reflect the processing of that information. The major problem of representation of locations is the selection of reliable referents or landmarks. Once a food location is known, however, it must be exploited before it is discovered by competitors. Naturalistic observations indicate that search is involved in hoarding or caching, both during hiding and recovery of gathered food. The foraging animal may expand or constrain search depending on the density of food at a known location.

Selection of Cues for Approaching Locations

What is the most direct way to represent the bearing of an unseen location? Its direction can be encoded with reference to a visible landmark. This solution can involve two distinct forms of representation. First, the landmark serves as a proximal symbol for the unseen location. Second, the landmark exists in spatial relation to the location. For example, consider an organism searching for a previously encountered food source. A large tree on the horizon might serve as a useful landmark to *symbolize* the location of the food source. However, the symbolic function of the tree must be supplemented by information about where the food source is *in relation to* the tree.

Some species apparently rely upon very simple relations, in which the vector for approaching an unseen target is given by the act of orienting to its landmark. If the goal were under a distinctive tree, the direction of locomotion is the direction of perception. The wasp apparently approaches the location of its home nest in this direct manner, yet, at the site of the nest, may encode the burrowed entrance in relation to a configuration of several landmarks (Alcock, 1975; Tinbergen, 1951). The strategy is limited because it depends upon the availability of conspicuous landmarks *at* the target site. This is not generally problematic when an organism is caching obtained food, because the site of the cache is its own choice. However, when an organism consistently caches food near landmarks, it risks losing food to a competitor that uses (or discovers) the same system. And, of course, organisms are faced with search problems other than recovering a cache.

A particularly interesting case is that of foraging by honeybees. This species is faced not only with the problem of food search, but also with the problem of communicating the results of that search to other members of the hive. As is well known, the strategy of the honeybee is to employ a moving referent—the sun— and to encode and communicate the bearing and distance relationships among food source, hive, and sun (von Frisch, 1967). In this case, the symbolic component of the representation of space is simple, involving only three symbols. The relational component of the representation is more complicated, involving distance and continuously changing bearings.

The system includes some natural generality: The sun is distinctive over a variety of different terrains and cover. Furthermore, the relational component of spatial representation can be singularly mapped into a communication that preserves the essential information. In the case of European honeybees (*Apis florea*), one system translates the angle between the food location and the sun's azimuth into a displacement from the vertical, and distance information into intensity of body movements.

There is a risk associated with reliance on a small number of orientation cues. For example, one of the cues used by the honeybee, the sun, may be occluded by clouds. On such occasions, when a honeybee is attempting to recruit foraging at a new food site, it dances with reference to the position of the sun as it appeared at that time on the previous clear day (Dyer & Gould, 1981). In other words, the backup system for communication of orientation involves a response that encodes a remembered celestial event. The symbol is more abstract than a landmark.

Many species have redundant systems that are used in response to environmental instability, such as increases in predation, or incomplete or ambiguous information in any one orientation system. Able (1980) reviews several examples. For instance, most crabs move about in familiar surroundings in reference to celestial cues, but switch to landmarks if they are persistently pursued. Similarly, some species of harvester ants use scent trails to return to their nests after foraging. When there are other colonies of ants nearby, scents are not distinguishable, and a return to the wrong colony can be fatal. Consequently, the forager may use sunlight as a directional cue, and as a tertiary system, the presence of landmarks. Adaptations to information deficits include switching from one cue to another (e.g., from the sun, when occluded, to wind direction in beetles and scorpions). Adaptations to information ambiguity include simultaneous integration of cues to achieve a compromise direction. For example, after switching from occluded sun to direction of light polarization, the desert ant employs wind direction to resolve the ambiguity of component vectors of polarized light.

In summary, there are two fundamental references for spatial locations. In the simplest, a landmark is approached directly. In the second, the approach vector may be to one side of an immediately perceivable cue. The information for an unseeable location is fundamentally indirect, a representation, and can be translated into symbolic form for communication or retention.

Hiding and Recovery of Obtained Resources

The ability of an organism to return to an occluded food source clearly implies that the location can be represented in some form. Frequently, the requirements of the animal cannot be fulfilled at a single location. The animal may be capable of representing several sites and also may be able to retrieve this information on future forays. These memorial abilities are most evident in species that cache food for later consumption.

Species that cache exhibit different levels of precision in hiding and recovering food. To illustrate this point, we will describe diverse behaviors of food-hoarding birds. Observations by Haftorn (1956) indicate that some tit species cache food over large but circumscribed areas. The areas themselves are apparently the unit remembered; the tit delimits search within the area, but does not otherwise indicate memories for particular locations. What is stored and retrieved, then, is information about a relatively large sector within which the probability of finding a cache is high. Food in the sector is dense relative to the distribution in the surround, where the distribution of resources may be homogeneous or patchy. Foragers other than the hoarding bird may, of course, discover the sector by sampling methods, but the hoarding bird has the advantage of delimiting it in memory.

Other species may store and retrieve much more specific information. In the simplest case, food may be gathered and placed in a single cache. For example, the acorn woodpecker usually selects a large tree for its complete collection (Roberts, 1979). In this case, the memory load is minimal, the process of gathering ensures repeated approaches to the site, and the spatial dispersion of recovery efforts is minimal. Nevertheless, there is a large risk in using only one cache. If a competitor discovers the site, the stored food may be plundered completely.

Scatter-hoarding is a strategy that reduces this risk, yet may be different than hoarding in sectors. Birds that are scatter-hoarders store items in several separate caches and seem to encode individual sites rather than areas. Ethological descriptions suggest that memory for unique sites is indicated because the birds directly approach rather nondescript locations. Single seeds may be isolated with a few probes into a broad bed of moss, or single nuts may be uncovered with minimal scratching on a large and homogeneous snowdrift.

Shettleworth and Krebs (1982) have recently reported experimental observations of marsh tits given 12 seeds to hoard in a large aviary containing 97–100 prefabricated hiding sites. Shettleworth and Krebs focused their analysis on the way these seeds were later recovered. They found that recovery was remarkably good. For example, the birds recovered about eight seeds after searching little more than 30 sites. The performance indicated that search was not a random process; Shettleworth and Krebs suggest that the efficiency can be attributed to specific memories for food locations. They note that the probability of visiting a particular location during search is higher when a seed has been cached in that location than when the location is empty. On some control trials, seeds were moved after the bird had hidden them. Recovery performance dropped in two ways: The birds visited twice as many sites (increasing travel), and the number of seeds recovered was less than when their location was preserved. Performance during these control trials indicated the birds did not use olfactory or other subtle cues allowing direct perception of the current location of the seeds. Furthermore, the numerous searches at locations where a bird had hidden seeds could not be completely explained by assuming a search path that recapitulates its order of preference for visiting sites. It appears that memories for environmental cues serve to direct recovery of caches made by the marsh tit.

Although the data of Shettleworth and Krebs (1982) deal with a specialized gathering and hoarding species, some general points can be made: First, even within a relatively homogeneous array of hiding places, individual birds showed preferences for visiting some sites over others. For example, when allowed repeated opportunities to cache seeds, marsh tits tended to use a more restricted sample of sites than would be expected if hiding trials were independent. Shettleworth and Krebs note how such a bias might improve recovery performance, although they demonstrate that it does not by itself account for the high levels of recovery that were obtained.

Second, it is possible that preference for particular places might be spatially structured, so that preferred places form a sector. Indeed, inspection of representative depictions of the performance of the marsh tits suggests, post hoc, the existence of a sector in the center of the room (See Fig. 9.1). Such a sector could represent a higher-order organization of individual locations, analogous to the grouping of perceptually structured information by humans (Dempster, 1981). Grouping of information improves its recallability; if the methods for grouping are unknown, memory capacity for isolated items might be overestimated.

Finally, the fact that marsh tits apparently demonstrate both spatial preferences and specific memories of hiding places indicates an interplay. The multiplicity of strategies possibly allows for adaptive response to two requirements of efficient hiding. First, the location of each cache must be remembered; otherwise, the gathering is wasted effort. Second, the location must be sufficiently indistinguishable to avoid detection by thieves. For example, another scatter-hoarding bird, the Clark's nutcracker, apparently groups caches near prominent landmarks, such as rocks or logs. While these referents might facilitate recall, non-hoarding competitors often constrain their search to sectors near such obvious landmarks (Vander Wall, 1982). The hoarder seems to reduce the risk of a competitor's discovery of a cache by hiding food in locations not spatially contiguous to landmarks, but nevertheless remembered by idiosyncratic rela-

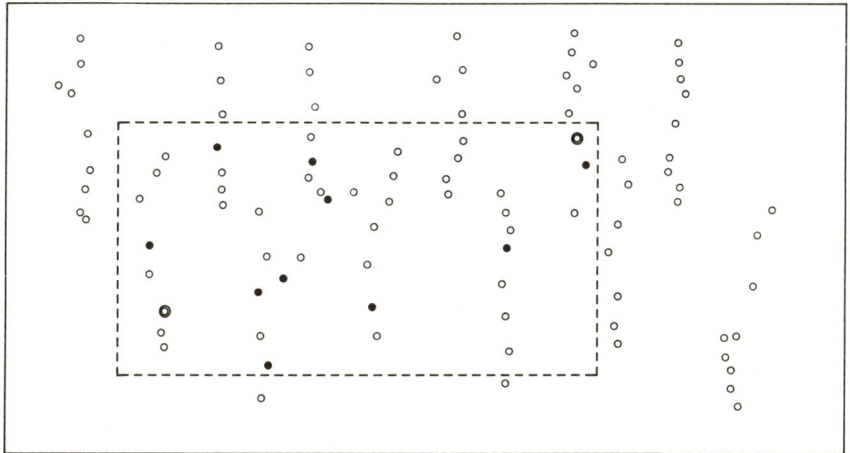

FIG. 9.1. A schematic of the test aviary depicted on p. 108 of Shettleworth (1983). The schematic presents a side view of the configuration of circular hiding sites; the ceiling of the room is represented by the uppermost solid line. Hiding sites were holes drilled in branches that were hanging from the ceiling or anchored to the floor. The dashed rectangle delimits a sector that encompasses the sites used by one marsh tit for hoarding 12 seeds. The two ringed circles indicate sites where a hidden seed was not recovered; completely filled circles indicate a successful search. Eighteen of the 24 holes inspected during the search phase were in the designated sector.

tionships to these cues. Specific memories provide a backup to the spatial grouping strategy.

In summary, search behavior can be directed in reference to general or particular memories. A memory of a sector represents an area where sites are concentrated. Individual sites may also be memories, such as the tree containing a single cache. More capacity could be required for memories of multiple sites. Nevertheless, grouping and hiding algorithms may be available to some species and combined in various strategies both to retain information for sites and ensure that the information is not apparent.

Directing Search to Locations with Abundant Resources

The law of effect (Thorndike, 1911) holds that a response will be strengthened if it is followed by reinforcing consequences. A contingent reward ensures that the probability of repetition or maintenance of the response is increased. As we shall illustrate, this law is not strictly true in situations in which reinforcing consequences are spatially distributed. Resources are unevenly distributed or patchy in most natural environments, so that after a food source has been depleted, repetition at that particular locale of the chain of searching and procuring responses is inefficient. It is time to move on.

Premature or excessive movement may be inefficient too, especially if resources are rare. Behaviors that allow foraging within a still-productive area are termed *win-stay* strategies. As we shall see, they are characterized as strategies because they usually involve something different than a repetition of a previously successful response. They allow the searcher to move on, but not out of the patch.

Constraining Search. Two simple win-stay strategies can be observed in the movements of foraging bees. Leaving one flower for another can involve both a new direction and flight distance. The bearings of any two successive flights are usually positively correlated; there is a tendency for a forward progression, although there may be several different vectors for flights. The generally forward direction of the foraging path may reflect that flowers are rare and easily depleted food sources. Both Pyke (1978) and Heinrich (1979) have determined that changes in the direction of flight are associated with the resources available from flowers on an inflorescence. An inflorescence is the arrangement of flowers on a branch or axis of a single plant. The number of flowers sampled on an inflorescence is an index of the reward value of the area. There is a positive correlation between the angular deviation of the departing flight path (relative to the flight path that allowed arrival on the flower) and the number of flowers visited on an inflorescence (Pyke, 1978). Distributions of directional change are different for bees foraging in rich versus depleted patches of clover (See Fig. 9.2). In the rich areas, they tend to head off in all directions (including backwards) with approximately equal probability. In areas of scarcity, they tend to move much more forward than backward.

Similarly, although most bees tend to visit the flower that is the nearest neighbor to the previously visited flower, bumblebees at least are known to adjust their intervisit flight distance in response to the quantity of nectar most recently obtained. Pyke (1978) found a negative correlation between the distance of a departing flight and the number of flowers sampled on an inflorescence: If only one flower had been visited, the bees flew twice as far to the next inflorescence than when three or more flowers of the same inflorescence had been visited.

The net effect of these changes in directional and distance responses is that bees tend to remain in food-rich patches and move through areas containing little reward. The algorithms for movement during search are similar to those of foraging thrushes (Smith, 1974). With both birds and bees, then, win-stay strategies involve novel responses to constrain behavior spatially.

Expanding Search. An alternative strategy, *win-shift*, may be predominant under different ecological conditions. A predator may be quite successful at search, localizing an area abundant with prey. Nevertheless, when foraging

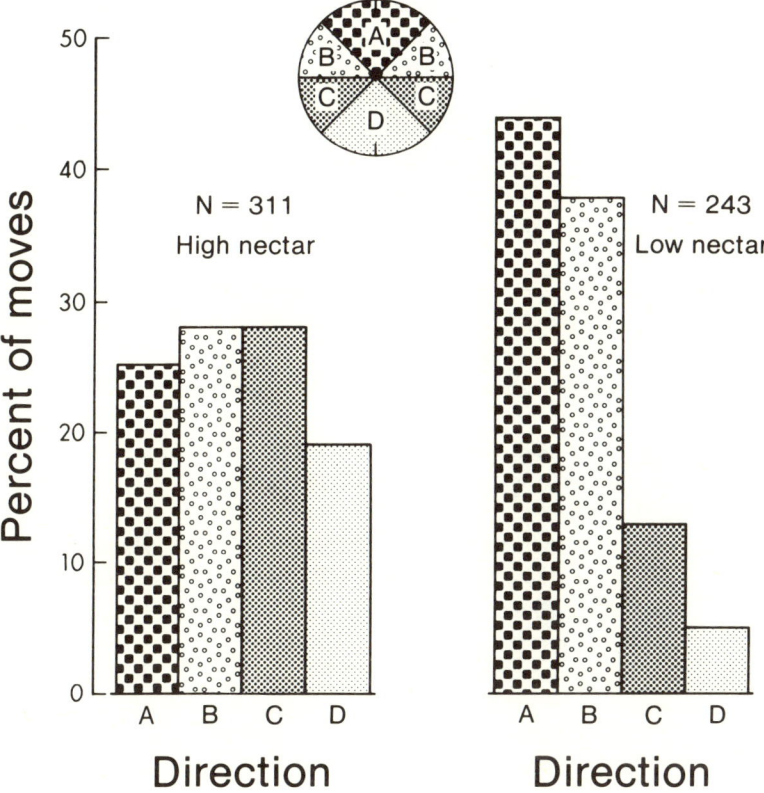

FIG. 9.2. Histograms representing the distribution of turning angles used by bees to depart from a clover head. The angle used to arrive at the clover is designated by checkering (A); symmetrical deviations are designated in the pie chart. The histogram on the left represents flight directions in a patch that had been screened for two days prior to the observations, and the histogram on the right represents flight directions in a depleted patch (Redrawn from Heinrich, 1979).

activities deplete the resources within a patch, it is useless to continue in the area, and an exit followed by an immediate return can be fruitless as well. For example, floral nectar is a food resource for some birds that is only slowly regenerated within clusters of flowers. The amakihi, a nectar-feeding bird of Hawaii, seems to adjust its pattern of search to these natural contingencies. Its prey is the luscious blossom of the mamane tree, and clusters of these blossoms seem to be exploited as a unit. Kamil (1978) found that individual birds avoided repeated visits to the same cluster and temporally patterned those returns that did take place. The revisits to a specific cluster occurred about one hour after an initial visit. Our estimates from Kamil's measurements indicate that about 84% of the nectar content of a cluster can be produced in one hour.

Kamil (1978) also suggests that it is unlikely there are botanical cues to indicate that a blossom has been visited. Amakihi that intrude into an area where another amakihi has been foraging do not avoid blossoms that have been emptied. It is possible that the resident forager uses a movement algorithm to distribute visits, or physically marks exhausted sites with some personal cue, but these strategies do not seem to be obvious to competitors or naturalist. Kamil suggests the possibility that the amakihi has memories for specific clusters, although one nonrepetitious search path could involve hundreds of individual memories.

There appear to be two separate uses of site memories by marsh tits. One, inferred from behavior similar to that of the amakihi, is apparent during recovery of seeds. The march tit avoids revisits to hiding sites that had been exhausted during its earlier feeding. Revisits to the most recently emptied sites are extremely rare; a second search at a location was observed to be more likely after 30–34 other locations had been emptied, but even after these interpolated activities, marsh tits only revisited sites on approximately 2% of the opportunities to do so (Shettleworth & Krebs, 1982).

The second use of site memories is inferred from the behavior of the marsh tit during hoarding. Shettleworth & Krebs (1982) used a clever manipulation to reveal win-shift hiding strategies. Individual birds were given eight seeds to hide in the open aviary described previously. One hundred hiding places were available. Two to 3 hours after this initial placement, a bird was given an additional eight seeds to hoard. Shettleworth & Krebs observed that an individual bird rarely revisited a site used as a cache in the first hoarding. Instead, it preferred to approach and use sites that were unfilled. The effect of this strategy is to produce scatter-hoarding, reducing the likelihood that all gathered resources will be discovered by a competitor. It is interesting to note that a second hoarding task requires a response that is opposite to that shown in the recovery task described earlier. Recall that when the marsh tit was recovering previously hidden seeds rather than storing new ones, it approached rather than avoided previously visited sites.

The processing of a large number of memories for specific sites tagged with either approach or avoidance responses could presumably involve extensive cognitive capacities. Before attributing such capacities to any organism, comparative investigators have used experimental methods to isolate simple algorithms that could mediate spatially organized behavior. The work of Olton and his colleagues (recently summarized in Olton, Handelmann & Walker, 1981) illustrates the approach with reference to the win-stay strategies used by foraging rats.

The general characteristics of the behavior should now be familiar. In the initial paradigm devised by Olton (Olton & Samuelson, 1976), rats were placed in the center of a radial-arm maze. All arms led to baited food locations, and the rat was free to run down any arm at any time. After choosing an arm and completely consuming the bait at its terminus, an individual rat rarely chooses the arm again once it returns to the center platform of the maze.

There are a number of ways the rat could avoid fruitless repetitions in this situation. It might use a response algorithm. For example, it might always turn to the left after emerging from an arm, choosing the immediately adjacent arm and circumnavigating the maze in a clockwise routine (cf. fish: Roitblat, Tham, & Golub, 1982). Such a response algorithm requires a minimum of travel and only three memorial items: a recent memory for the last arm visited, a memory for the turn direction, and a primacy memory for the first arm visited. The response algorithm could be difficult to observe if it were inconsistently executed or if choices were occasionally determined by a landmark cue. It is also possible that a systematic but idiosyncratic alternation scheme (e.g., crossing the maze) could serve to delineate sectors for choice. Several investigations (reviewed in Olton, Handelmann, & Walker, 1981) have attempted to disrupt any such response algorithms, by forcing the rats to choose certain arms before allowing them to choose freely, and confining them to the center platform of the maze after each choice. With both of these procedures, rats avoid repetitions just as well as they do in the free choice procedure, and the interpretation is that the animals do not have to use any form of response strategy to remember where food locations had been exhausted. This interpretation may be presumptuous, because even a simple tendency such as the rat's disposition to turn away from the arm it just emerged from (Olton, Collison, & Werz, 1977) could affect choice probabilities, and the most recent choice could be predominant information during a delay.

There is stronger evidence to suggest that the organization of the rat's search is based on memories for environmental cues, such as landmarks in the room containing the maze. The evidence comes from a demonstration of differential performance (Olton & Collison, 1979). A radial maze was constructed so that it could be rotated after the rat had returned from an arm and was on the central platform. After rotation, different arms of the maze pointed to the same locations in the test room. In one condition, rats were rewarded for choosing each spatial location once irrespective of the arm in that location. These rats performed at their usual high level of accuracy. In another condition, rats were rewarded for choosing each arm once irrespective of its relation to room cues. These rats performed at chance levels, indicating they did not use minute cues on the apparatus, personal scent markings, or the absence of bait odors to identify arms they had previously traversed. As a result of these and other experiments, it appears that rats execute a win-shift strategy in reference to memories for distant landmarks (Olton, 1978).

In summary, we have illustrated divergent search strategies shown by organisms with the common problem of localizing food sources. Successful search may involve spatially constraining activities (win-stay) or it may involve movement to other areas (win-shift). The determinants of these different behaviors seem to lie in the ecological requirements of search, a topic we consider in detail in the next section. A variety of possible mechanisms have been considered that would allow an organism to approach or avoid previously visited sites. One strategy, a habitual pattern of movement, allows spatial choice without assuming much about memorial capacities. There is accumulating evidence, nevertheless, that some organisms process a number of memories for individual locations and referential landmarks.

AN OPTIMAL FORAGING ANALYSIS OF SEARCH

When resources are spatially distributed, their exploitation becomes energetically demanding. Ethologists and comparative psychologists have become increasingly interested in explaining spatial behaviors in terms of these energy demands, frequently drawing upon models and concepts from microeconomic theory (Sibly & McFarland, 1976). As an overview, these models and concepts are intended to provide an explanatory framework for the variety of spatial representations and behaviors surveyed in the preceding section. More specifically, the idea is that forms of search are explicable by reference to their possible role in promoting the organism's fitness. One consideration involves what an organism gains from a search activity relative to what it loses. There is an algorithm that optimizes this trade-off.

Benefit/Cost Considerations

The guiding heuristic of a microeconomic analysis of foraging is the putative optimality of natural selection. Because the efficiency of gathering and using resources affects the reproductive fitness of the organism, these activities should presumably be finely tuned so as to increase the benefits of a choice of behaviors relative to their costs. It should therefore be possible to predict the emergence of a spatial strategy by specifying this benefit/cost relation for each organism's environmental niche.

In principle, the benefits can be specified by reference to the specific resources obtained at a place. Meeting grounds provide reproductive opportunities, nests provide offspring concealment, caches provide caloric reserves, and so forth. Indeed, it has been suggested that a common currency of benefits could be devised, based, for example, on energy units (Maynard Smith, 1978; Sibly & McFarland, 1976). Whatever the merits of these attempts, it seems obvious that benefits accrue when the organism encounters a resource as a result of a search process.

More problematic are the costs. The most apparent are those energetic requirements of finding, handling, and consuming the resource. We term these immediate energetic costs *direct costs*. Psychology has long been concerned with such direct cost considerations; witness its earlier concern with the law of least effort (Solomon, 1948). More subtle are the concomitant but indirect costs of a behavior brought about by its effects on the organism's opportunity to engage in other activities, risk of predation, or lost reproductive opportunities. Such *opportunity costs* have recently been addressed by ethologists in terms of general fitness benefits. Last, and most difficult to assess, are the costs associated with a more sophisticated psychological process. An omniscient behavior strategy might indeed maximize benefits, but it could require enormous amounts of information or processing to effect. We will refer to these as *complexity costs*. Short of some general guidelines such as parsimony, there has been little theoretical analysis of the costs of complex systems. As a start, Bremermann (1974) has suggested that it is possible to measure the complexity cost of an automaton in terms of quantifiable energy units. An automaton is a conceptual device that accomplishes a specified function, such as the execution of a reflex by a neural arc.

These considerations of optimality are especially pertinent in foraging situations such as the ones we have surveyed. When food sources are sampled by personal visits, complex tradeoffs of costs and benefits arise. Clearly, the organism receives benefit when a rich food source is discovered. But search requires energy. A search path that minimizes distance traveled might reduce most energy costs, but could also increase the risk of repeat visits to depleted areas. This trade-off, in turn, might be potentially solvable by purposive delays or distributions of returns, but optimal solutions might require complex decisions with large memorial demands. Even given an efficient rule for exploitation, environments are not static, and a fixed strategy may render the organism obsolete. In view of the uncertainties associated with evaluating direct costs, opportunity costs, and complexity costs, a prospective account that predicts spatial strategies seems difficult to obtain. Instead, at this time, ethologists and sociobiologists are attempting to demonstrate a congruence between the ecological and economical demands on an organism, and the presumed efficiency of observed behaviors.

For example, given a completely homogeneous spatial distribution of food sources, a simple response algorithm is quite efficient. If the distribution is large, such as a meadow of clover blossoms, an algorithm that avoids backtracking can provide a high rate of return (Pyke, 1978). A movement algorithm also does not require much complexity costs, so it could be used by organisms with rudimentary nervous systems (e.g., bees). In addition, in more complex organisms, a movement algorithm may be automatic, permitting allocation of processing to exploration, wariness, or the reduction of other opportunity costs.

Spatially clumped food sites are a more variable problem. If the distance between sites is relatively large, an organism might achieve better returns with short trips within a patch, even at the risk of repeat visits to depleted food sources. Furthermore, it is possible to direct search via an algorithm of only moderate complexity that is congruent with this ecology. In their observations of bumblebees, Waddington and Heinrich (1981) reported three possible mechanisms mediating the win-stay behaviors we described previously. The variability of flight directions after a successful visit to an inflorescence could be due to the extended circular motions of the bee while repeatedly probing a flower, to the loss of memory of the arrival vector due to time spent on the flower, or to decision processes affected by a sensitivity to the fullness of the flower relative to others.

For other species in patchy environments, both the direct cost of travel and the opportunity costs of risked revisits might be excessive. For example, hummingbirds have high metabolic rates that could make such costs very high. For such animals, the complexity costs of more complicated decision algorithms might be affordable.

The Marginal Value Algorithm

The problem of searching patchy environments has an optimal solution that follows from benefit/cost considerations. The change of benefits from an activity relative to the change of direct costs is known as the marginal returns of that activity. The maximum returns from the environment are gained when the predator remains in a patch only as long as its rate of return (benefits relative to direct costs) within the patch is larger than its average rate of return across all patches (Charnov, 1976). In other words, the predator will optimize foraging when it switches patches shortly after the marginal returns within a patch drop below marginal returns from the environment as a whole. The analysis is consequently referred to as the *marginal value algorithm*.

Observations of animal behavior in patchy environments indicate that foragers are sensitive to the variables that enter into a marginal value analysis (see Krebs, 1978, for a review). However, it has yet to be established that choices are determined by such an analysis. Notice that the optimal solution (optimal in the sense of reducing direct costs and opportunity costs) increases the complexity cost of the decision rule. To utilize the marginal value algorithm, the forager must be sensitive to both the local rate of return within a patch, and the global rate of return across all patches. In a sense, there must be a "working memory" for returns within a patch, and a "long-term memory" for returns from the environment as a whole; because these terms have other connotations, we will refer instead to *local* versus *global* memories. To employ the marginal value algorithm, an organism needs global memories to set the threshold for abandoning a patch and local memories to determine if that threshold has been reached in the current patch.

An important consideration would be the number of experiences that are represented in local and global memories. Krebs (1978) has suggested that the threshold for abandonment might be either fixed or variable, depending upon the size of a hypothetical memory window of n previous experiences with patches. If n includes all patches visited during the lifespan of the individual, then the threshold is fixed; if it is a sample of fewer experiences, then the threshold would vary in accordance with the encountered densities of food in the remembered patches. In other words, a large value of n would provide stable estimates of environmental returns, at the cost of increased demands for representation of global memories. Smaller values would allow for forgetting of some memories, but might result in variable threshold estimates.

Similarly, local memories represent returns within a patch. Since the patch itself is depleted as the organism forages, local memories must allow for good estimates of return rate as rate decreases. Obviously, the estimate is more precise if the sample size is large; however, if the sample includes too many early experiences in the current patch, the estimate will be biased by the higher rate of return available upon entering the patch. Orians (1981) has suggested that the window of local memories might be analyzable in such terms, leading to a theory of optimum memory span for directing search.

The marginal value algorithm is an efficient approach to the foraging problem under certain conditions. It provides a solution to the trade-off of the direct costs of moving to a new patch relative to the opportunity costs of staying within an increasingly depleted patch. Furthermore, it does this with the modest complexity cost of processing global memories for rate of return across patches and local memories for rate of return within a patch. However, it is an algorithm that is applicable only when search involves random encounters with goal objects within a patch (Krebs, 1978).

A perfectly nonredundant search is possible if the forager can identify or remember each food site that has been visited. Under these conditions, the organism can exploit the entire patch before leaving it. This strategy reduces the opportunity cost of staying within a patch, but can increase complexity cost through greater demands on memorial representations or on algorithms that reduce revisits. As we have seen, independent investigators have suggested that mnemonics underly the nonrepetitive search behavior of the amakihi, marsh tit, and rat. Thus, complexity costs may be affordable for a variety of species.

In the analyses presented here, we have generally treated the optimal solution to the problem of foraging as unique. This might be a plausible outcome in cases of fairly stable environments. However, in situations where ecological contingencies vary, a strategy or behavior that is optimal in one setting may be risky in another. For example, the Clark's nutcracker may remember caches dug in the soil in reference to configurations of pebbles or nearby twigs. These landmarks may be occluded for long periods, or even distorted, when snow and ice are extreme.

Real (1980) has suggested that behavioral adaptations might serve to avoid risks under conditions of environmental uncertainty. The optimal strategy may be flexibility, a set of strategies, each of which is optimal with respect to a set of environmental conditions. A broad range of strategies allows for contingencies; there is no overreliance on a single strategy that can become ineffective as the environment changes. One interpretation of Real's analysis is that the foraging strategy exhibited by organisms in variable environments is easily susceptible to modification.

In summary, considerations of optimal foraging theory suggest that search behaviors are governed by interactions of the ecology and psychology of the organism. The ecology will specify the direct and opportunity costs of search behaviors. The psychology of the organism will determine the complexity costs. The organism can be viewed as allocating and organizing search effort subject to these costs. In some cases involving simple organisms and regular environments, the search strategies might be quite fundamental. In more complex settings, permitting elaborate psychological processes, the strategies might be many and variable. In each case, we view the forager as responding to trade-offs in the cost of search relative to its benefits.

THE DEVELOPMENT OF HUMAN SEARCH STRATEGIES

The requirements of foraging seem especially pertinent to the spatial problem-solving abilities of the human species, because hominids have gained their subsistence by farming only for about 10,000 years (Pfeiffer, 1978). The anthropological record suggests that early humans established large territories with a wide variety of food types. The territories contained both animate prey and plants, which had to be harvested in different ways. Wild fruit and vegetables had to be located, gathered, prepared, and stored. Locations of fish and game also required continual exploration, and the pursuit, capture, and dressing of these protein sources often involved activities spread over considerable areas. Hence, orientation and navigation were integral to the search for food.

There is comprehensive evidence of unique human adaptations to meet these varying requirements. To illustrate this point, we consider two contemporary hunter-gatherer societies that evince different solutions to the problems of navigation while foraging. The solutions differ from those we have surveyed in the animal literature, in that they involve more obvious use of cognitive processes and intraspecies communication. In addition, we see that certain spatial mnemonics and strategies are mediated by cultural practices that preserve safety and productivity. Nevertheless, we argue that different cultural solutions to the problems of search exhibit commonalities when viewed as convergent adaptations.

For example, we see that hunter-gatherer peoples are sensitive to some of the extraordinarily subtle environmental cues that animals use to navigate. It seems likely that the same environmental contingencies provided the impetus for responding to these cues. In other words, the costs of effort, risk avoidance, and information processing have resulted in analogous solutions to the economics of foraging. Our thesis is that human search abilities are fundamental skills concerned with landmark use, hunting, and hoarding.

The Ulgunigamiut: Use of Landmarks in an Arctic Environment

The Ulgunigamiut are a native Inuit group whose home is the territory near Wainwright, one of the most northerly points of Alaska (Nelson, 1969). The arctic basin is a bleak environment of tundra and sea ice. Both are snow covered for about 9 months of the year. The land is generally flat and featureless, sometimes broken by river lagoons, upturned rocks, and shoreline cliffs. The sea, when it is covered by ice, is a chaotic mass of different types of ice, ranging from densely packed ice blocks and ridges to flat aprons of newly frozen leads. Although the variation in ice features provides some natural landmarks, they are frequently unreliable: Winds and currents move the sea ice relative to the land, and the weather of the region may occasionally obscure visibility beyond a few meters. Within this environment, the Ulgunigamiut hunters must orient and navigate over large distances and time periods. Furthermore, specific routes of travel are often rendered useless, either by the movement and rotation of the ice pack, or by the opening of a large, impassable lead of open water across the path of travel.

Nevertheless, the ecology of the region has sufficient diversity to provide a variety of protein sources. At different times of the year, cod, ducks, geese, fox, polar bears, white whales, ringed and bearded seals, walrus, and caribou can be harvested from land or sea. The abundance of each type of prey is seasonally determined, leading to cyclical or sequential patterns of hunting.

The Ulgunigamiut are remarkably efficient in exploiting these resources, despite the demanding environment. Nelson (1969) describes many of the social and psychological adaptations of these people which permit them to cope with the severe restrictions on navigation. Although these adaptations are cultural, they exhibit many of the features of the processing of spatial information exhibited by wild animals.

In winter, seals are hunted in open leads on the pack ice. As low-lying terrain features, leads in the ice are not directly visible over long distances. When available, the Ulgunigamiut employ meteorological features as indices of leads. Open leads of water produce certain atmospheric effects visible for long distances (15–30 km). These features, like distant landmarks, symbolize the location of hunting areas. Furthermore, the relation of the lead to the symbol is directly given by orientation to these features. For example, on clear days, steam clouds and fog banks hover over open leads. On cloudy days, features of the ice are reflected on low-lying clouds, and appear as colored patterns in the sky. This "sky map" can, to the experienced eye, directly indicate the location of an open lead, and may even delineate the configuration of the lead and the type of ice surrounding it.

More indirect is the use of environmental features that are not produced by events at a location, but reveal referential cues. A feature often used in this way is the arctic wind, especially in cases of poor visibility, when landmarks are not available. In this case, a vector or bearing is specified in relation to an immediate event, such as the blowing of fur around the head of the hunter's parka. Although the constancy of the arctic winds make this a reliable feature, the hunter must be alert to slight changes in direction or the cessation of the wind. The hunter may then rely on the drift patterns of snow, which provide a cumulative index of wind direction. The direction of water currents and swells and the flight paths of birds can also be used to reckon bearings.

In some cases, bearing information is provided by configural stimuli. That is, the reliability of the landmark depends upon the co-occurrence of other cues. An example of this is the direction of stellar landmarks, which show regular movements relative to fixed points on the land. These movements can provide directional information when they are accompanied by temporal information. For example, the handle of the constellation known as the big dipper (*Ursa Major*) parallels the horizon at 6:00 p.m., and if it is noted that the constellation is directly to the east at that time, the information can be used on subsequent days to guide travel. Hence, not only must there be remembrance of the patterning of the celestial event, there must be an independent judgment of time. Anthropologists have noted that the Ulgunigamiut have traditionally shown excellent capacity to estimate temporal duration and time of day, and contemporary hunters own watches, constantly adjust and refer to them, and hardly ever bother with compasses or spatial units of distance such as meters or miles.

Nelson's (1969) observations indicate that the Ulgunigamiut employ sophisticated techniques to extract bearing information from an environment that appears featureless. The information is then used in a variety of strategies for navigation. As noted, the drift of the ice pack and the possibility of open leads across a path makes specific route learning difficult. Nelson noted that on several occasions the Ulgunigamiut did not retrace a route, but navigated across large and novel spaces in order to return from a hunt. They planned such traverses in a way that exploits natural "catch features" of the environment. For example, if a hunting party is returning to a village on the coast, it will head not for the village itself, but for a point south of it. When the coast is reached, the party then knows the village is to the north. This strategy minimizes the risk of error that might result from a direct return; as Nelson notes, if the party had traveled straight toward the village and missed it, it would not know which direction to go to find it. Instead, at the outset of the return, a Euclidean spatial inference is made, involving the locations of the party, catch feature, and village. Paradoxically, the safest approach is considered to be away from the line of least distance.

The Ngatatjara: Search for Food and Water in a Desert Environment

The Gibson Desert of Australia is the home and hunting ground of the Ngatatjara people (Gould, 1969). The desert environment places considerable constraint on the Ngatatjara ecology. There is continuous uncertainty about water, for both the

Ngatatjara and their prey. This tends to localize both an important resource itself and some of the major foodstuffs. Despite its harsh appearance, the desert supports a variety of possible food sources. Some, such as lizards, grubs, and shrubs, are easily gathered from known vegetation patches. Others, such as kangaroos and emus, demand wide-ranging hunting forays. Because of the heterogeneous distribution of edible vegetation, game, and water, the Ngatatjara are mobile and sensitive to the large-scale spatial configuration of their environment.

While living with the Ngatatjara, Gould (1969) was especially impressed by the memories for sites demonstrated for him by these aboriginal hunter-gatherers. The Gibson Desert is not a well-defined entity, at either the macro or micro level. It forms part of a continuous series of deserts that cover approximately half a million square miles; the boundaries of these deserts are geographically arbitrary. Gould accompanied hunting parties and asked individuals to describe their path and destination as well as those of other places they had walked. An aborigine could freely recall more than 400 places with water—rock clefts and hollows in trees where rain collects, as well as ground holes, blinds, and gorges (Pfeiffer, 1978). Trees and rock formations that were completely indistinguishable to the naive traveler were anticipated and identified as they walked. The hunters represented their memories as a series of spatiotemporal associations, a living record of the sequence of events encountered during past travels. The routes across the desert were usually discussed in reference to shared names for locations and historical treks. Some of these treks were also represented in carvings or paintings on the faces of rocks at a waterhole or blind. The representations are idiosyncratic field maps, cues for the hunter and a small number of his totem cult. The elements on these maps are usually a rectilinear course of turns and landmarks. Waterholes are usually represented as geometric forms, and may form the hub for a few radiating paths. Although some routes were estimated to consist of over 400 miles of travel, they usually covered both the length and breadth of an area rather than bisecting it. These routes rarely crossed themselves and are reminiscent of the patterns of movement of insects and animals that sample broad environments (see Fig. 9.3).

External stores, social communication, and attentional strategies aid in the recollection of vital places. Veteran hunters among the Ngatatjara carve the representations of a significant track on their personal weapons. The procurement of these weapons involves recall of distant wood sources by several hunters, as well as instruction and modeling of techniques of construction. Gould (1969) also noted that significant landmarks are often encoded through directed attention to features, such as a backward scan to a full water site as the hunter leaves it.

All three of the mnemonic strategies are combined in some of the dramatic rituals of the Ngatatjara. Tribal history is recorded in sacred myths called the "dreamtime." In periodic ceremonies, totemic groups review the religious iconography of the dreamtime. The substance of the ceremonies is a review of the layout of past events, secret places and incidents occurring on legendary hunts or

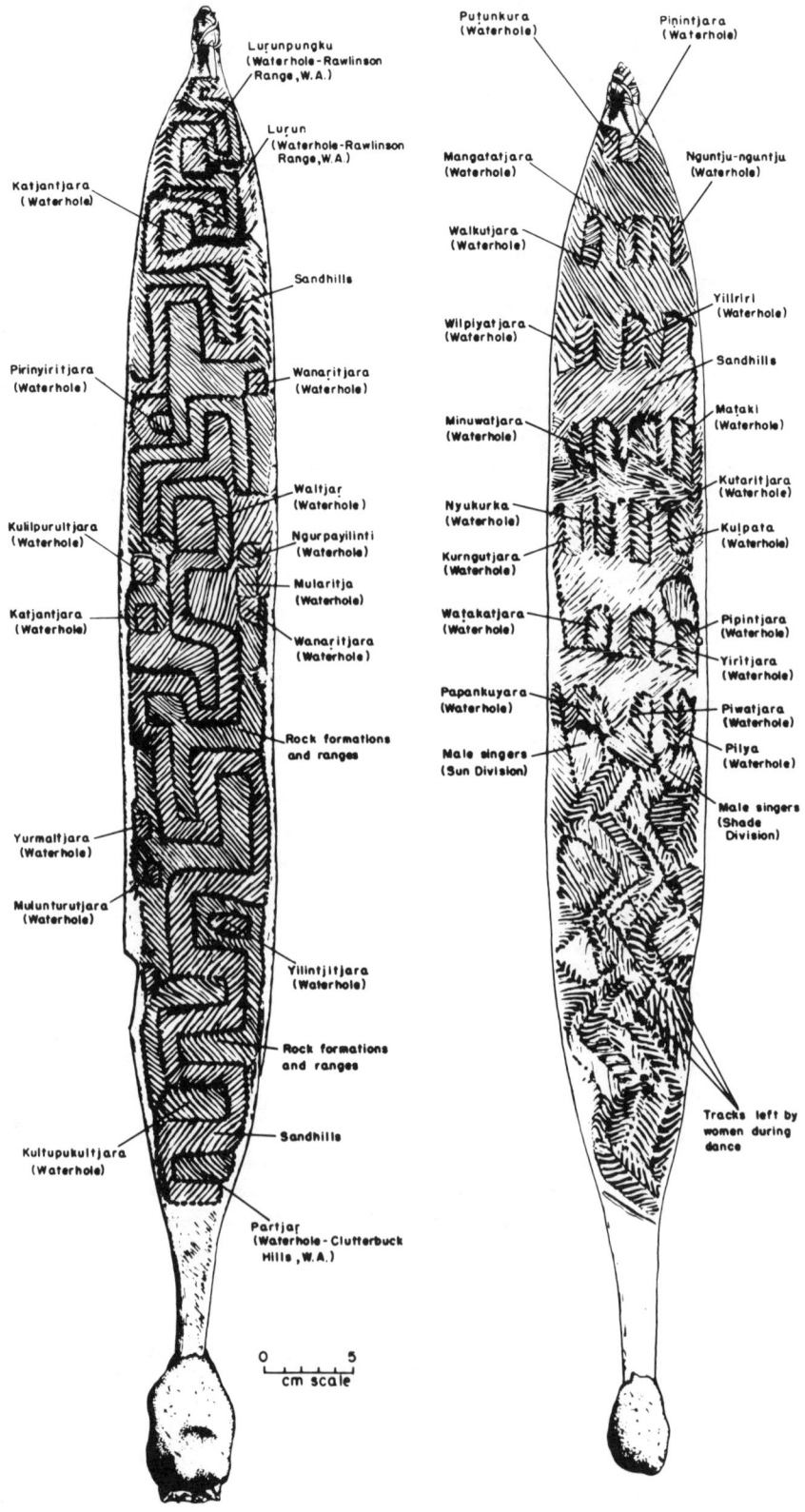

travels. The style of the ceremonies evokes varied emotional reactions: fear, laughter, isolation, and camaradarie. Names and locations are reinstated through various media: carvings on sacred boards, rock paintings, arrangements of stones, oral histories, and dances. The elements of each primarily encode the locations of waterholes and their interrelated paths. During the ceremony, these elements are reviewed through a communal knowledge base, in which lodge elders correct any variations of detail. Another interesting feature of the ceremonies is a recoding of the information through body painting, in which the landmarks of the myths and sacred boards are self-transcribed into designs on the body. Some artistic license in representation is permitted, but the older members of the totem lodge must approve the veracity of the design. All of these activities occur during periodic but intense emotional arousal and in the context of a significant site.

During these ceremonies, young men are initiated into the rituals of the lodge. The ceremonies seem designed to allow new members to link specific environmental knowledge. The Ngatatjara seem to have devised an inverse form of the well-known mnemonic, the method of loci. In the method of loci, known spatial configurations serve to reconstruct memories of objects or events. Among the Ngatatjara, sacred objects and ritualistic sequences of events serve to reconstruct memories of spatial configurations.

As a general characterization of the spatial representational and problem-solving strategies of contemporary hunter-gatherers, we note that the search practices of the Ulgunigamiut and Ngatatjara seem to reflect requirements of their particular ecologies. Both peoples demonstrate a keen sensitivity to subtle cues that permit them to distinguish landmarks and bearings. Navigational procedures and spatial knowledge are communally taught. Yet, the teachings of the Ngatatjara seem to emphasize names for locations and pictorial representations of traditional routes and sites. The archival nature of these depictions seems suitable for an environment that is geographically stable. In contrast, the Ulgunigamiut do not seem to rely on external representations of their landscape, although Inuit people are capable of producing maps (Sutton, 1932). Their communal reviews stress contemporary incidents in nightly conversations. Furthermore, the Ulgunigamiut regularly employ attentional and navigational heuristics to compensate for the variability in local features. It is interesting to consider that the relatively static schemes of the Ngatatjara are advantageous for exploiting the historical regularities of sites for resources. The strategies of the Ulgunigamiut may be optimal in conditions of extreme seasonal variability or environmental uncertainty.

FIG. 9.3. Decorated spear-throwers (Gould, 1970). The designs represent waterholes and other features of the desert along tracks of legendary animals. Drawings were provided through the courtesy of R. A. Gould.

Hiding and Recovery of Objects by Children

To this point, we have examined comparative and phylogenetic characteristics of search behaviors. We have illustrated human navigation abilities in the context of extant hunter-gatherer societies that exhibit many of the features of orientation seen in other species. We have noted that the processing of directions and places by humans is sufficiently flexible to represent varied ecologies.

This view of human spatial abilities is based on cross-cultural evidence comparing different solutions to the problem of localization. However, orientation is just one component of behaviors that interact with search processes. Once a resource has been found, it can be cached for subsequent use. The ability to cache requires selecting appropriate sites, remembering their locations, and recovering their contents. In light of the sophisticated hoarding abilities of animals, we suggest that there may be behavioral analogies in humans.

The possibility poses several questions: Does the organization of human search behavior reflect the spatial and economic requirements of hoarding? Are children flexible in their use of strategies to hide and recover resources? What is the interplay between mnemonic processes that represent cache locations and problem-solving strategies that direct search?

In this section, we describe how laboratory studies of persons of different ages can address questions such as these. From our perspective, the problem associated with foraging provide a framework for posing tasks in controlled settings, in which more detailed analytic tools can be deployed to isolate and identify spatial strategies and to chart their ontogenetic development. In developmental investigations, these tasks are usually presented to the child as games similar to an Easter egg or treasure hunt (Cornell & Heth, 1983, in preparation; Wellman, Somerville, Revelle, Haake, & Sophian, 1984).

For example, in our recent work (Cornell & Heth, in preparation), we have examined how children organize their hiding and recovery strategies in a large, naturally furnished children's laboratory containing 100 designated hiding places. These hiding places were small envelopes placed around the perimeter of the room and grouped into clusters of three (with one exception, see Fig. 9.4). In the next sections, we describe how we used this layout with two children and an adult.

Aaron (8 years, 2 months). The task was presented to Aaron as a number of treasure hunts. On each hunt, he was given a bag of 20 nickels. He was guided around the room and shown each of the 34 clusters of hiding places. Then, he was told to hide each of the nickels in an envelope of his choice and informed that he would return later to find and keep as many nickels as he could. He was warned that there were 100 hiding places and he would only be allowed to search 34 times. After hiding the nickels, he was taken to another room to watch television. Thirty minutes later, he was brought back to the center of the chil-

9. A COMPARATIVE DESCRIPTION OF SEARCH 237

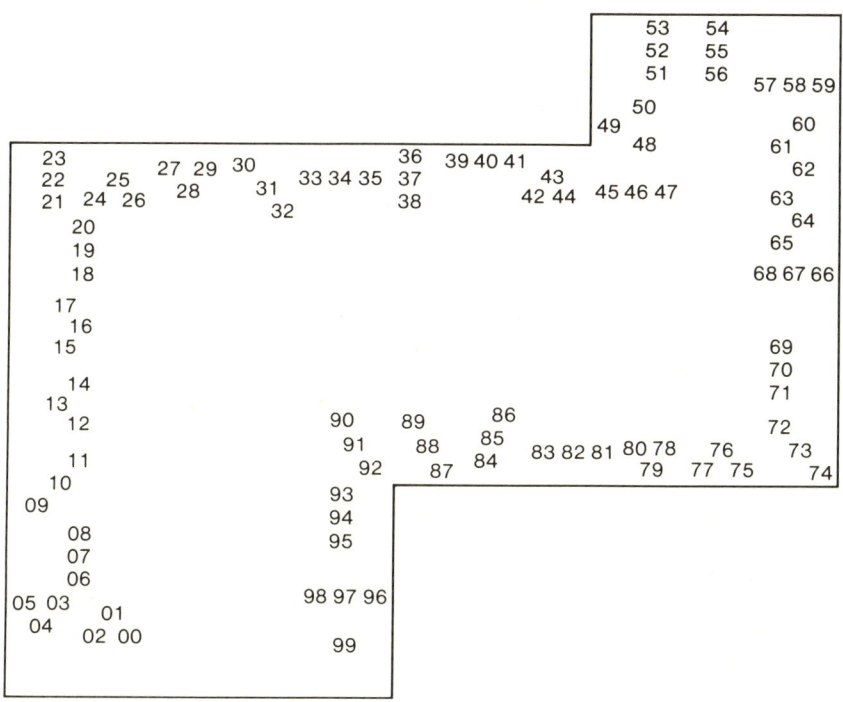

FIG. 9.4. A schematic of the overhead configuration of hiding places (envelopes) in the children's laboratory. Adjacent envelopes within clusters of three were approximately 20 cm from center to center. Adjacent clusters were approximately 100 cm from center to center. Envelopes were placed either on the floor or on tables, shelves, and ledges of other furniture, which were located along the walls of the room.

dren's laboratory and allowed to approach any location in any order he chose. Each time Aaron looked in an envelope was scored as a choice, and the serial number of each choice was announced. The envelopes were carefully positioned and checked after each choice to ensure that there were no obvious cues that they contained a nickel or had been manipulated.

This procedure was repeated three more times, constituting four treasure hunts in which Aaron hid and then searched by himself. Aaron's pattern of choices is represented in Table 9.1 as locations used for hiding and then for search during each of these four initial hunts. The leftmost column is the serial enumeration of choices (a maximum of 20 nickels hidden and 34 searches). The columns for each hunt refer to the specific locations numbered in Fig. 9.4. At the bottom of the table are descriptive statistics representing the number of nickels found, envelopes chosen but not having contained a nickel (intrusions), envelopes chosen, but having been previously emptied (repetitions), and finally,

TABLE 9.1
Patterns of Choices by Aaron During Hiding and Search Phases
of the Five Treasure Hunts by Himself

	Hunt									
	1		2		3		4		5	
Serial Order	Hiding	Search	Hiding	Search	Hiding	Search	Hiding	Search	Hiding	Search
1	33	07	78	33	35	33	78	55	35	33
2	88	06	80	34	34	34	79	56	34	34
3	93	99	79	35	33	35	80	76	33	35
4	99	78	76	07	36	32	77	75	36	26
5	06	73	77	06	37	31	76	77	37	25
6	05	33	75	05	38	30	75	72	38	38
7	14	88	69	01	32	29	72	73	39	37
8	16	39	70	78	31	28	74	74	40	36
9	22	42	71	80	30	27	73	80	41	39
10	27	22	33	79	28	36	69	79	42	40
11	31	27	34	82	29	37	70	78	44	41
12	34	24	35	77	27	38	71	82	43	43
13	38	89	21	76	26	21	68	68	30	44
14	78	65	22	75	25	22	67	67	31	42
15	73	53	23	69	24	23	66	66	32	28
16	65	58	13	70	21	24	65	64	28	29
17	67	61	14	71	22	25	64	63	29	27
18	58	46	12	64	23	26	63	65	27	30

238

19	61	67		61	16	16	56	52	26	31
20	51	69	06	43	17	17	55	51	25	32
21		80	07	26				58		
22		82		21				61		
23		16		22				70		
24		24		23				71		
25		97		14				69		
26		05		12						
27		91		13						
28		82								
29		53								
30		51								
31		61								
32		67								
33		27								
34		35								

Summary Data

Found		15		20		20		20		20
Intrusions		13		7		0		5		0
Repetitions		3		0		0		0		0
Repeated-Intrusions		3		0		0		0		0

Behavioral Organization

Clustering	1.0	1.0	.00	.00	.00	.00	.00	.00	.00	.00
Scattering	.05	.16	1.0	1.0	1.0	1.0	1.0	1.0	1.0	1.0
Sectoring	1.0	.99	.11	.04	.00	.00	.00	.00	.00	.00

envelopes that never contained a nickel but had been previously searched (repeated intrusions). The bottom rows labeled *Clustering, Scattering,* and *Sectoring* refer to three patterns of spatial organization of behavior that we have isolated using Monte Carlo techniques. Clustering refers to a tendency to group hidings or searches within one of the a priori spatial arrangements of three contiguous hiding places. Scattering refers to a tendency to avoid hiding or searching at more than one location within a cluster. Sectoring refers to a tendency to group choices into contiguous segments, across several clusters. Each entry represents the proportion of 10,000 Monte Carlo simulations that demonstrated at least as strong a tendency as the child's data. Low values indicate that the child's choices evince a much stronger tendency than the random simulations. A more detailed description of these forms of idiographic analyses is presented in Cornell & Heth (in preparation).

The general features of Aaron's performance can be interpreted as follows. On the first hiding, he distributed the nickels around the room. His tendency to hide only one nickel within a cluster of three was stronger than 95% of the random Monte Carlo simulations. His selectivity is similar to the scatter-hoarding behaviors we have surveyed in some species. Upon returning, he found a substantial number of nickels. There are several ways to evaluate the recovery performance. A Markovian model of choice, assuming completely random search, would predict that over 34 choices, 5.8 nickels would be found. Corroborating this theoretical value, data from control children in another study who had no knowledge of where objects were hidden found a mean of 6.2 in 33 such searches. The empirical data of naive search indicate that there were no obvious cues in the room or on the envelopes that could help search. Hence, we can conclude that on the first treasure hunt, Aaron showed reliable capacity to recover hidden objects.

Notice, however, that there were some errors in producing the finds on this hunt. Aaron used all 34 search attempts permitted. Of the 19 extraneous searches, most of them were at sites that had not been used for hiding. It can also be noted that there is no apparent spatial pattern in the choices Aaron made during this first hunt. When searching, his initial choices were often correct, but did not duplicate the sequence of choices made in hiding. In short, on the first hunt, the high number of finds was likely determined by memories for individual sites.

The second hunt was a new sequence of hiding and searching. Aaron was much more efficient this time, finding all 20 of the nickels in 27 searches. Both his pattern of hiding and search indicated a spatial organization of choice. When hiding the items, he tended to place nickels together, in clusters of three. He filled six clusters. None of the Monte Carlo simulations showed this pattern. Notice how Aaron's pattern could be exploited during search, if clusters are exhausted as a unit. If the first choice within a cluster is positive, the neighboring choices will also be positive; if it is negative, the neighbors will be too. Aaron seemed to use the feedback from negative choices, never searching more than once at an empty cluster.

While searching on the second hunt, Aaron exhibited the emergence of a new organization of behavior, in which choices were limited to a spatially circumscribed part of the larger area. We consider this sectoring tendency to be an independent strategy (Cornell & Heth, in preparation). As in clustering, we identify it relative to a set of 10,000 Monte Carlo simulations of random spatial choices. Only 4% of these simulations showed a sectoring tendency as strong as Aaron's during the search phase on the second hunt. As is apparent in Table 9.1, Aaron did not execute this strategy to its fullest extent, because he tended to leave some gaps between sites.

The clustering strategy was also apparent on the third hunt, but with the additional feature that the clusters were adjacent, in a sector. The combined strategies of clustering and sectoring further reduce the task of memorizing locations, because Aaron would only have to remember the boundaries of the sector and a rule for searching within those boundaries (e.g., exhaust all the clusters). The combined advantage of clustering and sectoring can be seen in Aaron's excellent performance in the third and fourth hunts.

In our view, Aaron's responses to this task exhibit increasing sophistication with the advantages of strategic organization of choices. In our earlier work, we documented rapid adoption of gathering strategies by children as young as 3 years of age (Heth & Cornell, 1983). Here, spatial strategies emerged during both hiding and recovery. At the completion of four hunts, Aaron's search performance was quite high, and he was very pleased with the ease of his profits.

Aaron versus Andy (6 years, 9 months). Aaron's mercantile abilities were severely taxed in our next variation of this task. For the next four hunts, we informed Aaron that there would be competition in his recovery of hidden treasures, in the form of a playmate, Andy. After Aaron hid the nickels, Andy was allowed into the laboratory for 34 searches. He could keep all of Aaron's nickels he could find; Aaron would then be allowed in to search for the remainder. Notice that this task captures some of the ecological characteristics of the competitive situations we have described earlier. As the hoarder, Aaron must be able to recover the objects he has hidden, but he must also prevent his competitor from finding them. The interaction of these requirements is apparent in the performance of Aaron versus Andy, summarized in Table 9.2.

On his fifth hiding, Aaron retained his use of clustering and sectoring, presumably as a mnemonic aid. Andy, when given the opportunity to search for Aaron's treasure, was faced with the necessity of searching efficiently and making each of his choices count. Our statistical analyses indicated that Andy organized his search by clustering and sectoring, avoiding repetitious searches by

TABLE 9.2
Patterns of Choices by Aaron and Andy During Hiding
and Search Phases of the Four Competitive Treasure Hunts

	Hunt												
	5			6			7			8		
Serial Order	Aaron Hiding	Andy Search	Aaron Search	Aaron Hiding	Andy Search	Aaron Search	Aaron Hiding	Andy Search	Aaron Search	Aaron Hiding	Andy Search	Aaron Search
1	69	38	16	35	86	35	72	21	80	39	36	09
2	70	37	80	34	85	34	74	23	65	40	37	10
3	65	36	78	33	84	33	73	20	62	41	38	11
4	64	39	79	21	87	99	76	19	71	42	39	07
5	63	40	77	22	89	17	75	18	70	43	40	08
6	76	41	09	23	90	21	77	78	69	44	41	06
7	77	43	05	16	91	23	80	79	73	89	42	89
8	75	44	64	17	92	24	79	80	72	88	43	88
9	80	48	67	99	95	89	78	72	74	87	44	87
10	78	49	70	09	98	07	71	73	76	14	47	16
11	79	50	71	08	97	40	70	74	75	12	46	26
12	34	47	69	94	96	41	69	71	77	13	45	91
13	35	46	82	93	99	39	68	70	83	09	49	03
14	33	45	21	95	01	37	67	69	82	10	48	01
15	21	65	22	41	00	36	66	67	81	11	50	00
16	23	63	23	40	02	24	65	66	65	06	51	02
17	08	64	34	39	03	26	63	68	64	07	57	39

09	51	33		04	12		47	63		58	41
10	52	35		05	19		46	67		59	42
03	53	38		06	27		45	68		60	21
	56	01	42	07	28	64	48	66	08	64	24
	55	99	43	08	29	61	51	71	01	67	26
	54	44	89	09	42	62	57	70		76	16
	58	43		10	44		58	69		75	99
	59	87		11	94		59	46		77	95
	60	86		12	95		61	47		85	03
	61	16		13	89		62	45		88	32
	62	26		14	92		60	51		87	33
	67	93		16	90		63	52		89	34
	68	98		17	87		64	53		93	35
	66	39		18	89		65	60		94	26
	77	36		19	88		81	61		95	25
	76	31		20	41		82	62		99	24
	75	27		22	40		44	55		98	96

Summary Data

Found	6	11		8	10		17	3		9	7
Intrusion	28	20		26	15		17	11		25	16
Repetitions	0	0		0	4		0	0		0	0
Repeated-Intrusions	0	1		0	1		0	0		0	5

Behavioral Organization

Clustering	.00	.00	.00	.00	.00	.00	.00	.00	.00	.00	.00
Scattering	1.0	1.0	.26	1.0	1.0	1.0	1.0	1.0	1.0	1.0	.99
Sectoring	.01	.00	.08	.37	.00	.00	.00	.00	.01	.00	.02

moving from left to right at the back of the room. Andy's score was 6 nickels discovered, close to the theoretical chance level and indicating that there were no obvious cues at sites Aaron had chosen.

Finally, Aaron was given the opportunity to recover the objects he had hidden. He correctly searched at 13 locations; two of these had been raided by Andy, leaving Aaron with a profit of 11 nickels for his 34 searches. This performance can be compared to the third hunt, in which Aaron likewise used clustering and sectoring during his hidings. An especially interesting aspect of the difference in performance is that Aaron's sectoring strategy began to weaken during the search phase of the fifth hunt. Nevertheless, the number of repetitions during the fifth search was still very low. Even though Aaron did not search at all of his caches, he remembered where he had checked during the recovery phase. Note also that intrusions generally occurred later in search, indicating that memories for hidings still controlled performance early in recovery.

On the sixth hunt, Aaron did not use a sector during hiding, but did during search. The results were similar to those following the disparate use of sectoring in the fifth hunt. On the seventh hunt, however, Aaron returned to the sectoring strategy for both hiding and search phases. The risk of this strategy in the competitive situation was immediately demonstrated. Andy's tendency to constrain his searching overlapped Aaron's sector of hidings. The result was that Andy found 17 of the 20 hidden nickels. When Aaron returned, he searched correctly at 18 of the locations; however 15 of these had been previously emptied by Andy.

Aaron was visibly upset over this outcome. On the next hunt (number eight) he tended to retain his sectoring strategy, but completely avoided the locations used on the seventh hunt. He furthermore did not use a concentrated sector, but tended to hide the nickels in three separate areas. This time, Andy found only 9. Aaron recovered 7, and also searched 6 places that had been emptied by Andy.

Aaron's overall performance had dropped in the four competitive hunts relative to the four hunts by himself. A possible explanation for this decrement is that repeated tests increase interference of retrieval of memories for recent hiding places. To test this possibility, Aaron was allowed one final noncompetitive hunt, presented in Table 9.1 as Hunt 9. Performance was essentially identical to the highest attained in his earlier solo hunts.

As a result of these observations, we suggest that without a competitor Aaron quickly developed efficient strategies for hiding and recovering the nickels. However, these same algorithms are vulnerable to competition. Clustering and sectoring condense the distribution of treasures. A competitor directing search in accord with the marginal value algorithm would be expected to stay within these rich areas. Indeed, on Hunt 7, Andy's behavior appeared to be sensitive to the local rate of returns.

David (37 years, 9 months). An interesting feature of Aaron's performance is that despite his success with the noncompetitive situation, he had not solved the trade-offs of a hiding strategy that is easy to recall, but also resistant to competition. Perhaps Aaron had encountered a problem in which the development of a more sophisticated spatial strategy would involve repeated attempts. It is also probable that a more sophisticated strategy requires complexity costs that are readily addressed by older children or adults.

As a case in point, we posed this problem to a university colleague. Intrigued by the challenge of developing an easily remembered but nonvulnerable strategy, he volunteered to hide and recover 20 cat's-eye marbles. His hidings began in one corner of the room and proceeded counterclockwise. An inspection of his choices and subsequent conversation indicated that he chose a single hiding place within a cluster. The specific hiding place was determined by a sequence, analogous to a repetitious cycle of choosing the rightmost (or front), middle, and leftmost (or rear) envelope in a cluster. Some clusters were skipped, apparently because their configuration did not allow an obvious distinction between front and middle (e.g., the triangular configuration of hiding places 75, 76, and 77 of Fig. 9.4). Other clusters were skipped for idiosyncratic reasons, which seemed to be memorized. The result was a series of hidings that looked random, but which could be decoded knowing the proper algorithm and exceptions.

When David later searched for these marbles, he recovered all 20, but made 10 intrusions. The intrusions seemed to be due either to failures to remember the ill-defined clusters he had skipped or to minor distractions that caused him to forget his place in the cycle of right, middle, left. Amused by these intrusions, he suggested that a better algorithm would have been one that was not as easily disrupted by the inconsistency of the environment. There are, for example, many number progressions (e.g., Lorge & Thorndike, 1954) that could be used provided that the ordinal properties could be mapped onto an arbitrary configuration of sites. If different sites served on different hunts as the start of the number series, decoding could be impossible for a competitor.

In summary, human responses to the requirements of search can be determined by complex and flexible strategies. Representations of routes and locations are usually pictographic or verbal; however, spatial information is preserved and communicated in the arrangements of elements in a variety of media. Spatial organizational strategies are applied to delineate large- and small-scale areas and may be combined with movement and feedback algorithms to remember places visited and sites of resources.

CONCLUSIONS AND PROSPECTUS

In our survey of natural manifestations of search we have noted several analogies between animal and human behavior. As a start, we reviewed search as the primary component of foraging, a universal spatial problem. Methods of localizing resources in patchy environments appear to be similar across different species. Nevertheless, the types of information specifying a place and the processes used to encounter locations vary in complexity. We have described representations of sites that may involve simple contiguities with visible landmarks, as well as other representations that may involve compound dimensions of time and topography. We have also considered that patterns of movement can be regulated by recursive response algorithms, whereas other forms of travel seem to require calculation and inference. In other words, although there appear to be correspondences in the goals and structure of behaviors of different organisms, the underlying mechanisms may be quite different.

Such limitations of analogical analyses are easily demonstrated, yet most theorizing in biology and psychology begins with comparative descriptions (Beer, 1980; Hazen, 1983). The major example is evolutionary biology, which has progressed from Darwin's observations of similarities to methods of mathematical and experimental prediction. In reference to our less expansive topic, we regard the analogies surveyed here as valuable heuristics for the isolation of mechanisms of human search and a characterization of their development.

The crux of our analysis is the efficiency of various spatial behaviors. A common theme of both the ethological and anthropological observations is the putative optimality of a given behavior or strategy in response to an environmental requirement. Unfortunately, field observations can only reveal the outcome of ecological interactions. Laboratory studies of search behavior can provide more substantive evidence of causal determinants by manipulating factors presumed to affect optimality.

Accordingly, we suggested that studies of the development of search abilities could be devised to provide an ecological and economic analysis of solutions. As an example, the problem we posed to a child and an adult combined two requirements of hoarding: selection of sites to be remembered during search, and avoidance of a competitor's detection of those places. We found that grouping strategies emerged and were modified in response to these requirements.

Earlier, we had outlined different types of costs relative to such spatial strategies. It seems appropriate to consider in conclusion how these might be expanded into directed research topics.

One type is the direct cost of search effort, which is sometimes estimated in energy units. It has been noted that children's search behaviors are affected by "least distance" choices (Wellman, et al., 1984). Additional research could profitably examine other effects of search effort. For example, the distance or effort of travel between patches should affect the amount of time spent searching within a patch. Thus, if a child is searching for an object in one area, his or her "give up" time should be directly related to the functional distance to another plausible resource site.

Another cost of importance to efficient search is the opportunity cost of searching in one area when other areas are more productive. Opportunity costs increase as an individual stays within a patch and depletes its resources. Opportunity costs also increase as resources regenerate or otherwise increase at alternative sites. Consequently, we would expect children to be sensitive to information revealing the relative returns of searching. Sophian and Sage (1983) illustrate such sensitivities in infants who observe that some occluders within a set of hiding places are sites for attractive toys. It seems possible to arrange search tasks that allow an estimate of children's memories for local rates of returns.

Perhaps the most interesting possibility would be to assess conjointly the different types of cost. For example, if we increase the direct energetic costs of search, would we find a greater tendency of children to pay the complexity cost of a more complicated "least distance" solution? The work of Fabricius and Wellman (Chapter 3 of this volume) points to such trade-offs. Or, in the foraging problem, simply reducing the number of searches allowed places greater emphasis on the opportunity costs of wasted choices. With only a few opportunities to search, effortful travel and mnemonic strategies seem warranted. The benefit of our emphasis on interdependent costs is the capacity to relate these manipulations within one framework, reflecting both the ecology and psychology of the searcher.

ACKNOWLEDGMENTS

Preparation of this chapter and our research cited herein were supported by Grant A0267 to E. Cornell from the Natural Sciences and Engineering Council of Canada. We thank Deborah Hay and Lorri Broda for their conscientious help in testing children. We thank Jeff Bisanz for his help with the manuscript.

REFERENCES

Able, K. P. (1980). Mechanisms of orientation, navigation, and homing. In S. A. Gauthreaux (Ed.), *Animal migration, orientation, and navigation* (pp. 283–373). New York: Academic Press.

Alcock, J. (1975). *Animal behavior: An evolutionary approach.* Sunderland, MA: Sinauer Associates.

Beer, C. G. (1980). Perspectives on animal behavior comparisons. In M. Bornstein (Ed.), *Comparative methods in psychology* (pp. 17–64). Hillsdale, NJ: Lawrence Erlbaum Associates.

Bremermann, H. (1974). Complexity of automata, brains, and behavior. In M. Conrad, W. Guttinger, & M. D. Cin (Eds.), *Physics and mathematics of the nervous system* (pp. 304–331). Berlin: Springer-Verlag.

Charnov. E. L. (1976). Optimal foraging: The marginal value theorem. *Theoretical Population Biology, 9,* 129–136.

Collier, G. H. (1981). Determinants of choice. In D. Bernstein (Ed.), *Nebraska Symposium on Motivation* (Vol. 29, pp. 69–127). Lincoln: University of Nebraska Press.

Cornell, E. H., & Heth, C. D. (1983). Spatial cognition: Gathering strategies used by preschool children. *Journal of Experimental Child Psychology, 35,* 93–110.

Cornell, E. H., & Heth, C. D. (In preparation). The organization of hiding and recovery of objects by children.

Dempster, F. N. (1981). Memory span: Sources of individual and developmental differences. *Psychological Bulletin, 89,* 63–100.
Dyer, F. C., & Gould, J. L. (1981). Honey bee orientation: A backup system for cloudy days. *Science, 214,* 1041–1042.
Gould, R. A. (1969). *Yiwara: Foragers of the Australian desert.* New York: Charles Scribner's Sons.
Gould, R. A. (1970). Spears and spear-throwers of the western desert aborigines of Australia. *American Museum Novitates,* No. 2403, 1–42.
Haftorn, S. (1956). Contribution to the food biology of tits, especially about storing of surplus food: Part IV. A comparative analysis of *Parus atricapillus L., P. cristatus L.,* and *P. ater L. Det Kgl Norske Videnskabers Selskabs Skrifter,* No. 4.
Hazen, N. L. (1983). Spatial orientation: A comparative approach. In H. L. Pick & L. P. Acredolo (Eds.), *Spatial orientation: Theory, research, and application* (pp. 3–37). New York: Plenum Press.
Heinrich, B. (1979). Resource heterogeneity and patterns of movement in foraging bumblebees. *Oecologia, 40,* 235–246.
Heth, C. D., & Cornell, E. H. (1983). *Gathering behavior of preschool children.* Paper presented at the Biennial Meeting of the Society for Research in Child Development, Detroit, MI.
Kamil, A. C. (1978). Systematic foraging by a nectar-feeding bird, the amakihi (*Loxops virens*). *Journal of Comparative & Physiological Psychology, 92,* 388–396.
Krebs, J. R. (1978). Optimal foraging: Decision rules for predators. In J. R. Krebs & N. B. Davies (Eds.), *Behavioural ecology: An evolutionary approach* (pp. 23–63). Sunderland, MA: Sinauer Associates.
Lorge, I. & Thorndike, R. L. (1954). *The Lorge-Thorndike intelligence test, Levels A-H.* Boston: Houghton Mifflin.
Maynard Smith, J. (1978). Optimization theory in evolution. *Annual Review of Ecology and Systematics, 9,* 31–56.
Nelson, R. K. (1969). *Hunters of the northern ice.* Chicago: University of Chicago Press.
Olton, D. S. (1978). Characteristics of spatial memory. In S. H. Hulse, H. F. Fowler, & W. K. Honig (Eds.), *Cognitive processes in animal behavior* (pp. 341–373). Hillsdale, NJ: Lawrence Erlbaum Associates.
Olton, D. S., & Collison, C. (1979). Intramaze cues and "odor trails" fail to direct choice behavior on an elevated maze. *Animal Learning and Behavior, 7,* 221–223.
Olton, D. S., Collison, C., & Werz, M. A. (1977). Spatial memory and radial arm maze performance of rats. *Learning & Motivation, 8,* 289–314.
Olton, D. S., Handelmann, G. E., & Walker, J. A. (1981). Spatial memory and food searching strategies. In Kamil, A. C., & Sargent, T. D. (Eds.), *Foraging behavior: Ecological, ethological, and psychological approaches* (pp. 333–354). London: Garland Press.
Olton, D. S. & Samuelson, R. J. (1976). Remembrance of places passed: Spatial memory in rats. *Journal of Experimental Psychology: Animal Behavior Processes, 2,* 97–116.
Orians, G. H. (1981). Foraging behavior and the evolution of discriminatory abilities. In A. C. Kamil & T. D. Sargent (Eds.), *Foraging behavior: Ecological, ethological, and psychological approaches* (pp. 389–405). London: Garland Press.
Pfeiffer, J. E. (1978). *The emergence of man.* New York: Harper & Row.
Pyke, G. H. (1978). Optimal foraging: Movement patterns of bumblebees between influorescences. *Theoretical Population Biology, 13,* 72–98.
Real, L. A. (1980). On uncertainty and the law of diminishing returns in evolution and behavior. In J. E. R. Staddon (Ed.), *Limits to action: The allocation of individual behavior.* New York: Academic Press.
Roberts, R. C. (1979). The evolution of avian food storing behavior. *American Naturalist, 114,* 418–438.

Roitblat, H. L., Tham, W., & Golub, L. (1982). Performance of *Betta splendens* in a radial arm maze. *Animal Learning & Behavior, 10,* 108–114.

Shettleworth, S. J. (1983). Memory in food-hoarding birds. *Scientific American, 248,* 102–110.

Shettleworth, S. J., & Krebs, J. R. (1982). How marsh tits find their hoards: The roles of site preference and spatial memory. *Journal of Experimental Psychology: Animal Behavior Processes, 8,* 354–375.

Sibly, R. M. & McFarland, D. J. (1976). On the fitness of behavior sequences. *American Naturalist, 110,* 601–617.

Smith, J. N. M. (1974). The food searching behavior of two European thrushes. II. The adaptiveness of the search patterns. *Behaviour, 49,* 1–61.

Solomon, R. L. (1948). The influence of work on behavior. *Psychological Bulletin, 45,* 1–40.

Sophian, C., & Sage, S. (1983). Developments in infants' search for displaced objects. *Journal of Experimental Child Psychology, 35,* 143–160.

Sutton, G. M. (1932). *Memoirs of the Carnegie Museum: The exploration of Southampton Island, Hudson Bay.* Pittsburgh: Carnegie Institute.

Thorndike, E. L. (1911). *Animal intelligence: Experimental studies.* New York: Macmillan.

Tinbergen, N. (1951). *The study of instinct.* Oxford: Clarendon Press.

Tolman, E. C. (1932). *Purposive behavior in animals and men.* New York: Century.

Vander Wall, S. B. (1982). An experimental analysis of cache recovery in Clark's nutcracker. *Animal Behaviour, 30,* 84–94.

von Frisch, K. (1967). *Dance language and orientation of bees.* Cambridge, MA: Harvard University Press.

Waddington, K. D., & Heinrich, B. (1981). Patterns of movement and floral choice by foraging bees. In A. C. Kamil & T. D. Sargent (Eds.), *Foraging behavior: Ecological, ethological & psychological approaches* (pp. 215–230). London: Garland Press.

Wellman, H. M., Somerville, S. C., Revelle, G. L., Haake, R. J., & Sophian, C. (in press). The development of comprehensive search skills. *Child Development.*

10 Mathematical Models of Search

David R. Cross
Henry M. Wellman
The University of Michigan

In recent years there have been increased attempts to use mathematical models to understand the development of cognition (Anderson, 1980; Brainerd, Howe, & Desrochers, 1982; Wilkinson, 1982). In fact, in the current volume one chapter proposes a mathematical model for assessing children's developing rule use (Sophian, Larkin, & Kadane) and others exploit log-linear (Wellman, Fabricius, & Sophian) or Monte-Carlo (Heth & Cornell) modeling techniques. There is nothing particularly novel in these attempts; mathematical models have a classic place in psychological theorizing (Luce, Bush, & Galanter, 1963; Miller, 1964; Restle, 1971) and the expected gains from such endeavors are well known. These include most prominently (a) that such models require analytic specificity and thus encourage theoretical clarity and rigor, (b) that once formulated such models can generate new nonobvious predictions, and (c) that mathematical models enable the separation of response components that are difficult or impossible to distinguish otherwise—as in the separation of sensitivity from bias in signal detection models.

In developmental research on human search (e.g., the chapters in this volume cited above) mathematical models have thus far been used essentially to allow the investigator to distinguish response components. However, the problem content of the research—search—lends itself to mathematical treatment as well, affording the possibility of more substantive models. As researchers have increasingly recognized (Koopman, 1946/1980; Wellman & Somerville, 1982), the searcher's task is at heart one of optimization—limited resources in the terms of looks, distance traveled, or locations searched must be efficiently allocated in order to effectively find the search target. Solving for optima characterizes the psychological problem but is itself a well-formulated mathematical problem.

A brief consideration of the nature of search problems substantiates this characterization. A search problem involves a *searcher,* a *target,* a *search space,* and a set of *search operations*—pursuing, uncovering, visually inspecting—that enables the searcher to find the target or know its whereabouts. The searcher could be a navy plane on submarine patrol, a search and rescue team, an animal foraging for food, a man searching for his lost keys, or a child finding Easter eggs. Whereas the searcher is most often characterized as an active agent, the target can be either active or inactive. If active, the target can be attempting to evade the searcher, attempting to find the searcher (e.g., a child separated from his or her parent), or moving haphazardly with regard to the searcher. The search space can assume many different forms; it could be ocean, wilderness, a house, or a backyard.

It is possible to distinguish two general approaches or strategies to the solution of search problems (Wellman & Somerville, 1982). In the first of these, *comprehensive search,* the searcher plans to search the entire search space or distribute search effort equally across the space. In the second, *selective search,* the searcher plans to avoid searching certain areas of the search space or at least defer searching them until more promising regions are searched first. Each of these strategies typically requires optimization—searching all locations but with the least possible effort, or narrowing search so as to reduce effort but still include the target's probable location. Selective and comprehensive search strategies are differentially appropriate depending on the amount of information available to the searcher prior to searching. It is thus possible to distinguish, by analogy, two sorts of search problems. In comprehensive search problems the searcher has no information about the location of the target other than that it is located within the search space. Thus, optimally, he or she should search comprehensively. Conversely, in selective search problems, the searcher has some prior knowledge of the whereabouts of the target. In this case, optimally, he or she should search selectively. Since efficient search solutions require optimization, search problems and processes afford mathematical treatment. Indeed, several mathematical conceptions of optimal search exist.

This chapter has two aims. One is to review extant mathematical conceptions of optimal search. These conceptions allow the computation of optimal search allocations, both in comprehensive and selective search problems. Although these formulations prescribe optimal search allocations, they do not model human search processes themselves. Nevertheless, they prove instrumental to an understanding of human search and its development in three ways. First, they help clearly define the nature of the task domain. Mathematical formulations of search complement psychological treatments by emphasizing those aspects of the problem—the premises or search information—on which optimal performance must be based. Second, mathematical search formulations can at times be applied directly as models of human search behavior. We present several examples of this. Third, even when not directly applicable the formulations we review can inspire psychological models of search. We propose an example of this sort later in the chapter.

Partly as a result of this review, a second yet primary aim of this chapter is to argue for one particular approach to modeling search behavior. To anticipate, we advocate qualitative/graphical models of human search. In such models, graphs, rather than algebraic formulas, constitute the modeling medium. Further, the assumptions and predictions are typically qualitative rather than precisely quantitative. This approach, we argue, has unique advantages for theorizing in developmental psychology.

There are two distinguishable but overlapping approaches to representing search mathematically: search theory and optimal foraging theory. The following two sections review these approaches. Our emphasis is on illustrating different models rather than formally presenting the theories. In a third section of the chapter we comparatively evaluate these approaches in terms of their applications to human search. It is there that we argue that a qualitative/graphical approach to modeling search behavior suits the current needs of developmental psychologists especially well. In a final section we formulate a qualitative/graphical model for an important question concerning the development of human search skills.

SEARCH THEORY

Background

Search theory is a branch of operations research that provides methods for calculating optimal solutions to many practical search problems. The foundations of search theory were laid during World War II as part of the navy's effort to protect the Atlantic convoys destined for Great Britain. The navy's task was to locate enemy submarines using small numbers of men, ships, and planes. The corresponding search problem was to allocate these meager resources in such a way that the probability of finding the enemy submarines was maximized; such an allocation of limited resources represents an optimal search plan. Solutions to the wide variety of search problems posed during the second World War (Koopman, 1946/1980, 1956a, 1956b, 1957) are at the core of search theory. Much of the early work following the war was reviewed by Dobbie (1968). Later, Stone (1975) presented the first mathematically comprehensive and systematic treatment of search theory, and this remains a major reference in the field.

Calculating an Optimal Search

The fundamental problem when planning an optimal search is to maximize the probability of finding the search target given a known, limited amount of available effort. Determining an optimal search plan is a five-step process:

1. Propose a *detection function*. This is the probability that the target will be detected with a given allocation of effort in its vicinity. One way to think of the detection function, and the thinking that originally lay behind the search theory approach, is that the searcher can direct a certain number of "glimpses" at the target. On each glimpse there is a specified probability that the target will be detected, and if more glimpses are directed at the target then the cumulative probability of detecting the target will increase. The detection function relates the number of glimpses to the probability of detecting the target.

2. Propose a *target density*. This is the a priori probability density for the location of the target in the search space and must be proposed by the searcher on the basis of his or her search information. In a comprehensive search problem the target density is uniform over the search space. In a selective search problem the searcher knows that some portions of the search space are more likely than others to contain the target and this knowledge suggests the functional form of the target density.

3. Determine the total *search effort*. Typically this is known a priori; it is determined by the resources available to carry out the search. For example, in a search and rescue mission there are only a finite number of man-hours available before it becomes too dark to search.

4. Incorporate 1, 2, and 3 into the *effectiveness function,* which when maximized yields the optimal *search plan*. Maximizing the effectiveness function guarantees the searcher the greatest possible rate of return (in terms of probability of detecting the target) for a given expenditure of effort. The resulting prescription for allocation of effort over the search space is the optimal search plan. For example, in comprehensive search problems (where the target density is uniform) the optimal search plan is one that distributes effort as evenly as possible over the search space (Stone, 1975). For selective search the effectiveness functions are more complex and optimal search plans are more prescriptive, as we will see.

5. Determine the *probability of finding* the target based on the optimal search plan found in 4. The quality of this estimate depends on the assumptions made in 1 and 2. For example, if the target is actually more difficult to detect than is assumed in 1, then the probability of finding the target will be overestimated in 5. Or, if the target density in 2 misrepresents the actual location of the target, then the probability of finding will again be overestimated.

Examples

There are many interesting applications of search theory to the problems of society: search and rescue, the detection of diseases, searching for minerals, and so forth (see Haley & Stone, 1980). In addition, we are aware of two applications where search theory has been used as a model of behavior (Hoffmann, 1983;

Shaw, 1978; Shaw & Shaw, 1977). The study by Hoffmann is an investigation of the search behavior of a wood louse that inhabits the arid and semi-arid deserts of North Africa. Search is a naturally occurring problem for this animal because it occasionally loses its burrow and can only remain outside for short periods of time. As a consequence, its survival depends upon being able to search effectively for its home.

As Hoffmann (1983) explains, the desert isopod *Hemilepistus reamuri* lives in a burrow, which it shares with a mate and other family members. These woodlice must leave their shelter in order to forage for food and clean or enlarge the burrow. Although they are able to unerringly return to the vicinity of the burrow, small navigational errors sometimes cause them to miss by a few centimeters. A woodlouse can only detect the burrow when very close because detection requires contact with the burrow by the animal's antennae. When the animal becomes lost it can be seen searching for the burrow entrance in a "peculiar" way and only finding it after a substantial search effort. It is this "peculiar" search behavior that Hoffmann attempts to model using search theory.

We present a brief verbal description of Hoffmann's model here; a more complete mathematical formulation is provided in Appendix 1. The detection function (step 1) employed by Hoffmann is the exponential distribution function. According to this function the probability of detection is an increasing function of search effort spent in the vicinity of the target, but the rate of increase declines as more and more effort is expended. In addition to effort, the probability of detection is influenced by the quality of the detection apparatus—in this case the isopod's antennae. This feature—the instantaneous probability of detection—reflects the frequency with which the antennae oscillate and the sensitivity of the antennae's chemoreceptors.

The exponential detection function lends itself well to modeling target detection. In particular, it has the property of "forgetfulness." Thus, it is assumed that information the animal has gained searching in the vicinity of the burrow is lost as it later searches with additional intensity. This detection function is also subject to the law of diminishing returns, which dictates that each small increment in search intensity is not going to increase the probability of detection as much as previous increments of the same size.

Hoffmann chose the bivariate normal density as the target density (step 2). The center of the density is the point in the search space where the isopod begins its search. According to this density the most likely locations for the entrance are in the immediate vicinity of the starting point, and the likelihood of the entrance being at any given point decreases as the distance from the starting point increases. These are reasonable assumptions since the woodlouse, when lost, usually begins searching at a point near its burrow.

The amount of search effort (step 3) available to the woodlouse is determined by how long it can remain outside its burrow. Although it is well adapted to its arid environment, it cannot search indefinitely. The optimal search plan will be a prescription for allocating the isopod's limited effort in a way that maximizes its probability of finding the entrance to its burrow.

The optimal search plan (step 4) is determined by the detection function, target density, and effort available for search, and is obtained by maximizing the effectiveness function. The optimal search plan for the woodlouse is to initially concentrate its search near the starting point and only search the outlying areas if the initial search is unsuccessful. There is a circular limit beyond which the animal should not search at all, and the radius of this circle grows gradually larger with time. Within the prescribed circle, the isopod should concentrate its search relatively more on the central areas, but less and less effort will be expended on these areas as the restrictive circle grows.

The effectiveness of the isopod's search (step 5) will be determined by the effort expended in the vicinity of the burrow. If more time is spent searching in the correct location then there will be a corresponding increase in the probability of detection as determined by the detection function. In this case, search effectiveness will be largely determined by how close the entrance is to the starting point of search, since the closer regions will be searched with greater intensity.

Hoffmann carried out two tests of the model. The first of these tests was to compare the cumulative probability of finding the burrow as predicted by the model with the cumulative frequency of detection actually observed. In carrying out his experiments Hoffmann varied the starting distance from the burrow and recorded the number of times the isopods located the burrow within the time limit. The fit of the observed curves with the predicted curves was considered acceptable, since there were no statistically significant differences between the frequencies at each time point. However, the values of two parameters (i and w in Appendix 1) were chosen so as to make the correspondence between the fitted curves and predicted curves as close as possible, because Hoffmann was unable to obtain independent estimates of these parameters. For this reason the second test carried out by Hoffmann is especially important.

The optimal search plan prescribes that *H. reamuri* should search close to the starting point and not move away from this position too rapidly. The model predicts that an isopod searching optimally will contain its search within the specified radius, so that the spatio-temporal characteristics of the isopods' search can be compared with this limit. In these tests also the observations compare favorably with the predictions: The mean maximal distance of the animals remained below the limit predicted, for a search duration of up to 800 sec. On the basis of these goodness-of-fit tests, and on other tests that ruled out other non-optimal models, Hoffmann concluded that *H. reamuri* searches optimally for its burrow.

One series of studies exists that has used search theory to model human behavior, specifically the allocation of attention required to detect objects in the visual field (Shaw, 1978; Shaw & Shaw, 1977). In all of these studies the subjects' task was to detect stimuli presented tachistoscopically in different visual locations according to a known probability distribution function. In the first study (Shaw & Shaw, 1977) the measured response was proportion correct; in the second pair of experiments (Shaw, 1978) the measured response was reaction time. In order to test the hypothesis that adults allocate their visual attention flexibly and optimally, Shaw and Shaw used search theory to build a model of optimal performance in this domain and then compared the performance of their subjects with predictions from this model.

The visual detection model is, with two exceptions, little different than the model formulated by Hoffmann. One difference is that the target densities were controlled by the experimenters and were part of the experimental design—the densities varied from study to study and also between conditions within a study. Another difference is that the model was instantiated differently for different response measures. For example, the probability of correct responding was derived from the model when the response measure was correct identification, but the expected mean reaction time was derived when the response was reaction time. Otherwise, the search models of Hoffman and Shaw and Shaw are similar (e.g., both use an exponential detection function) and are based on the foundations of search theory as laid out by Stone (1975). The mathematical details of Shaw's (1978) model are presented in Appendix 2.

Shaw and Shaw compared the performance of their subjects to predictions from the model for each of the subjects individually. In all of the studies the goodness-of-fit tests indicated an acceptable fit of the observations to the model's predictions for most of the subjects. In the first study (Shaw & Shaw, 1978), the conclusion was that adult humans were able to allocate their attention optimally to the visual field. The results of the second study (Shaw, 1978) were interpreted in the context of specific models of human information processing.

We earlier asserted that several benefits can accrue from the use of mathematical models for researching search behavior. An obvious strength of search theory is its quantitative precision. This precision indeed helps define the task by emphasizing crucial features of the problem necessary to estimate optimal performance. As is specifically clear in Hoffmann's work, this precision also requires a large amount of data about the organism in question (its foraging habits, the detection radius of its antennae, etc.) as well as a number of reasonable but contestable assumptions (e.g., the exponential detection function, the bivariate normal target density). The specificity is required in order to sufficiently characterize the needed equations. Nonetheless, Hoffmann still had to estimate the values of the two parameters using the same data that were used to test the model. Furthermore, these values were estimated so as to maximize the fit of the data to the model's predictions. Our comments are not meant to detract from the value of Hoffmann's work, but only to illustrate the point that the quantitative precision of models is not without costs. The next section on foraging theory provides a useful contrast to search theory in this regard, because it includes a set of less quantitative models of optimal search.

OPTIMAL FORAGING THEORY

Background

Optimal foraging theory (Krebs, 1978; Pyke, Pulliam, & Charnov, 1977; Schoener, 1971) encompasses a diverse range of mathematical models that have been used by behavioral ecologists to study the foraging behavior of animals, e.g., their search for food. It is assumed in these models that the evolutionary fitness of the foraging animals is a function of the efficiency with which they are able to forage. Foraging efficiency, usually measured in terms of the organism's net rate of energy intake, contributes crucially to the fitness of the organism and thus tends to be optimized by selective pressure. Foraging models have certain similarities with search theory. Most importantly, in both, the searcher/forager seeks to maximize some return while at the same time minimizing some cost, i.e., both are optimization models.

The Marginal Value Model

One problem facing the foraging animal is the problem of where to search and for how long. Usually food or prey are not uniformly distributed in the foraging environment, but instead occur in patches. The forager must make decisions about which of these patches to forage and how long to remain in each patch. Presumably there is a combination of patches and foraging times that maximize the forager's rate of energy intake, and this constitutes the optimal foraging strategy. If patch quality cannot be predicted prior to feeding in the patch, then the foraging problem becomes one of deciding how long to stay in the current patch.

The capture rate of prey or food in a patch will usually decrease with time spent in the patch due to the depletion of resources and other depressive effects of the forager's presence. If the forager remains too long in one patch, then the capture rate will drop below that which could be expected if it moved on to another patch. On the other hand, if the forager fails to stay long enough, then it will spend too much time traveling between patches. In general, the optimal solution is to stay until the capture rate in a patch—the marginal capture rate—drops to the average capture rate for the environment as a whole (Charnov, 1976).

10. MATHEMATICAL MODELS OF SEARCH

The graphical model, presented in Fig. 10.1, is the general solution to this search problem. The optimal solution—T_{opt}—is determined by two features of the environment: the distance between patches and the density of prey within patches. These features are specified in the model by the parameter t and the function $f(T)$, where t is the average time required to travel between patches and $f(T)$ relates the net energy gain, E, to the time spent searching in a patch, T. $f(T)$ is the within-patch energy gain averaged across all patches in the environment. Its generally decreasing slope specifies that depletion occurs: It takes more time to find prey as more and more prey are captured.

The optimal time spent in a patch—T_{opt}—can be derived from Fig. 10.1 as follows. Suppose B is a point on $f(T)$. The slope of the line AB then defines the average rate of return for the corresponding T, given t and $f(T)$, because the rate of return is simply the net energy gained divided by the total time taken. Net energy gained is $E = f(T)$ and total time is $t + T$, so the slope of AB is simply the ratio of $f(T)$ to $t + T$ (viz. "the rise over the run") for any point B on $f(T)$. The optimal position for B—defining T_{opt}—is where AB makes a tangent to $f(T)$, as

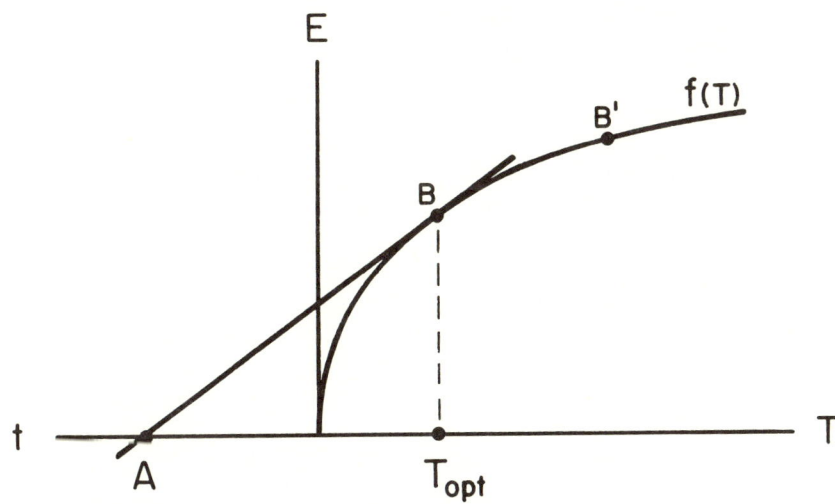

FIG. 10.1. Marginal value model. E is net energy intake, T is time spent in a patch, and t is the average travel time between patches. The function $f(T)$ represents the average net energy intake accross all patches in the environment, and A indicates the average travel time between patches in the environment. The point B is where the line drawn from A just touches $f(T)$, and the corresponding value of T—T_{opt}—is the optimal time in a patch. The slope of the line AB—$f/(t + T)$—is the average capture rate for the environment, which is maximized by choosing point B on $f(T)$. If any other point on $f(T)$ were chosen, B' say, then the average capture rate would be less. (From Charnov [1976]. Used by permission of Academic Press.)

depicted in Fig. 10.1. That is, T_{opt} will always correspond to the point where AB just touches $f(T)$. If any other time were chosen as the foraging time in a patch, then the average net energy gain—the slope of line AB—would be less than with T_{opt}. This can be seen, for example, by considering a time to the right of T_{opt}. If such a point is chosen instead of T_{opt}, corresponding to B' say, then when the line AB' is drawn its slope will be less than the slope of AB, indicating a lesser capture rate.

Since t and $f(T)$ determine T_{opt}, then changes in their value or form, respectively, will change the optimum time to be spent in a patch. Thus, if the patches are widely spaced, then the average travel time between patches will be relatively large. Similarly, if prey are sparse within a patch, then the function $f(T)$ will be relatively flat. In either case, the average rate of net energy intake will be small because the forager will have to spend a large portion of his time either traveling between patches or searching for prey within a patch. Notice that the effect of large travel times—increasing T_{opt}—can be read directly from Fig. 10.1. As point A moves to the left, point B moves to the right for a given $f(T)$: If a predator is going to spend a lot of time traveling between patches, then it had better make the most of a patch while foraging in it. Low prey densities have a similar effect on the optimal leaving time because point B moves to the right in Fig. 10.1 as $f(T)$ flattens out. Again this is a reasonable solution: If a predator is in a resource-poor environment it should not leave any one patch too soon because the expected capture rate in the next patch is so small.

The marginal value model (Fig. 10.1) lends itself to both qualitative and quantitative predictions. Qualitatively, one need specify nothing about the form of the curve $f(T)$ except that the slope consistently decreases, i.e., that the patch is depleted. If the distance between patches increases then T_{opt} should increase, regardless of the exact form of $f(T)$. Similarly, if the prey density in patches increases, then T_{opt} should decrease. For quantitative predictions, it is necessary to specify exactly the form of $f(T)$. The study discussed below features tests of both qualitative and quantitative predictions of the model in Fig. 10.1.

We will illustrate the marginal value model with an experimental study of the foraging behavior of great tits (Cowie, 1977). In his study Cowie held $f(T)$ constant and experimentally varied t in order to determine the affect of this manipulation on the birds' foraging behavior. Cowie's birds foraged in an aviary containing artificial trees; each tree supported six patches, which were cups of sawdust with hidden pieces of food. There were two conditions, identical except for the time and energy costs of traveling between patches. In the "easy" environment, the patches were covered with cardboard lids that were easy to remove, whereas in the "hard" environment, the patches were covered with lids that were difficult to remove. Travel times between patches —t—were longer in the hard environment because it took the birds longer to remove the lids between foraging bouts.

According to the marginal value model T_{opt} should be smaller in the easy environment than in the hard environment. This is because in the hard environment t will be large and the point of contact between AB and $f(T)$ will move to the right. Conversely, in the easy environment t will be small and the point of contact will move to the left. In addition, the model predicts that the average capture rate (slope of AB) will be greater in the easy environment than in the hard environment. Both of these qualitative predictions were supported by Cowie's data: The birds spent significantly more time within a patch in the hard environment than in the easy environment and their average capture rate was significantly larger in the easy environment than in the hard environment.

In addition to these qualitative tests, Cowie also carried out a quantitative test of the marginal value model. He used the model to define the relation between T_{opt} and t, and then compared this ideal relation with his observations of the birds. Cowie assumed that the functional form of the average net energy intake—$f(T)$—is a negative exponential function; based on this assumption Cowie was able to derive the mathematical relation between T_{opt} and t (see Appendix 3). This relation makes it possible to test the model quantitatively, but first one of the parameters of $f(T)$ (m in Appendix 3) had to be estimated. Cowie calculated the mean number of prey caught as a function of the time spent searching in a patch, and chose the values for $f(T)$ that gave the best fit of $f(T)$ to these data. Using these fitted values, Cowie concluded that the predicted relation between mean time spent in each patch—T_{opt}—and mean travel time—t—compared favorably with the mean foraging times of the birds.

The Diet Breadth Model

Another issue facing a foraging animal is the number of prey types to search for and include in its diet. Presumably, there is some optimal number of prey to include in the diet: Including either greater or fewer prey types would decrease the fitness (i.e., net rate of energy intake) of the foraging animal. For example, some food types may be so energetically expensive to capture and/or yield so little energy once eaten that they should be excluded from the diet. This is the issue of optimal diet, and one of the models used to study optimal diets is the *diet breadth model*. According to the diet breadth model the number of prey types in an optimal diet is a function of two conflicting behaviors on the part of the predator. On the one hand the forager must spend time searching for prey, and on the other must spend time pursuing and capturing the prey once it is found or encountered. If the animal forages for only a small number of prey types, then a larger amount of time will be spent searching and a relatively small amount of time will be spent pursuing. Conversely, if the animal forages for a large number of prey types then a smaller amount of time will be spent searching but a relatively large amount of time will be spent in pursuit.

These assumptions are captured in the graphical model in Fig. 10.2. This model does not specify the exact mathematical equations of the curves but only assumes that they are generally increasing or decreasing. Now, if the prey are ranked according to their net energy return per time spent foraging, then the optimal diet occurs at that point where the reduction in search cost by adding another prey type is matched by an increase in pursuit cost (MacArthur & Pianka, 1966). This point is the intersection of ΔS and ΔP in Fig. 10.2.

There are two simple yet important consequences of the diet breadth model. First, if the search costs increase, then the diet breadth should also increase. In graphical terms, this corresponds to moving the ΔS line in Fig. 10.2 upwards, in which case the point of intersection will move to the right. The second consequence is that if the pursuit costs are increased, then diet breadth should decrease. This corresponds to moving the ΔP line upwards, in which case the point of intersection will move to the left. Notice that costs of both types can change either as a result of changes in the forager's behavior or changes in the environment (e.g., increased abundance of prey and increased search efficiency will both decrease search costs). In practice, this model is rarely used to attempt precise predictions about the number of prey types included in an optimal diet, i.e., the precise point of intersection of the two admittedly weakly specified lines. Nevertheless, the more qualitative comparative predictions are quite useful, e.g., that increasing search costs should increase diet breadth.

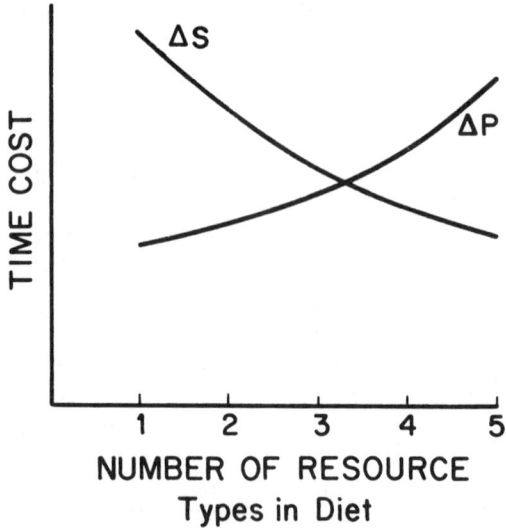

FIG. 10.2. Diet breadth model. Resources are ranked by their value to the forager in terms of net energy intake. The ΔS curve plots decreasing average search costs, and the ΔP curve plots increasing average pursuit costs, as an increasing number of resource types are added to the diet. The optimal diet breadth occurs at the point where the increases in pursuit costs are greater than the decreases in search costs when one more resource type is added to the diet. (From MacArthur & Pianka [1966]. Used by permission of The University of Chicago Press.)

Although there have been many tests of the diet breadth model (see Pyke et al., 1977), we focus on a study by Winterhalder (1981a, 1981b). This is an anthropological study of the foraging behavior of modern Cree Indians. The site of Winterhalder's study was a small Cree settlement in northern Ontario, Canada. Although the Indians were able to purchase food at a local store, they engaged in hunting, fishing, and trapping for both cultural and economic reasons. Food captured in the wild is considered by these Indians to be healthier than food available in stores, and being a proficient hunter is a highly desirable trait for the male members of the community. The hunters were also able to supplement their incomes by selling the pelts from many of the animals they captured. It is evident from ethnographic data and from interviews with the elders of the community that the foraging behaviors of these indians are little different from the foraging behaviors of their ancestors.

The boreal environment of northern Ontario contains a wide variety of potential resources, including moose, caribou, beaver, muskrat, hare, grouse, and fish. These species are generally of low density, scattered, and either solitary or in small groups. This distribution of prey types leads to the expectation that the Cree will expend considerable time and energy searching for prey, and as a consequence leads to the hypothesis (based on the diet breadth model) that they will have a generalized diet breadth. Winterhalder did in fact find that the Cree foraged for a wide variety of species, but this is not a very strong test because the quantitative predictions of the model are imprecise. Winterhalder carried out a stronger test that illustrates the power of foraging models when focusing on qualitative comparisons across situations.

In the past three centuries there have been several technological advances that have affected the efficiency of Cree hunting. In the 18th century the Cree acquired rifles and traps, which greatly increased their pursuit efficiency. Later, in the 20th century, the Cree acquired outboard motors and snowmobiles, which have greatly increased their search efficiency. According to the diet breadth model, these advances should have consequences for optimal diet breadth. Specifically, increasing use of rifles and traps in the 18th century should have decreased the cost of pursuit relative to search and thus should have increased diet breadth. Later the increase in snowmobiles and motorized boats in the 20th century should have increased search effectiveness and thus led to a historical decrease in diet breadth. Winterhalder cites a variety of historical evidence that supports the second of these predictions. According to this evidence a hunter is now more likely to pass up less desirable prey such as beaver or squirrels and spend more time searching for more desirable prey such as moose than was his counterpart of 20 or 30 years ago.

Two functions that foraging models have performed in Winterhalder's research deserve emphasis. First, the different models have helped to focus on the aspects of the foraging problems that are necessary for optimal foraging. For example, the models indicate that the optimal forager must be sensitive to the net rate of energy intake when choosing prey and patches. Furthermore, it is crucial that the forager allocate his time among the various search operations in such a way that he maximizes his energy intake. These are variables that may not have been obvious to anthropologists as important features of the Indians' foraging, and even if these variables had been considered, then the foraging models certainly have helped researchers to better formulate the relations among these variables. Second, as a result of focusing attention on the crucial features of the foraging task, foraging models have helped anthropologists generate new and more informative research. Winterhalder was able to go beyond an ethnographic description of Cree foraging behavior and generate testable hypotheses.

A COMPARISON OF FORAGING THEORY AND SEARCH THEORY

A common feature of the search and foraging models described above is that they each are optimization models (Maynard Smith, 1978). The simplest form of optimization involves maximizing (or minimizing) the value of some variable—the optimization criterion—which is a function of one or more other variables. What makes optimization problems interesting is that there are usually a number of factors to consider, coupled with constraints on optimization, e.g., limits on the time or effort available. So, for example, the optimization problem in search theory is to maximize the probability of finding the target given a fixed amount of effort or time, where the probability of finding the target is a function of the probability of detection, the target density, and the allocation of search effort. The optimization problem in the diet breadth model is to maximize net caloric intake given a fixed amount of effort, where the rate of energy intake is a function of time spent searching and time spent pursuing. In both cases, optimization yields a solution which, other things being equal, is a strategy that will be more effective than all other strategies available to the organism.

There are, however, some major differences between search theory and optimal foraging theory that make each lend itself to different sorts of applications. A convenient scheme for conceptualizing these differences is to evaluate models in terms of their generality, realism, and precision (Levins, 1966; see also Coombs, 1983). The goal of modeling is to represent a complex system in such a way that the essential and nontrivial features of the system are retained while at the same time providing a representation that is analytically tractable. Ideally, a model would simultaneously achieve generality, realism, and precision, but most types of models sacrifice at least one of these three qualities. For example, classic models in physics sacrifice realism to generality and precision. Frictionless gases or acceleration in a perfect vacuum do not exist, but in describing these ideal situations physicists can precisely capture very general properties of matter, even though they must ignore a wealth of very real factors of acute concern to engineers (e.g., coefficients of friction).

Models based on search theory sacrifice generality to precision and realism. Precise optimal solutions to very real problems are generated, but the calculational models that allow this rest heavily and specifically on the details of a particular problem (target density), organism (detection function), and situation (available effort). Furthermore, these models are really only useful when target detection is a critical feature of the search problem. Although search theory is a powerful tool for this type of problem, the emphasis on target detection limits the generality of search models.

Optimal foraging models of the graphical/qualitative sort sacrifice quantitative precision to realism and generality. As a consequence of this lack of quantitative precision, the predictions are most often expressed as inequalities between different environments or experimental treatments. Because of their generality, the models of foraging theory have been applied to the foraging behavior of a large number of species (see, for example, Kamil & Sargent, 1981) exhibiting a wide variety of foraging behaviors (see Charnov, 1976, and Orians & Pearson, 1977, for additional models not discussed here).

We wish to argue that the qualitative/graphical approach to modeling seems particularly useful for advancing our understanding of the development of human search abilities. This approach, although essentially unemployed in psychological theorizing, has some important advantages. A primary advantage of these models is that they are qualitative (Krantz, 1974):

> The formulation of a theory in terms of a few qualitative laws, the intuitive meanings of which are fairly transparent, aids the testing and the development of theory. It concentrates observations on critical points, where small but systematic deviations may be theoretically meaningful—where systematic violations may suggest alternative qualitative laws.

and

> In many cases the formulation of qualitative laws suggests experiments that are intrinsically simple and interesting, . . . but which might be very hard to arrive at otherwise. (p. 171)

In short, mathematical precision should not be confused with theoretical precision. Krantz's point[1] is that theoretical precision is possible—perhaps even more likely—in the absence of quantitative precision. Conversely, a quantitatively

---

[1]There is a fundamental difference between Krantz's qualitative laws and the kinds of qualitative models we have been discussing. The difference lies in the fact that Krantz's laws are based on an axiom system (see Krantz, Luce, Suppes, & Tversky, 1971, Ch. 1) and the models of foraging theory are based on the optimization of quantitative variables (see Schoener, 1971). In practice, we think this difference is of little consequence, because the procedure for testing models is similar in both cases. In the case of measurement theory, the axioms yield qualitative tests such as independence and cancellation (Krantz & Tversky, 1971). In the case of foraging theory, we use only the qualitative features of the models (Levins, 1966) to derive qualitative tests such as the comparative tests carried out by Wintehalder. Both approaches share the advantages of qualitative testing as described in the quote from Krantz.

precise result does not necessarily mean the result is theoretically accurate or meaningful (cf. Dawes & Corrigan, 1974). In the case of search theory, if used theoretically, the meaningfulness of the optimal search plan is undermined by the need to make questionable or arbitrary assumptions or estimates of unknown parameters.

One of the reasons why Krantz and others (e.g., Krantz, 1972; Krantz & Tversky, 1971) have argued for a qualitative approach to theorizing in psychology has been their dissatisfaction with the goodness-of-fit tests that are so often used with quantitative mathematical models. Hoffmann, Shaw and Shaw, and Cowie all used goodness-of-fit tests to compare the predictions of their models with their observations. There are three problems with goodness-of-fit tests in this regard (cf. Anderson & Shanteau, 1977). First, there are usually a large number of alternative models that will fit the data acceptably according to one of these tests. A related issue is statistical power: A goodness-of-fit test with inadequate power may fail to reject a model because of noisy data. For example, in Hoffmann's study there are numerous models with different combinations of parameter values that would give an acceptable fit to the data, and Hoffmann's test may lack the power necessary to reject any one of these. Second, goodness-of-fit tests, by providing a false sense of security, can induce the investigator to overlook theoretically important features of the data. For example, a close look at the curves in Hoffmann's study will reveal discrepancies between the pairs of predicted and observed curves; this suggests that some feature of Hoffmann's model is incorrect. The same point could be made for Cowie's results. These findings are potentially as interesting as the result of a nonsignificant goodness-of-fit test. Finally, even when the model is rejected by a goodness-of-fit test, the test provides little information about what aspects of the model are incorrect. On the other hand, qualitative tests can often be constructed to concentrate statistical power on the differences between alternative models, and thus are maximally informative.

A secondary, though still important, advantage of qualitative/graphical models is that they are graphical. Graphics like algebraics is a tractable analytic medium. The benefits of graphics are becoming increasingly obvious to statisticians, who have recently begun to show serious interest in the graphical display of information (e.g., Chambers, Cleveland, Kleiner, & Tukey, 1983; Wainer, 1984; Wainer & Thissen, 1981). A major benefit of graphics is made clear in the following (Tufte, 1983):

> What is to be sought in designs for the display of information is the clear portrayal of complexity. Not the complication of the simple; rather the task of the designer is to give visual access to the subtle and difficult—that is, the revelation of the complex. (p. 191)

We do not claim that these advantages are absolute. All models involve simplifying assumptions, some of which are likely to be arbitrary and/or erroneous. All have costs as well as payoffs. Furthermore, qualitative and quantitative models play complementary and mutually supporting roles in psychological theorizing, and will prove useful in different contexts. Our argument for the use of qualitative/graphical models is thus especially state-dependent.

Given the state of our knowledge on the development of human search, the advantages of more qualitative models seem high and the costs low. A contrast to search theory is again informative. In search theory there are many important parameters to measure, estimate, or assume. In the case of the measurable ones, research is only beginning to investigate them and their measurement will require independent programs of research in themselves. As an example, envision the research necessary to understand and measure children's developing visual detection capabilities. On the other hand, the graphical models of optimal foraging seem to allow for more ignorance; they allow the investigator to ignore potential variables of unknown or uncertain influence while concentrating on only a few focal factors.

The costs of doing this are twofold. First, the models' conclusions are essentially qualitative (Levins, 1966):

> we . . . resort to very flexible models, often graphical, which generally assume that functions are increasing or decreasing, convex or concave, greater or less than some value, instead of specifying the mathematical form of an equation. This means that the predictions we can make are also expressed as inequalities as between tropical and temperate species, insular *versus* continental faunas, patchy *versus* uniform environments, etc. (p. 422)

However, as noted above there are complementary advantages to qualitative predictions. In addition, in developmental psychology our predictions are often, as yet, qualitative. Thus we are specially in need of simple, general models that allow derivation of qualitative tests. Indeed, at this point we would expect reasonably general models to hold only qualitatively and to be actually contradicted in detail, in many situations, because of unknown and unmeasured factors. We can readily admit to knowing little about some potentially important determinants of behavior. Thus, somewhat like the physicist, too much information in our models at this point may only obscure the larger picture we seek.

A related asset, and cost, of such simplified qualitative models is that they depend on the use of "sufficient parameters" (Levins, 1966). The concept of sufficient parameters is similar to the statistician's concept of a sufficient statistic, which is a statistic that contains all of the information in the data necessary for achieving a particular goal. Likewise, sufficient parameters are the parameters actually included in a model and each of them is a proxy for several lower order parameters not included in the model. The loss of information is necessary in order to make the model practically useful, and the hope of the modeler is that the critical features of the system being studied have been captured by the sufficient parameters. A consideration of the nature of detection serves to underscore this point. Detection, the less-than-perfect probability of seeing a target given that it is there, is a fundamental component of search theory, along with the less-than-perfect probability of the target being in any specific place. Indeed, if the object is perfectly detectable and/or has a known location, the whole theory is obviated. (Note, however, that psychological search problems may still remain for the searcher, e.g., Wellman, Somerville, & Haake, 1979). Of course, detection is also at issue when a predator searches for prey. Yet in the diet breadth model, for example, this (plus other considerations) is subsumed in the less specific, qualitative claim that search decreases relative to pursuit as prey become more numerous.

"The sufficient parameter is a many-to-one transformation of lower level phenomena. Therein lies its power and utility, but also a new source of imprecision" (Levins, 1966, p. 429). If several things combine to determine "search" in the diet breadth model, the consequences of the model cannot tell us about the influence of one versus the other of those subordinate phenomena. In addition, models can be posed based on higher order parameters which may prove uninformative or illegitimate. Of course this is also a problem with more specific parameters, e.g., in applications of search theory.

In short, that qualitative/graphical models allow one to ignore many specific parameters and yield only qualitative comparative predictions constitute both the limitations and assets of the approach. The assets, however, seem well suited to our current state of knowledge in researching human development generally and the development of human search abilities specifically. Further, as was evident in the quote from Krantz above, such qualitative models allow one to focus an experimental test on just that feature of the theory that requires research. To underscore these putative advantages we propose a testable qualitative/graphical model specifically relevant to current questions concerning the development of search processes.

A PROPOSAL

Recall the distinction between comprehensive and selective search strategies. A clear dilemma facing the searcher is when to use which—when should I search all locations and when should I search by going primarily or first to a select few? Of particular interest developmentally is when children might understand these distinctively different approaches and use them appropriately. This question has been studied in part: When faced with obvious comprehensive search problems even 3-year-olds search differently than when faced with selective problems (e.g., Wellman, et al., 1979). The tests here have involved either situations containing no constraining target information (and thus requiring comprehensive search) or situations containing all information necessary to determine where the target is (and thus requiring selective search).

In contrast, real-world search problems are most often probabilistic; the searcher has some uncertain and insufficient knowledge and must decide how to search. An example occurs when my keys are missing and I believe they are probably in the upstairs bedroom. I go to look in the bedroom, but as I go I look on the table in the downstairs hall and also detour to glance in the bathroom. I do this because it is not impossible that the keys are there and those places are only slightly out of my way. This behavior represents a combination of comprehensive and selective tendencies, while being neither completely comprehensive (searching everywhere) nor selective (searching first and directly in the bedroom). Do such searches occur with any frequency, are they reasonably optimal, and if so, when are children able to search in such intelligent manners? We propose a graphical optimization model that covers these situations, and then show how it could be used to investigate these questions.

A basic assumption of the model is that a searcher possesses general strategies that partly specify how he or she will solve search problems. We make no claim whether the searcher can state these strategies or define the search information that dictates them; nevertheless we assume that the searcher will respond in systematic ways to search problems, based on systematic differences in the search information that characterize the search problems. More specifically we assume there are two general strategies—selective search and comprehensive search. We further assume that search information can be used to define a continuum of problems ranging from those that perfectly specify the location of a target to those specifying only that the target is somewhere in the search space. The model describes how a searcher would act if he or she were appropriately matching behavior to information. It is thus a model of optimal search. The model will be used primarily to make qualitative predictions about optimal behavior. When children's behavior at some age matches the model's predictions, inferences can be drawn concerning their search strategies, their understanding of the pertinent search information, and their ability to choose optimal strategies given the search information. When children's behavior differs from the model, inferences can be made about whether they possess partial skill or no skill at all, and the nature of information processing limitations causing nonoptimal performance. Utilizing the model in this fashion depends on assuming that the development of human search ability is, in part, a process of increasingly optimal and efficient problem-solving development. This general assumption is, we believe, well supported by a host of current studies (Wellman & Somerville, 1982).

If children fail to search according to the model at some age, or at all ages, alternate models can be proposed. These alternate models could also be based on optimal search considerations; they could be optimization models incorporating an alternate currency (e.g., redundant searches rather than distance traveled) and/or different sufficient parameters. That is, failure to search according to the model does not mean the searcher searches nonoptimally, under *some* perception of the problem. In fact we suspect that some tendency toward optimal search performance is invariant across a very wide age range, although the variables and models capturing this tendency probably vary greatly with age. The model to be presented does not depend on this background assumption in any strict sense, but this assumption further motivates our interest in and special consideration of optimal search models.

The general model holds across many situations but it is best developed with a specific search space and problem. Consider the square search array shown in Fig. 10.3. The searcher begins searching at point S and there are three locations—L, X, and R—in the search space that could potentially contain the target. The angle θ determines the shape of the array; in Fig. 10.3, $\theta = 90°$, hence the four vertices form a square. We will let the length of the sides be k, so that the diagonals, as diagonals of a square, have length $\sqrt{2}k = 1.41k$.

An important factor that determines the optimal search strategy is the target density, that is the probability that the item is in some one of the locations. This density can be determined completely by focusing on the probability that the target is in location X, call this $P(X)$. Then, to keep things simple, let the

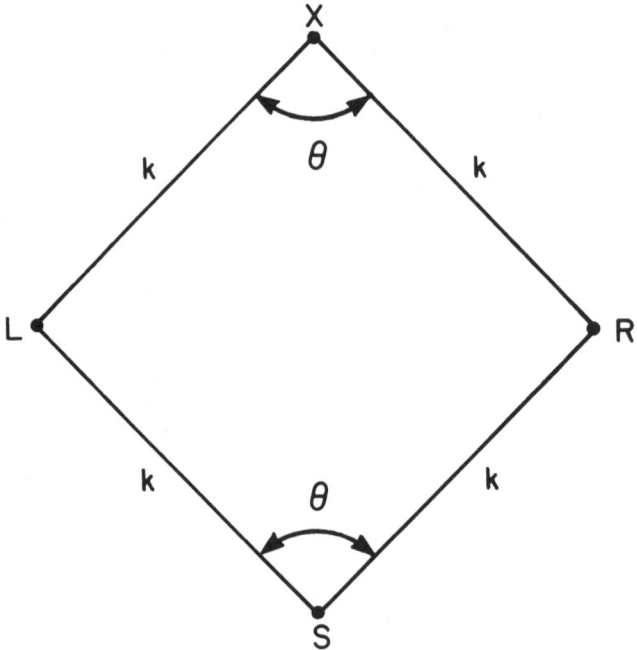

FIG. 10.3. Search space. S is the starting point of search and L, X, and R are possible target locations. k is the size parameter and θ is the shape parameter of the search space. The figure is drawn with $\theta = 90°$, but the distance between S and X can be varied by increasing or decreasing the value of θ.

10. MATHEMATICAL MODELS OF SEARCH 271

probability of the target being in L or R be equal, so that $P(L) = P(R) = (1 - P(X))/2$. Now, when $P(X) = 1/3$, the item is equally likely to be in any of the three locations, and when $P(X) = 1$, the item is at X. The values between 1/3 and 1 constitute a continuum of probabilistic search problems.

Consider now the distance traveled, D, by the searcher. In searching the space the searcher can move from any one point to any other. We will require the searcher to begin at S and return to S when finished. The search problem is thus to minimize the distance traveled to find the object and return to the start. There are two obvious strategies for the searcher. One strategy—S(X)—calls for first going to point X, which is an appropriate strategy if $P(X) = 1$. Another strategy—S(L)—calls for first going to point L and continuing in order to all locations if needed, which would be called for if $P(X) = 1/3$. Using S(X) means the searcher traces the path SXLRS or equivalently SXRLS (since $P(L) = P(R)$); when using S(L) the searcher traces the path SLXRS or equivalently SRXLS. Other paths are possible, but these two seem the most natural, and strategic ones illustrating the essential approaches to this search problem. Obviously, S(X) corresponds to a selective search strategy and S(L) corresponds to the most reasonable comprehensive search strategy—since it is the shortest path visiting all locations.

The expected distance, $E(D)$, for these two strategies will vary depending upon $P(X)$. Figure 10.4 displays $E(D)$ as a function of $P(X)$. Most importantly, considering the unbroken lines first, note that the expected distance for S(X) decreases relative to S(L) as $P(X)$ increases. This is the general graphical form of the model. Given regular search arrays of the general "circular" sort depicted in Fig. 10.3, then as $P(X)$ increases, the cost of the selective strategy S(X) decreases faster than the cost of the comprehensive strategy S(L) (which often in fact increases) so that the two curves intersect at some point. This becomes clear if we look at how $E(D)$ is determined in our concrete example. Suppose that the searcher adopts S(L) for the search problem in Fig. 10.3. Then the searcher's path will be SLS with probability $P(L)$, SLXS with probability $P(X)$, and SLXRS with probability $P(R)$. The length of path SLS is $2k$, the length of path SLXS is $3.41k$, and the length of path SLXRS is $4k$. It follows that the searcher's expected distance is $E(D) = P(L)2k + P(X)3.41k + P(R)4k$. Suppose instead the searcher adopts S(X) for the problem, then, in a similar fashion, $E(D) = P(X)2.82k + P(L)3.41k + P(R)4.82k$. Notice if the problem is selective $P(X) = 1$ and $P(L) + P(R) = 0$. Thus for S(X), $E(D) = 2.83k$, and for S(L), $E(D) = 3.41k$, as graphed in the unbroken lines of Fig. 10.4.

Figure 10.4 shows us exactly what we should expect, namely that a selective search strategy—S(X)—works best for a search problem where the target's location is known ($P(X) = 1$), and that a comprehensive search strategy—S(L)—works best for a problem where the target could be anywhere ($P(X) = .33$). In addition, corresponding to our intuitions again we see there is a range of $P(X)$ where S(L) is superior to S(X) and vice versa. Indeed, according to Fig.

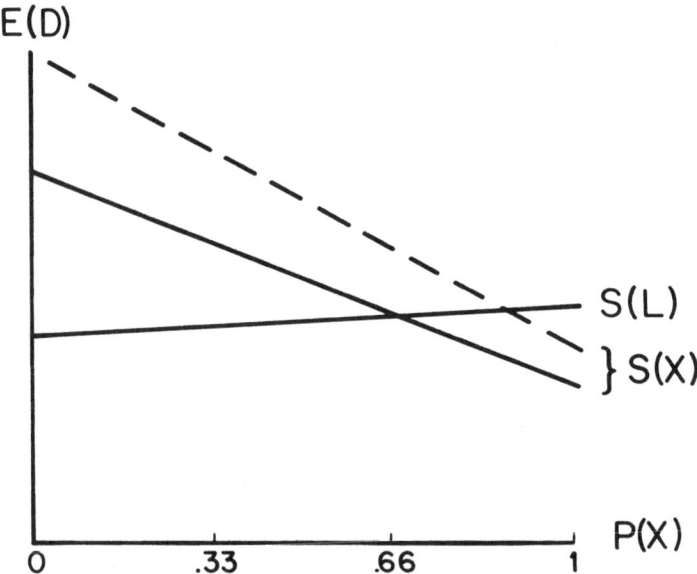

FIG. 10.4. Search model. $E(D)$ is the expected distance traveled, and $P(X)$ is the probability of the target being in location X. The S(X) line plots expected distance traveled using strategy S(X), and the S(L) line plots expected distance traveled using strategy S(L) or S(R). The solid lines are for $\theta = 90°$, and the broken line is for $\theta < 90°$. If $\theta = 90°$, S(L) is a more efficient strategy when $P(X) < .66$, but S(X) is more efficient when $P(X) > .66$. Decreasing θ has the effect of making S(L) more efficient for a wider range of $P(X)$ values.

10.4, S(L) is a more efficient strategy when $P(X) < .66$, S(X) is a more efficient strategy specifically when $P(X) > .66$. and the two strategies are equally efficient when $P(X) = .66$.

Figure 10.4 shows how $E(D)$ is affected by changes in $P(X)$, but the expected distances and hence the costs of the two strategies are also influenced by changes in the shape of the search space. For example, what if the square search array in Fig. 10.3 were squashed by decreasing θ while keeping k the same? The distances SL and SLX (or SR and SRX) would remain the same but the distance SX would increase. The influence of this is represented graphically by the dotted line in Fig. 10.4. Since SX is the prime determinant of the distance traveled using strategy S(X) and SL similarly determines S(L), the effect is to raise the cost of S(X) relative to S(L). Note that doing so moves the intersection point of S(L) and S(X) to the right. In fact, in general increasing θ moves the point of intersection in Fig. 10.4 to the left, and decreasing θ moves the point of intersection to the right. This corresponds to our intuitions about the problem: When θ is large, the distance between S and X is small relative to the distance between S and L and so the cost of going to X first is relatively small; when θ is small, the distance between S and X is large relative to the distance between S and L and so the cost of going to L first is relatively small. It is easy to see that for very small θ the searcher may as well choose L or R first for any type of search problem because these points are right on the way to X.

An important feature of this search model, and the qualitative approach, is that we do not have to test precise mathematical predictions, but can test the model via qualitative comparisons across situations. This is important because we would not expect adults, much less children, to apprehend precisely that the intersection point for the problems depicted in Fig. 10.4 is .66. Testing the quantitative value of such a point thus seems unreasonable. On the other hand, it is reasonable to test subjects' appreciation of the changes in costs of the two different situations, and hence changes in the intersection point as shown in Fig. 10.4. To see this, consider the following experimental design. Suppose each searcher is presented with nine search problems corresponding to the nine cells of a 3 × 3 factorial design. One of the factors is $P(X)$ with values .33, .66, and 1; the other factor is θ, with values 30°, 90°, and 150°. When faced with these nine search problems, an efficient searcher will always use S(L) when $P(X) = .33$ and will always use S(X) when $P(X) = 1$. When $P(X) = .66$, the efficient searcher will choose S(L) when θ = 30° and will choose S(X) when θ = 150°; when θ = 90°, he should be indifferent between the two strategies since $E(D)$ is the same in both cases.

In short, as a consequence of using a qualitative/graphical approach, we avoid comparing the performances of our subjects with quantitative features of the model. Instead, what we do is look at changes in the frequency with which subjects choose a strategy across particular search problems. For instance, if the subjects are sensitive to the selective/comprehensive aspect of the problem information they will be more likely to choose S(L) when $P(X) = .33$ than when $P(X) = 1.00$. Similarly, if they are sensitive to the trade-offs between S(X) and S(L) they will choose S(X) more often when θ = 150° than when θ = 30°.

We have not yet undertaken a direct experimental test based on this model, but we possess data from earlier studies that provide indirect support and information. In two studies (Haake, Somerville, & Wellman, 1980; Wellman et al., 1979) we have used similar procedures in two different search spaces when demonstrating that preschool children can search logically and effectively. Both search spaces were large outside playgrounds of roughly rectangular shape and contained a variety of play equipment. In each case eight obvious natural locations were identified (e.g., the seesaw) that formed a rough semicircular pattern. Preschool children searched the eight locations for an object (e.g., a lost camera) in two different conditions. In one, a comprehensive search condition, the object was equally likely to be at any location (the child was told it could have been left anywhere). In the other, a selective search condition, the object was known by inference to be at one of the central four locations (locations 3–6), and not at locations 1, 2, 7, or 8. This was inferable since the children had just visited all locations, in order, and on this circuit the camera was last shown to be present at location 3 and first shown to be absent at location 7. Information of this sort specifies with high probability that the item is in the critical central locations—that is, at or after the point where it was last seen but before the point where it was first noticed missing. In both these studies children tended to search comprehensively (going from 1 to 8 or 8 to 1 in order) in the comprehensive condition, but differently and selectively (spending a majority of their first four searches on location 3–6) in the selective condition. Although these comparisons were significant in each study, a comparison across studies proves relevant to the current discussion and model.

One of the playgrounds used was a typical, flat, two-dimensional terrain. For the other the terrain formed a "bowl." In this case, the play equipment was on the lip of the bowl occupying the roughly circular edge of the playground, and the middle of the playground contained a fairly steep depression. These differences between the two playgrounds are more complex than those used earlier to illustrate the model, but the effect is similar. In essence, the shape of the spaces is different such that in one space (the flat terrain) the direct distance from the start to a location in the critical area (e.g., S to location 3, analogous to SX in Fig. 10.3) is much shorter than the distance to that location via a comprehensive route (e.g., S to 1 to 2 to 3, analogous to SLX in Fig. 10.3). In the bowl, however, these two distances and their related efforts are more equal (since S to 3, analogous to SX, bows down and then up). In short, the expected cost—distance traveled—of a selective strategy relative to a comprehensive strategy is higher for the bowl than for the flat space. In terms of the model this means that the line S(X) in Fig. 10.4 is moved up relative to the line S(L), as shown by the dotted line. Obviously, the intersection point of the two lines thus shifts to the right for the bowl space in comparison to the flat space. In other words, comprehensive search should be retained as the preferred strategy in the bowl for a larger $P(X)$ compared to the flat space.

$P(X)$ was not varied in either of these studies, however, since children had to infer $P(X)$ from remembered information and both memory and inferential processes are likely to vary across the children, then $P(X)$ probably varies across children within a study. In short, across studies more children should be likely to search comprehensively in the selective condition for the bowl versus the flat terrain.

In fact, comparing performance across the two spaces, preschool children were less likely to give up a comprehensive route for a selective one in the bowl space than in the flat, as predicted. Specifically, in the comprehensive search conditions of each study, children were most likely to search comprehensively; 68% and 54% of the children in the bowl and flat spaces, respectively, adopted a comprehensive search pattern, $\chi^2(1) = .38$, n.s. In the selective search conditions, 36% versus 4% of the children in the bowl versus flat spaces searched comprehensively, $\chi^2(1) = 13.46$, $p < .01$. In short, while most children searched selectively in the selective condition of both studies and most searched comprehensively in the comprehensive condition, still, as predicted by the model, children were less likely to give up comprehensive search within the bowled search space than within the flat one.

The original studies focused on the straightforward prediction that performance would be different in clearly comprehensive (i.e., $P(X) = P(L) = P(R)$) situations as opposed to clearly selective ones (i.e., $P(X) = 1$). The current model allows us to account for the heretofore puzzling fact that although still in the minority, comprehensive search was more likely in the selective search condition of one study than the other. This account is posed as an implication of the model, and was nonobvious without it. Substantively, it suggests that preschoolers' search may be even more intelligently optimal than we previously conceived.

SUMMARY AND CONCLUSIONS

In this chapter we began by reviewing extant mathematical models of optimal search and ended by proposing a model of our own. Along the way we argued that qualitative/graphical models of the sort involved in our proposal might prove particularly informative for developmental research.

We devoted a substantial portion of this chapter to reviewing extant models for the reasons outlined briefly in the introduction. First, these models help to further define and analyze the problem domain. Essentially, search poses the organism with an optimization problem, where decisions must be made between competing response options, which themselves define a system of cost trade-offs. An essential question for humans, then, is their developing sensitivity to the competing factors and trade-offs involved and their ability to compound these together to arrive at optimal solutions. In addition, these models all highlight the geometric quality of search problems. An essential, though sometimes unacknowledged, ingredient of all the models reviewed concerns the actual or perceived a priori spatial distribution of search target(s). For example, the workings of our model depend on the shape of the search space; the marginal value model depends on the patchy distribution of prey; search theory models depend on whether the target densities are uniformly or unevenly distributed and if unevenly distributed the character of this distribution. In each case characterization of the search space—its nature and representation—dictates an essential part of the problem.

A further aspect of search problems is especially clear in optimal foraging models. These models highlight the fact that search itself is only part of the problem facing the searcher. For example, in the diet breadth model (or simply search for a lost pet) once a movable target is found it must be pursued, or in our model, once found, the target must be returned to a certain point. These larger concerns partly dictate the nature of optimal search solutions. In a similar fashion, search theory highlights the importance of target detection in all search problems. Indeed, in the only application of search theory to modeling human behavior that we are aware of, the resulting model is wholly a model of visual detection (Shaw, 1978; Shaw & Shaw, 1977). Sometimes, of course (e.g., in the sorts of problems most often studied in developmental research on search), the probability of detecting the object if it is there is unity. But this is also an essential part of the problem: Perfect detectability allows the searcher to ignore the concerns of detection and concentrate wholly on the probable location of the target(s) in space. In sum, by the features they encompass or highlight and by the solutions they yield, these models define search and help us understand its nature and its analysis as well as its behavioral importance and development.

Second, the models reviewed can be applied directly to further understand certain cases of human search behavior. An example of this is the research by Winterhalder on Cree hunting. Similarly the research by Shaw and Shaw represents a direct application of search theory to the study of human perception.

Third, even where these models cannot be applied directly to human search endeavors, they provide a pool of resources for formulating models of human search and search processes. Reasonable theories of human behavior are rarely, if ever, created in isolation. Later, more valid models are the offspring of less perfected predecessors, and often borrow some appropriate components, or solutions, from yet other models and theories. The pool of models reviewed here provides a foundation for furthering the task of modeling human searches. To illustrate this, we ended the chapter by proposing a model of one aspect of human search that borrows from models in foraging theory, but that was especially formulated to address a specific problem in our understanding of human search and its development.

Although admittedly in need of testing and further development, this proposed model also illustrates some of the advantages of attempting to model human search and its development. Specifically, the model provides a hypothetical analysis of human behavior within a tractable modeling language. In this case the language is primarily a graphical one. But in any event the model can be used to deduce testable predictions, at least some of which are nonobvious.

All attempts to model behavior force the researcher to arrive at plausible, tractable analyses of the domain in question. However, different sorts of models have different characteristic levels of precision, realism, and generality. They thus have different strengths and weaknesses. We argue for not ignoring the advantages of models that are appropriately imprecise and that are flexible enough for testing general developmental hypotheses; that is, we argue for the development of qualitative, general models of human search and its development.

ACKNOWLEDGMENTS

This work was supported in part by grants from NICHD to the second author. The authors would like to thank Mary Kaiser, Warren Holmes, and Frank Yates for helpful comments on previous drafts of this paper.

REFERENCES

Anderson, N. H. (1980). Information integration theory in developmental psychology. In F. Wilkening, J. Becker, & T. Trabasso (Eds.), *Information integration by children* (pp. 1–145). Hillsdale, NJ: Lawrewnce Erlbaum Associates.

Anderson, N. H., & Shanteau, J. (1977). Weak inference with linear models. *Psychological Bulletin, 84,* 1155–1170.

Brainerd, C. J., Howe, M. L., & Desrochers, A. (1982). The general theory of two-stage learning: A mathematical review with illustrations from memory development. *Psychological Bulletin, 91,* 634–665.

Chambers, J., Cleveland, W., Kleiner, B., & Tukey, P. (1983). *Graphical methods for data analysis.* Boston: Duxbury Press.

Charnov, E. L. (1976). Optimal foraging, the marginal value theorem. *Theoretical Population Biology, 9,* 129–136.

Coombs, C. H. (1983). *Psychology and mathematics: An essay on theory.* Ann Arbor: University of Michigan Press.

Cowie, R. J. (1977). Optimal foraging in great tits (*Parus major*). *Nature, 268,* 137–139.

Dawes, R. M., & Corrigan, B. (1974). Linear models in decision making. *Psychological Bulletin, 81,* 95–106.

Dobbie, J. M. (1968). A survey of search theory. *Operations Research, 16,* 525–537.

Haake, R. J., Somerville, S. C., & Wellman, H. M. (1980). Logical ability of young children in searching a large-scale environment. *Child Development, 51,* 1299–1302.

Haley, K. B., & Stone, L. D. (1980). *Search theory and applications.* New York: Plenum Press.

Hoffmann, G. (1983). The search behavior of the desert isopod *Hemilepistus reaumuri* as compared with a systematic search. *Behavioral Ecology and Sociobiology, 13,* 93–106.

Kamil, A. C., & Sargent, T. (Eds.). (1981). *Foraging behavior: Ecological, ethological, and psychological approaches.* New York: Garland Press.

Koopman, B. O. (1956a). The theory of search, Part I. Kinematic bases. *Operations Research, 4,* 324–346.

Koopman, B. O. (1956b). The theory of search, Part II. Target detection. *Operations Research, 4,* 503–531.

Koopman, B. O. (1957). The theory of search, Part III. The optimum distribution of searching effort. *Operations Research, 5,* 613–626.

Koopman, B. O. (1946/1980). *Search and Screening.* New York: Pergamon Press.

Krantz, D. H. (1972). Measurement structures and psychological laws. *Science, 175,* 1427–1435.

Krantz, D. H. (1974). Measurement theory and qualitative laws in psychophysics. In D. H. Krantz, R. C. Atkinson, R. D. Luce, & P. Suppes (Eds.), *Contemporary developments in mathematical psychology: Vol. 2. Measurement, psychophysics, and neural information processing* (pp. 160–199). San Francisco: Freeman.

Krantz, D. H., Luce, R. D., Suppes, P., & Tversky, A. (1971). *Foundations of measurement: Vol. 1. Additive and polynomial representations.* New York: Academic Press.

Krantz, D. H., & Tversky, A. (1971). Conjoint-measurement analysis of composition rules in psychology. *Psychological Review, 78,* 151–169.

Krebs, J. R. (1978). Optimal foraging: Decision rules for predators. In J. R. Krebs & N. B. Davies (Eds.), *Behavioural ecology; An evolutionary approach* (pp. 23–63). London: Blackwell Scientific Publishers.
Levins, R. (1966). The strategy of model building in population biology. *American Scientist, 54,* 421–431.
Luce, R. D., Bush, R. R., & Galanter, E. (Eds.). (1963). *Handbook of mathematical psychology.* New York: Wiley.
MacArthur, R. H., & Pianka, E. R. (1966). On optimal use of a patchy environment. *American Naturalist, 100,* 603–609.
Maynard Smith, J. (1978). Optimization theory in evolution. *Annual Review of Ecology and Systematics, 9,* 31–56.
Miller, G. A. (1964). *Mathematics and psychology.* New York: Wiley.
Orians, G. H., & Pearson, N. E. (1977). On the theory of central place foraging. In D. J. Horn, G. R. Stairs, & R. D. Mitchell (Eds.), *Analysis of ecological systems* (pp. 155–177). Columbus: Ohio State University Press.
Pyke, G. H., Pulliam, H. R., & Charnov, E. L. (1977). Optimal foraging: A selective review of theory and tests. *The Quarterly Review of Biology, 52,* 137–154.
Restle, F. (1971). *Mathematical models in psychology: An introduction.* New York: Wiley.
Schoener, T. W. (1971). Theory of feeding strategies. *Annual Review of Ecology and Systematics, 2,* 369–404.
Shaw, M. (1978). A capacity allocation model for reaction time. *Journal of Experimental Psychology: Human Perception and Performance, 4,* 586–598.
Shaw, M., & Shaw, P. (1977). Optimal allocation of cognitive resources to spatial locations. *Journal of Experimental Psychology: Human Perception and Performance, 3,* 201–211.
Stone, L. D. (1975). *Theory of optimal search.* New York: Academic Press.
Tufte, E. (1983). *The visual display of quantitative information.* Cheshire, CT: Graphics Press.
Wainer, H. (1984). How to display data badly. *American Statistician, 38,* 137–147.
Wainer, H., & Thissen, D. (1981). Graphical data analysis. *Annual Review of Psychology, 32,* 193–241.
Wellman, H. M., & Somerville, S. C. (1982). The development of human search ability. In M. E. Lamb & A. L. Brown (Eds.), *Advances in developmental psychology* (Vol. 2, pp. 41–84). Hillsdale, NJ: Lawrence Erlbaum Associates.
Wellman, H. M., Somerville, S. C., & Haake, R. J. (1979). Development of search procedures in real-life spatial environments. *Developmental Psychology, 15,* 530–542.
Wilkinson, A. C. (1982). Theoretical and methodological analysis of partial knowledge. *Developmental Review, 2,* 274–304.
Winterhalder, B. (1981a). Optimal foraging strategies and hunter-gatherer research in anthropology: Theory and models. In B. Winterhalder & E. A. Smith (Eds.), *Hunter-gatherer foraging strategies: Ethnographic and archeological analyses* (pp. 13–35). Chicago: University of Chicago Press.
Winterhalder, B. (1981b). Foraging strategies in the boreal forest: An analysis of Cree hunting and gathering. In B. Winterhalder & E. A. Smith (Eds.), *Hunter-gatherer foraging strategies: Ethnographic and archaelogical analyses* (pp. 66–98). Chicago: University of Chicago Press.

APPENDIX 1

Following Hoffmann (1983), the **detection function** (step 1) is the exponential distribution function,

$$b(\mathbf{x}, z) = 1 - e^{-iz}, \text{ for } i > 0 \text{ and } z \geq 0,$$

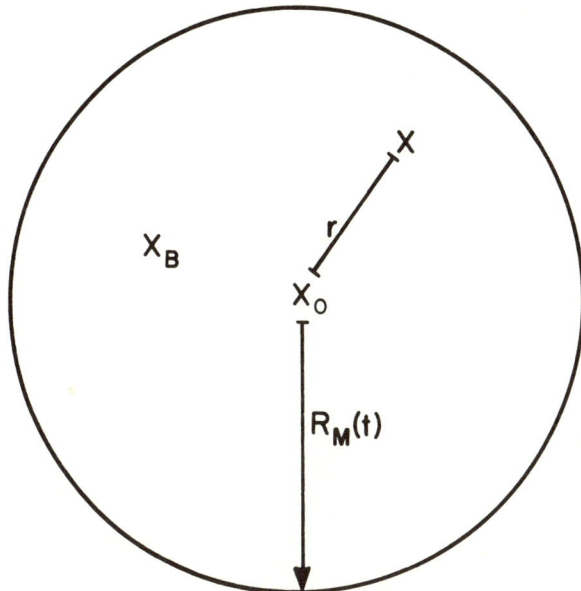

FIG. 10.5. Hoffmann's search space. x_0 is the starting point of search, x is the current point of search, and x_B is the location of the burrow. $r = \|x\|$ is the distance between the starting point and the current point of search. $R_M(t)$ is the search limit prescribed by the optimal search plan.

where **x** is a two-dimensional vector representing the location being searched (see Fig. 10.5), z is the search intensity at point **x**, and i is the instantaneous probability of detection. The detection function is the conditional probability of detecting the target with search intensity z given that the burrow is at point **x**. Notice that $b(\mathbf{x}, 0) = 0$; that is, the isopod cannot detect the entrance if it has not searched at its location, **x**.

It is assumed in this model that the probability of detecting the entrance increases by the amount $i\Delta z$ when the animal searches at the entrance with small intensity Δz. Furthermore, it is assumed that if an isopod has already searched at the burrow with intensity z and then returns after searching elsewhere, then it has lost the information gained from previous search. If it searches at the entrance with additional intensity Δz, then it will fail to detect the burrow with the same probability $(1 - i\Delta z)$ as in the beginning. It follows that the probability $(1 - b(\mathbf{x}, z + \Delta z))$ that the animal will not detect the burrow although it searches there with intensity $z + \Delta z$ is given by

$$1 - b(\mathbf{x}, z + \Delta z) = (1 - b(\mathbf{x}, z))(1 - i\Delta z).$$

From this it can be seen that the form of the detection function is derived from the fact that the probability of not detecting the burrow with intensity z is the product of the n probabilities of not detecting the entrance with small intensities Δz_j, $j = 1, \ldots, n$, where $\sum_{j=1}^{n} \Delta z_j = z$. Now, the asympotic form of the detection function is as follows:

$$b(\mathbf{x}, z) = 1 - (1 - i\Delta z_1)(1 - i\Delta z_2)\cdots(1 - i\Delta z_n)$$

$$\rightarrow 1 - (e^{-i\Delta z_1})(e^{-i\Delta z_2})\cdots(e^{-i\Delta z_n}) \text{ as } \Delta z_j \rightarrow 0, j=1 \ldots, n$$

$$= 1 - e^{-iz}.$$

The **target density** (step 2) chosen by Hoffmann for the search problem posed to *H. reamuri* is the two-dimensional normal normal distribution:

$$p(\mathbf{x}) = \frac{1}{\sqrt{2\pi w^2}} e^{-r^2/2w^2},$$

where $r = \|\mathbf{x}\|$, the length of the vector $\mathbf{x}$. Such a density seems reasonable because in natural settings the woodlouse usually finds its way back to the burrow, and if it goes astray at all, the search most probably starts at a point $\mathbf{x}_0$ near the entrance. The density $p(\mathbf{x})$ has its maximum at $\mathbf{x}_0$, and declines rapidly with increasing distance from this point.

It is assumed (step 3) that *H. reamuri* has time t to search for its burrow. In real life the woodlouse can only remain outside its burrow for about 16 hours before it dies from exposure, so 16 hours is the approximate time limit in its natural environment. In order to relate the time available, t, to the variables z and $\mathbf{x}$, we need to introduce the notion of a **search plan**. In general, a search plan,

$$d(\mathbf{x}, t) = z,$$

gives the intensity z that the animal should expend searching at point $\mathbf{x}$ if the total duration of the search must not exceed the time t.

Now, the total **search effort** is given by

$$C[d] \equiv \int_{\mathbf{x}} c(\mathbf{x}, d(\mathbf{x}, t))d\mathbf{x}$$

$$= \int_{\mathbf{x}} c(\mathbf{x}, z)d\mathbf{x}$$

$$= t,$$

where $c(\mathbf{x}, z)$ is the time required to search at point $\mathbf{x}$ with intensity z. $C[d] = t$ can be thought of as a constraint on the search plan d; d must allocate effort over the points in the search space in such a way that the total time spent searching does not exceed t. In Hoffmann's research, $c(\mathbf{x}, z) = z/2av = kz$, where a is the detection radius of the antennae and v is the search velocity of the louse. In particular for *H. reamuri*, $a = 2$ cm and $v = 2$ cm/sec, so that $k = 1/2av = 1/8$ sec/cm².

For a given target density and detection function, the optimal search plan $d_{opt}(\mathbf{x}, t)$ is the plan that maximizes the probability of finding the target in time t, where the probability of success is given by

$P[d] = \int_X p(\mathbf{x})b(\mathbf{x},d(\mathbf{x},t))d\mathbf{x}.$

Since search in one location does not effect the detection probability or search cost in another location, it is sufficient to optimize the search plan locally at each point in the search space (Stone, 1975). The **effectiveness function** determines whether it is advantageous to increase the search intensity z at point $\mathbf{x}$ by the increment Δz. This function, $p(\mathbf{x})b(\mathbf{x},z) - \lambda c(\mathbf{x},z)$, relates the increase of success $- \Delta z\, \partial/\partial z\, p(\mathbf{x})b(\mathbf{x},z) -$ to the weighted increase of the search costs $- \lambda \Delta z\, \partial/\partial z\, c(\mathbf{x},z)$. The weight λ, called the marginal rate of return, is the ratio of the increase in probability of detection to the increase in cost of search for an increment in search intensity of Δz; that is,

$$\lambda = \frac{\dfrac{\partial}{\partial z} p(\mathbf{x})b(\mathbf{x}, z)}{\dfrac{\partial}{\partial z} c(\mathbf{x}, z)}.$$

To calculate the optimal search plan (step 4), one needs to maximize the effectiveness function. When *H. reamuri* attempts to find its burrow after missing it by a small distance, the optimal search plan obtained by maximizing the effectiveness function (for details, see Hoffmann, 1983, Appendix) is

$$d_{opt}(\mathbf{x}, t) = \begin{cases} \dfrac{1}{i}\left[\left(\dfrac{it}{k\pi w^2}\right)^{1/2} - \dfrac{r^2}{2w^2}\right], & \text{for } r \le R_M(t); \\ 0, & \text{for } r > R_M(t); \end{cases}$$

where

$$R_M^2(t) = 2w^2\left(\dfrac{it}{k\pi w^2}\right)^{1/2}.$$

In words, the optimal search plan requires that the woodlouse search only within a small circular region with radius $R_M(t)$ and center $\mathbf{x}_0$. The size of this circle increases slowly with time, reflecting the fact that unsuccessful search in the closer regions makes it increasingly more profitable to search in the outlying areas.

Finally (step 5), the cumulative **probability of finding** the burrow by time t given that the animal uses a particular search plan depends on the intensity $d(\mathbf{x}_B, t)$ with which the animal has searched at the location of the burrow, $\mathbf{x}_B$. Hence, the effectiveness of the search is given by $CPD = b(\mathbf{x}_B, d(\mathbf{x}_B, t))$. If the starting point is at a distance r_0 from the burrow, $r_0 = \|\mathbf{x}_0\|$, the probability of finding the entrance in time t using the optimal search plan is given by

$$CPD(t, r_0) = \begin{cases} 1 - \exp\left[\dfrac{r_0^2}{2w^2} = \left(\dfrac{it}{k\pi w^2}\right)^{1/2}\right], & \text{for } r_0 \le R_M(t); \\ 0, & \text{for } r_0 > R_M(t). \end{cases}$$

APPENDIX 2

Following Shaw (1978), the **detection function** (step 1) is the exponential distribution function,

$$g(j, \phi(j,t)) = 1 - e^{-\phi(j,t)},$$

where j is the discrete location being searched, t is the time spent searching, and $\phi(j,t)$ is the amount of information processing capacity allocated to location j by time t. The detection function is the conditional probability of detecting the target with capacity allocation $\phi(j,t)$ given the target is at location j.

The **target density** (step 2) is a discrete mass function determined by the experimenter. For example, in one experiment, there were two conditions corresponding to two target densities; in both conditions the target could appear at any one of six locations. In the first condition the target density—PF1—was such that the target would appear at two of the locations each with probability .25 and at the other four locations each with probability .125. In the second condition the target density—PF2—was such that the target would appear at three of the locations each with probability .25 and at the other three locations each with probability .083.

It is assumed (step 3) that the rate—v—at which capacity is available for processing is constant over time; the total amount of capacity (viz. the total **search effort**) accumulated by time t is

$$\Gamma(t) = vt.$$

The capacity rate for each location—which need not be constant in this model—is

$$\gamma(j, t) = \frac{d\phi(j, t)}{dt}.$$

It follows from the definition of $\phi(j, t)$ and $\gamma(j, t)$ that

$$\phi(j, t) = \int_0^t \gamma(j, t)dt.$$

It is further assumed that the fixed rate of capacity is partitioned without waste; that is,

$$v = \sum_{j=1}^{n} \gamma(j, t),$$

where n is the number of target locations. With these assumptions it follows that the total amount of capacity is simply the sum of the capacities allocated to the n target locations:

$$\Phi(t) = \int_0^t v\, dt$$

$$= \int_0^t \sum_{j=1}^n \gamma(j, t)\, dt$$

$$= \sum_{j=1}^n \int_0^t \gamma(j, t)\, dt$$

$$= \sum_{j=1}^n \phi(j, t).$$

To simplify the presentation we adopt the following convention: Number the n target locations so that $p(1) \geq p(2) \geq \ldots \geq p(n)$. In the above example the numbering for PF1 would be $p(1) = p(2) = .25$ and $p(3) = p(4) = p(5) = p(6) = .125$; similarly, the numbering for PF2 would be $p(1) = p(2) = p(3) = .25$ and $p(4) = p(5) = p(6) = .083$.

The optimal **search plan** (step 4) for allocating attention to the visual field with a discrete target density is to allocate the capacity rate to the most likely target location until the posterior probability of the target being in this location falls to the prior probability of the target being in one of the less likely locations (Stone, 1975). For PF1, the optimal search plan is to divide v evenly between the two locations with $p(i) = .25$ until $t = t_0$, where t_0 is the time when the posterior probability of the target being in locations 1 or 2 falls to the prior probability of the target being in any of the other four locations. t_0 can be solved for by setting these two probabilities equal to one another:

$$p(2)e^{-1/2vt_0} = p(3);$$

solving for t_0 yields

$$t_0 = \frac{2}{v} \ln 2.$$

Similarly, for PF2,

$$t_0 = \frac{3}{v} \ln 3.$$

After t_0 the optimal search plan calls for dividing v evenly between all six locations for both PF1 and PF2.

Notice that t_0 is greater for PF2 since $3 \ln 3 > 2 \ln 2$. This means the optimal subject should wait longer for PF2 than for PF1 to begin allocating capacity to all six target locations. Hence there will be a greater difference in reaction times between the high probability locations and the low probability locations for PF2 than for PF1; that is, $\overline{RT}_1(.125) - \overline{RT}_1(.25) < \overline{RT}_2(.083) - \overline{RT}_2(.25)$, where $\overline{RT}$ stands for mean reaction time, the subscript indicates the target density, and the probability indicates the target location. This inequality is a testable consequence of the model and the experimental design. Shaw (1978) found this prediction to be supported by the data in both of her experiments.

When using the search plan ϕ, the **probability of finding** the target (step 5) is

$$P[\phi(j, t)] = \sum_{j=1}^{n} p(j)(1 - e^{-\phi(j,t)}).$$

Since the measured response is reaction time, a more useful quantity is the mean time to find the target:

$$E[t|\phi] = \int_0^t \{1 - P[\phi(j, t)]\} dt.$$

Note that increasing $P[\phi(j, t)]$ decreases $E[t|\phi]$; in fact, it can be shown that the search plan maximizing the probability of finding the target also minimizes the mean time to find the target (see Shaw, 1978, p. 589).

When the target is in location j, the mean time to find the target is given by

$$E_j[t|\phi] = \frac{1}{v} \left[\sum_{i=1}^{j} \left(1 - \ln\left(\frac{p_j}{p_i}\right)\right) + \sum_{i=j+1}^{n} \left(\frac{p_i}{p_j}\right) \right].$$

(The details of this derivation are in Shaw, 1978, Appendix B.) Notice that this expectation will be small when p_j is large relative to the p_i, and that it will be large when p_j is relatively small. Furthermore, $E_j[t|\phi]$ depends only on v and the target densities. If an estimate of v can be found, then this expectation can be used to test the model, since the target densities are known quantities.

In both target densities there are two types of target locations, call them a and b, with distinct probabilities such that $p_a > p_b$. Furthermore, let n_a and n_b be the number of locations with probabilities p_a and p_b, respectively. For example, in PF1 $p_a = .25$, $p_b = .125$, $n_a = 2$, and $n_b = 4$. Similarly, in PF1 $p_a = .25$, $p_b = .083$, $n_a = 3$, and $n_b = 3$. It follows from the above expression for $E_j[t|\phi]$ that the expected difference in mean processing time for the two types of locations is

$$E[t|b] - E[t|a] = (1/v)(n_b(1 - p_b/p_a) + n_a \ln(p_a/p_b)).$$

By replacing the expectations by sample estimates, we obtain the following estimate for v:

$$\frac{1}{v} = \frac{\overline{RT}(p_b) - \overline{RT}(p_a)}{n_b(1 - p_b/p_a) + n_a \ln(p_a/p_b)}.$$

Shaw used the data from both target densities to estimate v, then used this estimate to predict the difference in mean reaction time for each of the two target densities. Consequently, the fit of the model was evaluated for each subject by comparing $E[t \mid b] - E[t \mid a]$ with $\overline{RT}(p_b) - \overline{RT}(p_a)$ for each target density separately. The results of these goodness-of-fit tests were nonsignificant for most of the subjects, and Shaw concluded that the model provides a good account of reaction times in a visual detection task.

APPENDIX 3

The relation between T_{opt} and t can be derived in the following manner (Cowie, 1977). First, in order to represent the feature of diminishing returns within a patch, the average net energy intake is assumed to be negative exponential function of the form

$$f(T) = l(1 - e^{-mT}),$$

where l and m are constants. It follows that the rate of energy intake after a stay of length T is

$$\frac{df}{dT} = lme^{-mT}.$$

An optimal forager should leave a patch when its capture rate falls to the average capture rate for the environment as a whole. This occurs when

$$\frac{df}{dT} = \frac{f}{t + T_{opt}}.$$

In other words, at T_{opt} the instantaneous gain rate within a patch (slope of f) is equal to the overall gain rate for the environment (slope of AB in Fig. 10.1). Substituting yields

$$lme^{-mT_{opt}} = \frac{f}{t + T_{opt}}$$

$$= \frac{l(1 - e^{-mT_{opt}})}{t + T_{opt}},$$

and rearranging terms gives

$$t = \frac{1}{me^{-mT_{opt}}} - \frac{1}{m} - T_{opt}.$$

11 Controlling Sources of Variation in Search Tasks: A Skill Theory Approach

Roberta Corrigan
University of Wisconsin-Milwaukee

Kurt Fischer
University of Denver

The attempt to search for objects that are lost or hidden is a basic, human ability. During late infancy and early childhood, major changes occur in the types of behaviors that children will exhibit when searching. Although most theoretical frameworks acknowledge these changes, they differ greatly in their explanations of why they occur. For example, within Piaget's theory of cognitive development, changes in search behaviors are offered as evidence that children have begun to "think," i.e., that they have acquired "object permanence," which is a manifestation of the capacity for "mental representation" (Piaget, 1954). Mental representation, as measured by object permanence, is assumed to be completely absent in children younger than 18–24 months. Although thought processes clearly continue to develop beyond the age of 2, Piaget's account of cognitive development does not provide a description of the continuing development of search behaviors because search is of interest only as an indicator of the categories of space, time, object, and causality.

Alternative conceptualizations have viewed infant search as a measure of spatial perception and representation (Acredolo, 1978; Bremner, 1978a, 1978b; Butterworth, Jarrett, & Hicks, 1982) or a model of problem-solving abilities (Wellman & Somerville, 1982). The current chapter examines infant and preschool search behaviors within still another perspective: the skill theory framework of Fischer (1980; Fischer & Corrigan, 1981; Fischer & Pipp, 1984). The theory describes the sources of variation that an individual must control in order to successfully solve a particular search task in a particular environmental context. In particular, we examine the general hierarchical structure of skills and the transformation rules required to move from one developmental level to another. Other conceptualizations of search behaviors are contrasted with skill theory, and data from our own and others' laboratories are reviewed to try to isolate the types of skills necessary to perform different search tasks. Finally, we outline the steps necessary to interpret these findings within a skill theory framework. As background, a brief description of skill theory is first presented.

SKILL THEORY

Hierarchical Structure

According to Fischer (1980), a skill is a physical or mental behavior that is under an individual's voluntary control and is affected by environmental factors because actions always occur in a particular context. Skills develop through a series of three tiers of qualitatively different types: sensorimotor, representational, and abstract. Each tier consists of four levels: single sets, mappings, systems, and systems of systems. At the first level, the person can control variations in only a single action, representation, or abstraction at one time. At the second level, the person can relate two or more actions, representations, or abstractions at the same time. At the third level, a person relates two or more second-level skills to form a system. The final "systems of systems" level is both the fourth level of one tier and the first level of the succeeding tier. Thus, cognitive development consists of a sequence of three tiers all containing the same subsequence of four levels, for a total of 10 levels across the lifespan, as shown in Table 11.1. The levels of most concern in this chapter are Levels 2 through 5, which span the sensorimotor and representational tiers and which have been the focus of our research on search.

During the sensorimotor tier, infants understand only what they can act upon physically and perceptually. Skills within the sensorimotor tier are combined and differentiated to form skills of increasing complexity until the fourth sensorimotor level, which is the first representational level. Here the infant comes to understand (represent) simple properties of objects independent of his or her actions upon them. As development proceeds through the representational tier, single representational skills are combined and related to form skills of increasing complexity, in a process that parallels development in the sensorimotor tier.

Skill theory emphasizes that the developmental levels should not be viewed as discrete stages. Children do move through general optimal levels that are defined in terms of the upper limit on the children's information processing capacities. However, there is variation below that upper limit in the types of skills that will be used so that the children are never at the same level for all skills. Experience with different skills and the type of task involved in measuring them exert a major influence over the level of skill displayed. Children are not at one general developmental level across skills, but they display skills that are at a particular level for a particular task.

TABLE 11.1
The Ten Developmental Levels Described by Skill Theory

Tier	Level		Structure	Modal Age of Emergence
Sensorimotor	1	1	Single sensorimotor action	2–4 months
	2	2	Sensorimotor mapping	7–8 months
	3	3	Sensorimotor system	11–13 months
Representational	4 1	4	System of sensorimotor systems = Single representation	18–24 months
	2	5	Representational mapping	4–5 years
	3	6	Representational system	6–8 years
Abstract	4 1	7	System of representational systems = Single abstraction	10–12 years
	2	8	Abstract mapping	14–16 years
	3	9	Abstract system	adulthood
	4	10	System of abstract systems	adulthood

Adapted by permission of the publisher from Fischer, K., & Corrigan, R. A skill approach to language development. In R. Stark (Ed.), *Language behavior in infancy and early childhood.* Copyright 1981 by Elsevier Science Publishing Co., Inc.

Combining Skills

The process of movement from one level to another is described by a series of transformation rules. The particular steps that a person moves through during the gradual development of a new skill level are specified by five transformation rules. Only two of the rules, intercoordination and compounding, are discussed in this paper to illustrate how two or more search skills can be combined to form new, more complex skills. Other researchers have also suggested that combining skills is a major cognitive developmental process (e.g, Bruner, 1973; Halford, 1982; Piaget, 1952).

Skill theory defines any combination of skills that produces a new skill that is still within the same level as *compounding*. Combinations of skills that produce a skill at the next level of development are called *intercoordination*. "Intercoordination means reciprocol coordination. Two lower level skills become coordinated with each other and thereby produce a new higher-level skill" (Fischer, 1980, p. 499).

Intercoordination cannot occur under all circumstances. A person's optimal level, the upper limit on the most complex type of skill that he or she can produce, dictates whether or not the intercoordination rule can be applied. If two skills are already at the optimal level, then intercoordination is blocked, but skill development can proceed via either the compounding process or other transformations.

Predicting Sequences of Skills

Our basic approach to research on skill development has been, first, to try to identify the particular skill or concept of interest and to determine the simplest task that can demonstrate it. Then, sequences of steps in the development of that concept are generated by beginning with that minimal task and using the transformation rules to devise tasks that differ in complexity by only one additional rule. Finally, separate tasks are used to assess each step in the sequence and the accuracy of the sequence is then checked by determining whether individuals' patterns of performance on the tasks form a Guttman scale.

Thus far, skill theory has been useful in describing development in a number of diverse areas including self-recognition in infancy (Bertenthal & Fischer, 1978), pretend play (Watson & Fischer, 1977), understanding of social roles (Watson & Fischer, 1980), and arithmetic skills (Fischer, Hand, & Russell, 1983). Presumably, similar sequences of steps can be generated for search skills. At the present time, however, our research is still at the earliest stages, in which we have attempted to identify the component skills involved in various search tasks by clarifying those tasks. There is a major difference between (1) generating a sequence of tasks, beginning with the simplest possible task as we have done in the previously cited research, and (2) analyzing tasks that are used by other researchers, which may not conform to the minimal task rule, as we have done thus far with search tasks. Most tasks are inherently ambiguous until they are redone to reduce that ambiguity. That is, many tasks cannot be clearly labeled as requiring one level of skill versus another. They can be solved via multiple strategies. Task complexities that are only peripherally relevant to the core concept being investigated will obscure the level of skill that the child might produce under more optimal circumstances. Before deriving and evaluating developmental search sequences, we have found it useful to clarify commonly used tasks, because incorrect task analyses and complex tasks have interfered with the interpretation of the skills that a person must actually use in solving those tasks (Fischer, 1980).

Although developmental literature on search provides useful clues about the skills necessary for solving particular tasks, it is important to remember that the interpretation of research results will vary with the theoretical assumptions of the interpreter. Before we review some of the research on search skills, as interpreted within a skill theory framework, the next section of this Chapter contrasts the skill theory approach with several other theoretical approaches that examine search behaviors.

THEORETICAL APPROACHES TO SEARCH

There are a number of theoretical frameworks that provide alternative explanations for the changes in search behaviors that occur during infancy and early childhood. This section of the chapter does not attempt to comprehensively review all these approaches, as they are adequately described in other current reviews (e.g., Bremner, 1982; Harris, 1983; Schuberth, 1983). Instead, we have chosen to illustrate some of the major assumptions of a skill theory approach to search by comparing it to those approaches that have particularly salient points of contrast with skill theory. The major issues addressed are (1) whether development involves structured wholes or domain specific knowledge; (2) whether search can be viewed as a general paradigm for problem solving; (3) how to describe and define mental representation from a Piagetian versus a skill theory perspective; or (4) from a cognitive psychology (information processing) versus a skill theory perspective. Through the following sections, the question of whether development is best viewed as continuous or stage-like or both is also discussed.

Search as a Measure of Object Permanence, Spatial, Causal, and Temporal Relations

Piaget viewed search behaviors as an index of children's understanding that objects are permanent entities. Objects are permanent in the sense that they maintain stable relationships in space and exist whether or not they are acted upon. If a screen covers an object, a child knows that it still exists in space because it retains its position relative to the child, other objects in the room, and so on. An object that moves in space is still the same object because movement is one transformation (among many others) that is irrelevant to permanence. For Piaget, children's concepts of objects are intimately related to their ability to represent the object in space and to their general understanding of causality and time. Children cannot be said to have a notion of a permanent object until they can understand its displacements in space.

Piaget assumed that this "structure d'ensemble" was very general and applied across domains. In contrast, skill theory does not assume that a person possesses a general level of competence. Fisher and Pipp (1984) argued that even though the onset of a new skill level means that the child has a capacity to build a skill with the structure of the new level, he or she is not competent at that level until the necessary skills are constructed or learned. Skill theory views unevenness in development as commonplace, with a person functioning at different levels in different skills.

Empirical evidence supports the notion that skills in different domains are likely to develop unevenly (e.g., Bates, Benigni, Bretherton, Camaioni, & Volterra, 1979; Kopp, O'Connor, & Finger, 1975; Watson & Fischer, 1977). Synchrony between task domains is usually low. For example, Uzgiris and Hunt (1975) found low correlations among their seven scales of sensorimotor development (object permanence, means-end, vocal and gestural imitation, causality, object relations, and development of schemes). They interpreted this to mean that the scales were more independent "than a stage theory encompassing all of early psychological development would require" (p. 134).

In the area of search, skill theory maintains that children learn search skills in a variety of contexts in which they have had to follow objects visually and reach for objects manually. Children do not have a general search skill that has developed uniformly across different contexts. Instead, they develop search skills in a variety of task environments.

Search involves multiple task domains. Skill theory defines a task domain as a series of similar tasks that share the same core group of skill components, but differ in other specific, measurable skill components. In other words, a task domain encompasses behaviors that involve roughly the same tasks. This definition of a task domain is stringent compared to most common interpretations of the term domain. *Any* change in content or procedure, except those that result from the application of at least one of the five transformation rules described previously, will produce a different task domain by skill theory's definition. For example, searching for an object that has been lost en route from the kitchen to the bedroom is a different task, requiring different skills, than searching for an object that has been invisibly displaced under three screens by an adult examiner.

Within each task domain, development across levels is likely to proceed independently. Suppose, for example, that task domain A included task 1 involving skill components a, b, and c and task 2 involving skill components a, b, c, and d. Task domain B included task 3 involving skill components 1, 2, and 3 and task 4 involving skill components 1, 2, 3, and 4. Even if both tasks 2 and 4 from different domains were hypothesized to involve skills at the same cognitive level, it is unlikely that the child would produce those skills at the same time developmentally.

Within skill theory, the notion of a task domain can be contrasted with that of a skill domain. A skill domain is a broad grouping of behaviors across task domains. One criterion for defining a skill domain is that a number of task domains will share skills that develop in very rough synchrony. In the example cited above, if skills a, 1, and 2 developed in approximate synchrony, they might belong to the same skill domain. Examples of skill domains involved in search might be temporal ordering skills or spatial skills.

Thus, a skill theory approach dictates that solution of different types of search tasks involves different types of skills. There is no reason to suppose that the same skills will be required for all tasks, nor that they will necessarily develop congruently across task domains. Instead, the skill theory approach attempts to specify the minimal skills an infant must control in order to solve a particular task. That is, skill theory analyzes which skills an infant or preschooler uses to successfully retrieve an object that is hidden under one or more screens in a particular task. The answer will depend both upon factors such as the complexity and familiarity of the hiding task and the cognitive level of the child, which will set the upper limit on the type of skills that can be displayed in optimal circumstances.

Search as a Model of Problem-Solving Abilities

Like Piaget, Wellman and his colleagues (Sophian, 1982; Sophian & Wellman, 1983; Wellman & Somerville, 1982) have viewed search behaviors as a coherent set of abilities. But instead of viewing search as an index of a formal structure, as does Piaget, they view search as a paradigm for problem solving. In the conclusion of a recent paper, Wellman and Somerville (1982) argued that

> the relation between search problem solving and problem solving in general is stronger than we have yet asserted. Search may constitute not only an example of, but also a model for, problem solving . . . the solution of *any* problem is envisaged as a search, a search for a solution that is at one or another location in a symbolic problem space. (p. 81)

Following Newell and Simon (1972), problem solving is seen as a set of procedural skills in which an initial state is transformed into a goal state. Search involves the same components as any other problem-solving situation. Development in search is seen as the gradual addition and use of factors guiding more efficient search rather than a stage-like progression. That is, strategies such as selective and comprehensive search are not developmentally ordered, but are present in some form at early ages.

As we noted in the previous section, skill theory does not view search as a coherent set of abilities. Search is not one task domain. The solution of different tasks requires very different cognitive skills. It remains an empirical question whether the different task domains constitute one or more skill domains. In addition, search is not simply a set of procedural skills, but solution of different tasks may index qualitatively different structures, e.g., sensorimotor versus representational. Although we agree with Wellman that skill structures show fine, continuous gradations as they develop, we also agree with Piaget that they show rapid, discontinuous spurts at certain points. (For a lengthy discussion on how development can be both continuous and discontinuous at the same time, the reader is referred to Fischer, Pipp, & Bullock, in press.)

Search as a Measure of Mental Representation

Within Piaget's theory, successful search on Stage VI invisible displacements tasks is seen to be a measure of mental representation. Representation is necessary to understand the permanent object within the framework of space as a group of displacements; it is also needed to understand the effects of movement, time, and causality on the object. With representation, the child can expand his knowing into the past and into the future, to objects and events that are not immediately present.

Structuralist theories such as Piaget's view representations as procedures for constructing symbols (Scholnick, 1983). The use of symbols (mental representation) is necessary for thinking to occur. In addition, Piaget argued that sensorimotor children lack concepts. That is, they are missing a declarative knowledge base; thinking is purely procedural (Mandler, 1983).

A radical change in the organization of knowledge occurs at the beginning of the preoperational period when the child's action schemes are interiorized through imitation and become preconcepts. These preconcepts are represented by symbols. According to Piaget (Piaget & Inhelder, 1969), the first true symbols are internalized imitations. The first completely internalized imitation is the mental image.

> With the mental image . . . imitation is no longer merely deferred but internalized, and the representation that it makes possible, thus dissociated from any external action in favor of the internal sketches or outlines of actions which will henceforth support it, is now ready to become thought. (p. 56)

Unfortunately for the Piagetian position, there is no empirical evidence available to appraise either the assumption that mental images evolve through imitation or the assumption that the first symbols are internalized imitations (Mandler, 1983). Instead, there is evidence suggesting that preschool children do not exclusively represent information in the form of images (Kosslyn, 1978).

Skill theory uses the term *representation* somewhat differently from Piagetian theory. Representation is a particular organization of skills. The term is used to label one tier in the sequence of 10 levels described by skill theory (see Table 11.1). Skill theory defines single representations (Level 4) as systems of sensorimotor systems; that is, skills that have developed out of the intercoordination of at least two Level 3 sensorimotor skills. For example, one system might involve the understanding that when the child pushes a ball in different ways, she can watch it roll in different ways. A second system might involve the understanding that when someone else varies their pushing of the ball, the child can also see it roll differently. The intercoordination of these systems results in the understanding that one characteristic of balls is that they roll (Fischer, 1980).

Representation is the use of one sensorimotor system to cognitively evoke another; it allows a child to perform one sensorimotor system while thinking about another. For example, the child can think about characteristics of objects while performing other action systems. People, objects, and events can then be viewed as having characteristics that are independent of the child's sensorimotor systems.

The intercoordination of sensorimotor schemes to form higher level schemes, and ultimately, to form representational structures is implicit in Piaget's theory. However, skill theory makes the transformations explicit and specifies step-by-step how sensorimotor skills become representational skills. Skill theory also agrees with the Piagetian position that there is a major reorganization in thinking that occurs around 20 to 24 months of age (between Levels 3 and 4). However, we do not agree with Piaget that the nature of the change in thinking that occurs between Levels 3 and 4 can be specified in terms of a single factor such as the interiorization of action through imitation or the onset of imagery or the onset of other types of symbols.

Instead, skill theory defines the change structurally. Empirically, the change from Level 3 to Level 4 is described in terms of a major, rapid or sharp change in the form of the developmental curve (Fischer, 1983). When children reach a new optimal level (upper limit of performance), they show a cluster of spurts in performance across many domains (Fischer, 1983; Fischer, Pipp, & Bullock, in press). Empirical evidence for this shift from sensorimotor to representational skills comes from several researchers investigating a variety of tasks (e.g., Corrigan, 1983; McCall, 1983; Wolf & Gardner, 1981).

Thus, there is evidence for a stage-like shift at about the same age that Piaget noted its occurrence, but the mechanism to explain that shift has yet to be elaborated. Although we label Level 4 as representational, this does not imply that representation is limited to a particular type of symbol use or that symbolization cannot occur at Level 3. Although many representational skills do involve symbolization, in skill theory any behavior or task that requires the intercoordination of two or more sensorimotor systems is defined as representational. For example, when children simultaneously classify a simple shape such as a triangle into two color categories such as red and green, they are controlling one system for the color red and a second system for the color green. Because they are intercoordinating two sensorimotor systems, they are using representational skills, but these skills do not necessarily require symbolization (Fischer & Jennings, 1981). Similarly, symbol use can occur prior to Level 4. For example, Level 3 skills can be used to produce single-word and even two-word utterances under some conditions (Fischer & Corrigan, 1981).

A Different View of Representation: Search as a Measure of Spatial Concepts

A second group of researchers has also investigated infants' search behaviors on object permanence tasks as measures of spatial representation. In contrast to Piaget, these investigators believe that notions of an object's permanence and spatial understanding of that object should be investigated separately, and they have only investigated infants' perceptions or conceptions of space (Acredolo, 1978; Bremner, 1978a, 1978b; Butterworth et al., 1982). Although they do not always agree among themselves about the assumptions that underlie their theorizing (Liben, 1981; Schuberth, 1983), they do tend to use the term representation in a way that is consistently different from both Piagetian and skill theory.

Representations are generally viewed as static (though selective) copies of external data (Scholnick, 1983). Representation refers to the spatial information stored in an individual's brain in the form of propositions, relations, S-R bonds or other formats, and to knowledge about or consciousness of that information (Liben, 1981). That is, representation refers to knowledge and how it is organized and recalled (Mandler, 1983). The structure of the environment and the task or event constitute the basis for representation (Cocking, 1983).

In keeping with their definition of representation, many researchers discuss 6- to 8-month-old infants' search abilities and errors in terms of mental representation. They ask, when, why, and under what circumstances infants represent information about the spatial location of objects in relationship to each other (allocentrically). Infants who define spatial information totally in reference to their own bodies are said to be responding egocentrically rather than allocentrically. One controversy in the literature centers on whether egocentric responding precedes allocentric responding as a child develops, or whether both are present at an early age.

In contrast, skill theory is not concerned with labeling infants' capacities as egocentric or allocentric, but asks instead what skills children use in solving particular search tasks. Because skill theory defines representation structurally as the intercoordination of two sensorimotor systems, mental representation cannot emerge until Level 4 (around 20 months). In contrast to other viewpoints, representation is *not* used as a synonym for the way information is encoded, stored, or retrieved from memory. Although infants with Level 2 skills can clearly recall information about their own search movements, and possibly about the search movements of the hider, they cannot, by definition, *represent* the object and its position in space. That is, they cannot perform one sensorimotor system while thinking about a second one.

Summary

This section of the chapter has compared a skill theory approach to analyzing search behaviors with several other views of search. In contrast to other frameworks, skill theory views search behaviors as involving multiple task domains. Skills in different domains may develop independently from each other and they are task specific. Successful search for hidden objects in object-permanence-type tasks may occur using either sensorimotor or representational structures, depending upon the optimal cognitive level of the child and the nature of the task.

The next section of the chapter examines the literature on children's search for clues to the types of skills they are controlling, as interpreted within the various theoretical orientations, including skill theory. We also describe experimental research from our laboratories investigating search during late infancy and early childhood. Although we have not yet predicted and tested sequences of search skills, we can roughly assign some of these behaviors to skill levels based on ages, stages, and an analysis of the general types of skills that children should be able to produce at a given optimal level. These assignments can then serve as hypotheses for future research.

TOWARD A SKILL THEORY ANALYSIS OF SEARCH: LEVELS 2 THROUGH 5

The Onset of Manual Search for Hidden Objects

At approximately 8 months of age, infants begin to reach inside a container or under a cloth to retrieve an object that they have seen hidden there. Before this time, even infants with the manual skills necessary to pick up either an object or an obstacle separately (Bower, 1982; Willats, 1984) apparently do not lift the obstacle for the purpose of retrieving the object.

To illustrate this lack of intentional search in younger infants, Willats (1984) hid an object behind a cup for one group of 6-month-olds and presented the cup with no object hidden behind it to a second group. Infants in the first group mouthed, shook, banged, manipulated, or fixated the cup and either ignored the hidden toy or touched it as an afterthought without grasping it or picking it up. Infants in the no-toy group behaved no differently than children in the hidden-toy group, suggesting that the infants were not expecting to find a hidden toy.

The observation that intentional search begins at 7 to 8 months is consistent with a skill theory description of the Level 2 skills labeled sensorimotor mappings, which begin to appear at the same age. Infants with Level 2 skills can relate two components within or across the same sensory modality and coordinate two Level 1 single set skills to form a more complex skill, for example looking-grasping-a-particular-object or reaching-grasping-the-same-object. Infants with Level 2 skills can also relate their actions of seeing, hearing, or feeling another person to other simple actions. For example, at Level 2 an infant might predict that when she looks at her mother's face bending over her, she will soon be picked up.

Infants with the simplest Level 2 skills do not search under screens for hidden objects because infants cannot yet keep in mind the goal of reaching-grasping for the hidden object while first removing an obstacle. Later in development, a more complex Level 2 skill comes about as a result of the compounding transformation. The ability to remove an obstacle (screen) in order to retrieve an object seems to require a multiple component Level 2 skill such as looking at the screen as an index of the object, grasping the screen and removing it in order to look at and grasp the object.

The A not B error: The Onset of Allocentric Responses and the Decline of Egocentrism

Although infants around 8 months of age can manually search for an object hidden under one screen, they often display the so-called Stage IV or A-not-B error when multiple screens are present. To test for the A-not-B error, experimenters ask an infant to search for an object at location A on one or more trials. The object is then hidden in a new position (B) and the infant who makes the error searches for the object where it was last found rather than where it was last hidden.

Explanations of the A not B error vary with the theoretical framework of the researcher. In keeping with his position that cognition involves structures of the whole, Piaget (1954) argued that the A not B error in Stage IV stems from children's incomplete object concept, incomplete memory, and incomplete spatial localization of the object. Place and action are inextricably linked. The infant searches where the object was last found because the object only exists in the action context within which it has been inserted. Egocentric responding is not replaced until Stage V of the sensorimotor period when the child is no longer bound by what he has previously done, but can take account of what he has seen.

In contrast to Piaget's position, researchers working within the "spatial concepts" framework described previously have attempted to determine whether an infant who errs is searching at the same place where the object was retrieved or is making the same motor response that was previously successful. Using the A not B or related tasks, researchers move the infant or the screens where the object was previously seen or hidden in order to hold allocentric position constant while varying egocentric position or vice versa. They ask at what age and under what circumstances allocentric responding based on place can be elicited; alternatively, they ask when egocentric responses based on previous actions decline.

Results indicate, first, that infants sometimes exhibit allocentric responses and sometimes exhibit egocentric responses, even within the same test situation (Butterworth, 1975, 1977). Depending upon the task, errors may not be due to previous experience at all; 9-month-old infants are equally likely to search at a third screen where the object was never hidden or found (Sophian & Wellman, 1983). In addition, the age at which allocentric responses first appear varies greatly from one study to the next from as early as 6 months (Rieser, 1979) to as late as 16 months of age (Acredolo, 1978). Likewise, the offset of egocentric responding has been placed as early as 12 months and as late as 24+ months. Are there differences among experiments that may help account for these large age differences?

For example, compare the following two experiments, which attempted to establish the youngest age that allocentric responses can be produced. Both Rieser (1979) and Acredolo and her colleagues (1978; Acredolo & Evans, 1980) trained infants to look in one direction every time a buzzer sounded in order to observe an interesting visual event. The infants were then rotated 180° and retested. Rieser found that 6-month-old infants could use landmark information to encode the location of the display. In contrast, Acredolo found that even with the environmental support of very salient landmarks (a panel of flashing lights and stripes), 6-month-olds did not respond allocentrically. However, 80% of the 9- and 11-month-olds responded allocentrically with the presence of salient landmarks. Not until 16 months of age did allocentric responding predominate when no landmarks were present.

Two factors seem to account for the difference in infants' responses in the different experiments. Presence or absence of salient landmarks clearly affected the production of allocentric responses. Once an infant realizes that a landmark is a clue to the object's position, updating the position of the object while moving through space is made easier. It is not necessary for the infant to code the position of the object in space: he or she can simply code it as by the landmark window. However, even with salient landmarks present, 6-month-olds showed allocentric responses in one experiment, but not in the other. In this case, the type of movement of the infant may have been the important factor (Pick & Lockman, 1981). In Rieser's (1979) study, the infants remained in the same location but were rotated around their line of sight. In Acredolo's (1978) study, the infants were moved across the room before being rotated 180°.

In more traditional manual search tasks in which an object is visibly hidden under one of two screens, different tasks have also produced different results with respect to egocentric or allocentric responding. In these studies, variables that have affected infants' search also include landmark information such as cover color or background color of the table (Bremner, 1978a; Butterworth, 1977; Butterworth et al., 1982) and movement information such as whether the baby is moved or the table is moved (Bremner, 1978b; Bremner & Bryant, 1977).

Thus, research investigating both the onset of allocentric responses and the decline of egocentric responses illustrates that different tasks can produce different types of responding. From a skill theory perspective, the wide variation in demonstrating allocentric or egocentric responses is to be expected. It is impossible to pinpoint the onset or decline of a concept or ability independent of the task on which it is measured. Children cannot be labeled allocentric or egocentric at only a particular age or level, nor does egocentric responding disappear miraculously at a given point in time. Instead, the task itself partially determines the level of response that the child will produce.

One of the major tenets of skill theory is that environmental supports are critical for the development of skills. The environment plays an essential role in skill formation making decalage a widespread phenomenon. That is, many types of environmental factors can influence the level of skill displayed by a child. Of course, making comparisons across studies only allows speculation as to which factors caused differences in results. What is needed is a direct examination of sources of decalage in search behavior.

Jackson, Campos, and Fischer (1978) attempted to show that task demands were responsible for the decalage between search for hidden people (person permanence) in 6- to 9-month-old infants. They varied the amount of practice infants had on search tasks by including both cross-sectional and longitudinal groups; they varied search procedures by having infants search either behind screens in an apparatus that resembled a puppet theatre or under screens in a standard object permanence task; and they varied the type of objects that were searched for by including both familiar and unfamiliar people and familiar and unfamiliar toys. Practice and task variables affected infants' performances two to three developmental steps (for comparison purposes, approximately one Piagetian stage). The least important variable was type of object hidden (object vs. person). As would be predicted within a skill theory framework, children who were more likely to be functioning at their optimal level (because of practice or other environmental supports) were more likely to show higher degrees of synchrony across tasks. The authors concluded that there is not a unitary ability called "person permanence" that is independent of the type of task used to assess it. The same can also be said for "egocentrism."

In sum, at least two task factors have been iolated that seem to consistently and systematically affect infants' responses on A not B tasks: type of landmark and type of movement. The central issues in interpreting the A not B error and task variations that alter its occurrence have varied across theoretical orientations: (1) Piaget suggested that children should be characterized as egocentric because their underlying sensorimotor schemes, organized within a structure of the whole, prevent them from going beyond their own actions; (2) "spatial concept" theorists suggest that children should be characterized as egocentric or allocentric responders because of their underlying spatial representations; (3) skill theory suggests that children should not be characterized as egocentric or allocentric at all. Instead, we argue that children must control different sources of variation to solve different tasks and will therefore exhibit different types of errors under different circumstances. In other words, infants' behaviors on different tasks can be explained in terms of skill levels and transformation rules instead of adult labels such as egocentric or allocentric.

Search in Multiple, Visible Displacements Tasks

Beginning at around 12 months of age, Piaget found that infants could successfully retrieve an object that was visibly displaced under three screens and left under the last screen. Unfortunately, the exact nature of the skills involved in Piagetian Stage V tasks is difficult to ascertain because of the way they are usually administered. Because examiners using Piaget's Stage V tasks always leave the object under the last screen touched, the tasks fail to disentangle the effects of the path of movement of the hand/object and the point of transfer of the object under the screen (Jennings & Jennings, 1983). Thus, we suggest that Stage V infants cannot understand the relationships between the screens, the objects, and the examiner's hand as Piaget's analysis suggested they could.

In one attempt to disentangle the effects of the hand's movement and the point of transfer of the object, Sophian and Sage (1983) investigated 13- and 21-month-olds' search behaviors on a visible non-displacement task. Three screens were present, but one was irrelevant to the task. The examiner visibly hid the object at one location. She then moved her empty hand to the second location, with the fact that the hand contained no toy fully visible to the infant. The 13-month-olds exhibited chance-level search on this task. They also restricted their search only to relevant locations at a chance level. Contrary to expectations derived from Piaget's theory, the visibility of the object as it was transferred under the screen was not a sufficient clue to promote accurate search.

On the other hand, the 21-month-olds correctly searched significantly more than would be expected by chance. They also restricted their search to the relevant screens. In our estimation, the 21-month-olds could simply use a rule that told them to search under the first screen the examiner touched. In order to do this successfully on the first trial, they had to separate the hand's movement from the object's movement. In other words, they could distinguish "hand-with-object" from "hand-without-object." They did not have to follow the sequence of the object, but had to ignore the movements of the hand when it did not contain the object.

However, in some circumstances, the empty hand clue may not be salient enough to override other factors. Jennings and Jennings (1983) investigated 12-, 15-, 18-, and 24-month-olds' ability to reach for an object that had been hidden following a sequence of one, two, or three visible displacements. In order to test the effects of the hand's and object's movement and the point of transfer of the object under the screen, Jennings and Jennings varied the paths of movement of the object (three screens with six possible orders) and varied the point where the object was transferred from the hand to the screen (screen touched first, second, or last). They asked whether children used the visibility of the displacement to guide search in conditions where the hand continued its path of movement after the object had been visibly transferred under a screen.

Results indicated that across conditions, even 24-month-olds showed a low level of accurate first search on the visible displacements task. Children did not search where they saw the object transferred under the screen independent of the path of the hand's movement (first, second, or last screen touched) and the spatial location of the screens (right, mid, left). Although location was not relevant to where the object was actually transferred, it was a strong influence on search at all ages. The importance of order clues increased with age and by 24 months they were used in conjunction with visual information about the transfer of the object. Like the 21-month-olds in the Sophian and Sage (1983) study, 24-month-olds in this study could sometimes distinguish hand with and without object. On some occasions, other variables interfered with correct search. All three factors—location, order, and visibility—influenced search, but they had different weightings in different age groups. The interaction of all these factors meant that when the object was hidden under the last screen touched, both 18- and 24-month-olds tended to choose the correct screen.

Successful search for visibly displaced objects in Piaget's Stage V tasks (typically solved by 12- to 18-month-olds) does not occur because children can understand the relationship between the screens, the target objects, and the examiner's hand, but because the examiner always leaves the object under the last screen touched. Jennings and Jennings (1983) concluded that 2-year-olds are just beginning to distinguish one point in an event from another. Children pay attention to the ends and beginnings of events and do not yet completely control ordinal position.

In a variant of the visible displacements problem, Jennings (1981) investigated whether children between 18 months and 5 years of age could recreate the visible path of the adult's hand. Children were asked to imitate one of six sequences where the model made toy animals visibly hop to three different locations without disappearing behind occluders. The imitation task is advantageous over traditional search tasks because the production of a full sequence is not terminated by finding the object. Accurate imitation indicated that the children remembered the action sequence and could recreate its order in space.

None of the 18-month-olds imitated exact three-step sequences. Two-, 3, and 4-year-olds also did not preserve the ordinal information required to represent an object's displacements in space. Two-year-olds exactly imitated an average of only 8% of the total sequences. Although 50% of their responses were three-step sequences, the majority of them involved moving the object in an adjacent right to left or left to right pattern. Over 90% of 3- and 4-year-olds' responses were three-step sequences indicating that they understood something about the "threeness" of the array, but the majority of the responses were incorrect (only 31% and 41% of their total responses were exact imitations). Not until 5 years of age did children consistently coordinate sequence with spatial location in their three-step sequences in order to exactly match the movement pattern presented by the examiner (81% of their total responses were exact imitations).

In the experiments discussed thus far, several variables appeared to play a role in children's search for visibly hidden objects: (1) the pattern of the experimenter's hand movements (with or without the object) in relation to the spatial location of the screen, right, middle, or left; (2) the spatial location where the object is visibly transferred under the screen; (3) the order that the hand touches various screens, first, middle, or last; (4) the order in the sequence when the object is visibly transferred, first, middle, or last touched; (5) whether or not the hand's movement is irrelevant to the location of the object, i.e., in sequences where the hand continues to move after the object is hidden; and (6) the fact that patterns of the first five variables across trials are irrelevant to the solution of the task, i.e. prior information must be disregarded. These variables interact in complex ways in different tasks to produce a wide age variation in when children will be successful in their search for visibly displaced objects.

Invisible Hidings and Displacements: Can Infants Represent the Entire Path of an Object?

Another variable that has traditionally been assumed to influence children's search is the lack of visibility of the object at the point when it is transferred under a screen. Sometime after 13 months of age, Piaget (1954) observed that his children would search for an object that was visibly hidden in a container, then transferred invisibly under a screen. He also noted that it was difficult to interpret this occurrence. It could be due to the onset of "true" representation as he defined it: "from the moment when the vanished object is displaced according to an itinerary which the subject may deduce but not perceive" (p. 94). It could also be due to trial and error learning or "practical learning" (p. 92).

Piaget therefore introduced an invisible displacements task with multiple screens to provide a surer measure of representation. He further argued that success on this task requires that the child infer the hider's "system".[1] He cited his daughter Jacqueline's hesitations during the task and her touching of the screens in the order of hiding as evidence that she was mentally retracing the sequence of the hidings. He described her behavior as follows: "By searching for the object only under the last screen under which I slid my closed hand, Jacqueline follows a system and follows it consciously; given the growing interference of memories (the test is repeated ten times) she finds herself obliged each time to retrace the order I followed in order to recall under which screen I passed my hand last" (Piaget, 1954, p. 92).

Piaget's use of the term *system* is ambiguous (Jennings, 1981; Jennings & Fischer, 1983). It is not clear whether he is referring to the pattern of hidings within a trial (e.g., from right to middle to left screen) or the pattern of hidings across trials (e.g., always search under the last screen touched), or both. He certainly suggests that the child infers the object's path through space from the movements of the hand. However, because the object could logically be left under any screen on Trial 1, the child must also build up a pattern across trials in order to consistently search under the last screen touched.

Let us begin by examining the most complex interpretation of Piaget's term system. This use would imply that the child retraces the order of hiding of the object within a trial and learns across trials that the object is left in a particular ordered position or spatial location in the series (e.g., the last screen touched or the middle screen). This interpretation of a system seems to be the one adopted by many researchers. For example, Uzgiris and Hunt (1975) asked infants to "systematically" retrace the path of the examiner's hiding in a three-screen invisible displacements task by searching in reverse order from last, through middle, to first screen. This supposedly indicates that the child represents the path of the hiding within a trial. The search occurs only after the child has "established an expectation that the object is to be found under the last screen" (Uzgiris & Hunt, 1975, p. 163), having found it there successfully on at least two previous trials. However, Uzgiris and Hunt did not actually test the assumption

---

[1]Piaget's use of the term *system* does not correspond to the skill theory use. Piaget uses the term within the context of his group of displacements as a rough synonym for an orderly, complex pattern. The term has been adopted by other researchers who talk about *systematic* search, so it has been retained here. In a later section of this chapter, *A skill theory interpretation: Levels 3, 4, and 5*, skill theory's structural definition of *sensorimotor system* and *system of sensorimotor system* is explicated.

that the infant was tracing the entire path of the object. At least part of that assumption has already been called into question by the previously reviewed research on visible displacements suggesting that 2-year-old children do not completely follow the order of the hider's movements, even when the object remains visible (Jennings, 1981). The problem is complicated when the object is invisibly transferred under the screens, such that children learn patterns of variables across different hiding trials (systems) in order to correctly solve the task. Even if they do so, the patterns they learn may not involve the entire path of the object.

Cross-trial Systems. Jennings and Fischer (1983) investigated children's cross-trial systems on a three-screen, sequential invisible displacements task. Although in similar tasks the object is usually hidden under the last screen the experimenter touches, it could be left under any screen (first-touched, second-touched, last-touched). In addition, in a three-screen task, the hider's hand could follow any one of six possible routes, depending upon which particular screen was first, second, or last touched. If the hider followed a consistent route on repeated trials, a child might build up a "system" for the pattern of hidings across trials, as suggested by Piaget.

Jennings and Fischer tested 18 children at both 24 and 42 months to investigate the interaction of the order in which the screens were touched with the place that the object was ultimately hidden. Children were randomly assigned to one of three groups in which an object was always left at the screen the hider touched first, second, or last, across all six paths of hiding. These 12 trials were followed by 6 trials in which identical target objects were secretly hidden at each of the three screens so that the child's first choice always revealed the target.

The first question addressed in the study was whether results were due to the "system" acquired across trials, or were due to search biases exhibited by infants on the first trial. On the first trial, the object could have been left under any screen, so children should have searched equally at all locations. Instead, 28% searched under the first screen, 11% under the second screen, and 61% under the last screen touched. Spatial location biases, which could not be separated from order effects, were also evident. First trial preferences for left, middle, and right screens, respectively, were shown by 19%, 25% and 56% of the children.

Further information about search biases came from the six trials in which the child's first reach always yielded the target object. Children's choices could be guided by location variables (right, middle, or left screen), order variables (first, second, or last screen touched by the experimenter), or both. Children were scored as exhibiting location, order, or mixed tendencies based on the variable that guided four out of six choices. In the 2-year-old group, 9 children exhibited location tendencies and six order tendencies, with the remainder showing mixed tendencies, whereas in the 3½-year-olds, the results were reversed, with 10

TABLE 11.2
Total Reaches to Each Screen Touched by Each Treatment Group
for Both Age Groups

			24 Months Screen Touched				42 Months Screen Touched		
	Screen		1st	2nd	Last		1st	2nd	Last
Treatment Group:	where object was hidden	1st	38	14	11	1st	27	17	28
		2nd	9	14	42	2nd	9	13	49
		Last	17	10	38	Last	16	5	51

children exhibiting order tendencies, 4 location tendencies, and the remainder showing mixed tendencies.

Information about the children's systems across trials came from the first 12 trials. Children in both age groups, regardless of experimental condition, tended to reach at the last screen touched during the first 12 trials. Table 11.2 shows the total number of reaches for each treatment group for each age. For five of the six groups, there were no significant differences between biases exhibited on the first trial compared to later trials. Only 2-year-olds in the first-screen-touched condition showed any tendency to modify their "last-touched" biases. Results were therefore not due to any learning of a system across trials, but reflected the order biases of the children on the first trial.

In both age groups, 44% of children's total reaches across experimental conditions were to the middle screen during the first 12 trials (compared to 25% to the left screen and 31% to the right screen), indicating another source of search bias that was not based on the path of movement of the object. Thus, both order of screens that the hand touched and spatial position of the screens affected screen choice for both age groups, regardless of where the object was actually hidden.

In summary, children as old as 3½ showed no evidence that they were using complete hiding systems based on the position of the object in an ordered sequence. Even when children could not logically choose one screen over another, for example on the first trial or when they did not see the object hidden, they still exhibited spatial and order biases. These biases could lead an observer to falsely infer that the child is tracing the path of the object within each trial and learning across trials where the object has been hidden (Piaget's system).

Other evidence that young children have difficulty with temporal order comes from a study by Somerville, Niedrowski, and Haake (reported in Somerville & Haake, this volume). They investigated the influence of the spatial location of objects on children's recall of the temporal order in which the objects had been presented. Three-year-olds were unable to recall the order of three items except when they were arranged in a corresponding linear array. Four- and 5-year-olds also expected the temporal order to correspond to a right-to-left order. Only the 6-year-olds could recall the order of presentation of the three objects regardless of the spatial arrangement.

Finally, other research investigating the pattern of hiding across trials also suggests that children are not representing all points in the path of movement of the object. For example, Corrigan (1981) found that a simple change in the order of presentation of invisible displacements items affected 2-year-olds' abilities to successfully retrieve hidden objects, suggesting that they were not representing the path of the objects' displacements. In particular, one group of children was asked to search for an object hidden for a block of three trials in one direction followed by a block of three trials in the other direction; a second group of children saw the object hidden in alternating directions for six trials. The first group did significantly better than the second. If children were really representing the entire path of the object's displacements, then there is no reason to suppose that they would find anything substantially more difficult about the second method of presentation.

Sensorimotor Search Strategies. If infants are not inferring the entire path of the object and building up a system over trials, what are they doing when they successfully retrieve a hidden object in an invisible displacements series? In many circumstances, simpler, sensorimotor search strategies may be sufficient to ensure success. Children may use very simple strategies such as persistently pulling the screens until they uncover the object by chance or by searching in adjacent screens. They might use a strategy of searching where they last saw movement, or they could simply search in a particular spatial location regardless of where the object is actually hidden. It should be emphasized again that children should not necessarily be expected to display the same search strategies in different variants of invisible displacements tasks. Different tasks may require different skills for their solution. Nevertheless, any of these strategies may make children appear to be representing the entire path of a displaced object across trials when they are only using less sophisticated strategies.

Bertenthal and Fischer (1983) tested whether infants' apparent systematic behavior was actually the result of lower level strategies. They tested 12- to 24-month-old infants on invisible displacements tasks with three to five screens. Systematic search was operationally defined (similar to Uzgiris & Hunt, 1975) as search beginning with an end screen and moving through at least two adjacent screens before the object was retrieved. Systematic search was low in the invisible displacements task, ranging from 0 to 20% across the ages tested. Corrigan (1981) also found that only 17% of the children in her study engaged in systematic search for hidden objects. Systematic search, indicating that the child can recreate the hiding sequence, appears to be a difficult phenomenon to elicit. Similarly, in the Bertenthal and Fischer study, infants were also tested on a parallel cognitive task, seriation of nesting cups, where systematic behavior was defined as nesting of the cups in sequence from largest to smallest or vice versa. Systematic seriation occurred in only 2 out of 180 trials.

Instead of systematic behavior, Bertenthal and Fischer found that children showed persistent behavior. Persistence in search (number of screens searched) increased significantly between 15 and 21 months of age and also between 21 and 24 months, resulting in a significant increase with age in the number of trials that children successfully retrieved the object. Similarly, older children showed increasing persistence and more success in seriation. However, the more screens (or cups) that were present, the less successful were the children in searching or seriating.

Other evidence for sensorimotor search strategies on a variant of invisible displacements tasks comes from Haake and Somerville (in press). They invisibly displaced an object under one screen, then showed the infant that the object was either present or absent before they moved the closed hand under a second screen. At 12 months, infants in the object absent condition searched correctly on only 39% of the trials and on 58% of the trials in the object present condition (both chance levels). Instead, they searched nonlogically using spatial location clues (right vs. left) or information about the time in the sequence that the hand touched the screen (first or last touched) even though this information was not adequate to ensure solution of the task.

Another very simple search strategy, which may lead the observer to attribute sophisticated behaviors to the infant, involves searching at locations that the experimenter has touched. Sophian and Sage (1983) found that both 13- and 21-month-olds were equally proficient at solving invisible displacements tasks with two screens, with 80% and 93% correct search at the two ages. However, they defined correct search differently than it is usually defined. In traditional Piagetian tasks, the object is always left under the last screen touched. Logically, the object could be under any screen, but infants are expected to learn a pattern across trials and search directly under the correct screen. Instead, Sophian and Sage had three screens present, moved the closed hand to two of the locations, and left the object in either of the locations that the hand had traveled to, so either location could be correct. Infants had to ignore the irrelevant location, but could then use a simple strategy such as "search at both locations the examiner touches" to correctly retrieve the object.

More Complex Search Strategies. Although they do not follow the entire ordered path of the object across trials (Piaget's systems), infants by about the age of 2 can use more complex strategies than the sensorimotor search strategies described in the previous section. The children can pay attention to the ends and beginnings of events in invisible displacements tasks and can build up simple patterns of information across trials to infer the hiding strategy of the examiner without learning the order of the entire path of the object. Supporting this hypothesis, Bertenthal & Fischer (1983) found that 24-month-olds searched in end screens more frequently than chance, but 12- to 18-month-olds did not. To test whether the infants were basing their end screen search on their observations of the experimenter, Bertenthal and Fischer compared infants who watched the experimenter hide the toy with those who were presented with screens under which the toy had already been hidden. Infants at both 16 and 24 months tended to search under middle screens when they did not see the experimenter hide the toy. When infants saw the toy hidden, 16-month-olds searched equally often under all screens, but 24-month-olds tended to search under the end screens.

Other results are also consistent with the suggestion that children in the second half of the second year can sometimes use prior information to infer simple hiding strategies. In the Haake and Somerville (in press) two-screen displacements task, infants had to ignore prior information in the object present condition (the object had already been found). In the object absent condition, they had to ignore the second, irrelevant hand movement. By 18 months of age, 10 out of 15 infants correctly and consistently retrieved the object in the correct location (77% of the time in the object absent condition, 80% in the object present condition).

Of course, the ability to build up patterns of information across trials will be task dependent. The Haake and Somerville (in press) task was further complicated by adding two additional screens (Somerville & Haake, this volume). The experimenter's hand was opened between screens 2 and 3 to show the child that the object was present (had not yet been hidden) or absent (had already been hidden). In this task, the object could logically be under either of two screens, one of the first two (in the object absent condition) or one of the last two (in the object present condition). Results indicated that only 29% of the 2-year-olds limited their search to one of the two correct screens. This percentage rose to 45% at age 30 months and 50% by age 5.

The converse of showing that more complicated tasks will be solved at later ages is to show that tasks involving greater environmental supports (to simplify them) will be solved at earlier ages. Skill theory predicts that environmental support enhances optimal performance. Bertenthal and Fischer (1983) found that even 18- and 21-month-olds, who were given practice in searching on a series of simpler tasks prior to the invisible displacements task, showed a higher proportion of end screen search on the displacements task. This procedure is the normal course of events when administering an object permanence series (Uzgiris & Hunt, 1975) and may account for the finding that children in longitudinal studies with repeated practice on simpler tasks display more advanced object permanence skills than children in cross-sectional samples (Corrigan, 1978, 1983). Corrigan (1981) also found that practice on invisible displacements tasks alone affected performance. However, she found that although too few trials inhibited performance in 18-month-olds, there was a limit on the number of trials that had an effect in producing change. On the other hand, 24-month-olds continued to benefit from increased practice until they reached ceiling.

It has become apparent in the discussion thus far that determining what factors children actually use in retrieving hidden objects is not an easy matter. In addition to the problem that the same tasks can be solved with multiple strategies, methodological differences among studies can also exacerbate difficulties with interpretation. Even researchers using the "standard" invisible displacements tasks have differed in how they administer the tasks, the number of occluders they use, the direction of displacement of the object, the number of trials necessary to "pass" the task, and so forth (Corrigan, 1979).

Determining whether the child is representing the entire ordered series of locations visited by an object in an invisible displacements task requires that the position of the screens and the order of the screens touched by the experimenter be systematically varied (Fischer & Jennings, 1981) and that sufficient controls be instituted to rule out the possibility of random responses or responses that require only lower level sensorimotor skills.

Summary of Research Evidence, Visible and Invisible Displacements

The previous two sections of this chapter examined skills required to successfully search for objects hidden in both visible and invisible displacements tasks. In contrast to a Piagetian view, which labels these Stage V and Stage VI behaviors, respectively, data seem to suggest considerable overlap in the skills involved in solving both tasks. This section of the chapter summarizes the results from studies using both visible and invisible displacements tasks, organized by age rather than type of task.

Between 11 and 13 months children begin to search for an object that is visibly hidden in a container, then invisibly hidden under a single screen (Piaget, 1954; Uzgiris & Hunt, 1975). This task provides little information about the search strategies the child may be using, leading researchers to introduce multiple-screen displacements tasks. In a two-screen, invisible displacements task with a third, irrelevant screen present, infants at the same age will restrict their search to the locations visited by the hand. They show no preference for searching under one relevant screen versus the other—any screen the hand has touched will do (Sophian & Sage, 1983). This behavior is perfectly logical so long as the infants are really using the hand's movement as an index of the object's movement. However, even if the object is visibly rather than invisibly hidden, infants cannot ignore irrelevant hand movements (Sophian & Sage, 1983), suggesting that they are paying attention to the movements of the hand rather than using these movements to infer the location of the object. Similarly, if the presence or absence of the object is signaled by opening the hand between the two screens in the invisible displacements task, the majority of 12-month-olds display "non logical" search based on spatial location or temporal order of the movements and fail to consistently retrieve the hidden object (Haake & Somerville, in press). The movements of the hand thus seem to be a major variable directing search at the beginning of the second year, with the visibility of the object itself less important for the child.

Sometime around 18 to 24 months, children begin to differentiate points in the movement sequence of the hand. In particular, they start to pay attention to beginnings and ends, though they cannot yet follow an entire sequence. In both visible and invisible displacements series, they begin to choose the correct screen if the object is hidden under the last screen the experimenter touches (Bertenthal & Fischer, 1983; Jennings & Jennings, 1983). When there is no hand movement to cue the children's search, they show spatial localization biases and search under the middle screens (Bertenthal & Fischer, 1983).

By 18 to 21 months, children can probably ignore irrelevant hand movements in limited settings where there are only two screens present (Haake & Somerville, in press; Sophian & Sage, 1983). Such movements are still confusing to children in situations where the order of movement of the hand does not correspond exactly to the linear spatial array of the screens, whether the object is visibly or invisibly displaced (Jennings & Fischer, 1983; Jennings & Jennings, 1983). In four-screen displacements where the presence or absence of the object is signaled by opening the hand between the first two and the last two screens, 2-year-olds will ignore irrelevant hand movements and limit their search to the two correct screens. However, they show nonlogical screen preferences within those locations. In short, infants can now discriminate relevant from irrelevant hand movements, at least in conditions where they must only discriminate right from left and where the order of the movements corresponds to the linear spatial arrangement of the screens. In some circumstances, they also build up patterns of information from previous trials (sometimes erroneously) to try to infer the location of the object (Bertenthal & Fischer, 1983; Corrigan, 1981).

Even at 42 months, children have difficulty understanding the entire movement sequence of the hand and object (Jennings & Fischer, 1983). Not until sometime between 4 and 5 years does the situation seem to improve significantly. By 5 years, 81% of children could reproduce the exact movement of the hand that had been visibly transporting an object to three locations (Jennings, 1981). In the four-location hiding task described by Somerville and Haake (this volume), 5-year-olds seemed to understand that either of the two screens was equally logical, as evidenced by their lack of preference for one screen over the other.

In sum, children cannot be neatly labeled as being at "Stage V" or "Stage VI" based on their performances on visible and invisible displacements tasks. Instead, children at around 12 months of age can readily solve some invisible displacements tasks using simple search strategies, and children at 42 months still have difficulty with some visible displacements tasks. What is needed is a better method for describing the sources of variation that children must control in order to solve both types of displacements tasks. Skill theory provides such a characterization.

A Skill Theory Interpretation: Levels 3, 4, and 5

The search behaviors described thus far as necessary for solving both visible and invisible displacements tasks fit nicely within a skill theory description of Levels 3 and 4.

Sensorimotor Search Strategies: Level 3. An 11- to 13-month-old infant with Level 3 skills can relate two or more aspects of two or more actions at the same time. That is, the infant intercoordinates two sensorimotor mappings into a system. For example, infants can coordinate several aspects of their own actions with several aspects of what they perceive in another person. In order to qualify as a sensorimotor system, at least two variations must be controlled for each of the two coordinated actions. One example of a sensorimotor system is the classic Piagetian Stage V behavior in which an infant produces variations in one behavior (e.g., dropping a toy in different ways) in order to observe variations in a second behavior (e.g., watching how it hits the ground).

Level 3 search skills may be required to solve either visible or invisible displacements tasks. When 18- to 24-month old infants solve a visible displacements task by searching under the last screen touched (Jennings & Jennings, 1983), they are probably using Level 3 skills. Level 3 skills may also be involved in invisible displacements tasks where the infant does not have to infer the location of the object, but simply searches persistently or uses the global movements of the hand as an index of where to search, e.g., at the last place where movement was seen.

Wellman and Somerville (1982) argued that the findings of Sophian and Sage (1983) refuted the skill theory notion that children may be using sensorimotor skills (such as looking where you last saw movement) to solve invisible displacements tasks. Recall that Sophian and Sage found that both 13- and 21-month-olds could solve two-screen invisible displacements tasks by searching persistently under both of the two screens touched by the experimenter and ignoring the third screen that was not touched. In a second, visible non-displacement task, the 21-month-olds, but not the 13-month-olds, were able to ignore the irrelevant movements of the empty hand as it moved to a second screen after leaving the object under a first screen.

The results are consistent with a skill theory interpretation. The younger infants could simply have used a rule such as "look where you last saw movement" in both tasks, since they correctly searched at chance level on the visible non-displacement task, but not the invisible displacements task. The 21-month-olds searched correctly at above-chance level on both tasks. This required an additional distinction of "hand-with-object" from "hand-without-object" on the non-displacement task. The invisible displacements task still required only the global movement rule, or perhaps a more refined rule such as "search at both locations the adult touches." The infants obviously could not use a rule such as "look under the last screen touched" and be correct in their search.

The discrepancy in interpretation between Wellman and Somerville (1982) and skill theory appears to stem from differing definitions of the term representation. Because we do not equate representation with recall, a task such as the Sophian and Sage task may require recall and still require only Level 3 skills. Significantly, the one Sophian and Sage task that required that the infant represent the path of an object's motion and infer its location (a transposition task where the object was hidden under one of two cups, after which the two cups were transposed) was solved at a chance level by both the 13- and the 21-month-olds.

This example illustrates the importance of a careful task analysis to determine the nature of the skills that a child uses to perform a given task. Not all "invisible displacements" tasks will require the same skills for correct solution. Seemingly minor variations in the tasks can alter the strategies necessary to solve them.

More Complex Search Strategies: Level 4. At Level 4, which emerges around 18 to 24 months, skill theory suggests that infants first become capable of representing simple properties of objects independent of their actions upon them. This results when two sensorimotor systems are intercoordinated. Representation also allows the child to use one Level 3 system while thinking about another. For example, when pretending that a doll is cooking breakfast, the child is using his Level 3 systems to act out the cooking movements and manipulate the doll while relating these actions to the Level 3 systems needed for real-life cooking activities.

Fischer and Jennings (1981) argued that searching under the last screen a hider touches may involve representational skills if the child is intercoordinating a Level 3 finding system (seeing the adult hide the object, seeing the screens, reaching for the object under the screens, etc.) with a Level 3 hiding system. The child detects a simple hiding strategy of the examiner and fits his or her search to that hiding behavior. The child uses representation to infer the hiding strategy of the examiner over trials; the examiner consistently hides the object in a particular location, even though the child does not actually see it being hidden there.

In the Bertenthal and Fischer (1983) study, consistent end screen search thus occurred at the same age that skill theory hypothesizes that single representations emerge. Because the 24-month-olds modified their search based on the hiding of the experimenter, they appeared to be using Level 4 skills to represent the simple, covert hiding strategies of the experimenter. Infants were not simply using preexisting biases, but were using a pattern of hidings across trials.

Inferring the Entire Path of the Object: Level 5. Infants with Level 4 skills cannot yet intercoordinate different representations and relate them to each other (a Level 5 skill). Within the search task, this means that they cannot represent the sequential invisible displacements of an object. The traditional Piagetian Stage VI task, where the examiner hides an object in a container and then displaces it sequentially, while hidden, under a series of screens, is usually regarded as a measure of the ability to infer the location of the object from the path of movement of the hand. Piaget described the child as following a "system" of the experimenter's hidings. The research reviewed previously in the section "can infants infer the entire path of the object across trials" suggests that the 2-year-old infant is *not* using the Level 5 skills that Piaget's term "system" implies. Instead, skill theory predicts that various versions of the invisible displacements task are either measuring complex Level 3 search behaviors (such as persistent search), or simple Level 4 representations (such as those described by Bertenthal and Fischer, 1983 or Fischer and Jennings, 1981), but not children's multiple representation of events.

Children with Level 5 skills can relate variations in one representation to variations in a second representation, although they still lack the ability to consider both aspects simultaneously. Skill theory predicts it is not until Level 5 that children can represent sequential invisible displacements of an object. Data from Jennings (1981), Jennings and Jennings (1983) and Jennings and Fischer (1983) appear to support this hypothesis.

A SKILL THEORY APPROACH TO SEARCH: WHERE DO WE GO FROM HERE?

One problem with search tasks such as traditional three-screen visible or invisible displacements tasks is that they can be solved using different combinations of complex skills. That is, children can produce behaviors that look identical but that involve very different strategies.

The use of tasks such as those used by Piaget and other investigators thus violates one of the basic principles described in the previous section of this chapter on predicting or explaining developmental sequences in skill theory: The researcher should purposefully design the simplest possible task that can elicit a particular behavior. Beginning with this simple task, the transformation rules can be applied to predict a complete developmental sequence. Each step in the sequence should then be tested using the same basic task and procedure, incorporating only the minimal changes that are necessary to determine the differences between steps.

Lacking this fine-grained task analysis, it is very difficult to determine whether the different tasks used across the studies cited in this chapter are even in the same task domain. Certainly, some of the same skills seem to be required for solving the various tasks, but the tasks do not map directly onto one another in the most optimal way.

Nevertheless, making comparisons across different tasks, and looking at the different strategies that can be used to solve the same task, are certainly necessary exercises in the initial phases of predicting developmental sequences. In particular, we are in a much better position to identify the types of skills that are and are not involved in solving different types of displacements problems than we were even 5 years ago, when most research was limited to replicating the ordinality of Piaget's sequence. With this new knowledge and our general predictions about developmental levels, it should now be possible to design a minimal task and to generate and evaluate developmental sequences of search behaviors within that task domain, using finer-grained task analyses than have previously been reported.

CONCLUSION

This chapter has traced the development of search behaviors during infancy and early childhood within the skill theory framework of Fischer (1980). Skills during this age period develop through a series of five levels of two qualitatively different types (sensorimotor and representational). Movement from level to level occurs through the process of intercoordinating or combining skills at one level to form skills at the next highest level. The characteristics of skill structures at each level and the transformation rules describing the transitions from one type of skill to another can be used to predict sequences of skills that can then be tested experimentally.

In contrast to Piaget's theory, skill theory does not view infant search behavior solely as a measure of object permanence, which in turn is a reflection of underlying representational structures. Instead, skill theory argues that different types of search skills develop independently and that each search task must be examined separately to analyze the types of skills necessary for its solution. Children do not develop uniformly across different skills.

In contrast to most information processing approaches to cognition, skill theory predicts that along with the gradual accretion of skills that typifies development, there are also fundamental changes in the organization of behaviors at certain times. At the beginning of each of the three tiers of skills described by skill theory, new types of structures appear. However, these structures will not be produced under all circumstances. If children are tested on difficult tasks, with little practice, and with minimal environmental support, they will not show the stage-like developmental spurts that can be produced under conditions that make optimal performance more likely.

Skill theory thus provides an original interpretation of developmental data because it reconciles opposing theoretical perspectives. Development is seen to be both gradual and abrupt, continuous and discontinuous, and controlled by both the child and the environment. Because of the unique point of view of skill theory, the questions that we are interested in addressing are often different from those posed by other theoretical orientations. For example, general labels such as *egocentric*, which have been applied to characteristics of children as they attempt to solve A not B tasks, are not appropriate within a skill theory perspective. Although their optimal level constrains the upper limit on the skills that they can produce, children will produce skills at multiple levels depending upon their past experiences, practice, the type of task they are tested on, and other characteristics of the environment.

Skill theory emphasizes the need for careful task analyses to determine what skills are necessary to solve a particular task administered in a particular way. This need is particularly salient when multiple visible and invisible displacement tasks are examined. This chapter has reviewed the affects of various variables such as the path of movement of the hand versus the object, the point of transfer of the object under the screen, the spatial location of the screens, and the use of information from previous trials to build up a system for the pattern of hidings across trials. These variables are often confounded in displacements tasks as they are usually administered. As a result, children can often solve the same task via multiple strategies and they will appear to be using more sophisticated skills than they are actually capable of producing.

Research from our own laboratories reveals that the same search task, a sequential invisible displacements task with multiple screens, can be solved using either Level 3, 4, or 5 skills. Using Level 3 skills, children may be persistent in searching and retrieve the object in the last place where they saw movement, especially when it is the end screen. Level 4 representations are required for successful search when the child infers that the examiner hid the object in a particular location even if the child did not see it being hidden there. Finally, children with Level 5 skills may solve the task by representing the object's sequential displacements through space. Because sequential invisible displacements tasks can be solved with skills from so many different levels, they are difficult to interpret. As a result, we have concluded elsewhere that their use as a measure of representation is premature (Corrigan, 1981), and that other tasks such as pretend play, self-recognition, and classification provide "more valid" measures of representation (Bertenthal & Fischer, 1980).

Despite these reservations about invisible displacements tasks as they are currently devised and administered, search tasks remain of interest because humans everywhere lose or misplace objects and must search to find them. It is perhaps for this reason that theorists such as Piaget afforded special status to search tasks as measures of mental representation, and other authors such as Wellman and Somerville (1982) have viewed search as a model for general problem-solving behaviors. Although acknowledging that search is an important human activity, skill theory views search activities as neither more nor less significant than any other type of behavior engaged in by young children. The same methods that have allowed the prediction of developmental sequences of other types of skills are certainly available within skill theory to predict sequences of search skills. In addition, skill theory provides the tools for determining how the optimal cognitive level of the child will interact with tasks of differing complexity, in search tasks or in any other cognitive tasks. Skill theory thus provides a consistent theoretical framework for making sense of the many sources of variation the child must control when searching for hidden objects.

ACKNOWLEDGMENTS

Portions of this chapter were prepared while the first author was supported by the School of Education Office of Research, University of Wisconsin-Milwaukee. Preparation of the chapter was also supported by a grant from the Carnegie Corporation of New York to the second author. The statements made and views expressed are solely the responsibility of the authors. We would like to thank Sybillyn Jennings for her thoughtful critiques of all versions of the manuscript and for the use of her unpublished data. We would like to thank Bennett Bertenthal for his major contributions to the joint research that is cited in this paper.

REFERENCES

Acredolo, L. (1978). Frames of reference used by children for orientation. *Developmental Psychology, 14,* 224–234.

Acredolo, L., & Evans, D. (1980). Developmental changes in the effects of landmarks on infant spatial behavior. *Developmental Psychology, 16,* 312–318.

Bates, E., Benigni, L., Bretherton, I., Camaioni, L., & Volterra, V. (1979). *The emergence of symbols.* New York: Academic Press.

Bertenthal, B., & Fischer, K. (1978). The development of self-recognition in the infant. *Developmental Psychology, 14,* 44–50.

Bertenthal, B., & Fischer, K. (1980). Toward an understanding of early representation. *Proceedings of the 1979 UAP/USC Ninth Annual International Conference on Piagetian Theory and the Helping Professions.* Los Angeles: University of Southern California.

Bertenthal, B., & Fischer, K. (1983). The development of representation in search: A social-cognitive analysis. *Child Development, 54,* 846–857.

Bower, T. G. R. (1982). *Development in infancy* (2nd ed.). San Francisco: Freeman.

Bremner, J. (1978a). Spatial errors made by infants: Inadequate spatial cues or evidence of egocentrism? *British Journal of Psychology, 69,* 77–84.

Bremner, J. (1978b). Egocentric vs. allocentric spatial coding in nine-month-old infants: Factors influencing the choice of code. *Developmental Psychology, 14,* 346–355.

Bremner, J. (1982). Object localization in infancy. In M. Potegal (Ed.), *Spatial abilities: Development and psychological foundations.* New York: Academic Press.

Bremner, J., & Bryant, P. (1977). Place versus response as the basis of spatial errors made by young infants. *Journal of Experimental Child Psychology, 23,* 162–177.

Bruner, J. (1973). Organization of early skilled action. *Child Development, 44,* 1–11.

Butterworth, G. (1975). Object identity in infancy: The interaction of spatial codes in determining search errors. *Child Development, 46,* 866–870.

Butterworth, G. (1977). Object disappearance and error in Piaget's Stage IV tasks. *Journal of Experimental Child Psychology, 23,* 391–401.

Butterworth G., Jarrett, N., & Hicks, L. (1982). Spatiotemporal identity in infancy: Perceptual competence or conceptual deficit? *Developmental Psychology, 18,* 435–449.

Cocking, R. (1983). Early concept formation: Models from Nelson and Piaget. In E. Scholnick (Ed.), *New trends in conceptual representation: Challenges to Piaget's theory?* Hillsdale, NJ: Lawrence Erlbaum Associates.

Corrigan, R. (1978). Language development as related to stage 6 object permanence development. *Journal of Child Language, 5,* 173–189.

Corrigan, R. (1979). Cognitive correlates of language. Differential criteria yield differential results. *Child Development, 50,* 617–631.

Corrigan, R. (1981). The effects of task and practice on search for invisibly displaced objects. *Developmental Review, 1,* 1–17.

Corrigan, R. (1983). The development of representational skills. In K. Fischer (Ed.), *Levels and transitions in children's development.* San Francisco: Jossey-Bass.

Fischer, K. (1980). A theory of cognitive development: The control and construction of hierarchies of skills. *Psychological Review, 87,* 477–531.

Fischer, K. (1983). Developmental levels as periods of discontinuity. In K. Fischer (Ed.), *Levels and transitions in children's development.* San Francisco: Jossey-Bass.

Fischer, K., & Corrigan, R. (1981). A skill approach to language development. In R. Stark (Ed.), *Language behavior in infancy and early childhood* (pp. 11–16). Amsterdam: Elsevier.

Fischer, K., Hand, H., & Russell, S. (1983). The development of abstractions in adolescence and adulthood. In M. Commons, M. Richards, C. Armon (Eds.), *Beyond formal operations* (pp. 11–14). New York: Praeger.

Fischer, K., & Jennings, S. (1981). The emergence of representation in search: Understanding the hider as an independent agent. *Developmental Review, 1,* 18–30.

Fischer, K., & Pipp, S. (1984). Processes of cognitive development: Optimal level and skill acquisition. In R. Sternberg (Ed.), *Mechanisms of cognitive development.* San Francisco: Freeman.

Fischer, K., Pipp, S., & Bullock, D. (in press). Detecting discontinuities in development: Method and measurement. In R. Harmon & R. Emde (Eds.), *Continuities and discontinuities in development.* New York: Plenum.

Haake, R., & Somerville, S. (in press). The development of logical search skills in infancy. *Developmental Psychology.*

Halford, G. (1982). *The development of thought.* Hillsdale, NJ: Lawrence Erlbaum Associates.

Harris, P. (1983). Infant cognition. In M. Haith & J. Campos (Eds.), *Handbook of child psychology: Vol. 2. Infancy and developmental psychobiology.* New York: Wiley.

Jackson, E., Campos, J., & Fischer, K. (1978). The question of decalage between object permanence and person permanence. *Developmental Psychology, 14,* 1–10.

Jennings, S. (1981, August). *Do children recreate the hand's route in displacement tasks?* Paper presented at the American Psychological Association convention, Los Angeles, CA.

Jennings, S., & Fischer, K. (1983). *Sequential invisible displacements task study.* Unpublished manuscript, Russell Sage College.

Jennings, S., & Jennings, K. (1983, August). *Factors influencing search: Location, visibility, and sequence.* Paper presented at the American Psychological Association convention, Anaheim, CA.

Kopp, C., O'Connor, H., & Finger, I. (1975). Task characteristics and a stage 6 sensorimotor problem. *Child Development, 46,* 569–573.

Kosslyn, S. (1978). The representational development hypothesis. In P. Ornstein (Ed.), *Memory development in children.* Hillsdale, NJ: Lawrence Erlbaum Associates.

Liben, L. (1981). Spatial representation and behavior: Multiple perspectives. In L. Liben, A. Patterson, & N. Newcombe (Eds.), *Spatial representation and behavior across the lifespan*. New York: Academic Press.

Mandler, J. (1983). Representation. In J. Flavell & E. Markman (Eds.) *Handbook of child psychology: Vol. 3. Cognitive development*. New York: Wiley.

McCall, R. (1983). Exploring developmental transitions in mental performance. In K. Fischer (Ed.), *Levels and transitions in children's development*. San Francisco: Jossey-Bass.

Newell, A., & Simon, H. (1972). *Human problem solving*. Englewood Cliffs, NJ: Prentice-Hall.

Piaget, J. (1952). *The origins of intelligence in children*. New York: International Universities Press.

Piaget, J. (1954). *The construction of reality in the child*. New York: Basic Books.

Piaget, J., & Inhelder, B. (1969). *The psychology of the child*. New York: Basic Books.

Pick, H., & Lockman, J. (1981). From frames of reference to spatial representation. In L. Liben, A. Patterson, & N. Newcombe (Eds.), *Spatial representation and behavior across the lifespan*. New York: Academic Press.

Rieser, J. (1979). Reference systems and the spatial orientation of six month old infants. *Child Development, 50,* 1078–1087.

Scholnick, E. (1983). Why are new trends in conceptual representation a challenge to Piaget's theory? In E. Scholnick (Ed.), *New trends in conceptual representation: A challenge to Piaget's theory?* Hillsdale, NJ: Lawrence Erlbaum Associates.

Schuberth, R. (1983). The infant's search for objects: Alternatives to Piaget's theory of object concept development. In L. Lipsett & C. Rovee-Collier (Eds.), *Advances in infancy research* (Vol. 2). Norwood, NJ: Ablex.

Sophian, C. (1982). Selectivity and strategy in early search. *Journal of Experimental Child Psychology, 34,* 342–349.

Sophian, C., & Sage, S. (1983). Developments in infant's search for displaced objects. *Journal of Experimental Child Psychology, 35,* 143–160.

Sophian, C., & Wellman, H. (1983). Selective information use and perseveration in the search behavior of infants and young children. *Journal of Experimental Child Psychology, 35,* 369–390.

Uzgiris, I., & Hunt, J. McV. (1975). *Assessment in infancy*. Urbana: University of Illinois Press.

Watson, M., & Fischer, K. (1977). A developmental sequence of agent use in late infancy. *Child Development, 48,* 828–835.

Watson, M., & Fischer, K. (1980). Development of social roles in elicited and spontaneous behavior during the preschool years. *Developmental Psychology, 16,* 483–494.

Wellman, H., & Somerville, S. (1982). The development of human search ability. In M. Lamb & A. Brown (Eds.), *Advances in developmental psychology* (Vol. 2). Hillsdale, NJ: Lawrence Erlbaum Associates.

Willats, P. (1984). Stages in the development of intentional search by young infants. *Developmental Psychology, 20,* 389–396.

Wolf, D., & Gardner, H. (1981). On the structure of early symbolization. In R. Schiefelbusch & D. Bricker (Eds.), *Early language: Acquisition and intervention*. Baltimore: University Park Press.

Author Index

Numbers in *italics* denote pages with bibliographic information.

A

Able, K. P., 218, *247*
Acredolo, L. P., 5, 6, 8, 9, 10, 11, 12, 13, 14, 17, 19, 20, *23*, 28, 36, 41, 46, *51*, 56, 59, 62, 63, 64, *71*, 107, *121*, 172, *180*, 287, 295, 298, 299, *316*
Adams, A., *71*, 96
Adams, M. J., 96, *103*
Alcock, J., 217, *247*
Anderson, N. H., 251, 266, 277
Andreasson, C., 164, *183*
Anooshian, L. J., 29, *52*, 78, 83, *103*
Antell, S. E., 111, *121*
Appel, K. J., 107, *122*, 190, *213*
Ashmead, D. H., 152, *180*
Aslin, R. N., 54, *72*

B

Baisel, E., 66, *72*
Baker-Ward, L., 157, 162, 164, *182*
Bates, E., 291, *316*
Beach, D. H., 156, 163, *181*
Beale, I. L., 14, *23*
Beer, L. G., 246, *247*
Benigni, L., 291, *316*
Benson, J. B., 66, 67, *71*

Benson, K., 170, *181*
Berla, E. P., 30, *51*
Bertenthal, B., 53, 66, *71*, 82, *103*, 139, *148*, 290, 306, 308, 310, 312, 313, 315, *316*
Bespalec, D., 171, *183*
Bigelow, A. E., 30, 48, *51*
Bjork, E. L., 100, *103*, 189, 190, *213*
Blair, R., 169, *180*
Bluestein, N., 20, *23*
Borton, R., 54, *72*
Botkin, P. T., 18, *23*
Bower, T. G. R., 10, 16, *23*, 54, 55, 59, 67, *71*, *72*, 108, 113, *121*, *122*, 191, *213*, 297, *316*
Braine, M. D. S., 90, *103*
Brainerd, C. J., 1/2, *180*, 251, *277*
Bransford, J. D., 153, *180*
Bremermann, H., 227, *247*
Bretherton, I., 291, *316*
Bremner, J. G., 6, 7, 8, 10, 11, 13, 14, 17, *23*, 28, 37, 41, 46, *51*, 53, 56, 59, 60, 61, 62, 63, 64, 67, *71*, 107, 108, *121*, 190, *213*, 287, 290, 295, 299, *316*
Brodie, F. H., 30, *52*
Bronfenbrenner, U., 160, *181*
Brown, A. L., 90, 94, *103*, 107, *121*, 153, 155, 158, 163, 165, 166, 167, 168, 169, 170, 172, *180*, *181*, 189, *213*

AUTHOR INDEX

Bruner, J. S., 289, *316*
Bryant, P. E., 6, 7, 8, 10, 14, *23*, 53, 61, *71*, 96, *103*, 190, *213*, 299, *316*
Budwig, N. A., 143, *149*, 179, *183*
Bubatko, D., 168, 170, *181*
Bullock, D., 293, 295, *317*
Burton, S. G., 199, *214*
Bush, R. R., 251, *278*
Butterworth, G., 5, 6, 7, 8, *23*, 287, 295, 298, 299, *317*

C

Camaioni, L., 291, *316*
Campione, J. C., 153, 165, *180*
Campos, J., 53, 66, 68, *71*, *72*, 299, *317*
Campos, R., 53, 66, 67, *71*
Capuani-Shumaker, A., 81, 97, 100, *104*
Carpenter, P. A., 30, *51*
Case, R., 185, *213*
Cassiday, D. J., 153, 158, *181*
Cavanaugh, J. C., 170, *182*
Ceci, S. J., 160, *181*
Chambers, J., 266, *277*
Charnov, E. L., 228, *247*, 258, 259, 265, *277, 278*
Cheng, K., 27, *51*
Chinsky, J. M., 156, 163, *181*
Cleveland, W., 266, *277*
Cocking, R., 296, *317*
Cohen, L. B., 74, 100, *104*
Collier, G. H., 216, *247*
Collison, C., 225, *248*
Coombs, C. H., 264, *277*
Cooper, L. A., 41, *51*
Cooper, R. G., Jr., 111, 114, 119, *121*, *122*, 185, *214*
Corballis, M. C., 14, *23*
Cornell, E. H., 6, 10, 13, *23*, 59, *71*, 107, 108, 116, 117, *121*, 139, 140, *149*, 191, *213*, 236, 240, 241, *247*, *248*, 251
Corrigan, B., 266, *277*, 287, 295, 306
Corrigan, R., 73, 75, 100, *103*, 139, *149*, 308, 309, 311, *317*
Cowie, R. J., 260, *277*
Cultice, J. C., 156, *183*
Cummings, E. M., 100, *103*, 189, 190, *213*
Curtis, L. E., 111, 119, *122*, 185, *214*

D

Daehler, M. W., 168, 170, *181*, 189, *214*
Darby, B. L., 54, *72*

Dawes, R. M., 266, *277*
Day, J., 155, 171, *182*
Day, R. H., 12, *24*, 64, 67, *72*
DeLoache, J. S., 28, 48, *51*, 107, *121*, 151, 153, 155, 158, 163, 165, 166, 167, 168, 169, 170, 173, 174, 176, 177, 178, *181*, 189, *213*
Dempster, F. N., 220, *248*
Deregowski, J. B., 1, *23*
Descoendres, A., 110, *121*
Desrochers, A., 251, *277*
Diamond, A., 108, *121*
Dickerson, D. J., 56, 59, 61, *72*, 108, *122*
Dobbie, J. M., 253, *277*
Drozdal, J. G., 76, *103*
Dyer, F. C., 218, *248*

E

Eisenberg, P., 30, *51*
Evans, D., 8, 13, *23*, 56, 59, 64, *71*, 107, *121*, 298, *316*
Evans, W. F., 107, *122*, 190, *213*

F

Fabricius, W. V., 128, 132, *149*
Ferrara, R. A., 153, *180*
Finger, I., 291, *317*
Fischer, K. W., 75, 82, 87, *103*, 139, *148*, 185, *213*, 287, 288, 289, 290, 291, 293, 294, 295, 299, 303, 304, 306, 308, 309, 311, 312, 313, 314, 315, *316*, *317*, *318*
Fishbein, H. D., 18, *23*
Flavell, J. H., 18, 19, *23*, *25*, 76, *103*, 124, *149*, 155, 156, 157, 163, 175, *181*, *183*
Flook, J. P., 170, *182*
Ford, M. E., 4, *23*
Fox-Kolenda, B. J., 30, 48, *57*
Fraiberg, S., 29, 30, 48, *51*
Freedman, D. A., 30, 48, *51*
Freemen, N., 108, *121*, *122*, 191, *213*
Furth, H. G., 90, *104*
Fry, C. L., 18, *23*
Frye, D., 7, 8, *23*

G

Galanter, E., 124, *149*, 251, *278*
Gallistel, C. R., 27, *51*, 110, 112, *121*
Gardner, H., 295, *318*
Gebhard, P., 155, *183*

Gelman, R., 110, 111, 112, 114, 118, *121, 122*, 153, *181*
Gibson, E. J., 66, *71*
Gibson, J. J., 9, *24*
Gilliard, D. M., 165, *180*
Gleitman, H., 30, *51*, 175, *182*
Gleitman, L., 30, *51*, 175, *182*
Glucksberg, S., 4, *24*
Goldfield, E. C., 56, 59, 61, *71*, 108, *122*
Goldberg, S., 54, *71*
Golub, L., 225, *249*
Goodwyn, S. W., 68, *71*
Gould, J. L., 218, 232, 233, *248*
Grady, J. C., 170, *182*
Gratch, G., 7, 8, *24*, 54, *72*, 107, *122*, 189, 190, 191, *213*
Greenberg, C., 96, *104*
Griffith, S. B., 178, *181*

H

Haake, J. R., 76, 77, 78, 79, 81, 83, 87, 88, 91, 100, *103, 104*, 108, *122*, 127, 147, *149*, 186, 236, *249*, 268, 273, *277, 278*, 305, 307, 311, *317*
Hadkinson, B. A., 96, *104*
Haftorn, S., 219, *248*
Haley, K. B., 255, *277*
Halford, G., 289, *317*
Hand, H., 290, *317*
Handelmann, G. E., 224, 225, *248*
Harris, P. L., 6, 13, *24*, 106, 107, 108, 109, *122*, 153, 163, *181*, 290, *317*
Hartman, S. R., 78, *103*
Hasher, L., 154, 156, 171, 172, 173, *181*
Hayes-Roth, B., 124, 125, *149*
Hayes-Roth, F., 124, 125, *149*
Hazen, N., *182*, 246, *248*
Heim, A., 27, *51*, 53, 66, *72*
Heinrich, B., 222, 227, *248, 249*
Heiman, M. L., 140, *149*, 185, *214*
Held, R., 53, 66, *72*
Heldmeyer, K. H., 2, *24*
Heth, C. D., 6, 10, 13, *23*, 59, *71*, 107, 116, 117, *121*, 139, 140, *149*, 236, 240, 241, *247, 248*, 251
Hicks, L., 287, *316*
Higgins, E. T., 4, *24*
Hill, K. T., 74, 100, *104*
Hillstrom, K. E., 199, *214*
Hoffmann, G., 255, *277*
Horn, H., 170, *181*, 189, *213*

Howard, I. P., 4, *24*
Howe, M. L., 172, *180*, 251, *277*
Hughes, F. P., 19, *25*
Hughes, M., 118, *122*
Hunt, J. McV., 74, 100, *104*, 139, *149*, 291, 303, 306, 308, 309, *318*
Hutko, P., 19, *25*
Huttenlocher, J., 19, *24*, 27, 36, 41, 46, *51*, 187, *213*

I

Ihrig, L. H., 12, 13, 17, *25*, 62, *72*
Ihsen, E., 12, *24*, 64, *72*
Inhelder, B., 2, 3, 4, 16, 18, *25*, 36, *51*, 90, 91, 94, 95, *104*, 294, *318*
Istomina, Z. M., 156, *181*

J

Jackson, E., 299, *317*
James, G. A., 30, *51*
Jarrett, N., 287, *316*
Jarvis, P. E., 18, *23*
Jennings, K., 295, 300, 301, 302, 303, 304, 310, 311, 312, 313, *317*
Jennings, S., 75, 87, *103*, 300, 301, 302, 303, 309, 310, 311, 312, 313, *316, 317*
Johnson-Laird, P. N., 16, *24*
Jones, B., 30, *51*
Justice, E. M., 177, 178, 179, *182*

K

Kadane, J. B., 199, 203, *213*
Kalish, D., 10, *25*, 46, *50*
Kamil, A. C., 223, 224, *248*, 265, *277*
Kaplan, B., 3, *26*
Karttunen, M., 155, *183*
Keating, D. P., 111, *121*
Keiffer, K., 18, *23*
Kielgast, K., 19, *24*
Kingma, J., 172, *180*
Klahr, D., 110, 111, 114, *122*, 125, 145, 146, 147, *149*
Kleiner, B., 266, *277*
Koopman, B. O., 251, 253, *277*
Kopp, C., 291, *317*
Kosslyn, S. M., 2, *24*, 294, *317*
Kramer, J. J., 49, *51*, 74, 100, *104*
Krantz, D. H., 265, 266, *277*
Krauss, R., 4, *24*

Krebs, J. R., 2, *24*, 219, 220, 224, 228, 229, 248, *249*, 258, *278*

L

LaBerge, D., 172, *182*
Landau, B., 30, 49, *51*
Landers, W. F., 190, *213*
Lange, G., 178, *181*
Larkin, J. H., 199, *213*
Lasky, R., 9, *24*, 187, *213*
Laurendeau, M., 5, 18, *24*
LeCompte, G. K., 107, *122*, 190, *213*
Leonard, J. H., 30, *51*
Levine, M., 21, *24*
Levins, R., 264, 267, 268, *278*
Lewis, D., 18, *23*
Liben, L. S., 1, 3, *24*, 295, 296, *318*
Light, L. L., 172, 173, *182*
Lloyd, S., 108, *121*, *122*, 191, *213*
Locklear, E. P., 2, *24*
Lockman, J. J., 6, 7, *25*, 139, 140, *149*, 299, *318*
Lonardo, R., 168, *181*
Lorge, I., 245, *248*
Loughlin, K. A., 189, *214*
Lucariello, J., 176, *182*
Lucas, T. C., 7, *24*, 57, *72*
Luce, R. D., 251, 277, *278*
Lutz, R., 172, *182*

M

MacArthur, R. H., 262, *278*
Maier, N. R. F., 27, *51*
Mandler, J., 1, 2, 3, 16, *24*, 36, *51*, 155, 171, 172, *182*, 294, 295, *318*
Margileth, D. A., 30, 48, *51*
Marmor, G. S., 30, *51*
Masangkay, Z. S., 19, 20, *24*
Massar, B. M., 108, *122*
Maynard-Smith, J., 226, *248*, 264, *278*
McCall, R., 295, *318*
McCluskey, K. A., 19, 20, *24*
McFarland, D. J., 226, *249*
McIntyre, C. W., 19, 20, *24*
McKenzie, B. E., 12, 13, 14, *24*, 64, 65, 67, *72*
McKillip, J., 171, *183*
McLane, J. B., 143, *149*, 179, *183*
McNamee, G. D., 143, *149*, 179, *183*
Meacham, J. A., 160, 178, *182*

Meck, E., 112, 115, *121*
Meicler, M., 54, *72*, 107, *122*
Menzel, E. W., 2, *24*, 27, *52*
Millar, S., 29, 41, *52*
Miller, D. J., 74, 100, *104*
Miller, G. A., 16, *24*, 30, 48, *51*, 124, *149*, 251, *278*
Minskey, M., 21, *24*
Mischel, W., 124, *149*
Mitchell, D. B., 170, *182*
Montgomery, K. C., 10, *24*
Moore, M. K., 54, *72*
More, J. J., 199, *214*
Mounoud, P., 16, *24*
Muller, A. H., 54, *72*
Murphy, M. D., 90, 94, *103*
Myers, N. A., 155, 164, 170, *180*, *181*, *182*, 189, *213*

N

Nadel, L., 18, *25*, 46, *52*
Nadolny, T., 108, *122*
Neilson, I., 55, *72*
Nelson, K., 16, *25*, 107, *122*, 152, *182*, 231, 232, *248*
Newcombe, N., 2, 16, *25*, 28, 36, 46, *51*, 187, *213*
Newell, A., 127, *149*, 293, *318*
Newman, R. C., 30, *51*
Newport, E., 175, *182*
Niedorowski, L., 91, *104*
Norris, M., 30, *52*

O

O'Connor, H., 291, *317*
O'Keefe, J., 18, *25*, 46, *52*
Olsen, M. G., 172, *180*
Olton, D. S., 224, 225, *248*
Orians, G. H., 229, *248*, 265, *278*
Ornstein, P. A., 157, 162, 164, *182*

P

Palmer, S. E., 2, *25*
Papousek, H., 10, *25*
Park, D. C., 172, 173, *182*
Pasko, S., 171, *183*
Patterson, C. J., 124, *149*
Pea, R. D., 125, *149*
Pearson, N. E., 265, *278*

Perlmutter, M., 152, 155, 164, 169, 170, *180*, *182*
Pezdek, K., 172, *182*
Pfeiffer, J. E., 230, 233, *248*
Piaget, J., 2, 3, 4, 5, 7, 16, 18, *25*, 36, *52*, 53, 54, 66, *72*, 73, 74, 75, 90, 91, 94, 95, 96, 100, *104*, 105, 106, 117, *122*, 124, 138, 139, 140, *149*, 189, *214*, 287, 289, 294, 298, 302, 303, *318*
Pianka, E. R., 262, *278*
Pick, H. L., 2, 3, 4, 6, 7, 13, *25*, *26*, 112, *122*, 140, *149*, 172, *180*, 299, *318*
Pinard, A., 5, 18, *24*
Pipp, S., 287, 291, 293, 295, *317*
Potegal, M., 29, *52*
Presson, C. C., 4, 12, 13, 14, 17, 19, 20, 21, *24*, *25*, 41, *52*, 62, *72*, 187, *213*
Pribram, K. H., 124, *149*
Pufall, P., 14, 21, *25*, 90, *104*
Puglisi, J. T., 172, *182*
Pulliam, H. R., 258, *278*
Pyke, G. H., 222, 227, *248*, 258, 263, *278*

R

Ratner, H. H., 175, 176, 177, 179, *182*
Real, L. A., 229, *248*
Reeve, R. A., 153, *182*
Restle, F., 46, *52*, 251, *278*
Revelle, G. L., 127, *149*, 236, *249*
Rieser, J. J., 4, 5, 6, 8, 9, 10, 13, 14, *25*, 64, *72*, 107, *122*, 140, *149*, 185, *214*, 298, 299, *318*
Ritchie, B. F., 10, *25*, 46, *52*
Ritter, R., 157, *183*
Roberts, R. C., 219, *248*
Robinson, M., 125, 145, 146, 147, *149*
Roitblat, H. L., 225, *249*
Romano, N., 9, *24*, 187, *213*
Ross, G., 152, *182*
Rothkopf, E. Z., 171, *182*
Russell, S., 290, *317*

S

Sachs, J., 176, *182*
Sage, S., 99, 100, *104*, 188, 190, 191, 194, *214*, 248, *249*, 300, 301, 307, 309, 310, *318*
Salatas, H., 18, *25*
Samuelson, R. J., 224, *248*
Sargent, T., 265, *277*

Scharf, J. S., 78, *103*
Schmid, D., 66, *71*, *72*
Schneider, W., 172, *182*
Schoener, T. W., 258, *278*
Scholnick, E., 294, 295, *318*
Schuberth, R., 290, 295, *318*
Schulman, A. T., 171, *182*
Schwartz, A., 66, *72*
Seegmiller, D., 155, 171, *182*
Shanteau, G., 266, *277*
Shaw, M., 255, 257, 276, *278*
Shaw, P., 255, 257, 276, *278*
Shaw, R., 21, *25*
Shepard, R. N., 41, *51*
Shettleworth, S. J., 219, 220, 224, *249*
Shiffrin, R. M., 172, *182*
Sibley, R. M., 226, *248*
Siegel, A. W., 3, *25*
Siegler, R. S., 194, 195, 196, *214*
Simon, H., 127, *149*, 293, *318*
Sinha, C. G., 108, *121*, *122*, 191, *213*
Smirnov, A. A., 155, *182*
Smith, J. N. M., 222, *249*
Smothergill, D. W., 19, *25*
Soloman, R. L., 227, *249*
Somerville, S. C., 1, 22, *25*, 73, 76, 77, 81, 87, 88, 91, 96, 97, 100, *103*, *104*, 108, *122*, 123, 126, 127, 128, 147, 148, *149*, 152, 153, 156, 175, 178, *183*, 186, 236, *249*, 251, 252, 268, 269, 273, *277*, *278*, 287, 293, 305, 307, 310, 311, 312, 315, *317*, *318*
Sophian, C., 99, 100, *104*, 108, *122*, 127, 128, 137, 147, *149*, 185, 186, 188, 189, 190, 191, 192, 194, 195, 199, *214*, 236, 247, *249*, 251, 293, 298, 300, 301, 307, 309, 310, 311, *318*
Spaulding, P. J., 30, *52*
Spelke, E., 111, 128
Starkey, P., 111, 118, 119, *122*, 185, *214*
Stone, L. D., 253, 254, 255, 257, *277*, *278*
Strauss, M. S., 111, 119, *122*, 185, *214*
Sutton, G. M., 235, *249*
Svejda, M., 53, 66, *71*, *72*
Szeminska, A., 96, *104*

T

Templeton, W. B., 4, 14, *24*
Tham, W., 225, *249*
Thissen, D., 266, *278*
Thorndike, E. L., 221, 245, *249*

Thorndike, R. L., 245, *248*
Timmons, S. A., 19, *25*
Tinbergen, N., 217, *249*
Tolman, E. C., 10, *25*, 27, 46, *52*, 215, *249*
Tootle, H., 67, *72*
Trabasso, T., 96, *103*
Tufte, E., 266, *278*
Tukey, P., 266, *277*
Tversky, A., 266, *277*

U,V

Uzgiris, I. C., 7, *24*, 57, *72*, 74, 100, *104*, 139, *149*, 291, 303, 306, 308, 309, *318*
VanderWall, S. B., 220, *249*
Vinter, A., 16, *24*
Volterra, V., 291, *316*
Von Frisch, K., 218, *249*
Von Wright, J. M,. 155, 171, 172, *183*
Vygotsky, L. S., 179, *183*

W

Waddington, K. D., 227, *249*
Wainer, H., 266, *278*
Walker, J. A., 224, 225, *248*
Wallace, J. G., 110, 111, 114, *122*
Warren, D., 29, 30, *52*
Waters, H. S., 164, *183*
Watson, J. S., 10, *25*
Watson, M., 290, 291, *318*

Webb, R. A., 108, *122*
Wellman, H. M., 1, 22, *25*, 73, 76, 77, 78, 83, 101, *103, 104*, 123, 124, 126, 127, 128, 132, 147, 148, *149*, 152, 153, 156, 157, 158, 162, 175, 178, *181, 183*, 186, 189, 190, 191, 192, 195, *214*, 236, 246, *249*, 251, 252, 268, 269, 273, *277, 278*, 287, 293, 298, 311, 312, 315, *318*
Wenters, J., *24*, 187, *213*
Werner, H., 3, *26*
Wertsch, J. V., 143, *149*, 179, *183*
Werz, M. A., 225, *248*
White, S. H., 3, *25*
Wilensky, R., 145, *149*
Wilkinson, A. C., 251, *278*
Willats, P., 139, 140, 143, *149*, 297, *318*
Winterhalder, B., 263, *278*
Wishart, J. G., 55, 59, *72*, 108, *122*
Wolf, D., 295, *318*
Wright, J. W., 18, *23*
Wright, N. A., 107, *122, 213*

Y,Z

Yengo, L., 189, 190, *214*
Yonas, A., 2, 3, 4, *25, 26*, 113, *122*
Zaback, L. A., 30, *51*
Zacks, R. T., 154, 156, 171, 172, 173, *181*
Zechmeister, E. B., 171, *183*
Zelinsky, E. M., 172, 173, *182*
Zinchenko, P. I., 155, *182*

Subject Index

A

A not B error, *see* Perseveration

C

Cognitive Maps, 20, 29, 235
Cues, 10, 56, 129–131, 165–171, 217–219, 240, 301
  memory, 165–171
  orientation, 218
  picture, 168
  place, 10
  response, 10
  sighting, 129–131

D

Distance, 36, 126–138, 227, 233

E

Egocentrism, 1, 3, 6–10, 13, 46, 50, 62–65, 297–302
Event sequences, 90–95, 126

F

Foraging, 216, 217–230, 258–265

I

Inferences, 20, 73, 95–98, 185, 187–188, 308

L

Landmarks, 11, 31, 50, 63, 107–108, 166–170, 218, 220, 228, 231–232, 299
Logical abilities, *see* Inferences

M

Memory, 91–95, 151–180, *see also* Perseveration, Search strategies, and Spatial representation
Maps, 20, 27, 30, 35, 36, 233
Models, 135, 193–199, 207–211, 226–230, 240–241, 251–276
  comparisons between, 207–211, 264–268
  graphical, 265–275
  log-linear, 135
  monte-carlo techniques, 240–241
  optimal foraging, 226–230, 258–265
  rule-based, 193–195
  stochastic, 195–199

N

Number, 105, 109–120
  addition and subtraction, 117–120

Number (cont.)
  counting, 109, 112–116
  number conservation, 113
  number discrimination, 109–112
  subitizing, 110–112

P

Perseveration, 6, 7, 43, 61–63, 108–109, 189–191, 297–300
Planning, 123–148, 155, 216
Problem solving, 73, 123–126, 142–144, 178–179, 236, 269, 275, 293

R

Rules, 146, 193–211, see also Search strategies

S

Search strategies, 76, 83, 84, 87, 98–103, 121, 126–138, 155–165, 221–226, 230–245, 252, 253, 268–275, 297, 306–313
  comprehensive search, 103, 121, 126–137, 223–226, 252, 268–275
  exhaustive search, see comprehensive search
  indirect search, 137–138
  intentional search, 124–126, 297
  memory-based, 155–165
  selective search, 98–102, 222, 252, 268–275
  sensorimotor search, 306–307
Search tasks, see also Spatial tasks
  comprehensive, 126–137, 268–278
  hidden object, 297–300
  hide-and-seek, 153, 155, 158–165
  indirect, 137–138
  logical, 73–89
  multiple hiding, 162–163
  naturalistic, 76–79
Skill theory, 287–316
Spatial coding, see also Spatial representation
  allocentric, 1, 13, 298–300
  automatic, 171–174
  egocentric, 1, 3, 6–10, 298–300
  geocentric, 1, 9
  objective, 1, 5, 9, 62, 65
Spatial information use, 15, 20, 90, 151–180
Spatial knowledge, see Spatial representation
Spatial representation, 1–22, 27–30, 35, 41, 62, 65, 128, 187, 219, 293–296, 298–300, 309–313, 315
Spatial tasks, see also Search tasks
  hiding and finding, 80–86, 236–245
  invisible displacement, 55, 57, 58, 139, 188, 302–309
  map reading, 21, 35
  navigation, 29, 47
  perspective taking, 18, 21
  planning, 128–129
  rotation, 8–13, 28, 36–49, 56, 59
  shortest route, 139–140
  spatial coordination, 299
  three location, 191
  transposition, 56, 189, 199–201
Stage IV error, see Perseveration

T

Theories, see Models